MAN-MADE MORALS
FOUR PHILOSOPHIES
THAT SHAPED AMERICA

By the Same Author

THE FIRST AMENDMENT

WILLIAM H. MARNELL

MAN-MADE
MORALS

FOUR PHILOSOPHIES
THAT SHAPED AMERICA

DOUBLEDAY & COMPANY, INC.
GARDEN CITY, NEW YORK

The author is grateful to the following for permission to use copyrighted material.

Atlantic-Little, Brown and Company and Harold Ober Associates Incorporated for material from *Yankee from Olympus*, by Catherine Drinker Bowen. Copyright 1943, 1944 by Catherine Drinker Bowen. Reprinted by permission.

Beacon Press and Harold Ober Associates Incorporated for material from *Reconstruction in Philosophy*, by John Dewey. Reprinted by permission.

Putnam's & Coward-McCann for material from *The Quest for Certainty*, by John Dewey. Copyright © 1929 by John Dewey. Reprinted by permission.

Yale University Press for material from *Essays of William Graham Sumner*, edited by Galloway Keller and Maurice R. Davie. Reprinted by permission.

To Clare Lorinne Marnell

CONTENTS

INTRODUCTION

IF A BOOK, unlike beauty, is not its own excuse for being, then the place for the excuse is the Introduction. There is clearly evident in English history and, with due allowance for the fact that American history starts as a late development in English history, in American history as well a developing challenge to the ancient concept of natural law by the contract theory of society, which carries with it the concept of the man-made moral order. This book is a study of the historical origin and development of this conflict, a conflict which came into being in England three hundred years ago and still continues today. A by-product of the study and part of the book's excuse for being, it is hoped, is some light upon the causes of a certain perplexity and confusion visible today about the deeper meanings of the words *liberal* and *conservative*, a perplexity and confusion that extend to conflicting attitudes toward the Constitution present in both the people as a whole and in their Supreme Court. On the one hand there is the traditional concept of the American Constitution as a charter of government with a relatively fixed meaning that can be changed only by the established process of amendment. This concept can be approximately equated with *conservative*. On the other hand there is the newer concept of the Constitution as an instrument of government with a relatively flexible meaning that can be employed as changing circumstances dictate for the betterment of the national well-being. This concept can be approximately equated with *liberal*. It should follow that certainly the word *virtue* and possibly the word *truth* can be equated with neither.

If we are not mistaken, belief in natural law has never really succumbed to the challenge. It has become submerged, lingering better perhaps as by its nature it should in the instincts of man than in his explicit beliefs, and surviving better in the untutored thought of common man than in the cultivated philosophy of his intellectual betters. From time to time it has heard the call of a beleaguered people in England and America and come to their relief. It did so at the start of the nineteenth century when England was in a spiritual dead calm, it did so late in the nineteenth century when "The Cry of the Children" somehow pierced the blackened walls of factories in England and America, and if we are not mistaken it is doing so again in the civil rights movement.

Our primary concern, however, is not this submergence and reappearance of belief in natural law. It is rather the belief that began to replace it around 1660, became dominant around 1860, and is still potent as we enter the last third of the twentieth century. This is the belief that morals are man-made, that the moral foundations of society are man-made, and hence that right and wrong are values induced and created by observation and experimentation. It is our purpose to trace what history unquestionably reveals as the checkered course of the man-made moral order, and to show that the concept of Progress which lies at its heart has repeatedly proved itself a delusion and a snare. This implies no cynicism about the progress which we trust is a fact and not a slogan.

The history of England and America reveals that the concept of the man-made moral order has crested four times in the past three hundred years, and receded three. It has started each time with the hope and promise of reform; each time it has achieved a measure of desirable reform, but the impulse to reform each time has died away. It crested in the form of deism and its philosophic consequences in the eighteenth century, in the form of utilitarianism in the mid-nineteenth century, in the form of social Darwinism in the late nineteenth and early twentieth centuries, and in the form of pragmatism during the Depression. We shall be concerned with the rise and fall of belief in the man-made order in the English-speaking world through these three centuries. Other concepts of the man-made order have crested and receded elsewhere in the same period, and three most ominous ones in our own day and age: fascism, Nazism, and Communism. These are not our concern because they belong, as Chaucer would put it, "in an othere boke." Each has had its obviously profound effect on Anglo-American life, but no one of them has entered Anglo-American belief and the life that is based on belief.

Our starting point is the year 1660, the year when the first ripples of the successive waves of belief in the man-made order lapped on English shores. England had been through a Civil War, fought in the physical sense by relatively small bands of warriors but fought in the metaphysical sense on every ideological battlefield that dogged Roundheads and stubborn Cavaliers could occupy. The Roundheads had won the physical war, in the sense that such a war can ever be won, and Oliver Cromwell had been Lord Protector. But Cromwell had been dead for two years, and his actual if not technical successor

General Monk made one of the most statesmanlike and enduring decisions in English history. He knew that Puritans and Anglicans had to live side by side on some terms or other, and in the wise and prudent judgment of General Monk the most promising way was under a king with limited powers. Hence General Monk maneuvered the restoration of Charles II and set in motion the forces that generated the first manifestation of the man-made order in the English-speaking world.

An Introduction can also serve the gracious purpose of tribute. To a friend of nearly forty years' standing I owe my first interest in formal philosophy and most of my uncertain grasp upon it. Older colleagues retire first, which is their reward and our misfortune. I hope that I have learned enough from William J. Roche, Professor Emeritus of Philosophy at Boston State College, to carry me through to my own retirement. The greater debt, like the adequate tribute, can only be suggested. If everything that goes into the making of a book—the thought, the discussion, the planning, the encouragement, the analysis, the criticism—were considered part of the act of authorship, as properly they should be, my wife's name would appear with mine upon the title page. This, and vastly more, is acknowledged by the Dedication.

W.H.M.

The supreme law was born in all the ages, before any law had been written or any state had been established.

—Marcus Tullius Cicero, *De Legibus,* I.6.19

I say that natural knowledge, seeking to satisfy natural wants, has found the ideas which can alone still spiritual cravings. I say that natural knowledge, in desiring to ascertain the laws of comfort, has been driven to discover those of conduct, and to lay the foundations of a new morality.

—Thomas Henry Huxley, *On the Advisableness of Improving Natural Knowledge,* 1866

MAN-MADE MORALS
FOUR PHILOSOPHIES
THAT SHAPED AMERICA

I

THE DAWN OF REASON

GEORGE MONK, DUKE OF ALBEMARLE, had one inflexible rule of conduct: to be on the winning side. There is a shade less of cynicism in this statement than might seem likely; his own high abilities often made his the winning side. The side, however, had to be potentially the winning side before he was on it. He had done his practice fighting in the training school of the seventeenth century, the Low Countries, and he had learned its lessons well. He had shown his knowledge in Ireland in 1641, and when he finally made his decision and declared for the king, Charles I made him major general of the Irish brigade. But Monk had broken his own rule, for the side of Charles was not to be the winning side. Monk had three years in the Tower to contemplate his error.

Three years, taken from the best years of his life, was not too high a price for this error at a time when the price of an error tended to be a man's head. The Parliament needed his services as badly as had the king, and Parliament's price, that he accept the Covenant, was not too steep for one of his pliable moral code. He took the Covenant and served Parliament loyally and effectively for a decade and a half. In 1650, with six thousand men and the exhilaration of victory at Dunbar to spur them on, he conquered Scotland. In 1653 he defeated the Dutch in one of history's bloodiest naval battles. He allowed himself a brief recess for romance, and married his mistress, Anne Clarges, "ever a plain homely dowdy" according to Samuel Pepys in one of his kinder descriptions of the duchess of Albemarle. Then he settled down to five years of strong-handed government in Scotland, steadily whittling away at the power of the Presbyterian clergy who were thorns in the side of Cromwell. For enthusiasm, in the seventeenth-century meaning of the word, he had a bitter contempt with perhaps a bit of fear to whet the bitterness. When chance offered, he purged his forces of enthusiasts, and he forced the chance when he could.

Many years after the Civil War was safely over and the sun of Reason well above the horizon, Thomas Hobbes wrote his views on enthusiasm in his *Behemoth, or, The Long Parliament.* He makes clear the judgment he had long entertained, as had Monk and the other men of reason, that all the horrors of the Civil War had resulted from the theological aberrations, tinged with treason, of the Presbyterians, the Independents, and the Papists. The Presbyterians were the worst of the lot, Hobbes believed, since they held for the supremacy of the Church over the State and for freedom of individual interpretations of Scripture. The former to Hobbes was contrary to nature and the latter inimical to the peace. The Independents were nothing better than Presbyterians in the rudimentary stages, and all the lesser sects were breeders of chaos and foes of authority. The Papists made useful whipping boys for Hobbes. He could excoriate them to his heart's content, but one who read between the comfortably separated lines would read Church of England where Hobbes wrote Church of Rome. A plague on all the divided brethren who spoke with acrimonious tongues, on all who spread the gospel with fire and sword. They have been the devastation of England, the plague of the land. Theirs was the final folly, enthusiasm; only wisdom and reason could rescue the land from its effects. This was precisely the viewpoint of Monk. He was a cold and calculating man and a very able one, and there is nothing the cold and calculating man fears more than incalculable fanaticism. Scotland was a land of incalculable fanaticism during the Commonwealth period, and England only slightly less so.

When Oliver Cromwell died in 1658, Monk sat tight in Edinburgh. He knew as thoroughly as anyone in the British Isles that whatever the theory, the fact of Cromwell's rule was rule by the sword. Now it would be an open military dictatorship or open military chaos. It would be despotism in the saddle, or fanatics at one another's throat. It was fanaticism itself, the extravagant religious emotionalism that the seventeenth century called *enthusiasm*, which had to be quelled. That much Monk knew clearly. Civil government would have to control the army, and Parliament would have to comprise the civil government. Monk read that lesson in his own heart and the hearts of the English people. They were infinitely weary of war, and infinitely fearful of more war. But how to replace enthusiasm with reason was the paramount question.

There was always the possibility of a restoration of the king. Charles Stuart had written from exile in France to Monk as far back as 1655, and Monk had turned the letter over to Cromwell. Grenvil, the agent of Charles Stuart, won Monk's clergyman brother Nicholas to his side in July, 1659, and Nicholas conveyed to Monk the substance of another letter from the exiled king. In October Monk loudly denounced the idea of a restoration, and quietly pondered it. In midwinter, in York, he loudly denounced it again, but in the quiet of his private councils Monk carefully calculated the beat of the English pulse. He listened patiently as enthusiasts urged him to don the mantle of Cromwell, and as patiently when others proposed that the army restore the king. He listened patiently to those who feared that the army would restore the king, and smiled enigmatically when Parliament took him, if not to the top of a high mountain, at least to Hampton Court and said it would be his if he did its bidding. He had mapped out in his own mind the campaign, once he had decided to his satisfaction which would be the winning side. Enthusiasm was a potent danger, but it was not so strong as the fear of enthusiasm. The people wanted civil government by Parliament because they wanted peace. Monk knew that a free Parliament would restore the king, so Monk worked until he had achieved a free Parliament. In March for the first time he met Grenvil and sent by him to Charles the terms of restoration later made official in the Declaration of Breda. He allowed to all who would claim it, and many would, credit for the forthcoming restoration. In April he quietly accepted the thanks of Parliament, and expressed polite surprise when Grenvil gave him an official letter from the king. On May 29, 1660, Charles II entered London. Monk was present, on the winning side.

Thereafter Monk was laden with the honors and the titles
bestowed with such lavish prodigality by society upon its enig-
matic personalities after they have retired safely and permanently to the sidelines of life. Restoration society was not for the
likes of Monk, the rough soldier and consummate diplomat, and
his lackluster duchess. And so he became the Duke of Albemarle,
Master of the Bedchamber, Knight of the Garter, Master of the
Horse, and he lived in quiet comfort on his pension of seven
thousand pounds. He emerged in 1666 to save his country from
the Dutch, and retired to die of the dropsy in 1670. He was a
man of reason, one of the first great men of reason in the newly
dawning age.

THOMAS HOBBES

Another great man of reason was trying to reason a way to
national peace and harmony as early as the First and Second
Bishops' War of 1639 and 1640. While Pym and Hampden
headed His Majesty's far from loyal opposition and sent Straf-
ford and Laud to the Tower, Thomas Hobbes was trying to make
civil strife obsolete by grounding new and profoundly disturbing
doctrines of man and the state on utterly strange concepts of
what comprised natural law. While Parliament volleyed and
thundered, this peace-loving scholar in later middle life, who
according to Aubrey "used to study, and sitt, bare-headed, and
sayd he never tooke cold in his head, but that the greatest
trouble was to keepe off the flies from pitching on the baldnes,"
was quietly manufacturing in the name of peace bombs that
would not detonate until the nineteenth century. Thomas
Hobbes was the first man of thought in the Dawn of Reason, as
truly as the Duke of Albemarle was the first man of action. By
1640, the year of the Second Bishops' War and some years before the campaigns of the Civil War in the strict sense, he had
completed his doctrine of man.

Thomas Hobbes lives in literature and the history of thought
by his *Leviathan, or the Matter, Form and Power of a Commonwealth, Ecclesiastical and Civil,* which he published in 1651.
For a half century Hobbes had watched the forces gather that
would erupt into civil war. He saw the primary division between

Anglicans and Puritans grow inveterate and bitter, and the sub-divisions among the dissenter sects take on that venom so often found when differences are minor and inconsequential. He saw the Crown decline in strength and the might of Parliament grow until the precarious peace depended on an impossibly delicate balance of power. Some basic convictions gradually were brought home to him, convictions so basic that they horrified England until utilitarian philosophy and scientific materialism seemed to reaffirm them in the nineteenth century.

Hobbes became convinced that the state of nature is a state of war. He became convinced that man is by nature a selfish animal constantly in conflict with his fellows. His life would indeed be, in the most famous of his phrases, "solitary, poor, nasty, brutish, and short"[1] if he did not surrender a portion of his independence to his fellows in return for a commensurate sur-render in the name of mutual security. The social order rests on a solid foundation of fear. But that surrender would be in vain if it did not produce security, and Hobbes saw with perfect clarity that there is no security when the final resting place of power is not secure and universally acknowledged. What hap-pens when sovereign power is divided was writ large in the happenings in England in the years when *Leviathan* was being conceived and written. Leviathan, that symbol of the state, must by its nature be unique. Total power must be vested in a single focal point of power; sovereignty cannot be divided and remain sovereignty. *Leviathan* is the most eloquent plea for govern-mental absolutism in English literature.

But it is more than that. If it were merely a plea for govern-mental absolutism, it would be a historic landmark at best, re-membered for the brilliance of the prose style which even its bitterest detractors admit. In fairness to those detractors, they had read *Leviathan* far more carefully and understood it far more thoroughly than those who today confidently pin it down with the categorical phrase. Many of the detractors would quite will-ingly forgive the absolutism; some would applaud it. Seven-teenth- and eighteenth-century opposition to *Leviathan* rested on very different grounds indeed.

Perhaps the starting place might be the frontispiece of the first edition, the picture of a benign giant leaning over the horizon and looking placidly at a landscape of hills and dales and little towns. Regard that giant closely, and you see that his body is composed of an enormous number of human beings. He is the state, the multitude united in one person upon whom they confer all their power and strength. The contract is among the people, not between the people and the king or the assembly. Leviathan ultimately is all the individual human beings of the realm, and those human beings do not totally and permanently surrender their individuality when they merge it in a state for purposes of peace. They must obey their sovereign only so long as he can perform the role for which he was brought into being, to protect the people. If that power goes, his sovereignty goes with it. Hobbes did not write as a royalist or as a Parliamentarian. He wrote as a believer in the peace, and as one who believed that only total power vested in one sovereign, be he a man or an assembly of men, can keep the peace. Absolutism has no other reason for existence; the purpose of society can be achieved by nothing less than absolutism. But the state is not monolithic in Hobbes, as it has been in twentieth-century absolutism. It is still that multitude of tiny men, numerous beyond counting, who make up the body of Leviathan, in whom they live and have their possibility of being.

SELF-CENTERED MAN

What motivates these tiny human molecules that make up Leviathan? John Aubrey, whose *Brief Lives* is one of the minor delights for those who stray into the bypaths of seventeenth-century literature, records the amazed delight with which Hobbes discovered geometry. He was in a gentleman's library and happened upon Euclid open to *47 Element libri I.* "'By G——,' sayd he (He would now and then sweare, by way of emphasis), 'this is impossible!'" He traced the proposition back to another proposition, Aubrey tells us, and then farther back until convinced by demonstration of its truth. Geometry became the cornerstone of his philosophic method. Geometry explained what motivated the human molecules. Without motion there would be no sensation, without sensation no life. Therefore motion is the final, universal cause of human as well as physical phenomena. We react with an instinct for self-preservation to motions from the outside. Man is fundamentally self-centered, acting and reacting as external motivation affects his instinct for self-preservation. A sense reaction instigates a reaction in the mind; the mental reaction is an idea. We can be aware of mental images by imagination, we can recall them by memory. We can anticipate their logical sequence by prudence. Desire draws us to the image that we like, aversion turns us away from the image we dislike. We love what we desire and call it good; we hate what we dislike and call it evil. Good and evil are subjective, originating within us, corresponding to no objective reality.

There is a point beyond which prudence cannot calculate the logical sequence of images. Beyond is the unknown, and the unknown is the feared. Religion is the defense prudence contrives to meet the challenge of this unknown. "This perpetual fear, always accompanying mankind in the ignorance of causes, as it were in the dark, must needs have for object something. And therefore when there is nothing to be seen, there is nothing to accuse, either of their good, or evil fortune, but some power, or agent invisible: in which sense perhaps it was, that some of the old poets said, that the gods were first created by human fear. . . ."[2] Hobbes hastens to add that the gods were created and multiplied among the Gentiles by this process and by the personification of natural forces. Nothing he has said applies to revealed religion, above all nothing is hostile to Christianity. His detractors did not accept as valid this distinction between natural and revealed religion, nor did the seventeenth and eighteenth centuries in general. His contemporaries and their successors were not overconcerned with Hobbes the absolutist. Their archenemy was Hobbes the atheist, because the thought of Hobbes was atheism as the seventeenth century understood the term.

Still peering through the magic casements of geometry, Hobbes saw in action and reaction the explanation of human conduct in society. Man is a social being not by nature but by necessity. He lives in accordance with certain natural laws, but natural law to Hobbes is something far different from what it is to Grotius and Hooker. To Hobbes a law of nature "is a precept or general rule, found out by reason, by which a man is forbidden

to do that, which is destructive of his life, or taketh away the
means of preserving the same; and to omit that, by which he
thinketh it may be best preserved."[3] The fundamental law of
nature is ". . . that every man, ought to endeavour peace, as
far as he has hope of obtaining it; and when he cannot obtain
it, that he may seek, and use, all helps, and advantages of war.
The first branch of which rule, containeth the first, and fundamental law of nature; which is, to seek peace, and follow it.
The second, the sum of the right of nature; which is, by all
means we can, to defend ourselves."[4] There follows the second
law of nature: ". . . that a man be willing, when others are so too,
as far-forth, as for peace, and defence of himself he shall think it
necessary, to lay down this right to all things; and be contented
with so much liberty against other men, as he would allow other
men against himself."[5] And Hobbes, with his instinct for grounding his iconoclasm on traditional theology, sums it up in a
paraphrase: "That is the law of the Gospel: whatsoever you
require that others should do to you, that do ye to them."[6]

Thus natural law is reduced to an instinct for survival, with
such exercise of the mental powers of imagination, memory, and
prudence as that instinct elicits. The tradition of natural law is
turned topsy-turvy; in Hobbes the law does not depend upon
morality but morality depends upon the law. Men differ in their
moral concepts profoundly, but they do not differ in their instinct
for self-preservation. What we call moral laws are merely the
maintenance of attitudes beneficial to self-preservation. Hobbes
said it in the sixteenth century, and the social Darwinians would
say it in the nineteenth.

We are now reaching the heart of the thought of Hobbes, the
heart which his seventeenth- and eighteenth-century critics
understood and feared. Hobbes does not start with a concept of
law but with a concept of right. In the state of nature each man
has complete freedom, total right to do what he pleases in the
way he pleases. But the exercise of this total right brings him into
immediate and potentially fatal conflict with his fellow man, who
also has complete freedom. The price of survival is compromise,
and out of the fact of compromise emerges law. Law is the
codification of the compromise whereby man insures his survival. Society is the creation of men living under the compro-

mise, a creation necessary as the alternative to chaos. The concept of Hooker and Grotius, or indeed of Plato and Aristotle, is that the natural law exists independent of the human will. The concept of Hobbes is that natural law is the creation of the human will. Hooker and Grotius hold that law is antecedent to rights; Hobbes holds that rights are antecedent to law. The very term "natural law" is a misnomer in Hobbes; "natural rights" is a proper term. The thought of Hobbes is antithetical to the thought of Plato and Aristotle, of Hooker and Grotius. It is not antithetical to the thought of Hume and Rousseau. The road is a long and tortuous one, with many unexpected twists and turns, but the road to the modern concept of the man-made order starts with Thomas Hobbes.

There is, then, vastly more to *Leviathan* than an eloquent plea for absolutism. There is also a challenge to the historical concept of natural law. Law in Hobbes, as we said before, does not rest upon morality, but morality rests upon law. There are no fixed and unchanging natural laws except in the sense that the instincts and impulses that comprise to him the "laws" of nature are fixed and unchanging. Right and wrong are not absolute and objective; they are relative and subjective. Man makes right, not God. Society does not result from the nature of man; it results from man's despair of survival on any other terms. There is no such thing as *the people;* there are only individuals living in juxtaposition by surrendering the necessary part of their individual rights to the sovereign of their creation. The sovereign, whether it be a king or a parliament, has unquestionable authority so long, but only so long, as it can give the individuals living under it the protection for which they brought it into being. This authority extends to the interpretation of religious truth as well as to the codification of civil law.

The theories of Hobbes horrified his contemporaries and his concept of the moral order assailed the fundamentals of their belief. Thomas Hobbes had no followers but a few crackpots, found every man's hand turned against him, and was refuted in 109 books between 1650 and 1700 according to Samuel I. Mintz's "Checklist of Anti-Hobbes Literature and Allusion in England."[7] Hobbes was the universal enemy of all right-thinking men of all shades and diversities of right thought, and yet went

on influencing thought if only by way of reaction until he enjoyed a belated and bifurcated triumph in the political philosophy of Jeremy Bentham and James Mill and the psychology of
David Hartley and David Hume. Thus old Thomas Hobbes, who
was born prematurely on Good Friday in 1588 when his mother
was alarmed by reports of the Spanish Armada, who became the
favorite secretary of Francis Bacon, whose entire intellectual
horizon expanded at the age of forty when he discovered
geometry, who Aubrey says used "to sing prick-song every night
(when all were gone and sure nobody could heare him) for his
health, which he did beleeve would make him live two or three
yeares longer," who had few books and "was wont to say that if
he had read as much as other men, he should have known no
more then other men," who still played tennis at seventy-five
and died at ninety-two in at least a suggestion of the belated
odor of sanctity, and came to life again as a philosophic influence
in the nineteenth century, is for its modern form the "onlie
begetter" of the man-made order. With him in the realm of
thought, as with Monk in the realm of action, the story starts.

II

NATURAL RELIGION

ALL ENGLISH THOUGHT continues to be to the right of Hobbes until the nineteenth century. How true this is may best be illustrated by comparing with Hobbes the seventeenth-century thinker who rivaled him in devotion to absolutism. He is Robert Filmer, who like Hobbes was born in 1588. Filmer's birth was not hastened by news of the Armada, since the Filmers were not disconcerted by the mere mundane, but neither was his life prolonged by prick song. Filmer died in 1653.

Behind Robert Filmer was the stateliest line that that eminent dowager of counties, Kent, could produce. His father was lord of the manor of Little Charlton and later owner of all East Sutton. His mother was an Argall. His uncle Sir Samuel Argall established the beeline route to Virginia and, John Fiske reports,[1] in 1612 bribed the chief of the Potomac tribe to wink at the abduction of Pocahontas. His wife was Anne Heton, daughter of Queen Elizabeth's bishop of Ely. When his father died in 1629, as the oldest of eighteen children he became patriarch of East Sutton, the lord and master of his brethren, his menservants and maidservants, his relatives, retainers, and dependents of every degree. As Peter Laslett, his editor, well puts it, Filmer assumes in his readers the presuppositions of the head of East Sutton Park. *Patriarcha* was written by a patriarch.

Hobbes the absolutist is known to the twentieth century by the conclusion which he reached, and the significance of the ideological way stations that he occupied on his way to it is largely overlooked. Filmer, insofar as he is known at all, is known by his ideological way stations and not by the conclusion that he reached. It was the great misfortune of Filmer to base his argument in part upon a historical howler, and for the most important political writer of his age to capitalize upon it. John Locke actually never penetrated to the heart of Filmer's thought, nor indeed attempted to do so. Filmer was destroyed more easily than that.

Filmer is faintly remembered for his *Patriarcha,* which he withheld from print during his lifetime. Twenty-seven years after Filmer died, *Patriarcha* was hurried through the press with such haste that pages are misnumbered; it was to serve the same political purpose as Dryden's *Absalom and Achitophel,* and it served that purpose amazingly well. But the ideas of *Patriarcha* are to be found, often in more careful and logical development, in other works published during his lifetime. The most important are *The Anarchy of a Limited and Mixed Monarchy* (1648), *Observations upon Aristotle's Politiques touching Forms of Government* (1652), and *Observations concerning the Originall of Government* (1652).

FILMER'S DIVINE AUTHORITY

Filmer believed that society is natural and organic. It has its origin in the family. The father is its natural head. The role of patriarch is a natural extension of the role of father. The natural duties of a king are an extension of those of a father and a patriarch. Kings are either fathers of their people, or heirs of such fathers, or the usurpers of the rights of such fathers. That monarchy is the will of God is evident from the fact that it is the form of government He gave His chosen people. But this is merely historical confirmation of what is evident in the nature of things, since God established the family as the fundamental unit of society and patriarchal sovereignty is its logical development.

There are certain corollaries important in the thinking of Filmer. The moral authority of the father is the foundation of all authority on earth. "I see not then how the children of Adam, or of any man else, can be free from subjection to their parents. And this subordination of children is the fountain of all regal authority, by the ordination of God himself. From whence it follows, that civil power, not only in general is by Divine institution, but even the assigning of it specifically to the eldest parent. Which quite takes away that new and common distinction which refers only power universal or absolute to God, but power respective in regard of the special form of government to the choice of the people. Nor leaves it any place for such imaginary pactions between Kings and their people as many dream of."[2] The social contract therefore is a figment of the imagination. Hobbes's concept of society as something grounded on the instinct for self-preservation is historically false, and any theory of mixed government with sovereignty shared by king and Parliament is unsound. Society is a natural, organic growth; it is in no sense and from no viewpoint a thing of man's making. The cultural anthropologist, to whom the peripheral arguments of Filmer might seem primitive beyond even his previous experience, might well find himself in unexpected agreement with the central thesis of *Patriarcha*.

It was the peripheral argument on which Locke seized in the first of his *Two Treatises of Government*. Filmer accepted the Bible as the literally true and complete revelation of the divine will, the comprehensive record of history from the creation of the world to the death of the apostles, and the eternal and unchanging guide for all man's actions. God created Adam superior to Eve; man is eternally superior to woman. God literally gave the entire world to Adam. Adam, as father, was the sole ruler of the world, which was entirely his possession. When Adam died, his eldest son succeeded to his property and paternal authority. All patriarchs and all kings are descendants of Adam. There may be question as to the rightful heir to the throne, but there never can be question of the fact that there is a rightful heir. Some descendant of Adam is always rightful heir to the throne. Society does not arise from human consent, nor does human consent put one in society. Everyone is born into society; the social contract is a self-evident absurdity. So is the state of nature as a state antecedent to society. From the hour that Eve was created, society was. It was upon the thesis that in every society there is someone closest in blood to Adam and hence the rightful king that Locke gleefully pounced. He never attempted to rebut the real foundation of Filmer's argument, which is unaffected by the tissue of historical fabrication it is made to bear. He never attempts to rebut the concept of society as a natural and organic growth.

Precisely at this point we see the distinction between a believer in the divinely created order like Filmer and a believer in the man-made order like Hobbes. To the latter the social order is always something of man's making. Hence he is often uneasy about the nature of the moral code upon which the social order rests. He may go the full way with Hobbes, and say that morality depends upon law and not law upon morality. If he does so, he is severely logical and hence is distrusted by those who do not like to venture upon the sea of thought beyond the ideological breakwater. Or he may sacrifice some or all of his logic and attempt the compromise implicit in the belief that man made society but God made the moral code on which it rests. But he faces the need for another compromise when he attempts to reconcile the concept that man made society and hence in obeying the sovereign man is obliquely obeying himself with the concept that the principle of obedience to authority is of divine creation. The believer in natural law is saved these exercises in the illogical, even if he may have some others peculiar to himself. He believes that law rests upon morality, that society is natural and organic, and that the principle of obedience to lawful authority is an aspect of obedience to God.

Filmer was a believer in natural law. To argue that all the kings of Europe are lineal descendants of Adam and that the right of succession is a problem for the genealogist to solve certainly deserved the mockery of Locke. But to argue that society is natural and organic is not absurd, and Locke leaves Filmer's central thesis severely alone. Hobbes was a believer in the man-made order. To argue that society came literally into being by a compact based upon mutual fear and the instinct for self-protection is as absurd as Filmer's argument that the states of the modern world are the end products of Noah's division of the world among his sons. But to argue that morality is man-made and depends upon law is not absurd, however dangerous it may seem to one who believes in natural law. The philosophic defense of absolutism advanced in their several ways by Hobbes and Filmer has passed into the limbo of half-remembered political philosophy. The fundamental division between the thinking of the two men, one of whom holds that society is of man's making and the other that society is an organic development, is the most fundamental division in all social thought.

As for the historic importance of Filmer, it did not arise until he had been in the grave for nearly thirty years. In 1680 the forces that would strip the Catholic James, Duke of York, of his title to the throne were steadily mounting in power. Charles II was desperately in need of arguments to bolster his brother's title to the throne. But the arguments required would have to refute the claim that Parliament had the right to pass an Exclusion Bill. Filmer's unpublished manuscript was resurrected and hurried through the press. The arguments of *Patriarcha*, solid and absurd alike, became the rallying cries of the supporters of the Crown; the philosophy of monarchical legitimatism was extracted from it, and *Pater Patriae* (ironically, Father of his Country) made a rallying cry to set against "No Popish Successor." It succeeded until 1688, when the birth of a baby boy to the royal family swept into oblivion the philosophy of monarchical legitimatism. Now there was a Popish Successor with his whole life before him, and Protestant England could not stand that. James II went into exile and Filmer became a clay pigeon for the shafts of John Locke. The Whig thesis that government rests upon consent had triumphed. The Tory thesis of the divine right of kings quietly passed into history, and with it Filmer's *Patriarcha*. Everything in *Patriarcha* is dead except the central concept, but that central concept cannot die so long as belief in the divinely created order lives.

Hobbes and Filmer in their several ways had offered a hypothetical solution to the practical problem which beset General Monk. The difficulty was that in establishing absolutism there was a certain belling-the-cat quality. Perhaps "mutual fear brings peace," as the poet Blake would put it more than a century later, but mutual fear does not set up a universally accepted and respected sovereign. Indeed mutual fear totally precludes the possibility of his acceptance, except for the sort of acceptance imposed by fire and the sword, the kind that the Duke of Albemarle and the people of England did not want. Filmer's explanation of the origin of society had a comforting logic and simplicity about it, but they were deceptive. If there was to be any *Pater Patriae* within the realm of practical politics, it was to be Charles II who assumed the throne under terms as antithetical to the absolutist principles of Filmer as to those of Hobbes. The simple fact of the matter was that the English people had had their taste of absolutism and wanted no more of it, whatever might be its philosophic foundation. The Glorious Revolution of 1688 merely confirmed what the Restoration of 1660 established: absolutism whether of the right or of the left was a thing of England's past. The thought processes of neither Hobbes nor Filmer were dead, but their conclusions were.

THE CAMBRIDGE PLATONISTS

There had to be a compromise, and it had to be based on reason. The Age of Reason dawned in 1660; for the rest of the century the problem of reason, its nature, its foundation, its relationship to religion and its place in human life was to preoccupy thinkers and practical men alike. The term is chameleonic throughout the rest of the seventeenth century and the entire century that followed. Reason can mean anything from an intuitive perception of the divine wisdom down to ordinary common sense. It is the most elusive of terms with which to deal, the most eellike in its capacity for semantic squirming. This much, however, can be safely said: Reason is opposed to Enthusiasm. Monk and Hobbes were men of reason, and so was Filmer. But Monk's form of reason was consistent with England's destiny, Hobbes's and Filmer's forms were not. The future, then, in the realm of thought, which is not necessarily opposed to the realm of action, lay with those whose form of reason was consistent with that of Monk. In an age that sorely needed men of reason, certain of them wielded an influence on English thought that they would not have wielded under other circumstances. For example, there is that quiet group of academicians, the Cambridge Platonists. More by chance than design, their central concepts were on the main line of development in English thought. Before Tillotson and Locke there were Whichcote, Cudworth, and Henry More.

The Cambridge Platonists started with the sound Platonic

axiom that no faculty in man is higher than reason, since the divine reason is the highest attribute of God. The divine mind knows only ideas, the ultimate concepts in accordance with which all things that exist have their being. Human reason is, on the human scale, analogous to the divine reason. As Benjamin Whichcote put it, "To go against reason is to go against God; it is the self-same to do that which the reason of the case doth require, and that which God Himself doth appoint. Reason is the Divine governor of man's life; it is the very voice of God."[3]

LATITUDINARIANISM AND THE DEISTS

Since reason is the very voice of God, there can be no true conflict between reason and faith. Faith is mental assent to what reason produces; it may be a reluctant and delayed assent since the human will can be perverse, but it is an assent that cannot finally be denied. The Cambridge Platonists obviously could not accept the Calvinistic thesis that revelation is the only source of moral enlightenment. God reveals Himself to man partly through reason and partly through revelation, and there can be no essential conflict between the two. But this philosophical principle was in obvious conflict with the observable fact that men's convictions varied where the meaning of revelation was concerned. At this point their concept of reason as the voice of God is of particular importance. Since reason is the voice of God, it follows that the voice of conscience is an aspect of reason. But one cannot follow the voice of God as it speaks through conscience unless one is free to do so. Hence the Cambridge Platonists were, in the pejorative seventeenth-century phrase, Latitudinarians, and in the happier twentieth-century phrase, believers in religious tolerance. "God applies to our faculties, and deals with us, by reason and argument. Let us learn of God to deal with one another in meekness, calmness, and reason, and so represent God," pleads Whichcote (Aphorism 572).

From their latitudinarianism is derived their concept of the Church. They believed that morality is simple and, of necessity, within the understanding of the common man. The fundamental moral principles are revealed in Scripture and they are written in the heart of man. They are understood by reason, and the

moral principles that man apprehends by reason are modifica-
tions of the divine wisdom adapted to human reason. The
Church exists to aid man in attaining that moral goodness which
is the supreme goal of life. The church of their choice was the
Church of England, but it might not be the church that other
men of good will chose. If they were men of good will intent on
achieving the good life, that was all that mattered. They should
be free to choose the church that helped them best.

Thus the Age of Reason is promoted by these quiet academicians and reasonable men. Moral conduct is the important
thing, not dogma or ritual. There is no place for enthusiasm
in the make-up of men to whom reason is the voice of God
speaking to man through conscience for his moral guidance.
There is no place for the warfare of the sects in the thinking
of men to whom moral goodness is the supreme goal of life and
the church that leads the individual to the goal is the right
church for him. But this was the gospel that men of reason
of Monk's stamp wanted to hear. Let them be denounced as
Unitarians and vilified as atheists; "the latitude men" knew how
to live and let live, and that was the lesson England had to
learn. The practical answer wasn't absolutism; absolutism could
only have been achieved through despotism. The practical answer was toleration, emphasis on morality, guidance by the
clear light of reason and not by the murky flare of enthusiasm.
In the preceding age few would have heard the voice of
Cambridge Platonism. In this age these men of the ivory tower
were the ultimate realists.

As things developed, England paid abundant lip service to
their creed and little service of the heart. They were tolerant
by principle; the century to come would be tolerant by indifference. They believed that reason was the voice of God
speaking to the heart of man; the century to come believed
that reason was the voice of common sense talking to the selfish
instincts of man. To them morality had as its goal a mystical
union with God; to the century ahead morality meant the
application of the pleasure-pain calculus of Jeremy Bentham
and the other utilitarians. But at least England paid lip service
to their creed. Cheapened, coarsened, bandied about with cynical contempt, exploited with unabashed selfishness, still their

gospel of reason, morality, and tolerance was the gospel to which the eighteenth century paid lip service. And, of course, there were those in the century who paid it service of the heart. There always are.

That gospel was also preached by the deists. The distinction between the Cambridge Platonists and the deists is crystal clear in terms of theology and its lesser cousin philosophy. The distinction becomes blurred, however, when viewed in terms of influence and practical results. There is always a sense in which deism is an attitude of mind, and in that sense it does not differ profoundly from the attitude of mind to be found in the Platonists. The deists seldom had the academic accolade, and usually lacked an accolade of any sort. Some of them were much closer in spirit to the village atheists of the nineteenth century than to the thoughtful and reverent Cambridge Platonists. Yet at the heart of their gospel also were the eighteenth-century virtues: reason, morality, and tolerance.

As a movement in English thought, deism was short-lived. With one exception the chief deists were born in the quarter century between 1654 and 1679, and their activity was limited to a half century. The influence of deism, however, continued to be strong throughout the eighteenth century and can be said never to have entirely disappeared. One of them was born before the rest, born in the generation of Hobbes and Filmer, and he was the most intriguing personality of them all.

Edward Lord Herbert of Cherbury (1583–1648) was a man of affairs as well as the most constructive thinker among the deists. The triumphant progress of his life—an Oxford student at the age of twelve, the husband of an heiress at fifteen, the associate of Casaubon, Gassendi, and Grotius in his twenties, ambassador extraordinary to France at the age of thirty-seven—came to a sudden and total halt, and his last years were a dreary procession of disasters. He was on both sides in the Civil War and important to neither, and he died in its last days. His *Autobiography* is an amazing book. At every turn, as his editor Sidney Lee points out, Lord Herbert lauds to the skies his own handsome appearance, valor, and nobility of birth. The book is a parade of social triumphs recalled by a man living in the glories of a dead and buried past and so blinded

by the brilliance of his memories that he cannot see his genuine
and solid claims to fame. He is a strange figure in the history
of thought, this man who recorded himself as Osric and was
at heart Hamlet.

Lord Herbert laid the enduring cornerstone of deism. Attempt-
ing to do for natural religion what Grotius was doing for natural
law, he laid down five fundamental principles: (1) God exists;
(2) He must be worshiped; (3) worship is the cultivation of
moral virtue in a spirit of reverence; (4) one must repent his
sins; (5) there is an afterlife of reward or punishment. The law
and the prophets come to nothing more than this, and the
heathens outside the law accept the same fundamental charter.
This is natural religion. Everything else, be it rite or ritual,
dogma or doctrine, is the work of crafty priests. The history of
deism starts with Lord Herbert's *De Veritate* (1624), which
presents a faculty psychology, an epistemology, and a charter
of natural religion. Its complement is *De Religione Gentilium*
(1663), in which Herbert maintains that heathens also, under-
neath the absurdities and distortions of their belief, subscribe to
the same charter.

The concept of natural religion made possible a new theological climate in England. Faith, said the Cambridge Platonist,
is mental assent to what reason produces, not to what the theologian proclaims. Revelation can no more discredit reason than
reason can discredit revelation. Revelation and reason are twin
lights to guide man to a sound moral life, and each light strength-
ens the beam of the other. The deists held fundamentally to the
same position, but with a certain inclination in the direction
of reason. Reason among them tends to become the touchstone
that determines the accuracy of the interpretation of revelation.
The essence of religion is obedience to unchanging laws of
morality which are codifications of the will of God. But the
court of ultimate appeal does not reside in the tribunals of
theology; it rests in the individual human heart. Critical individualism as the cornerstone of religious faith was implicit in Protestantism from the start, but it required the conflicts and the
crises of the seventeenth century to give it an opportunity to
burgeon forth in England. It was, at least in a secular sense,
an entirely happy alternative to the battle of the sects.

JOHN LOCKE

The times called for the eighteenth-century virtues—reason, morality, and tolerance—but they called as well for the man to embody them. John Locke answered the call. Locke lived through the seventeenth-century conflicts and crises, and they affected his life and at times imperiled it as they did the lives of others. He was born a Puritan under circumstances best designed to promote a respect for Puritanism at its finest, for his own father embodied it. But his Oxford years, which were the years of the Commonwealth, left him with a hatred of what he deemed the intolerance and fanaticism of Presbyterian and Independent alike. He came through these years quietly, reaching his conclusions but keeping them to himself, and quietly established himself as a tutor at Oxford in 1661. He disliked scholasticism, lectured on Greek, dabbled in chemistry, and associated with the physician Thomas Sydenham and the physicist Robert Boyle. In 1666, with his meeting of Lord Ashley, later the first Earl of Shaftesbury, he had started down the road to disquiet and insecurity, to peril and to exile, to a triumphant private restoration, and to as secure a place in philosophy as any Englishman holds.

He lived at Exeter House as Lord Ashley's confidential secretary from 1667 to 1682, except for the years of exile. In 1675 Shaftesbury fell, and Locke found ill health a compelling reason to seek intellectual companionship with the men of science and of letters in the more urbane and stable land of France. He came back to London and to Shaftesbury in 1679, and was fearfully present in the electric days of 1681 when Shaftesbury tried to upset the succession of the Catholic James, Duke of York, to the throne in favor of the Duke of Monmouth, who was happily Protestant but unhappily illegitimate. Watching from some obscure niche in Somersetshire, he saw his master escape the gallows and flee to Holland. In 1683 Locke followed him to Holland, then a secure asylum for Europe's mavericks of thought, but not secure enough in Locke's judgment for him to use his own name. There he met William of Orange. Shortly after the Glorious Revolution of 1688, Locke returned to England in a private restoration of his own. Thereafter he was to know controversy,

but never again terror. He lived for fourteen years at Oates
Manor in Essex, the estate of Sir Francis Masham, whose wife
was the daughter of the Cambridge Platonist Ralph Cudworth.
The old link with the Ashley family was re-established, as the
secretary of the first Earl became the friend of his grandson, the
third Earl of Shaftesbury. He corresponded about science with
Sir Isaac Newton and about religion with the deist Anthony
Collins. He was a commissioner on the Board of Trade for four
years and then in 1700 (that "necessary century," the eighteenth,
did not start automatically with the tearing of a page from the
calendar) resigned from the Board of Trade to devote himself to
Biblical studies. He died on October 28, 1704, and he rests in the
parish church at High Laver.

There is always about Locke something suggestive of the man
caught "wandering between two worlds, one dead,/The other
powerless to be born. . . ." He held the future in his hands,
and had no idea of the treasure in his grasp. He was fearful,
darkly fearful, of the present. He wrote, and concealed the fact
that he had written. He published concepts that would remake
the world of Western man, and strove desperately to keep men
from knowing in whose mind they were conceived. "Other spirits
there are standing apart/Upon the forehead of the age to come,"
and John Locke was one of them. He stood there, often in fear
and trembling, because Locke had that hardest and perhaps
noblest kind of courage, the courage that must always fight
against fear as well as for truth.

Specifically in Locke the scientific revolution comes of ideological age. Before him were the pure scientists, Copernicus and
Tycho Brahe, Kepler and Galileo, Newton and Boyle, and the
scientist who was a philosopher as well, Descartes. The Coper-
nican-Cartesian universe, that machine of unimaginable dimensions made by an infinite Creator and operated by His objective
and unchangeable laws, is the universe of John Locke. It is a
fearsome universe to contemplate, but puny man has freedom of
the will within it. John Locke knew and accepted the axioms of
modern physical science, but he never believed that they obliter-
ated the human spirit.

Locke believed that men are born free and equal. He agreed
with Hobbes and against Filmer, that government came into

being through agreement. The patriarchal concept of Filmer, insofar as he treats it seriously, he dismisses as an imperfect and misleading parallel; the subservience of children to parents has a natural limitation of time and offers no model for society. The truth, according to Locke, is that all men are born free and equal because all men are born the property of God. "For Men being all the Workmanship of one Omnipotent, and infinitely wise Maker; All the Servants of one Sovereign Master, sent into the World by his order and about his Business, they are his Property, whose Workmanship they are, made to last during his, not one another's Pleasure."[4] Thus the equality of man rests upon the fatherhood of God; that is the true patriarchal system according to Locke, not the patriarchal system that Filmer conceived.

THE LIMITATIONS OF HUMAN LAW

Of what, then, does freedom consist? It consists of an order brought into being and perpetuated by law; ". . . the end of Law is not to abolish or restrain, but to preserve and enlarge Freedom. . . . Freedom is not, as we are told, A Liberty for every Man to do what he lists: (For who could be free, when every other Man's Humour might domineer over him?) But a Liberty to dispose, and order, as he lists, his Person, Actions, Possessions, and his whole Property, within the Allowance of those Laws under which he is; and therein not to be subject to the arbitrary Will of another, but freely follow his own."[5] What determines the limitations of law? The limitations of human law are determined by the law of Nature, which is the expression to man of the will of God revealed to man by the light of human reason: "The law of nature is the law of reason." Nothing in Locke is stressed more powerfully than the thought that reason is the mode of cooperation among men; it is his essential answer to the absolutism of both Filmer and Hobbes. Thus John Locke knew and accepted the axioms of modern political science in free societies, and believed that the human spirit flourished best under them.

"In the beginning all the World was America"; the phrasing is memorable, but the concept of the state of nature is conventional

enough. Locke held it, but unlike Hobbes did not think of the
state of nature as a state of war. The state of nature was simply
the state in which individuals retained the executive power over
their possessions. The fact of property made them merge their
rights into a state. "Though the Earth, and all inferior Creatures
be common to all Men, yet every Man has a Property in his own
Person. This no body has any Right to but himself. The Labour
of his Body, and the Work of his hands, we may say are properly
his. Whatsoever then he removes out of the State that Nature
hath provided, and left it in, he hath mixed his Labour with, and
joyned to it something that it is his own, and thereby makes it his
Property."[6] It is the protection of this property that motivates the
formation of the state. ". . . 'tis not without reason, that he seeks
out, and is willing to joyn in Society with others who are already
united, or have a mind to unite for the mutual Preservation of
their Lives, Liberties and Estates, which I call by the general
name, Property."[7] Thus John Locke knew and accepted the
axiom of nineteenth-century liberalism and twentieth-century
conservatism, that government exists to protect property.

But did he? It is precisely at this point that the need for
caution shows itself, as one decides what a germinal thinker
like John Locke did or did not know and accept. Locke believed
that the state exists to protect the lives, liberties, and estates of
its members, all embraced in the general name *property*. There
is nothing isolated in this comprehensive use of the term *property;* Laslett lists twelve other instances in the *Treatises* in
which he uses the word in the comprehensive sense. Indeed it
is the only philosophic sense in which he uses it; when he uses
property to mean physical possessions, he makes the fact perfectly clear. It is as though Locke conceived the attributes of a
man—his life as a member of a family, a society, a profession or
trade, a church; the ways in which he orders that life in its
several aspects; in a word, what later would be summed up, together with life and liberty, as "the pursuit of happiness"—as
distinguishable from the man himself although aspects of him
and therefore subject for merger with the attributes of other men
in a common society formulated and perpetuated for the common good. It is this philosophic concept of proverty which permits men, as Laslett succinctly puts it, to ". . . proceed from the

abstract world of liberty and equality based on their relationship with God and natural law, to the concrete world of political liberty guaranteed by political arrangements."[8] Thus John Locke knew and accepted the reverse axiom as well, the axiom of nineteenth-century conservatism and twentieth-century liberalism, that government exists to protect human rights. This is the sort of thing that should make one ponder the value of simple labels like "liberal" and "conservative."

The religion of John Locke is a sort of modified and limited deism. Belief in Jesus as the Messiah is necessary, but it must be united with a good life. In *Reasonableness of Christianity* he says, "Repentence is as absolute a condition of the covenant of grace as faith; and as necessary to be performed as that. These two, faith and repentence, i.e., believing Jesus to be the Messiah and a good life, are the indispensible conditions of the new covenant, to be performed by all those who would obtain eternal life."[9] Those who lived before His time had sufficient grace to attain salvation, those who have never heard of Him have an inner light clear enough to guide them. But Jesus makes the way clearer to man, the truth more evident to his vision, and aids him in the life. Hence the "reasonableness" of Christianity. God, a tender and patient father, has given man reason, and a law which can never be unreasonable. To aid man's frailty, He has given him a Redeemer. This is all the law and the prophets. "This is a plain, intelligible proposition; and the all-merciful God seems herein to have consulted the poor of the world, and the bulk of mankind: these are articles that the laboring and illiterate man may comprehend. This is a religion suited to vulgar capacities, and the state of mankind in this world, destined to labour and travail. The writers and wranglers in religion fill it with niceties, and dress it up with notions, which they make necessary and fundamental parts of it; as if there were no way into the Church, but through the Academy or Lycaeum. The greatest part of mankind have not leisure for learning and logic, and superfine distinctions of the schools. Where the hand is used to the plough and the spade, the head is seldom elevated to sublime notions, or exercised in mysterious reasonings. . . . And if the poor had the gospel preached to them, it was, without doubt, such a gospel as the poor could understand, plain and intelligible: and so it was, as we have seen, in the preachings of Christ and his apostles."[10] Thus John Locke knew and accepted the axiom of eighteenth-century Christianity, and much of Christianity of the centuries that followed, that religion is simply a way of life. It is the way to peace in heaven, and men of reason said it was the way to peace on earth.

In Locke, as in Hobbes before him, can be seen in broad outline the utilitarian pattern of thought which looms so large in nineteenth-century thought. "Nature, I confess, has put into man a desire for happiness and an aversion to misery: these indeed are innate practical principles which (as practical principles ought) do continue constantly to operate and influence all our actions without ceasing: these may be observed in all persons and all ages, steady and universal; but these are inclinations of the appetite to good, not impressions of truth on the understanding."[11] But Locke manages, in a way more creditable to his religious feeling than to his logic, to reconcile the fundamentals of utilitarianism with the concept of a divinely created moral order. "Good and evil . . . are nothing but pleasure or pain to us. Moral good and evil, then, is only the conformity or disagreement of our voluntary actions to some law, whereby good or evil is drawn on us, from the will and power of the lawmaker; which good and evil, pleasure or pain, attending our observance or breach of the law by the decree of the law-maker, is that we call reward and punishment."[12] That is to say, moral good gives pleasure because God ultimately rewards it; moral evil gives pain because God ultimately punishes it. The moral code is divinely created, but man's incentive to observe it is based on the utilitarian consideration of reward or punishment. Right and wrong are not eternal verities, and the limitation which natural law philosophers believe God's justice imposes upon His omnipotence is not recognized by Locke.

What is true in the divine order is true in the human. Locke accepts the compact theory but, unlike Hobbes, believes that the compact by its nature limits the power of the prince. Government exists for the welfare of the people, and it must justify its existence by the utilitarian test. The compact rests ultimately on the golden rule, and the golden rule rests ultimately on the sanctions devised by God. It is not true to say that in Locke right and wrong are of human determination, tested by the happiness or sorrow they produce. But it is true to say that right and wrong are of divine determination, tested for man by the eternal happiness or sorrow they produce. To government the test of utility is applied. To the compact on which government rests the same test is applied. To the moral code from which the compact is derived the same test is applied. John Locke was not a nineteenth-century utilitarian, but he knew and accepted in a framework of religion the axioms that in a secular framework would produce nineteenth-century utilitarianism.

To make of Locke merely a spokesman of the rising middle class is seriously to underestimate his significance in the history of thought. He did have that quick eye for a good investment often found beneath the pious brows of Puritans, but he seems to have mistrusted the trading class. As a doctor he was not particularly conscious of his professional status. The *Two Treatises of Government* may be read to justify the Revolution of 1688—certainly Locke would have encouraged such a reading—but it is a reading only of the surface. He was a political theorist, but so philosophic a theorist as safely to remove him from the arena of political science. There is a sense in which John Locke is so simple that to twist him into anything other than himself is to make him unconvincingly complex. Just as the thinking of Filmer is based upon a patriarchal concept, the fatherhood of man, so the thinking of Locke is based upon a different patriarchal concept, the fatherhood of God. From the fatherhood of God come the equality and liberty of man. From the equality and liberty of man come the social compact, and government by the consent of the governed. From the equality and liberty of man comes that complex of human attributes and possessions which Locke calls *property*, which government exists to protect. Religion is an awareness of the fatherhood of God, an awareness of His law and the sanctions by which He enforces it. But to make John Locke ultimately the prophet of democracy, or of economic conservatism (or economic liberalism, for that matter), or of eighteenth-century deism, or of nineteenth-century utilitarianism or twentieth-century indifferentism, is to confuse the corollaries of a philosopher's thinking with his fundamental axiom. Filmer was the man to be answered, and everything that the modern world considers modern in John Locke arises from the axiom with which he answers Filmer. It is the fatherhood of God on which rest the freedom and equality of man. That axiom is fundamentally consistent with natural law thought. But the law of God is determined by the will of God, and man obeys the will of God through respect for the divine sanction. When law depends upon will and not will upon law, the concept is not consistent with the concept of natural law, even when the will is the will of God.

Thus a new religious climate was brought into being, the climate which had to exist for the Age of Reason to exist. Absolutism had had its day, and England had no stomach for tyranny in any guise. Enthusiasm had had its day, and England had no stomach for a further war of the creeds. A common denominator of agreement had to be achieved in the contiguous realms of government and religion. Monk and those who thought like him had shown the way in the realm of government, and the lesson of 1660 was confirmed in 1688. The Cambridge Platonists and the deists, both those who wrote before Locke and those who followed him, showed the way in religion. It was the way needed, probably the only way that could exist short of an unearthly reformation of sinful man himself. The new way in government and the new way in religion found their philosopher in John Locke. By 1700 enthusiasm had subsided; emotionalism no longer threatened to reach flood stage and the level was steadily falling. Absolutism had passed from the English scene, and the pitched battles of the Crown and Parliament had subsided to the squabbles of the Tories and the Whigs. The angry Jehovah of Calvinism had mellowed to the benign Father of deism. The heroic age was over, in a land that had had more than its fill of heroics. England was ready for a prose age of reason and common sense, ready for that peace of the Augustans which is not quite the peace that passeth human understanding. The men of reason had triumphed. It remains to be seen what happened to reason itself.

III

"WHATEVER IS, IS RIGHT"

It was a comfortable if rather superficial Age of Reason that was ushered in as the fires of enthusiasm among Roundhead and Cavalier, Anglican, Puritan, and Papist died down to the twilight glow of latitudinarianism and deistic rationalism. The day was coming late in the century when they would flare up again, but the quiet glow was sufficient to light the furious feuds of the Whigs and the Tories, those eighteenth-century political struggles in which heat was a more than ample compensation for the lack of light. To Americans the political intrigues of the British eighteenth century have a nightmarish complexity, nor is it entirely certain that twentieth-century Britons are much better versed in the political ins and outs of their ancestors. We are fortunate in not having to plunge into that historical rain forest.

Some generalizations, however, are in order. The Tories were the eighteenth-century descendants of the seventeenth-century Anglicans and the ancestors of the nineteenth- and twentieth-century Conservatives. The Whigs were the eighteenth-century descendants of the seventeenth-century Puritans and the ancestors of the nineteenth- and twentieth-century Liberals. The *Concise Oxford Dictionary* defines *Tory* as a "member of the party that opposed the exclusion of the Duke of York (James II), inclined to the Stuarts after 1689, accepted George III and the established order in Church & State, opposed Reform Bill of 1832, & has been succeeded by the Conservative party." It adds something to the political flavor of the age to know that the word *Tory* comes from the Irish *toraidhe*, meaning "robber." The same source defines *Whig* as a "member of the political party that, after the Revolution of 1688, aimed at subordinating the power of the crown to that of Parliament & the upper classes, passed the Reform Bill, & in the 19th c. was succeeded by the Liberal." The reader may make what he wishes from the etymology of *Whig*. It comes from the Scottish *whiggamor*, the nickname of the Scots of the west who whigged (i.e. jogged) their mares to Leith for corn.

The Tories supported the Crown and the Whigs supported Parliament. The Tories went on pleasant Sundays to the Church of England, the Whigs rather more frequently to the nonconformist chapels. The Tories were oriented to a country economy, supporting agriculture and the landed gentry. The Whigs were oriented to a city economy, supporting trade and middle-class industry and banking. To the Tories England was Shakespeare's "precious stone set in the silver sea," and a strong Navy was the right defense for "this other Eden, demi-Paradise." The Whigs had a less romantic but far more aggressive and expansive foreign policy. Every baby born alive in that age was either a little Whig or a little Tory.

BOLINGBROKE

What it meant to be a Tory, however, had changed from the age of Filmer, and we may start our consideration of the age that John Locke and the Whigs brought into being by considering a Tory of the period. He is Henry St. John Viscount Bolingbroke (1678–1751). Bolingbroke was the grandson of a pious Puritan and the son of a notorious rake. He attended Eton with his lifelong political foe Robert Walpole and perhaps went on to Christ Church, Oxford. The life of young Bolingbroke offers evidence that there is more realism in Restoration comedy than one would imagine. He married the daughter of Sir Henry Winchescomb. She never ceased to love him however much reason she had to deplore him. Much of the time he lived with one described by Oliver Goldsmith as "the most expensive demi-rep of the kingdom."

He entered Parliament in 1701 and his oratorical powers soon won him prominence among the Tories. He became Secretary of War under Marlborough, and Marlborough brought out the best in Bolingbroke. Even his bitter enemies never denied the brilliance of Bolingbroke, and Marlborough elicited from him an enthusiastic dedication to his work not always in evidence. In 1710, after Queen Anne dismissed the Whigs, he became Secretary of State. His supreme service in the politics of the age was to engineer the Treaty of Utrecht (1713), which ended the War of the Spanish Succession. The glorious victories of Marlborough at Blenheim, Ramillies, Oudenarde, and Malplaquet were being nullified in the realm of power politics by the peril of a union between the crowns of Spain and the German empire. The Tories wanted peace, as did the English people, and Bolingbroke and the Tories believed that a peace fundamentally favorable to England was secured when the Treaty provided that the two lines of the Bourbon house might never inherit from each other nor the two crowns ever be worn by a single head.

From this moment, when Bolingbroke stood at the apex of his career in the complete confidence of the queen, his descent was sudden. He became involved in the affairs of James Stuart the Pretender, whose birth in 1688 had rocked the Empire and made entirely hypothetical Tory absolutism of Filmer's sort. The Pretender had made in 1708 one abortive attempt to claim his crown. He had fought the following year in the French campaigns in Flanders, and Parliament had set a price of 100,000 crowns upon his head. But his half-sister was the Queen of England, and Anne wanted her brother restored to the line of succession. In general the Tories inclined to the Stuarts, and to an extent now impossible to estimate Bolingbroke took part in the enterprise of formulating a Stuart restoration. So, at least, the Whigs believed, and some months after the death of Anne in August, 1714, Bolingbroke fled to France. Perhaps it was an error, but there is substantial evidence that the Whigs intended to impeach him for high treason and bring him to the scaffold.

The rest is twilight. He was involved in the stupidly conceived and poorly executed return of the Pretender to Scotland in 1715. None of the conditions he believed essential for a successful Stuart restoration were achieved, yet Bolingbroke was blamed and dismissed from the Pretender's presence after James Edward had slunk back to the safety of France. In 1723 a now harmless Bolingbroke was pardoned by the English government,

and for some years he divided his time between England and
France, where his second wife had a luxurious estate. For a
decade he attacked Walpole and the entire Whig philosophy of
government in a weekly called *The Craftsman*. These were his
Dawley years, the years of his friendship with Alexander Pope,
which won him a more secure place in literary history than he
holds in political. Around him gathered the literary wits of the
age, and its authentic geniuses, Swift, Pope and Voltaire, along
with Congreve, Gay, Arbuthnot, and the rest. After 1735 he spent
most of his time in France. The more removed he became from
practical affairs, the more philosophical became his writings, and
the more they merit a place in literary history. Like a vastly
greater writer, Edmund Spenser, Viscount Bolingbroke cultivated the flower of literary immortality in the graveyard of his
political hopes.

When we pass from his political disasters to his philosophical
views, we see the religious compromise fully developed. To be a
Tory usually meant that one was an Anglican, and to be an
Anglican often meant that one was receptive to deistic thought.
Bolingbroke held to the full deistic position, and opened important saliences from it of major importance in its subsequent
development. It was these saliences that made Dr. Johnson refer
to Mallet's 1754 edition of Bolingbroke's works as "the gun
charged against Christianity."

There is always something of the elegant amateur to Bolingbroke in his philosophical writings. They comprise four essays
"addressed to Alexander Pope" and enough "fragments or minutes of essays" to fill a substantial folio volume in Mallet's edition.
The advertisement to the latter states in part: "The foregoing
Essays, if they may deserve even that name, and the Fragments
or Minutes that follow, were thrown upon paper in Mr. Pope's
lifetime, and at his desire. They were all communicated to him
in scraps, as they were occasionally writ. . . . They are all nothing more than repetitions of conversations often interrupted,
often renewed, and often carried on a little confusedly."[1] Their
significance to Pope will be evident when we reach his *Essay on
Man*.

Bolingbroke held to the usual deist viewpoint on natural religion. "The religion of nature, and therefore of the God of nature

is (necessarily) simple and plain; it tells us nothing which our reason is unable to comprehend, and much less anything which is repugnant to it. Natural religion and reason are always agreed, and the whole economy of God's dispensations to man is of a piece."[2] He criticizes the writers on natural law, but tends to accept their premises, as he tends to accept Filmer's concept of the patriarchal origin of society. "On the whole, as fast as families united in larger societies, and the same plain and simple rules, the first rudiments of natural law, that had been sufficient under paternal government were so no longer, but required greater extension and a greater variety of application, philosophers and legislators arose, constituted governments, and made laws wisely and unwisely. . . . But there would have been no societies to whom laws might be given, no pretence to give them, no disposition to receive them, if there had not been a primaeval law, a law by which the families of men were governed in that state which we commonly call a state of nature and which laid the principles of future government in another state, to which they were advancing gradually. This primaeval law is that code wherein all the laws, to which God has subjected his human creatures, are contained. Civil laws are the glosses which sometimes explain and sometimes perplex it, which men make, and men may alter at their will; whilst the other remains immutable like that of God."[3] He then proceeds to use the argument from natural law to refute Hobbes's denial of a law antecedent to statute law. Bolingbroke was in no sense a believer in the manmade order.

FAITH IN PROVIDENCE

The main contributions of Bolingbroke to eighteenth-century thought, and the intellectual saliences which he opened in it, are his belief in general providence and his philosophic optimism. More than any other deist he recognized the central importance of providence in deism. "In asserting the justice of providence, I chuse rather to insist on the constant, visible, and undeniable course of a general providence which is sufficient for the purpose, than to assume a dispensation of particular providences. The atheist, who assumes that there ought to be such, complains that they are wanting. The theist, who admits that there are such, complains that they are insufficient. The former draws from what he assumes a pretence to cavil. The latter only grows inconsistent; for I would ask him if there are any such providences, why not more? He admits enough to break through and overturn the natural order and constitution of the physical and moral system. How comes it to pass that there are not enough to stop his mouth when he complains of the misery of man and the injustice of providence? The truth is that we have not in philosophical speculation, in any history except that of the Bible, nor in our own experience, sufficient grounds to establish the doctrine of particular providences, and to reconcile it to that of a general providence, which continues, and directs the course of things in the material and intellectual systems, as these systems were originally constituted by the author of nature."[4] Again and again he returns to this concept of general providence. "It is plain by the whole course of God's providence, that he regards his human creatures collectively, not individually, how worthy soever every one of them deems himself to be a particular object of the divine care. He has given them indifferently, and in common, the means of arriving at happiness in their moral, as in their physical state; and has left to them to improve these means, that they may obtain this end."[5]

Bolingbroke believed in the principle of plenitude, the concept of the great chain of being in which each being occupies its appropriate place. Man has his appropriate place in the great chain, but it befits man, in the humility born of wisdom, to look down to the animals from which he is separated by finite degrees rather than up to infinity. He did not believe that man was any more the final cause of creation than was any other created being. He believed that the doctrine of particular providence carried with it logically three other doctrines to which he could not give assent: belief in future rewards and punishments, belief in predestination, and denial of free will. He further felt that belief in particular providence only keeps alive that sectarianism whence come enthusiasm and all the evils it connotes. "To keep up a belief of particular providences serves to keep up a belief not only of the efficacy of prayer, and of the intercession of saints in heaven as well as of the church on earth, but of the several rites of external devotion. . . ."[6]

Hence Bolingbroke, unlike the other deists, is a philosophic optimist. He believed in God on the principle of causality. Certainly anticipating and presumably setting the model for Paley's Clockmaker Deity, he writes, "Carry a clock to the wild inhabitants of the cape of Good Hope. They will soon be convinced that intelligence made it, and none but the most stupid will imagine that this intelligence is in the hand that they see move, and in the wheels that they see turn. Those among them, who pretend to greater sagacity than the rest, may perhaps suspect that the workman is concealed in the clock, and there conducts invisibly all the motions of it. The first of these hottentot philosophers are, you see, more rational than atheists; the second are more so than the heathen naturalists, and the third are just at a pitch with some modern meta-physicians."[7] But once the Watchmaker God has created the universe on the principle of general providence, his work is complete. "To think worthily of God, we must think that the natural order of things has been always the same, and that a Being of infinite wisdom and knowledge to whom the past and the future are like the present, and who wants no experience to inform him, can have no reason to alter what infinite wisdom and knowledge have once done."[8]

From this it follows, in the logic of Bolingbroke, that an infinitely wise and powerful God who has created a universe to be operated on the principle of general providence could only have created the best possible of worlds. "Since infinite wisdom not only established the end but directed the means, the system of the universe must be necessarily the best of all possible systems. . . ."[9] That evil exists is, of course true, but it is not true that evil is the opposite of good. The view that evil exists is a true one, but a view that is incomplete; "the seeming imperfection of the parts is necessary for the real perfection of the whole."[10] Physical evils are merely the transient and impermanent results of a system directed by a general providence. Moral evil is the result of the misuse of free will. If we could see the universe in its myriad and magnificent entirety, we would see that this is the best possible of worlds. "Whatever is, is right."

These are among the saliences of thought that will be developed as the century progresses. Out of the concept of general
providence comes the concept frequently but inaccurately attributed to the early deists, the concept of the absentee God. It
is not really to be found in them, but it is to be found in Bolingbroke and will be found in others who come after him. Out of
the concept of general providence formulated by an infinitely
wise and just God comes the related concept of the perfect
system, the philosophic optimism of Alexander Pope's aphorism,
"Whatever is, is right." But observe the implications of the
doctrine of general providence and philosophy of optimism
where traditional religion is concerned. Obviously there is no
point to petitionary prayer, since God never employs particular
providence or changes by one jot or tittle for individual man the
general system He has created. Whatever is, is right, whether
one likes it or not. The individual cannot choose but to accept
it. When we have reached this point, the religious compromise
has become a religious surrender.

One might further point out that the political compromise
does not fare particularly well. Bolingbroke might believe that
ultimate authority comes from the people and that government
exists for the popular welfare. His democratic Toryism might
be instanced as another example of the instinctive alliance between the aristocracy and the common people against the middle
class. But the doctrine of philosophic optimism, the aphorism
"Whatever is, is right," is hardly a clarion call for reform. It may
be paradoxical that religious liberalism can lead down one
avenue of thought to a state of social and economic stagnation,
but it is a paradox that must stand. History illustrates it very
often.

Thus out of deism, in the hands of Bolingbroke, had evolved
a disbelief in particular providence and a belief in philosophic
optimism. Both beliefs tended to reduce deity to an absentee
status. Therefore both beliefs tended toward the concept of the
social order as something created by man in the absence of God,
although Bolingbroke himself did not believe in the man-made
order. Again we see illustrated the truth that the tenor of a man's
thoughts is often more influential and important than its content.
Reason was more firmly entrenched than ever as a result of

Bolingbroke's essays. Authority was routed. But the real paradox is that in the name of reform, reform was quelched. Again and again in the history of the man-made order we find that what starts as an argument for reform is distorted into a justification of the *status quo*. To the man who makes the order, "whatever is, is right."

SHAFTESBURY

The next stage is marked by the appearance of a rival for reason; it is reached in the essays of Shaftesbury. Anthony Ashley Cooper, third Earl of Shaftesbury (1671–1713), was the son of as intermittently distinguished a line as the peerage boasts. The first Earl was chancellor of England, co-author with his friend John Locke of the Carolina Constitutions, fomenter of Monmouth's Rebellion, and immortal as Achitophel in Dryden's *Absalom and Achitophel*, the greatest political satire in English literature. The seventh Earl was a noted Victorian philanthropist, and with a bit of Victorian artistic incongruity the bronze archer of the statuary group in Piccadilly Circus. On the other hand the second Earl, according to Dryden, was "born a shapeless lump, like anarchy." It is customary to think of Shaftesbury as the grandson of the first Earl, and to pass over with discreet silence the fact that he also had a father.

Shaftesbury was educated, in a fashion that later appalled him, at Winchester School, but his real education was in the salons and the galleries of the Continent. In 1695 he entered Parliament for Poole; a Whig by birth, education, and conviction, his vote really went for Parliamentary liberty and human freedom. His public life, however, was short and undistinguished. Shaftesbury was asthmatic and tubercular, and the problems London presents to both conditions are notorious. He soon retired to France and Holland, and to the intellectual company his grandfather and his own mentor John Locke had so much enjoyed. Shaftesbury was very much the student of Locke, but only to a limited degree a member of his school.

Shaftesbury's writing lifetime was brief, yet must have been intensive. He is a man of one book, *Characteristics of Men, Manners, Opinions, Times* (1711). Its first volume comprises essays on Enthusiasm and Freedom of Wit and Humour, along with one called "Soliloquy or Advice to an Author"; its second and far more important volume contains the heart of his philosophy, "Inquiry concerning Virtue or Merit" and "The Moralists"; the third is given over to "Miscellaneous Reflections on the Preceding Treatises and Other Critical Subjects." The "Inquiry concerning Virtue or Merit" was an early work, published by the deist Toland without Shaftesbury's consent in 1699. The other essays of the first two volumes were published separately between 1708 and 1710. Shaftesbury did much hard thinking and close writing during the last years of his short and disease-ridden life.

Shaftesbury had his private recipe for dealing with enthusiasm. The way to combat it is by ridicule; the only sound approach to problems of religion and morality is through good humor. "Gravity is of the very essence of Imposture." But behind his recipe lies something fundamental in his thinking. Like Bolingbroke he accepted the thesis of philosophic optimism, that an infinitely wise and good Creator would create only the best possible of worlds. "Good-humour is not only the best security against enthusiasm, but the best foundation of piety and true religion; for if right thoughts and worthy apprehensions of the Supreme Being are fundamental to all true worship and adoration, 'tis more than probable that we shall never miscarry in this respect, except through ill-humour only. . . . For there are so many arguments to persuade a man in humour that, in the main, all things are kindly and well disposed, that one would think it impossible for him to be so far out of conceit with affairs as to imagine they all ran at adventures; and that the world, as venerable and wise a face as it carried, had neither sense nor meaning in it. This however I am persuaded of, that nothing besides ill-humour can give us dreadful or ill thoughts of a Supreme Manager."[11]

That Shaftesbury should be poles apart from Hobbes follows quite obviously, and he devotes part of his "Freedom of Wit and Humour" to a refutation of Hobbesian morals and politics. Whereas to Hobbes the natural essence of life is nasty, brutish, and short, to Shaftesbury it is noble, beautiful, and enduring. Again there appears in incipient form a central thought that will be fully developed in the major essays. Shaftesbury lived and wrote in a neoclassical age when balance, order, symmetry, and proportion were the accepted artistic ideals. But they were the ideals of human life as well, and from the parallelism of the two there begins to emerge in this essay the most typical of all Shaftesbury's concepts, the analogy he saw between morality and art. "Of all other beauties which virtuosos pursue, poets celebrate, musicians sing, and architects or artists, of whatever kind, describe or form, the most delightful, the most engaging and pathetic, is that which is drawn from real life, and from the passions. . . . Let Poets, or the men of harmony, deny, if they can, this force of Nature, or withstand this moral magic. They, for their parts, carry a double portion of this charm about them. For in the first place, the very passion which inspires them is itself the love of numbers, decency and proportion; and this too, not in a narrow sense, or after a selfish way (for who of them composes for himself?), but in a friendly, social view, for the pleasure and good of others, even down to posterity and future ages."[12]

Like John Ruskin a century and a half later, a man whose thinking so closely resembles that of Shaftesbury, the Earl believed that only the good man could be the good artist and, conversely, that a good life is itself a work of art. "Such a poet is indeed a second *Maker;* a just Prometheus under Jove. Like that sovereign artist or universal plastic nature, he forms a whole, coherent and proportioned in itself, with due subjection and subordinancy of constituent parts. He notes the boundaries of the passions, and knows their exact tones and measures; by which he justly represents them, marks the sublime of sentiments and action, and distinguishes the beautiful from the deformed, the amiable from the odious. The moral artist who can thus imitate the Creator, and is thus knowing in the inward form and structure of his fellow-creature, will hardly, I presume, be found unknowing in himself, or at a loss in those numbers which make the harmony of a mind." And continuing with the thought that evil is not the opposite of good but its imperfection, "knavery is mere dissonance and disproportion. And though villains may have strong tones and natural capacities of action, 'tis impossible that true judgment and ingenuity should reside where harmony and honesty have no being."[13]

The pattern of thought developing in these essays comes to full development elsewhere in *Characteristics*. Man is a complex of passions and emotions ruled by reason. Reason ordains the characteristics of balance, order, symmetry, and proportion, which mark the virtuous life. But balance, order, symmetry, and proportion are the characteristics of art as they are of nature, which Shaftesbury often hymns in a way suggestive of the Romantic Movement. Hence the analogy between morality and art is a valid one. "To philosophise, in a just signification, is but to carry good-breeding a step higher. For the accomplishment of breeding is, to learn whatever is decent in company or beautiful in arts; and the sum of philosophy is, to learn what is just in society and beautiful in Nature and the order of the world."[14]

THE SANCTION OF MORALITY

There is, then, an analogy between the aesthetic sense and the moral sense. With this analogy we come to the very heart of Shaftesbury's thought. Shaftesbury rejected totally the doctrine of his teacher Locke that right and wrong are products of God's fiat. Accepting the natural law view that God's omnipotence is controlled by His justice, Shaftesbury held that right and wrong are objective entities to which God Himself is subject. Man has a moral sense whereby he knows and approves of what is right, knows and disapproves of what is wrong. This moral sense can and must be educated, even as the aesthetic sense which it so closely resembles. It is the guide and guardian alike of man in his quest for the good life, which is also the beautiful life. But before it is a developed sense it is an instinct, and that instinct is the root of all man's moral being. "'Tis impossible to suppose a mere sensible creature originally so ill-constituted and un-natural as that, from the moment he comes to be tried by sensible objects, he should have no one good passion towards his kind, no foundation either of pity, love, kindness, or social affection. 'Tis full as impossible to conceive that a rational creature coming first to be tried by rational objects, and receiving into his mind the images or representations of justice, generosity, gratitude, or other virtue, should have no liking of these or dislike of their contraries, but be found absolutely indifferent towards whatsoever is presented to him of this sort. A soul, indeed, may as well be without sense as without admiration in the things of which it has any knowledge. Coming therefore to a capacity of seeing and admiring in this new way, it must needs find a beauty and a deformity as well in actions, minds, and tempers, as in figures, sounds, or colours. . . . Sense of right and wrong therefore being as natural to us as natural affection itself, and being a first principle in our constitution and make, there is no speculative opinion, persuasion, or belief, which is capable immediately or directly to exclude or destroy it."[15]

There remains the problem of the sanction of morality. Shaftesbury rejects with contempt Hobbes's concept that the moral law is man-made and hence that the sanctions are those provided by statute law; indeed the refutation of Hobbes is the starting point of *Characteristics*, as it is of so many other philosophic treatises of that period. He rejects with equal vigor the thesis of John Locke that the source of morals is the will of God and that the principle of pleasure or pain depends ultimately on reward and punishment in the hereafter. Shaftesbury finds the true sanction to be the inner one, the approval or disapproval of the moral sense. With this inner sanction he couples the love and reverence due to a just God. The final test of the sanction is the way in which a course of action affects the general welfare. Universal benevolence is the attitude of the perfectly developed moral sense; the social virtues transcend the personal ones; to anticipate a phrase, "the greatest happiness of the greatest number" is the final goal of the good life. "To love the public, to study universal good, and to promote the interest of the whole world, as far as lies within our power, is surely the height of goodness, and makes that temper which we call divine."[16]

Shaftesbury is one of the most attractive figures in the history of English thought. He did study universal good and he did try to promote the interest of the whole world. He was a man of high idealism, and he had by instinct a benevolence as universal as the benevolence that he preached. Those who dismiss the graceful optimism of Shaftesbury as an optimism natural for a titled aristocrat of abundant means ignore the total picture.

Shaftesbury was titled, wealthy, asthmatic, and tubercular. There were other things than wine and roses in his life.

Yet Shaftesbury opened saliences of thought the further development of which would have horrified him. In Shaftesbury not reason but a moral sense is the touchstone of good and evil. Morality is by no means a matter merely of instinctive feeling to Shaftesbury. He did believe that the moral sense is present in man as an instinct, but he believed that it was an instinct that had to be trained, cultivated, and educated. There were those who came long after Shaftesbury to whom the instinct seemed all that mattered. "An act is right if I think it right" is a serious departure from the principle of authority; "an act is right if I feel it is right" is an even more serious one. Indeed strange fruit budded on the tree of deism. Certainly the benevolent Deity whom Shaftesbury reverenced would shield the Earl from recognizing Oscar Wilde as his ideological descendant, but the line of descent exists. Let the emphasis shift a trifle and "the good life is the beautiful life" becomes "the beautiful life is the good life." The Age of Reason had to allow some living room to the Age of Emotion.

The challenge issued to reason by emotion is not really to be found in Shaftesbury himself. To him the foundations of moral distinctions are in men themselves, and if the subcellar on which those distinctions rest is an instinct, the structure that houses them is erected by reason. Shaftesbury accepts, of course, the deistic fundamental that there is nothing incompatible in reason and revelation and nothing in the moral order that reason, operating through the moral sense, cannot encompass. Morality is independent of institutional theology. The ultimate test of the virtue of an act is its effect on the general welfare. The test is applied by the moral sense, which passes an immediate judgment on the consistency or inconsistency of the act with the general welfare. The criteria by which the trained moral sense makes its judgment are analogous to the criteria employed by the aesthetic sense. In a superficial way one might say that Shaftesbury believed morals to be a matter of good taste, but it is more accurate to say that he believed morals and good taste to have closely analogous criteria.

The two best reasoned and most mature expositions of Shaftesbury's thought are "An Inquiry concerning Virtue or Merit" and "The Moralists." Their fundamental purpose is to propound a system of natural theology grounded on philosophic optimism and venerating a God whose prime characteristic is universal benevolence. As is so often true in the history of thought, many of the disciples took the striking but superficial aspects of Shaftesbury's thought and ignored the foundations. To many of them morals are a matter of instinct and a branch of aesthetics. The disciples did not teach the true gospel of Shaftesbury, but they did teach a gospel; and as the eighteenth century progressed and the nineteenth approached, more and more listened to the new gospel. Before long the deistic repudiation of authority had bifurcated. To one branch, which we may for the sake of simplicity call the Bolingbroke branch, the guide to human conduct is human reason. To the other branch, which we may with less exactitude call the Shaftesbury branch, the guide to human conduct is human feeling. This division will necessarily persist so long as belief in the man-made order persists. A rational being has only two possible internal guides, the mind and the heart.

ALEXANDER POPE

There are two pitfalls more perilous than all others awaiting the historian of thought. Both pitfalls might be labeled *influence,* but in different senses. There is the influence that one writer exerts upon another. Such influence exists, but it is a difficult thing to estimate and often one inclines to attribute to personal influence what was, generally speaking, in the air. An idea is present in Bolingbroke or in Shaftesbury. It is also in Pope's *Essay on Man.* Therefore Pope got it from Bolingbroke or Shaftesbury. Toward influence of that sort it is well to entertain a healthy but not a universal skepticism. We often entertain willingly the thought of others when it accords with our own original thought. Pope might be influenced by a thought of Bolingbroke's because it was a thought he had anyway; he might be unaffected by a thought he met in Shaftesbury because it was a thought with which he was familiar and which he disbelieved. We do not contract ideas as we do diseases by exposure to others;

more often the ideas of others help us mold and modify the
thoughts we have ourselves. When literary and intellectual influences are thought of in this more subtle way, one tends to be
more respectful toward the reality of their existence.

The other pitfall concerns the amount of influence a piece
of writing exercises. There is a natural tendency for the com-
mentator to be carried away by his enthusiasm and to think that
the book which fascinates him fascinated the world when it was
published. Literature and philosophy endure after the societies
that produced them pass away. Hence the literature and philosophy of a period loom much larger centuries later than do other
aspects of contemporary life. The fallacy of thinking that the
same was true originally must be guarded against. We may think
of Elizabeth as Queen of England in the Age of Shakespeare.
How fantastic that would have seemed to the theatergoer of
1600!

So much by way of preface to Alexander Pope's *Essay on Man*.
The preface seems advisable because the poem is really indebted
to both Bolingbroke and Shaftesbury, even if it is indebted more
to the spirit of the times. It seems advisable because the poem
really was read and really did stimulate thought, discussion, and
acrimonious criticism in a way difficult to envisage in a century
in which poetry has ceased to elicit anything but coterie thought,
discussion, and criticism. But the *Essay on Man* is much more
than Bolingbroke versified, if it also is much less than Pope had
dreamed might come to pass.

The thought of Alexander Pope and the nature of his life is a
haunting one. He was the little hunchback of Twickenham,
four feet eight inches tall, his poor lungs pushed together to give
him those endless bouts of asthma that made him write of "this
long disease, my life." It was an age when people laughed at
hunchbacks, and people knew that a crooked body meant a
crooked mind, but people did not laugh in the face of Alexander
Pope. There was a fierce independence to Pope, and one can
understand the satisfaction of the stunted cripple who had
inherited some money but had made so much more with his pen
that no one could think he ran Twickenham on his inheritance.
There was a fine pride in Alexander Pope, not so fine as to
elevate him above the vindictive snarl when he was chivvied,

but a fine pride in his fine moments. Pope held a hand of low cards and the ace of trumps, and he knew it. It was his intention to play that ace of trumps with consummate care. He had the power to write the great poem of his age. Like Wordsworth who had the same dream and the same power, Pope achieved a magnum opus which is but a fraction of his dream, but it is an imposing fraction.

The great poem was to be in four books. The first would contain the *Essay on Man,* the second would treat knowledge and its limits, the third would be a treatise on the government of Church and State, and the fourth would be an analysis of morals couched in terms of the cardinal virtues. Pope seems to have conceived the work in 1723 and to have worked on it in 1730. He published the four epistles of the *Essay* in February, March, and May, 1733, and January, 1734. Again like Wordsworth's, Pope's dream died hard, and he continued to revise what he had written for the rest of his life. When every allowance is made for the unquestioned fact that Bolingbroke's company and fascinating conversation were an inspiration to Pope and the other fact that Bolingbroke did write out his thoughts for Pope and that they are extensive enough to fill more than a volume of his *Works,* a third fact remains incontestable. There is nothing to indicate that Bolingbroke was capable of the largeness of poetic vision necessary for the great poem Pope envisaged. Pope freely acknowledges his debt to Bolingbroke in the *Essay,* but the horizons of Alexander Pope were not within the vision of Lord Bolingbroke.

The *Essay on Man* is essentially a theodicy, a vindication of God's holiness and justice in the light of the existence of moral and physical evil. It is indebted to Leibnitz's *Théodicée* in the fact that it is a theodicy and in the fact that the Chain of Being is more important in the philosophy of Leibnitz than in any other philosophic system of the period, but not in any other sense. Pope no doubt knew the most systematic theodicy in English literature, Archbishop William King's *On the Origin of Evil* (*De Origine Mali,* 1702), and quite likely Pope's vindication of philosophic optimism is indebted to King, but Pope does not imitate King's systematic treatment of evil, and the subject matter of most of the *Essay* is foreign to King. Such concepts

as universal harmony, the duty of the individual to cultivate
universal benevolence, and the serenity of virtue which lets
Shaftesbury say, "Good humour is . . . the best foundation of
piety and true religion" are to be found in Pope, but Pope
discards the concept of the moral sense as analogous to the
aesthetic sense which lies at the heart of Shaftesbury's thought.

The truth is that Pope did in the *Essay* a compendium of ideas
in the air during his generation. A God of infinite wisdom would
create the best possible of worlds on the principle of plenitude;
man has the degree of perfection that he needs; a benevolent
God operates by general providence; imperfection is the effect
of incomplete vision; the ultimate goal is universal benevolence;
it is pride that breaks the Great Chain of Being and causes
chaos; the state of nature was one of peace; society came into
being on the patriarchal principle.

THE RULING PASSION

The most nearly original concept in the poem is that of the
ruling passion. In the first Epistle Pope labored to establish the
point that man's attitude toward the universe provides the
framework within which his ethical concepts are to be contained.
If that framework is properly constructed, man recognizes that
all things, taken together, are right. Within that framework man's
relationships with himself and with his fellow man can be developed. The first relationship of man is with himself; and the
ruling passion which each man has and the way that passion is
developed, trained, and regulated determine his success in
achieving an ordered life. Character, then, is something of an
artistic achievement. The concept must be as old as history: the
Romans thought of the sound mind in the sound body, Shaftesbury blends the moral with the aesthetic sense, Matthew Arnold
talks of Sweetness and Light, and every educational system on
record pays it at least lip service. Pope's contribution to it is the
concept of the ruling passion, that inner drive which takes a different form in every human being, differentiates men by giving
them personal objectives and, in the aggregate, gets the work of
the world done. Whether it really exists in all men is another

matter, but it certainly exists in the leaders of men. Pope was a leader of men, with his ruling passion poetry.

The *Essay on Man* adds nothing else of substance to deistic thought, yet its contribution to the dissemination of such concepts as philosophic optimism and universal benevolence was enormous. Others before him had erected their systems of morals and ethics outside the framework of institutional religion but inside the framework of natural religion. No one even approaching the position of Alexander Pope in literature had done so. No Cambridge Platonist was his rival with the reading public, and certainly no deist. Shaftesbury's *Characteristics* was hardly a rival in popularity to the *Essay on Criticism, The Rape of the Lock,* and the translations of the *Iliad* and *Odyssey.* As for Bolingbroke, he was not even in print when Pope did the *Essay on Man.* Pope, on the other hand, was the most celebrated name in contemporary letters long before he did the *Essay on Man.* One of the most fascinating, human, and sad poems in literature is Pope's *An Epistle to Dr. Arbuthnot.* As Pope wrote it, his aged mother was dying. With her death the last person who loved Alexander Pope would be gone. The *Epistle* is the sad reflection of that courted, admired, envied, feared, honored, hated little hunchback in whose life was every other emotion but tragically little love. For thirty years his villa at Twickenham was the leading literary shrine of England in a day when poetry had an importance it had never enjoyed before in the English-speaking world. It may well be questioned if any poet in English history, Tennyson included, has ever been accorded contemporary fame comparable to that of Alexander Pope. By that gauge must one measure the significance of the *Essay on Man* in establishing the Age of Reason and the rule of natural religion.

Now, we might pause and consider what point we have reached. Except for Thomas Hobbes no English thinker of the slightest consequence has indicated a belief in the man-made order. In one sense or another, belief in the natural law is still universal. It is, then, a tendency of which we have been speaking and not an accomplishment. The tendency of deism was to separate God and man, to relegate God to absentee status. Such concepts as general providence and philosophic optimism, with their overtones suggestive of Newton's ordered universe and that simple trust in the finality of science which marks the eighteenth century, reinforced man's reliance upon reason. Such related concepts as the essentially simple nature of true religion, the essentially simple nature of the moral order, and the assurance that man has a moral sense to guide his reason unerringly to the truth helped man down the road to a belief in the man-made order. But that belief is not to be found in the Cambridge Platonists, the deists, Bolingbroke, Shaftesbury, or Pope. They all believed, within the framework of deism, in an order that is divinely instituted. Unlike French deism, English deism always stays inside the framework of religion.

The point must be made as strongly as possible because we are approaching the Enlightenment proper, and few periods in history have been quite so beshadowed by commentary and controversy as the Enlightenment. In a sense Bolingbroke and Shaftesbury are products of the Enlightenment; so is Hume; so are Condorcet, Holbach, Voltaire, and Rousseau; so are Benjamin Franklin and Thomas Jefferson. Having said that, we have said little more than that all were born in the eighteenth century and felt the intellectual winds that blew across it. American thought has always tended to lag behind English and Continental thought. Benjamin Franklin and Thomas Jefferson were leaders of the Enlightenment in America; both were influenced by Bolingbroke. On the whole, Jefferson stands closer to Shaftesbury in his thinking than to anyone else mentioned. Both Franklin and Jefferson lived in France and knew the thinkers of the French Enlightenment, yet there is no evidence that either American really understood, as Edmund Burke did, the profound philosophic difference between the American Revolution and the French Revolution. Late in the eighteenth century, Franklin and Jefferson were such deists as Bolingbroke, Shaftesbury, and Pope were early in the century. Yet in all history no one would be less likely to accept as valid the aphorism "Whatever is, is right" than Thomas Jefferson—unless, of course, it was Benjamin Franklin. That is the difference between the Age of Stagnation, which we are about to consider, and the Age of Revolution which lies beyond.

IV

BEGINNINGS
OF THE ECONOMIC GOSPEL

NOT since we met the portentous figure of old Thomas Hobbes at the very start of our study have we met a confirmed and unqualified believer in the man-made order. We shall now meet two, Mandeville and Hume, and with them, by way of contrast, the chief follower of Shaftesbury and the man who best exemplifies the continuing development of the moral sense concept, Francis Hutcheson. Furthermore, in Mandeville and Hume we shall see exemplified the twin spirits of skepticism and positivism, spirits that grew in the nineteenth century and became rampant in the twentieth. At the end of this chapter we shall be farther down the road to full belief in the man-made order than we shall be again until we reach Jeremy Bentham and his followers in Chapter IX.

THE GRUMBLING BEEHIVE

Bernard Mandeville (1670–1733) was born in Holland, came to England, and settled down in London to the practice of medicine, for which he had been trained at Leyden. In 1705, when Marlborough's war with France was a matter of hot debate and the Tory charge was rampant that the war was carried on purely in the interest of the general and the politicians, when the air was blue with charges of fraud, bribery, and dishonesty, Mandeville took pen in hand and wrote some two hundred doggerel verses. He published them as a sixpenny pamphlet under the title *The Grumbling Hive*, and soon saw them pirated as a halfpenny sheet. London was fascinated, appalled, or titillated

according to individual preference by Mandeville's impudent
thesis that individual greed and self-seeking are indispensable if
a nation is to become strong and wealthy, that "private vices are
public benefits." It was bad enough that the charges against the
administration be true; this devil's disciple made the crimes
meritorious.

Once there was a hive of bees ruled by a limited monarchy,
just like England. The bees were like human beings and were
divided into the industrious citizens and the knavish officials, but
if the truth had to be told, there was also knavery among the
citizens in every occupation. Lawyers spun out cases for their
own gain, doctors fawned on the families of their patients for
larger fees; there were some idealistic, poverty-stricken clerics
who preached true religion but the collection went to their
superiors. Soldiers who avoided the battlefield prospered although those upon it lost arms and legs; courtiers feathered
their nests, and everyone prospered by dishonesty. There was
implacable justice in the hive, but only for poor bees. The result
was a magnificent state which prospered through its vices:

> The Root of Evil, Avarice,
> That damn'd ill-natur'd baneful Vice,
> Was Slave to Prodigality
> That noble Sin; whilst Luxury
> Employ'd a Million of the Poor,
> And odious Pride a Million more:
> Envy it self, and Vanity,
> Were Ministers of Industry;
> Their darling Folly, Fickleness,
> In Diet, Furniture and Dress,
> That strange ridic'lous Vice, was made
> The very Wheel that turn'd the Trade.
> Their Laws and Clothes were equally
> Objects of Mutability;
> For, what was well done for a time,
> In half a Year became a Crime;
> Yet while they alter'd thus their Laws,
> Still finding and correcting Flaws,
> They mended by Inconstancy
> Faults, which no Prudence could foresee.

Thus Vice nurs'd Ingenuity,
Which join'd with Time and Industry
Had carry'd Life's Conveniences,
Its real Pleasures, Comforts, Ease,
To such a Height, the very Poor
Liv'd better than the Rich before,
And nothing could be added more.[1]

Yet the bees were inconsistent enough to grumble at the vices which made them strong and prosperous. There was raised so inconsistent a cry for honesty that Jove swore in anger to rid the hive of fraud. He did so, and disaster followed. Honesty ruined the legal profession, now that the courts had nothing to batten on. The profit left medicine. Since all the clergy were now devoted to duty, not nearly so many were needed and clergymen were laid off left and right. With graft eliminated from government, public officials lost their only reliable source of income. Fashionable living was abandoned, wars were no longer fought for gain, people did not frequent taverns nor spend money on lavish clothes. The result was a blight on all economic activity, a great weakening of membership in the hive, and the ultimate necessity of the remaining bees to leave their comfortable quarters and take refuge in the modest security of a hollow tree. And the moral:

Then leave Complaints: Fools only strive
To make a Great and Honest Hive
T'enjoy the World's Conveniences,
Be fam'd in War, yet live in Ease,
Without great Vices, is a vain
Eutopia seated in the brain.
Fraud, Luxury and Pride must live,
While we the Benefits receive:
Hunger's a dreadful Plague, no doubt,
Yet who digests or thrives without?
Do we not owe the Growth of Wine
To the dry shabby crooked Vine?
Which, while its Shoots neglected stood,
Chock'd other Plants, and ran to Wood;
But blest us with its noble Fruit,

As soon as it was ty'd and cut:
So Vice is beneficial found,
When it's by Justice lopt and bound;
Nay, where the People would be great,
As necessary to the State,
As Hunger is to make 'em eat.
Bare Virtue can't make Nations live
In Splendor; they, that would revive
A Golden Age, must be as free,
For Acorns, as for Honesty.[2]

Very likely Mandeville meant nothing more than a *jeu d'esprit*. However, to view *The Fable of the Bees*, the two-volume work which grew out of the two hundred doggerel lines, as nothing but a *jeu d'esprit* is certainly to overestimate the endurance and volubility of any writer in pursuing literary flights of fancy. A distinction must always be borne in mind between *The Grumbling Hive*, the few doggerel verses of 1705, and the long prose treatises on economics and the social order which grew out of it. In 1714 he added *Remarks*, which comprise some two hundred pages of notes to his two hundred verses, and *An Inquiry into the Origin of Moral Virtue*. In 1723 he added *An Essay on Charity Schools* and *A Search into the Origin of Society*, and rounded off the work in 1729 with six dialogues, which required a volume by themselves, under the title *Fable, Part II*. In 1732 the work went through its eighth edition—it had thirteen editions in the eighteenth century—and in 1733 the author died. These bibliographical details are necessary because casual commentators on eighteenth-century literature constantly refer to Mandeville's work as a *jeu d'esprit*. *Jeux d'esprit* don't run to two thick, tightly printed volumes.

Bernard Mandeville was a perfectly serious writer on social and economic matters, with more than a touch of Bernard Shaw to his matter and manner. Like Shaw he delighted in taking the upside-down, inside-out view of life, not because such is the right view but because it is a way of concentrating attention on the uneasy truths of life comfortably hidden to the conventional view. His *Inquiry into the Origin of Moral Virtue*, which he added in 1714, is an answer to Shaftesbury's *Characteristics*, which appeared three years before. To Mandeville Shaftesbury was a treader on the clouds, his concept of virtue as universal benevolence mere Rock Candy Mountain thinking. The real source of virtue, according to Mandeville, is the psychological reaction which occurs when flattery plays on pride; ". . . the humblest Man alive must confess, that the Reward of a Virtuous Action, which is the Satisfaction that ensues upon it, consists in a certain Pleasure he procures to himself by Contemplating on his own Worth: Which Pleasure, together with the Occasion of it, are as certain Signs of Pride, as looking Pale and Trembling at any imminent Danger, are the symptoms of Fear."[3] Virtue is not something man achieves by listening to the voice of the moral sense but something achieved by listening to the voice of pride. Both Shaftesbury and Mandeville think of virtue as disinterested action. The difference is that Shaftesbury, who thinks of the moral order as of divine origin and revealed to man by the moral sense, bases his belief in disinterestedness upon man's moral duty to show universal benevolence; Mandeville, who thinks of the moral order as man-made, bases his belief in disinterestedness upon the utilitarian argument from pleasure. Later we shall meet the argument, in a much more dignified and philosophic form, in the utilitarians, but the argument is the same. A man does virtuous deeds of a disinterested sort because they make him feel better than do selfish deeds.

MAN AT WAR WITH NATURE

The full development of Mandeville's thought comes in the 1723 edition in which appear the *Charity Schools* and *Origin of Society* essays. The latter is an explicit answer to Shaftesbury. Again Mandeville rejects the idea of universal benevolence; it is admirable, but unrealistic. As for the moral sense, a man can lead so easy and comfortable a life that his passions are lulled to rest and he imagines that he has a natural virtue which in truth he does not have. If a person really has universal benevolence, he proves it by leading a life of action and not by basking in the pleasant sun of self-approval. No form of self-deception is quite so common as self-approval; "we are ever pushing our Reason which way soever we feel Passion to draw it, and Self-Love pleads to all human Creatures for their different Views, still furnishing every Individual with Arguments to justify their Inclinations."[4] The calm virtues recommended in *Characteristics* would never lead a man to a life of achievement; it is Pride that really moves the world. As for man's social instincts, Mandeville likes the company of educated gentlemen and dislikes the company of drunkards and boors. He cannot see that a liking for humanity is a virtue in itself. In short, the *pulchrum et honestum,* that union of the beautiful and true on which Shaftesbury's parallel between the aesthetic and the moral sense depends, is in no sense a constant. Mandeville concludes, "the *pulchrum et honestum,* excellency and real worth of things are most commonly precarious and alterable as Modes and Customs vary; that consequently the Inferences drawn from their Certainty are insignificant, and that the generous Notions concerning the natural Goodness of Man are hurtful as they tend to mis-lead, and are meerly Chimerical."[5]

As for nature, it is hostile to man in all its aspects, and man's constant preoccupation is the effort to protect himself from it. Blandly accepting the fall of man, Mandeville points out that the precise difference between man's state of innocence before the fall and after is that then he was at peace with nature and since has been at war with it. In the state of innocence man needed no trades or industries; trades and industries arise from the necessity man feels of freeing himself from the baneful and hostile state of nature. As for society, it is the body politic into which man is either subdued by force or drawn by persuasion. The family may be a natural social unit, but not even the patriarchal state could have grown peaceably from it. We live in society by what we can make out of others, although hypocrisy demands that we conceal it. "The Sexton would be stoned should he wish openly for the Death of the Parishioners, tho' every body knew that he had nothing else to live on."[6] All society is solidly grounded on hypocrisy.

A Search into the Origin of Society is the best presentation of Mandeville's thought. In it he rejects an absolute standard of morality, states his belief that pride which inspires self-aggrandizement is the true motivating force in life, dismisses the moral sense as a self-delusion induced by comfortable living in which one's real motives are concealed by satisfaction with one's lot, maintains that the state of nature is one of brute force, and concludes that society is the state into which man is lured or dragooned to escape from the state of nature. With good reason Leslie Stephen says that "his book was regarded as a kind of pothouse edition of the arch-enemy Hobbes."[7]

Something far more important, however, than Hobbes in motley is to be found in the *Charity Schools* essay, as indeed it is in the verses themselves. This is the implicit axiom that the *summum bonum*, the ultimate good of which man dreams and philosophers theorize, is worldly prosperity. Presented half-jokingly in the verses, the thought lies at the serious heart of the essay. *An Essay on Charity Schools*, which first appeared in the edition of 1723, is essentially a protest against what Mandeville thought the maudlin sentimentality that disguised Pride by calling it Charity, and failed to understand the nature of the true virtue, Pity. Sentimentality was taking a characteristic form in the multiplying of charity schools. Mandeville could see no evidence that they curbed either juvenile delinquency or adult crime; "I intend to examine into the real Causes of those Mischiefs so justly complained of, and doubt not but to make it appear that Charity-Schools, and every thing else that promotes Idleness, and keeps the Poor from Working, are more Accessary to the Growth of Villany, than the want of Reading and Writing, or even the grossest Ignorance and Stupidity."[8] Mandeville attributed the crime wave in London, which reached dangerous proportions in the early eighteenth century, to laxity of punishment, carelessness of property owners, and idleness. Lack of education he did not consider a cause. He suspected that the real reason for the foundation of the charity schools was not the uplift of the poor but the spread of sectarian religion.

What England really needed was a multitude of workers, since the abundance and price of commodities depend in large measure on the abundance and price of labor; "the surest Wealth consists in a Multitude of laborious Poor."[9] "To make the Society happy and People easy under the meanest Circumstances, it is requisite that great Numbers of them should be Ignorant as well as Poor. Knowledge both enlarges and multiplies our Desires, and the fewer things a Man wishes for, the more easily his necessities may be supply'd. The Welfare and Felicity therefore of every State and Kingdom, require that the knowledge of the Working Poor should be confin'd within the Verge of their Occupations, and never extended (as to things visible) beyond what relates to their Calling. . . . Reading, Writing and Arithmetick, are very necessary to those, whose Business requires such Qualifications, but where People's livelihood has no dependence on these Arts, they are very pernicious to the Poor, who are forced to get their Daily Bread by their Daily Labour. Few Children make any progress at School, but at the same time they are capable of being employ'd in some Business or other, so that every Hour those of poor people spend at their Book is so much time lost to the Society."[10]

Far be it from Mandeville, however, to appear a total reactionary. He favored an increase in the size of university faculties, the introduction of medical education at Oxford and Cambridge, the elimination of a tuition charge for those entering the ministry so that more of the poorer classes could afford the cloth, and the maintenance of fewer but better classical schools. He had a clear vision of the perfectibility of the classes, but was blind to the potential improvement of the masses. He returns to the thesis that it is the wage rate which determines the prosperity of a nation, a most intriguing anticipation of David Ricardo's wage-fund theory. When Mandeville voiced the thesis, as when Ricardo or any other member of the *laissez faire* school of the nineteenth century voiced it, the thesis meant precisely the opposite of what it ordinarily means today. To them the thesis that the wage rate determines the prosperity of the nation meant that the lower the wages are, the more prosperous the nation. Hence there must always be a surplus working force, to keep wages down and the nation prosperous, and the way to keep that surplus working force is to limit the education of the masses. Mandeville is shocked to hear that something resembling what a later age would call trade unionism was rearing its ugly head among London's footmen; ". . . a parcel of Footmen are arriv'd to that height of Insolence as to have enter'd into a Society together, and made Laws by which they oblige themselves not to serve for less than such a Sum, nor carry Burdens or any Bundle or Parcel above a certain Weight, not exceeding Two or Three Pounds with other Regulations directly opposite to the Interest of those they serve, and altogether destructive to the Use they were designed for."[11] Add to this that they had set up a mutual benefit fund and were pledged to take corporate action against any master who struck a footman, and the full measure of Mandeville's horror can be surmised. He concludes with his premise, that England must bring up enough of its poor in ignorance to provide a working pool large enough to undersell her competitors. "This is the Noble and Manly way of encountering the Rivals of our Trade, and by dint of Merit outdoing them at Foreign Markets."[12] There is enough work to be done in England to keep the laboring poor busy for three or four centuries.

Thus Mandeville accepts the aphorism "Whatever is, is right" in a strictly materialistic sense. What promotes the economic welfare of the state is right; private vices are public benefits. The division of society into the favored few and the laboring masses is right; the prosperity of the nation rests on the poverty of the poor. That prosperity should seep down through prodigal spending at the top until a trickle reaches even the working poor is right; not morally right since morals are not involved, but economically true and therefore economically right.

Mandeville is not important for what he thought and said, but he is tremendously important because as early as the first quarter of the eighteenth century this Dutch physician, who is quite oblivious to that need for moralistic protective coloration which Matthew Arnold assures us English Philistines always feel, preaches in stark simplicity the economic gospel by which a century later the Manchester school of economists will live and rule the land. The pothouse Hobbes has accepted fully the thesis of the man-made order, and accepted it in what will prove to be a characteristic form. The school of Bolingbroke, which never more than half accepts the thesis, may base morals upon reason. The school of Shaftesbury, which accepts it even less, may base morals upon feeling. But Mandeville, who accepts it fully, bases morals upon prosperity. Not even Thomas Hobbes does that. Of all the commentators on morals who wrote in the late seventeenth and early eighteenth centuries, Mandeville is the only one to make the norm of morality worldly success. In him the abdication of the absentee God of deism from responsibility for the moral standards of His children is complete.

FRANCIS HUTCHESON

Of the three persons considered in this chapter, Mandeville has as his dominant virtue a candor that disarms even while it appalls. There is not a more cheerfully amoral writer in English literature, nor one who takes fewer pains to conceal the fact. Hume has the dominant virtue of intellectual incisiveness, a penetrating clarity of mind that sees him through from his premises to conclusions from which he did not shrink, however much his century might do so. It has been well said that everything the French Revolution represents is implicit in David Hume. Francis Hutcheson has a lesser virtue, being a far smaller figure than Hume in the history of thought, and a smaller one, at least in this writer's perhaps perverse judgment, than Mandeville. Hutcheson's virtue is that he best exemplifies a pattern of thinking important in his day and age and very characteristic of it. He illustrates the development of the moral sense theory in a way that its originator, the far more original and powerful thinker Shaftesbury, does not.

Francis Hutcheson (1694–1746) was born in County Down, Ireland, of a line of dissenting ministers. He was educated at Glasgow, returned to Ireland, and opened a private academy in Dublin. He was soon known well and favorably in the city, and protected by Archbishop King against prosecution for keeping a school without subscribing to the episcopal canons. Everything by which Hutcheson lives in literature and thought dates to his Dublin days. In 1729 he was elevated to the post of professor of moral philosophy at Glasgow; he shed luster on the post until his death in 1746, but did no important writing.

Time has winnowed down to four essays, and perhaps even to two, the enduring part of Hutcheson's writing. In 1725 he did under a monumental single title the essays now known as an *Inquiry concerning Beauty, Order, Harmony, Design* and an *Inquiry concerning Moral Good and Evil*. The latter is really his central work and the final embodiment of his thought. It was expanded in 1728 into two essays and published under the title *Essay on the Nature and Conduct of the Passions and Affections* with *Illustrations upon the Moral Sense*."[13]

Hutcheson wrote to defend Shaftesbury against Mandeville. On the title page of the 1725 volume he states that in his essays "the Principles of the late Earl of Shaftesbury are explained and defended against the Author of the Fable of the Bees. . . ." This is a precise statement of contents. Shaftesbury's equation linking the moral and aesthetic sense is presented, his analysis of the moral sense reproduced, the principle of universal benevolence expounded, and the belief that the test of virtuous action is its beneficial influence on the general welfare upheld. But no student, not even so docile a one as Hutcheson, exactly reproduces the thought of the master. Shaftesbury believed that the moral sense is present in man from the start as an instinct, but he makes abundantly clear his belief in the necessity for training that moral sense and sharpening its perceptivity. Hutcheson stresses rather the instinctive nature of the moral sense: "The Author of nature has much better furnished us for a virtuous conduct, than some moralists seem to imagine, by almost as quick and powerful instructions, as we have for the preservation of our bodies. He has given us strong affections to be the springs of each virtuous action; and made virtue a lovely form, that we might easily distinguish it from its contrary and be made happy by the pursuit of it."[14]

In one sense the doctrine of Shaftesbury is merely modified, but in a much deeper sense it is fundamentally changed by Hutcheson. The concept of the moral sense as initially an instinct for right and wrong is something very native to the Christian tradition. It is usually called the voice of conscience. That Man has the necessity as well as the moral obligation to perfect his conscience is a fundamental of the Christian tradition, perhaps even *the* fundamental. Shaftesbury belongs to tradition in this respect. But in Hutcheson the moral sense seems perfected in itself. The implication is clear: man knows right from wrong by instinct and so he needs no moral guidance external to himself. If a man feels an action is right, then right it is—at least for him. Infallibility is universal. The moral sense does not have growth nor history, nor does moral judgment enter particularly into its operation. Hutcheson conceives of it as functioning immediately and instinctively. Couple with this Hutcheson's acceptance of the Shaftesburian equation between the moral sense and the aesthetic sense, and we have reached aesthethic morality. "The beautiful life is the good life." Feeling has supplanted reason as the moral norm of action, just as reason supplanted the orthodox tradition. All the world need do is await the birth of Oscar Wilde. Hutcheson even attempted to work out a sort of moral algebra for computing the moral worth of human actions. After laying down and developing six axioms or propositions for computing the morality of an act, he concludes, "That must be the perfection of virtue, where the moment of good produced equals the ability, or when the being acts to the utmost of his power for the public good; and hence the perfection of virtue in this case, is as unity."[15]

The true importance of Hutcheson in the history of thought, however, does not lie in his quite innocent and not thoroughly thought-out reduction of morals to feeling. He did not have followers enough, at least in his own century, to make this pattern of thinking important. His real significance lies in the fact that he is the chief link between the Shaftesbury school of intuitionists and the utilitarians. Hutcheson accepts fully the concept of universal benevolence as a moral duty. The concept is present in Shaftesbury, but in him the moral duty of universal benevolence comprises that aspect of duty inseparable from the concept of rights in all who hold fundamentally to a belief in the divinely created order. Again it may be questioned if Hutcheson understood the implications of his own thought, but in his moral algebra the real criterion of one's contribution to the universal well-being of the race becomes the utility of the contribution. "In comparing the moral qualities of actions, in order to regulate our election among various actions proposed, or to find which of them has the greatest moral excellency, we are led by our moral sense of virtue to judge thus: that in equal degrees of happiness, expected to proceed from the action, the virtue is in proportion to the number of persons to whom the happiness shall extend; (and here the dignity, or moral importance of persons, may compensate numbers) and in equal numbers, the virtue is as the quantity of happiness, or natural good; or that the virtue is in a compound ratio of the quantity of good, and number of enjoyers. In the same manner, the moral evil or vice, is as the degree of misery, and number of sufferers;

so that that action is best, which procures the greatest happiness for the greatest numbers; and that worst, which, in like manner, occasions misery."[16]

There is something very engaging about the picture of Francis Hutcheson, a thoroughly good man and professor of moral philosophy, painstakingly working out his moral algebra and writing it down in that involuted and confusing form which always results when people try to write like Euclid. No doubt in him the moral sense was instinctive, instantaneous, and infallible. In fairness to him, he never makes the explicit claim that it is such in all men, although it would be hard to keep the morally light of heart from reading that into his pages. No doubt every fiber of his moral being would recoil from the concept of aesthetic morality, but the man who maintains that the moral sense perceives virtue and vice as the eye perceives light and darkness invites it. In Hutcheson the role of moral judgment is logically reduced to determining the reason for the instinctive reaction of the moral sense; in Shaftesbury the moral sense had been an instinct capable of being educated into a moral judgment. Thus Hutcheson is much farther down the road to an intuitional moral code than Shaftesbury. In practice it is exceedingly difficult to differentiate between belief in an intuitional moral code and belief in the man-made order. Hutcheson is kept from going all the way down the road by his preoccupation with the benevolent affections; the benevolent affections always outrank the self-regarding affections in Hutcheson. "The ultimate notion of right," says Hutcheson, "is that which tends to the universal good."[17] A law of nature is "no more than a conclusion from observation of what sort of conduct is ordinarily useful to society."[18] Thus the principle of utility comes perilously close to replacing the law of God as the ultimate authority for Hutcheson.

Hutcheson never quite reaches this position. He holds that utility is the test of virtue, but he does not quite say that utility is the cause of moral approbation. He says that God has so organized His complex universe that He achieves harmony by making the benevolent affections dominate the moral sense. The aphorism "Whatever is, is right," as met in Bolingbroke, Shaftesbury, and Pope, really meant "Whatever exists in God's eternal order is right." In Mandeville and Hutcheson, in their several ways and with full recognition that each would be outraged (Mandeville would be amused) at the linking of their names, it comes perilously close to meaning "Whatever works is right." It simply remained for David Hume to take the next step and to say precisely that. In Hume utility is the cause of moral approbation.

DAVID HUME

When we come to David Hume (1711–1776), we sense how far the new spirit has moved in a century. Even the deplorable Hobbes had protected the flank by a careful if not necessarily sincere distinction between Christian religion and man-made religion, and had expended his not inconsiderable literary powers in praise of the former. Hume, free from theological predilections, hardly bothers to do so, and when he does, it is with a nod to the "zealots." In Hume's *Natural History of Religion* the implicit assumptions are entirely consistent with what will be nineteenth- and twentieth-century rationalism. To Hume, the old order had finished changing.

There is something very human about David Hume, ensconced as he is on the high Olympus of metaphysical speculation yet always peering anxiously down through the mists to see how he is regarded from below. Literary distinction was the breath of life for him, and he never seemed to consider how few are mentally equipped to follow an intellectual explorer over the horizons of human thought. Philosophy fascinated him from boyhood, and the most complete and austerely philosophic statement of his thought was composed before he was twenty-five. In 1739 he published the first two books of his *Treatise of Human Nature*, those that treat of the understanding and the passions, and the following year Book III, "Of Morals." There followed a dead silence. "Never literary attempt was more unfortunate; it fell dead-born from the press, without reaching such distinction as even to excite a murmur among the zealots," he says ruefully in the little eight-page autobiography which he wrote in April, 1776, as the shadows of death closed in on him. He later revised, simplified, and made the work far more readable in his *Enquiry Concerning Human Understanding* (1748) and *Enquiry Concerning the Principles of Morals* (1751), but for those prepared and willing to follow him the *Treatise* is the comprehensive expression of the thought of Hume.

Paradox though it is, the greatest philosopher of England's Age of Reason is an antirationalist. Hume accepts the thesis of Locke that innate ideas are an illusion, but parts company with Locke and Berkeley on the relationship between sensation and reason. Hume believed that experience, not reason, leads us to pass from the idea of one object to the idea of another. We start with an impression of an object. This immediate and direct impression dims to an idea of the object. We pass to the impression of a second object, and combine with this impression the impression of contiguity with the first. This impression of contiguity, repeatedly confirmed, becomes an idea of contiguity. If there is also an impression of succession, repeated confirmation will make this an idea of succession and hence of causality. It is experience and not reason that gives us the idea of cause and effect: "To consider the matter aright, reason is nothing but a wonderful and unintelligible instinct in our souls, which carries us along a certain train of ideas, and endows them with particular qualities, according to their particular situations and relations. This instinct, 'tis true, arises from past observation and experience. . . ."[19]

Hume is a philosophic skeptic, but the term requires defining and limitation. His skepticism extends to inference by insight, but not to inference from experience. Since one man's experience is very much like that of another, we all tend to come to the same conclusions about the world in which we live. Skepticism was Hume's cast of mind as he probed the metaphysical ultimates; he says himself his skepticism vanished when he left his study. The essential point to note, however, is the implications of experience as the foundation of knowledge and belief. Experience, and experience alone, teaches. Hence man has no guide but experience. This is the ultimate, logical conclusion of the old aphorism from which belief in the man-made order ultimately is derived: *Nihil est in intellectu quod non prius fuerit in sensu* ("There is nothing in the mind which was not previously in a sense perception"). Many never hear

Leibnitz's murmured corrective: *Nisi intellectus ipse* ("Except the mind itself").

The implications of Hume's belief are clearly visible in Book III of the *Treatise,* "Of Morals." Reason is inert and hence cannot be the source of moral judgments: "Since morals . . . have an influence on the actions and affections, it follows, that they cannot be deriv'd from reason; and that because reason alone, as we have already prov'd, can never have any such influence. Morals excite passions, and produce or prevent actions. Reason of itself is utterly impotent in this particular. The rules of morality, therefore are not conclusions of our reason."[20] Virtue and Vice are not matters of fact but objects of feeling. "Take any action allow'd to be vicious: Wilful murder, for instance. Examine it in all lights, and see if you can find that matter of fact, or real existence, which you call *vice.* In whichever way you take it, you find only certain passions, motives, volitions and thoughts. There is no other matter of fact in the case. The vice entirely escapes you, as long as you consider the object. You never can find it, till you turn your reflexion into your own breast, and find a sentiment of disapprobation, which arises in you, towards this action. Here is a matter of fact; but 'tis the object of feeling, not of reason. It lies in yourself, not in the object. So that when you pronounce any action or character to be vicious, you mean nothing, but that from the constitution of your nature you have a feeling or sentiment of blame from the contemplation of it."[21] One's emotional reaction to a situation is the adequate guide to conduct: "Nothing can be more real, or concern us more, than our own sentiments of pleasure and uneasiness; and if these be favorable to virtue and unfavorable to vice, no more can be requisite to the regulation of our conduct and behaviour."[22]

The natural next question is, What does Hume understand by morality? He denies that morality is a matter of fact; it is nothing that can be determined by the understanding. He does believe that vice and virtue may be likened to colors, sounds, heat and cold, which he holds are not qualities in objects but perceptions in the mind. Moral distinctions, therefore, are derived from a moral sense, and Hume falls into the pattern of thought set by Shaftesbury and Hutcheson. The moral sense can be absolutely trusted: "The distinction of moral good and evil is founded on the pleasure or pain, which results from the view of any sentiment, or character; and as that pleasure or pain cannot be unknown to the person who feels it, it follows, that there is just so much vice or virtue in any character, as every one places in it, and that 'tis impossible in this particular we can ever be mistaken."[23] Whatever mental quality in ourselves or others gives pleasure is virtuous; whatever gives uneasiness is vicious. This view is entirely consistent with Hume's treatment of the passions in Book II, in which he treats love, pride, humility, and hatred as indirect passions which arise from good or evil, pleasure or pain according as they are employed with their natural or usual force; "every immorality is derived from some defect or unsoundness of the passions."

Since moral distinctions arise from the natural distinctions of pleasure and pain and these distinctions are spontaneous and involuntary, free will in the full sense is an illusion. "As to free-will, we have shewn that it has no place with regard to the actions, no more than the qualities of men. It is not a just consequence, that what is voluntary is free. Our actions are more voluntary than our judgments; but we have not more liberty in the one than in the other."[24]

MORALITY AND UTILITY

There is a natural relationship between the ideas of virtue and justice, the natural obligation of justice being related to the sentiment of right and wrong. The link between the two is sympathy, the passion which causes uneasiness at the sight of injustice. This is as close as Hume comes to basing morals on utility in the *Treatise*. He goes the full way in *An Enquiry Concerning the Principles of Morals*. "It appears to be matter of fact, that the circumstance of utility, in all subjects, is a source of praise and approbation: That it is constantly appealed to in all moral decisions concerning the merit and demerit of actions: That it is the sole source of that high regard paid to justice, fidelity, honour, allegiance, and chastity: That it is inseparable from all the other social virtues, humanity, generosity, charity, affability, lenity, mercy, and moderation: And, in a word, that it is a foundation of the chief part of morals, which has a reference to mankind and our fellow-creatures."[25]

The foundation, then, of morality is utility and what man mistakenly considers to be religious principles have no relationship (except by clerical adoption) to the historical phenomenon called religion. Hume considered religion to be a phenomenon both historical and natural, and he wrote about it on the only foundation he considered firm in his *The Natural History of Religion* (1757). It is history and natural history at that, scientific history and not supernatural. History reveals to Hume that polytheism was the first form of religion. Primitive man does not believe in deity because of arguments from causation or design; "the first ideas of religion are not from a contemplation of the works of nature, but from a concern with regard to the events of life, and from the incessant hopes and fears, which actuate the human mind."[26] Primitive man believes in particular providence, and life is so diverse and contradictory that the concept of particular providence requires either a large number of competing deities interesting themselves in human affairs or one god with an impossibly contradictory nature. Surely the god who gives you victory in battle is not the god who makes the corn grow or the one who protects your wife in childbirth. Hume did not believe that man progressed steadily onward and upward from polytheism to monotheism, but rather that there was a natural flux and reflux between the two ideas. Perhaps the point was intended only for the edification of the zealots, but Hume even professed to believe that man shows his nobler side under polytheism.

In chapter thirteen he reverts to his chief contention. "The primary religion of mankind arises chiefly from an anxious fear of future events; and what ideas will naturally be entertained of invisible, unknown powers while men lie under dismal apprehensions of any kind may easily be conceived. . . . And no idea of perverse wickedness can be framed, which those terrified devotees do not readily, without scruple apply to their deity."[27] Thus, on the one hand, religion has its origin in the fear of the unknown. But the need to placate deity by praise leads the religionist to praise in the highest terms the deity whom he suspects of the blackest deeds. "Every virtue, every excellence, must be ascribed to the divinity, and no exaggeration will be deemed sufficient to reach those perfections with which he is endowed. . . . Here therefore is a kind of contradiction between the different principles of human nature, which enter into religion. Our natural terrors present the notion of a devilish and malicious deity: Our propensity to adulation leads us to acknowledge an excellent and divine."[28] And as men exalt their idea of deity, they both exalt their terror of his infinite power and they exalt their feeling of need to placate him by the ultimate in praise.

Actually it is not religion but the absolute needs of society which preserve systems of morals; "Nothing can preserve untainted the genuine principles of morals in our judgment of human conduct, but the absolute necessity of these principles to the existence of society."[29] Even if a religion were created in which the inculcation of true morality was the only objective, people would make churchgoing to hear the sermons at which these principles were preached the real test of morality.

How, then, is one to account for the presence of genuine codes of morality among men when religion does nothing to inculcate them? Hume's answer is essentially an appeal to the moral sense. A man does his duty to his family and friends because the moral sense impels him to do it; he never thinks of the performance of such duties as having a religious connotation. But the same is true of the duties which he performs for society in general; the moral sense and the principle of universal benevolence take away from the performance of such duties any sense of religious worth. But if the man is superstitious, after he has done his full duty to his family, friends, and society, he still feels that he has done nothing to serve God. "He considers not, that the most genuine method of serving the divinity is by promoting the happiness of his creatures. He still looks out for some more immediate service of the supreme Being, in order to allay those terrors, with which he is haunted. And any practice, recommended to him, which either serves no purpose in life, or offers the strongest violence to his natural inclinations; that practice he will the more readily embrace, on account of those very circumstances, which should make him absolutely reject it."[30] Hence the greatest crimes have coexisted with religious fervor, nor does the sincerity of a person's devotions shed any light on his morals. "Ignorance is the mother of Devotion: A maxim that is proverbial, and confirmed by general experience."[31]

In a curious way Hume's *The Natural History of Religion*, which undermines by its fundamental thesis the cornerstone of deism, is the logical, culminating document in the deist movement. The first article in the deist creed is that man originally had a clear and distinct idea of the one God, Creator and Preserver of the perfectly ordered universe which He rules by general providence; that is the meaning of "Christianity as old as Creation." This belief, of course, was rooted in the traditional Christian belief that the original truth is in the Old Testament and that all paganism is a corruption of it. Hence the theological problem is really one of historical research, the effort to recover that original, clear, and unsullied idea of God. In *The Natural History of Religion* Hume treats religion as a historical phenomenon. His approach would be acceptable to deists, but his conclusions appalling.

Harking back to Hobbes, Hume finds that religion arises from fear. He finds no connection between religion and morality, holding that the moral order arises from the moral sense and the passion of universal benevolence. The mysteries of religion exist for the benefit of the priests; the final mystery is utterly unfathomable. Belief in God is one thing, practice of religion is another. One must believe that God exists, but religion is entirely the creation of man. It sheds no light on the nature of man's relations with the Infinite, it does nothing to create for man a pattern of life on earth. Religion is the creation of man's fears, a constant allegory that tells in supernatural terms a tale of natural forces. The god or gods of religion are of man's making. Religion is a psychological and historical phenomenon, to be studied like all other psychological and historical phenomena. Deism has come in Hume to its only logical conclusion, the denial that there is any relationship between God and man that has been codified, or can be codified, in the form of religion.

Thus the pattern of thought that starts with Lord Herbert of Cherbury comes to its conclusion in the religious concepts of David Hume. Deism starts with the thesis that true religion is simply the good life led by the light of reason. The Church dwindles in importance, as deism undermines its reason for existence. When Bolingbroke adds the concept of general providence and Pope coins the aphorism of philosophic optimism, "Whatever is, is right," the point to petitionary prayer itself has disappeared. Man has been placed in the Clockmaker's universe to follow the light of reason to his eternal home.

But reason is not man's only compass. Shaftesbury adds an inner monitor, one that does not depend on conscious cerebration, the moral sense. It is not automatic and infallible, to be sure, as Shaftesbury conceives it. It is an instinct but one that requires training, and it has a sort of external guide and regulator in the aesthetic sense. No proponent of the moral sense goes so far as to say that it is automatic and infallible, and no proponent goes so far as to deny completely the freedom of the will to flout its dictates, but in Hutcheson the instinctive nature of the moral sense looms larger than in Shaftesbury, and in Hume it looms larger than in Hutcheson. In Hume the final moorings to a divinely created moral order are cast off; as we have already noted, utility becomes "the sole source of that high regard paid to justice, fidelity, honour, allegiance, and chastity . . . inseparable from all the other social virtues . . . a foundation of the chief part of our morals, which has a reference to mankind and our fellow-creatures."[32]

There is, of course, a profound difference between the theorizing of philosophers and the actual practice of men and women. For one thing, the message of the philosopher has a limited audience. On the other hand, it had a relatively larger audience in a reading century like the eighteenth than in a century less given to reading like our own. Of the philosophers and near-philosophers we have considered, Hobbes had much of the success that can attend intellectual scandal in an intellectually oriented age; Pope was the most widely read poet in English literature until Tennyson; Locke wrote the political bible for the triumphant Whigs, and Filmer for the defeated Tories; Mandeville enjoyed a *succès de scandale* something like that of Hobbes; a fair number of the diligent plodded their way through Shaftesbury; and Hume was read at least by those articulate people most receptive to new ideas. It was an age given to speculative interests, and if it was an age in which the masses did not read, it was also an age in which the masses did not influence governmental forms and ruling class social patterns. The people who ran England read Pope and Shaftesbury, Mandeville and Hutcheson, and some of them read Hume. So did the people who ran the American colonies.

As we have already pointed out, there was a far more cogent reason than intellectual appeal for the acceptance of deism and its corollaries. General Monk, the men of reason, all Englishmen except the most fanatical of the enthusiasts wanted a compromise that would end religious strife. Deism offered a way out, a way that would allow religion and religionists to survive in an atmosphere of tolerance. Hence the truly practical men were the ivory-tower academicians, the Cambridge Platonists and the deists who ranged the social spectrum from the titled Lord Herbert to the sincere, devout, and completely untitled Thomas Chubb. Give their thought the social éclat, the social prestige that milords Bolingbroke and Shaftesbury could supply, and let it become the vogue and be chiseled into memorable epigrams by Mr. Pope, "the first poet of our age," and its triumph is assured. England could survive only if Cavalier and Roundhead learned to live side by side. Deism offered a way.

We have seen the gradual fading of belief in the divinely created order as we considered successively the Cambridge Platonists, the deists, Bolingbroke, Shaftesbury, and Pope. We have seen belief in it disappear from the subconscious mind of Hutcheson, the cheerfully conscious mind of Mandeville, and the incisively analytical mind of Hume. But some rationale for the order that exists must be established by one who assumes the philosopher's robes. In a curious way the entire nineteenth-century development of the man-made order is foreshadowed in Hutcheson, Mandeville, and Hume. The school of intuitional morality that evolved historically out of German idealism is foreshadowed in its reliance upon the moral instinct in Francis Hutcheson. The school of utilitarianism, which made the greatest happiness of the greatest number its criterion of moral excellence, all studied directly or indirectly at the feet of David Hume. But the cheerful Philistines of the Victorian age whose criterion of moral worth was material success, who paid willing lip service to orthodox religion, the moral sense, or the utilitarian principle as circumstances dictated, but paid unfaltering and devoted heart service to their personal aggrandizement, were the sons of Bernard Mandeville. The philosophic future might be divided between the followers of Hutcheson and Hume, but the economic and political future belonged to the followers of Mandeville.

We may now pass to the other part of the compromise, the political part as it appears in the political philosophy and practice of the age. It was John Locke's supreme achievement to formulate the philosophy which the political compromise demanded, a philosophy which accepted the social contract and the concept of natural liberty and the equality of men. Insofar as the fatherhood of God and a moral order divinely instituted are fundamentals of his thinking, Locke belonged to one tradition. If our purpose were to develop that tradition, a consideration of Bishop Berkeley, Joseph Butler, and William Law would be in order. But it is the tradition of the man-made order we are tracing, and so our primary interest in Locke and his successors concerns the aspects of their thought which belong to it. They include the concept of the contract, the thesis that government exists to protect property, and the steadily growing inclination toward utilitarianism. We shall not meet another English thinker of the first order in whom the two traditions are fused until we come to Edmund Burke.

V

THE ERA OF STAGNATION

THE POLITICAL COMPROMISE was necessary but beset with problems. The first problem to be solved was the position of the Established Church within the State. The Clockmaker's universe would not run backward; time would not turn back to the days of James I. The Church might survive as an establishment, but it would have to share the realm of religion with the Dissenter churches and share the kingdom of religious thought with Calvinism, deism, and the spirit of Hume for which the name was not yet coined, agnosticism. Religious toleration had become an inevitable part of the political compromise. Put a less pleasant way, the spirit of the age demanded that religious faith yield to political expediency.

Let us start with the orthodox and, legally speaking, the official viewpoint, the one about to be discarded. The Church of England is a branch of the true Church founded by Christ, with the twelve apostles as its first bishops and their episcopal powers transmitted by apostolic succession to the bishops of the eighteenth century. As such it is a perfect fellowship and must have within itself the power necessary for its continuing existence and the performance of its divine mission. Out of this conviction developed the position and the actions of the Nonjurors. In 1689 some four hundred beneficed clergymen, the first of the Nonjurors, refused to swear allegiance to William and Mary, preferring to give up their benefices rather than take an oath which they felt left control of the Church in the hands of the State. Perhaps they were loyal to a dead past, but many of them paid a stern price of poverty for their determination

that the Church of Christ should not become the tool of
Parliament. There was obstinacy among the Nonjurors, there
was intolerance, but there was abundant courage and there was
nobility. Theirs was the historic and orthodox view, but the
eighteenth century was not to be theirs.

Let us turn to the viewpoint of the Dissenter churches. Underlying Calvinism in all its forms is one basic thesis: wherever the
message of salvation is honestly taught and sincerely heeded,
there is the true Church of Christ. The Church of Christ is not
a physical church but a church of the spirit, the spiritual union
of the faithful in their several congregations. From the Dissenter
viewpoint the claim of any single church to be the true Church
of Christ—and this was just as true when the claim was made in
Canterbury as when it was made in Rome—was a self-evident
absurdity. The apostolic succession was a fiction; the Real
Presence, a myth. The strength of the Dissenter churches being
what it was, it is not difficult to see why deism, with its basic
thesis that religion is a way of life and not allegiance to a creed,
provided a way out that was politically expedient to successive
kings and their ministers. Deism, therefore, made possible the
role played by those bishops of the Established Church who
were cooperative with kings and ministers by instinct or by
policy. Their view was unhistoric and unorthodox, but it fitted
the eighteenth century.

Such bishops were not above using the arguments of deism
when these arguments served worldly purposes. The most notorious instance in the eighteenth century was provided by Benjamin Hoadly, successively and triumphantly bishop of Bangor,
Hereford, Salisbury, and Winchester. Hoadly had shown a
capacity to win favor with kingdoms very much of this world
under both Anne and George I; his satirical "Dedication to
Pope Clement XI" (1715) in which he pokes fun at church
authority had the curious but instructive result of winning him
the see of Bangor, which he never visited during his six years
of incumbency. In 1716 came his once-celebrated *Preservative
against the Principles and Practices of the Non-Jurors both in
Church and State.* Its immediate occasion was the publication
of the papers of a distinguished Nonjuror, George Hickes; its
purpose was to proclaim the right of the state to every means

of self-preservation, including control of the actions of ecclesiastics. What mainly raised orthodox hackles was the explicit statement in it, by a bishop of the Church of England, of a primary clause from the canon of deism: a man's "title to God's favour cannot depend upon his actual being or continuing in any particular method, but upon his real sincerity in the conduct of his conscience and of his own actions under it."[1]

Hoadly capped the *Preservative* on March 31, 1717, by preaching before the king a sermon entitled "Nature of the Kingdom or Church of Christ." He denied that there is a visible Church of Christ, denied the reality of the apostolic succession, the power of excommunication, the sacrament of penance, and any meaning to the Eucharist beyond the symbolic. He denied of all the Christian churches that "any one more than another has authority either to make new laws for Christ's subjects, or to impose a sense upon the old ones, or to judge, censure, or punish the servants of another master in matters relating purely to conscience or salvation."[2] The king made sure that the sermon was promptly in print.

THE BANGORIAN CONTROVERSY

There followed the Bangorian controversy, one of the bitterest in English religious history, probably the most prolific of pamphlets, and now almost certainly the deadest. Some fifty-three controversialists ground out nearly two hundred pamphlets, the titles of which occupy eighteen pages in Hoadly's collected works. Hoadly himself did twelve between 1717 and 1720, with the net result that two royal chaplains who opposed his viewpoint and that of their king lost their posts and Hoadly got Hereford (1721). He was there for two years, during which Bishop Atterbury was tried for high treason. Atterbury, whose sermons as bishop of Rochester were High Church and higher in quality than average according to cognoscenti of the eighteenth-century sermon (the Duke of Wharton compared him to Christ at Emmaus, and Steele, more convincingly, says in *Tatler* No. 6 that Atterbury never attempted the passions until he had convinced the reason), had fallen into the habitual Tory booby-trap and supported the Pretender. Hoadly heartily agreed with the sentence of imprisonment and in a series of letters to the *London Journal* did all the damage he could to his episcopal colleague's reputation and character. This estimable service got him Salisbury (1723). Later his episcopal pen was at the service of the Crown in an attack on the Treaty of Vienna and a defense of the Alliance of Hanover. The see of Winchester was the not unfitting reward (1734).

In 1736 Benjamin Hoadly, reviewing his career as bishop of Bangor, Hereford, Salisbury, and Winchester, delivered his apologia for the edification and enlightenment of his subordinate fellow workers in the vineyard. He then continued in the rich and potent bishopric of Winchester to watch for a quarter century the political wisdom of his youth fructify into the solid comforts and ripe emoluments of age. He died in 1761 at the age of eighty-five, to join in eternity Thomas Ken, Bishop of Bath and Wells, a Nonjurist bishop of the saintly stamp, and his old foe Bishop Atterbury. Bishop Hoadly had established the fact that the way to success in the Church of England, under the political compromise, was to serve the king by proclaiming the deist doctrine that the foundation of faith is not objective dogma but subjective sincerity. Whether Hoadly himself had subjective sincerity is a matter for eternity to decide. He certainly fared better on earth than Bishop Atterbury, who went to jail and later to exile, or than Bishop Ken, whose life is part of the noble Anglican tradition of simplicity and renunciation which somehow survived the political compromise and reappeared in Keble, Pusey, and Newman. The lesson of Bishop Hoadly's success was not lost on the eighteenth century.

THE ALLIANCE BETWEEN CHURCH AND STATE

Warburton was the bishop who best formulated the theological foundation for the compromise. William Warburton (1698–1779) rose to be bishop of Gloucester in 1759. He had done his yeoman service two decades earlier in *The Alliance between Church and State* (1736). Warburton used as the basis of his political doctrine the teaching of Locke, proceeding with some ingenuity to argue from the theory of the social contract to a defense of the current state of affairs in England. Point after point in his attack on the concept of the High Church is drawn from Locke.

Warburton's thesis is that in the alliance between Church and State, the Church voluntarily gives up its sovereignty in return for the protection of the State. Church and State are distinct and the Church is necessary to the State, since only under the aegis of religion can the State perform fully its social purpose. But it is right that the State, as protector, be senior partner in the alliance; in justice the king is supreme, but the Church shares the legislative responsibility. Translated into tangible terms, this means that the king is active head of the Church of England and that bishops are members of the House of Lords. Erastianism is the name commonly applied to the subordination of religious to secular authority, a piece of nomenclature entirely unfair to the memory of Thomas Erastus, who merely opposed the implementation of moral judgments by the Church through ecclesiastical censures and punishments, particularly excommunication.[3] In the age of Walpole, Warburton's *Alliance* became something close to the accepted formulation of Erastianism, in the derived sense of the word. In practice the major partner tended to absorb the minor, as the Church tended to become a fairly pliable "moral sense" at the disposal of the State when it chose to look for moral guidance. Warburton's formulation was accepted by the age of Walpole because what Warburton argued for was what existed anyway. Whatever is, is right.

Thus the Church of England passed into the drabbest period in all its history, as bishoprics were filled with Whigs of the cloth and low churchmen tolerantly disposed toward Dissenters. This was the age of Bishop Hoadly and his kind, and the pen of the bishop of Winchester and way stations was steadily at the service of Walpole, in affairs of State quite as much as in affairs of the Church. By Walpole's side stood stout Bishop Gibson of London, whose sole test for preferment in the cloth was loyalty to the administration. So well did they do their work that Walpole could count safely on the votes of twenty-four of the twenty-six bishops in the House of Lords, enough to give him a majority on a contested issue. Small wonder that Bolingbroke called a bishop "a layman with a crook."

To return from the realities of Erastianism to the theories of

Locke is almost to return to an atmosphere of piety and devotion.
Locke wrote four letters on toleration, but the first (1689) makes
clear his entire position. Christianity is the true religion and it
is to be found in all the Christian churches; except in the
spiritual sense there is no Church of Christ. If God will not damn
a man for belonging to the church of his sincere conviction, then
man should not burn him for it. Sincerity, by general agreement, is a virtue and not a vice. The true way with Dissenters
should be to put them on the same level as members of the
Established Church; if the State stops oppressing churches of
the Calvinist tradition, people of the Calvinist tradition will
stop being thorns in the side of the State. A Church is a "voluntary society of men, joining themselves together of their own
accord, in order to the public worshipping of God in such a
manner as they judge to be acceptable to him, and effectual to
the salvation of their souls."⁴ The doctrine of a free church in a
free state does not imply legislative noninterference for its
success and it does imply a fairly uniform moral code in society
at large, but no theoretical shortcomings of the doctrine of Locke
are nearly so bad as Erastianism in practice. The American
colonists, who knew very well the eighteenth-century history of
the churches, were not to miss the point when the hour of self-
determination arrived.

THE AGE OF WALPOLE

This, however, was the hour of Erastianism. Walpole had
been disheartened by the excellent health and sturdy constitutions of the Tory bishops elevated by Anne, but in 1723 bishops
at last began to die. Before the year was over, London, Ely,
Winchester, Chichester, St. David's, and Rochester (by the
exile of Atterbury) were vacant. Walpole had a hierarchy to
create and he found in Edmund Gibson, Bishop of Lincoln, the
man to do his bidding. He dangled London before Gibson, and
on September 6 was able to write to Newcastle, "We grow well
acquainted. He must be Pope, and would as willingly [be] our
Pope as anybodies."⁵ Walpole went on calling Gibson his Pope,
an epithet which tickled Walpole and irritated Gibson, but if
Paris is worth a Mass, then London is worth an insult.

Walpole, indeed, became something of a connoisseur in the fine art of running a church. He found a weakness in the fact that so few clerics have the recommendation of ancestors and high connections. When you made a clerical appointment, you won the services of the cleric; but how much more aesthetically satisfactory it was if he had a relative in Parliament whose services you could win with the same stroke. Managing Peter's skiff was pleasant relaxation for one wearied with the ship of state. Walpole interested himself in deanships, prebendaries, and diaconates, nor did he disregard even the strategically placed curate. And then there were the Dissenters. They were outside the Church but they were Whigs, they were inside the government, and they had votes. The mantle of his particular type of tolerance covered the Dissenters very thoroughly. Walpole protected their position in the kingdom of England. They could look to their position in the kingdom of Heaven for themselves.

To appraise the ministry of Robert Walpole in terms of his attitude toward the Church would be the sort of special pleading that is a self-evident absurdity. But the Walpole who was the first minister in modern times to study finances and to put trade, both foreign and domestic, upon a rational basis; the Walpole who laid the cornerstone of later colonial policy, saw the wisdom of union with France, and envisaged European peace as most conducive to English well-being, and then went down to defeat rather than yield to the cry for war with Spain; the Walpole of rich personality and penetrating human insight who yet, says Chesterfield, was "inelegant in his manners, loose in his morals"; the Walpole who created in Houghton House one of the artistic triumphs of the century; in a word, the Walpole who dominated the politics of his part of the century as Pitt and Burke dominated theirs and is one of the great names if not one of the great men of English history is not the man of our concern. What we say of him is limited and one-sided, but it is necessarily so.

To the Walpole of our concern the Church was merely another instrument used to achieve the great purposes of his life, to assure the Hanoverian succession and to defeat the Jacobites. The total Whig triumph was his unwavering goal, and Church patronage was merely an aspect of the political patronage that

Walpole used to reach it. To say that the sort of thinking which began with the Cambridge Platonists and the deists made possible the use that Walpole made of the Church would be to attribute altogether too much to philosophic thought, altogether too little to human weakness. Yet with that concession the fact remains that the time-servers like Hoadly and Gibson used the arguments of deism to justify a cynical Erastianism. Perhaps Erastianism would have carried the field anyway, but the Cambridge Platonists and the deists, Pope and Shaftesbury and Hutcheson, and even Walpole's inveterate enemy Bolingbroke, had paved the way for its triumph by minimizing Church authority and dogma and exalting human reason and the moral sense. To give comfort and a leg up to a Hoadly or a Gibson was the farthest thought from their minds, but so it worked out.

And then one must look at the other side of the coin. John Locke took a modified deist position in his *Reasonableness of Christianity*, and wrote his letters on toleration from a deist viewpoint. The doctrine that emerges from his religious writings is the doctrine of a free church in a free state. Religious tolerance and, beyond tolerance, religious freedom can be traced to deism quite as truly as can any particular form that Erastianism took in the eighteenth century. By minimizing church authority and dogma and by exalting human reason John Locke paved the way for the triumph of free churches in a free state. The triumph would be achieved in the United States, where the Founding Fathers could take a clear, objective view of the theories of Locke and the practices of Erastianism, and reach their own conclusions. The long and intricate tradition which we are tracing bore many fruits, some wholesome and some obnoxious. Deism is alike the rationale of eighteenth-century tolerance and eighteenth-century Erastianism. Probably that is the best refutation of Shaftesbury, Hutcheson, Hume, and the entire moral sense school. The moral sense works splendidly in men of good will, but what does it do for the Walpoles, the Hoadlys, and the Gibsons?

When we turn from the problem of the relationship of Church and State to the purely secular problems of government and society, we see the age of Walpole in its true light. It was not an age of problems, and certainly not an age of solutions. It was an age of contentment. The ruling classes were sitting pretty and therefore sitting tight. Walpole had his philosophy of government: one gets power, one holds it, and one never forgets that the real way to hold a tight rein is to create the illusion that it is a loose one. Walpole knew when and where to be tolerant, and he knew with crystal clarity the outer limits of tolerance. His weakness, of course, was his greed for power and it drove many capable men into the ranks of the opposition, but his strength was so solidly grounded and yet so supple that he was able for years to brush aside opposition. The governing class was content to live and let live, so long as it could live on the highly advantageous terms that resulted from the Revolution of 1688, and so long as it need let live no peril more potent than the Jacobites. It was not an age to produce political theory, nor did a political theorist of the first order arise in England between Locke and Burke. At the most charitable, Bolingbroke is a theorist of the second order, and the contributions of Hume to political theory are at least overshadowed by his work in psychology and ethics. Yet both of these men offer insight into the development of the eighteenth-century concept of the man-made order; and, as the only political theorists of any significance in the period, their contributions to the political theory antithetical to the natural law cannot be ignored.

We saw in Chapter III the paradox whereby Bolingbroke's belief in general providence and his philosophic optimism change him from a reformer in intent to a defender of the *status quo* in practice. There is also something anomalous about his political theories. He was a Tory by birth and by conscious conviction, but some sort of subconscious conviction tended to upset his thought patterns. He never really believed that a restoration of the Stuart line was practical, and he despised the Pretender personally. A lifetime of venomous attack upon the Whigs left him with a contempt, not so much for the Whigs as for politics in general. He fought Walpole until fighting no longer seemed worth while. He knew that the politico-religious compromise that followed 1688 required a Tory compromise as well, and all through his writings he is groping toward that compromise without really reaching it. The closest he can come is his chimerical concept of the Patriot King. In the realm of philosophy, where he is not hampered by obtrusive political facts, he fully reaches it. In the writer's judgment, the traditional evaluation of Bolingbroke's work which elevates his political writing above his philosophical might well be reversed.

It is not hard to see why that traditional evaluation was made. Bolingbroke writes a strong, nervous prose, one of the first minor figures in English literature to write the prose that the great prose geniuses, Dryden and Swift, brought into being. But vigorous personal attack is more native to political writing than to philosophical. It is one thing to unload vials of wrath upon Robert Walpole; politicians are used to it. It is another thing to do it to Descartes. But Bolingbroke uses billingsgate on all and sundry, be they politicians or philosophers. That his prose style is better fitted to politics than to philosophy no one can deny.

When one examines the content of his political writing its thinness becomes apparent. There is the "Letter to Sir William Wyndham" (1717) in which he vindicates, sometimes by a bland disregard for facts, his conduct in the matter of the Stuart restoration. There are his essays in *The Craftsman* (1726–1736), admirable from the viewpoint of the connoisseur in political diatribe but adding little to political science. There is the "Letter on the Spirit of Patriotism" (written 1736, published 1749), more philosophic in tone and hence more praised, but in essence a melancholy jeremiad on Whig iniquities and Tory servility. Most worthy of consideration is *The Idea of a Patriot King* (written 1738, published 1749), a melange of Tory ideas and the political compromise.

In *The Idea of a Patriot King* Bolingbroke expresses a belief in the natural law and in the duty it imposes of obedience to the civil law. He believes that only the good king rules by divine right since the extension of the divine right to an evil king would be counter to the justice and goodness of God, and he believes in the limitations imposed by the justice and goodness of God upon His omnipotence, standard concepts in orthodox thought. But the influence of Locke is present even in Bolingbroke's own idealistic concept of the Patriot King. Bolingbroke believes that ultimate authority comes from the people; he believes that a limited, hereditary monarchy is the best form of government; he holds that the end of government is the welfare of the people, and that the Patriot King is the monarch powerful enough in personality and virtue to rise above partisan politics yet humble enough to exercise his authority with an awareness that it comes from the people. In a sense this most philosophic of his political writings is a repudiation of politics. The Patriot King is above politics, yet he is the servant of the people. The American concept that the President of the United States is President of all the people yet their servant is dimly foreshadowed in *The Idea of a Patriot King*, a treatise that John Adams, in particular, read carefully and thoughtfully. Thus at the end of the first third of the eighteenth century an outstanding Tory comes very close to accepting the political philosophy of John Locke, if not in its practical applications, at least in its theoretical foundation. The contributions of Bolingbroke to the man-made order were unintentional and oblique, but they reinforced the contributions of Locke.

ESSAYS MORAL AND POLITICAL

When we turn from Bolingbroke to Hume we find a new foundation for political theory. Hume's political thought is to be found chiefly in his *Essays Moral and Political* (1741–1742). The work was well received, had a second edition shortly, and a third in 1751. The first volume (1741) contains all the political essays. Hume relegates the divine right of kings to final oblivion. The social contract he dismisses as a hypothesis convenient enough for certain purposes and even tenable if rigidly defined, but as ordinarily understood simply a historical myth. As always, Hume is strongest in demolition, weakest in construction. Without ever evolving a philosophy of government or offering more than a mechanical pattern on which one might be organized, he does offer at least a motivating principle for government. It is the principle of utility.

Essay XII, "Of the Original Contract," clears the ground for the expression of his political convictions. First he divides political theorists into those who trace government to God and those who trace it to "a kind of original contract." The former consider the slightest deviation from tradition to be sacrilege: the latter reserve the right to resist the sovereign when he abuses the contract. Hume is willing to concede that God is the Author of government in the sense that government is included in the general providence by which He rules the universe. But the notion that this implies the divine right of kings is to Hume sheer nonsense. "The same causes, which gave rise to the sovereign power in every state, established likewise every petty jurisdiction in it, and every limited authority. A constable, therefore, no less than a king, acts by a divine commission, and possesses an indefeasible right."[6] As for the original contract, he is willing to follow Hobbes in the belief that men may originally have banded into society for self-protection. If this is what is meant by the contract, well and good, but Hume will not proceed farther. Society became firmly established, its institutions more explicitly formulated, the authority of its chieftain more generally respected because men saw increasingly the utility of it all.

Hume's real quarrel with the contract theorists is their affirmation "that all men are still born equal, and owe allegiance to no prince or government, unless bound by the obligation and sanction of a promise."[7] If that promise is not fulfilled by the sovereign, the contract theorists believe that the people have the right to rebel. But, Hume maintains, nowhere in the world do people actually think in such terms. They simply take obedience to government for granted: "Obedience or subjection becomes so familiar, that most men never make any enquiry about its origin or cause, more than about the principle of gravity, resistance, or the most universal law of nature. . . . Were you to preach, in most parts of the world, that political connexions are founded altogether on voluntary consent or a mutual promise, the magistrate would soon imprison you, as seditious, for loosening the ties of obedience; if your friends did not before shut you up as delirious, for advancing such absurdities."[8] One generation later the Battle of Lexington and Concord would be fought.

When he turns from what he disbelieves to what he believes, Hume as usual becomes less specific. He believes in the moral sense, which dictates man's duties to society. Among his duties are justice, which includes a regard for the property of others, and fidelity or the observance of promises. Justice and fidelity are natural duties, clearly related to the political or civil duty of allegiance. Allegiance rests on exactly the same foundation as fidelity: "If the reason be asked of that obedience, which we are bound to pay to government, I readily answer, because society could not otherwise subsist. And this answer is clear and intelligible to all mankind."[9]

And to whom is allegiance due? At this point Essay XII moves into a welter of classical references, with Germanicus jostling Drusus, Commodus rearing his besotted head, Julian, Pescennius Niger of Syria and Albinus of Britain raising their long muted voices until, Herodian tells us, Severus marched out of Pannonia to beat them down. And to what purpose this array of classical learning, which sends the twentieth century reeling and must have impressed even the eighteenth? "The general obligation, which binds us to government, is the interest and necessities of society; and this obligation is very strong. The determination of it to this or that particular prince or form of government is frequently more uncertain and dubious. Present possession has considerable authority in these cases, and greater than in private property; because of the disorders which attend all revolutions and changes of government."[10] When the whole procession of ghosts from the ancient domain that Gibbon was to make his own have sifted back into the lifeless pages of Herodian, the principle they illustrate slowly comes into view. "Whatever is, is right."

In Essay IV, "Principles of Government," Hume makes clearer the foundation of utility which he believes to be the true foundation of the social order. He starts with the thesis that since the governed always have numbers and strength upon their side, governors are supported by opinion. There are two kinds of opinion, opinion of interest and opinion of right. The former is utilitarian in the obvious sense: a government is most secure when the people are convinced that to support it is to their interest. Opinion of right is divided as right itself is divided, right to power and right to property. Right to power really means the right of the *status quo* to exist simply because it is the *status quo*: "Antiquity always begets the opinion of right."[11] As for the right to property, while Hume will not go so far as Harrington, who declared in *Oceana* that government exists to protect property, he does assert that it is one of the primary purposes of government. "Upon these three opinions, therefore, of public interest, of right to power, and of right to property are all governments founded, and all authority of the few over the many."[12] "That Politics May be Reduced to a Science" is the title of one of Hume's essays and presumably one of his convictions, but he does not attempt the reduction himself. He comes closest to it in Essay XVI, "Idea of a Perfect Commonwealth," but apart from an admirable mathematical symmetry which he gives its voting pattern, a symmetry that would certainly relegate gerrymandering to man's sinful past, it has little to recommend it, and certainly nothing practical.

The truth is that Hume had nothing constructive to offer in political theory, and the truth is clearest when he attempts in his "Idea of a Perfect Commonwealth" to present something constructive. Skepticism is by nature self-limiting. If society is nothing but a random grouping of individuals, history but a succession of events, forms of government but patterns created by chance, and all man's pitifully limited knowledge a small body of experience surrounded by limitless oceans of mystery, how can we construct a philosophy of society, history, and government? Logically and consistently Hume limits himself to the expression of the hope that a philosophy of government some day may be constructed. Meanwhile he can suggest an operating principle for government, the principle of utility. But the opinions of interest and right naturally favor the *status quo*, and therefore the *status quo* is to be favored on the principle of utility. Hence Hume leans toward a sort of skeptical conservatism, to what Leslie Stephen terms "that stagnation which is the natural ideal of a skeptic."[13]

Harold Laski goes farther, labeling the period we have been considering, which coincides approximately with the reigns of George I (1714–1727) and George II (1727–1760), "The Era of Stagnation."[14] It was an age in which those in a position to make their wills effective were immensely satisfied with life and opposed change as a matter of principle. It was an age in which deism and the skepticism which was its logical outcome bred the spirit of reaction, stifling any questioning of the fundamentals of society. Hence in the realm of politics it was the age of Walpole, in religion the age of Hoadly, in philosophy the age of

Hume. It was not an age of vital theorizing about the philosophic fundamentals of life, but what theorizing there was buttressed the pattern that had developed in English life. Complaisant and compliant bishops meekly accepted that subordination of Church to State called Erastianism, and found that the cynically meek also inherit the earth. Even bishops of the Church of England agreed with Locke that except in the spiritual sense there is no Church of Christ. Walpole manipulated the Church of England while Hume reasoned in his skeptical fashion until he reached the intellectual threshold of utilitarianism. It was an age in which the man-made order, in the names of modernity, enlightenment, reason, and progress, ground to a dead stop. One would indeed have to be daringly prophetic to predict that the century marked by such halcyon calm in the realm of politics and such unruffled optimism in the domain of thought would conclude with one of the most earth-shaking challenges to the social order in all human history.

VI

THE SCHOOL OF
MONTESQUIEU

THERE WAS a spirit moving the stagnant waters even in the age
of Walpole, Hoadly, and Hume. The new thought appeared first
in France, was given a philosophic depth by Edmund Burke,
spread to the American colonies, and helped bring into being
the United States of America. In part this spirit of the late
eighteenth century was derived from the concept of the man-
made order which we have traced through Hobbes, the Platonists
and deists, Bolingbroke and Shaftesbury, Hutcheson and Hume.
In part it was a return to the older concept of the natural law
and the divinely created order on which it rests. There is nothing
more important in the history of thought in the United States
than the line of demarcation between the spirit we have traced
from the compromise of 1660 and the spirit which is present in
the entire Judaeo-Christian tradition. In this and the following
chapter it is that line of demarcation we shall try to keep steadily
in view. Everything else is necessarily subordinate to this piece
of ideological surveying.

Our starting point is the great vaulted hall of the Chateau de
La Brède. On either side, in closets behind mullioned glass, are
incunabula, volumes with a value of their own and volumes
with a value from association with Montaigne and Malebranche.
At one end is the great fireplace and, to its right, an inscription
which the master of La Brède would only partially accept: AV
MAGISTRAT REN HVMBLE OBEISSANCE IL HA DE DIEV C'EST HONNEVR
ET PVISSACE ("Pay humble obedience to the magistrate; he has
his honor and power from God"). It is a massive and imposing

room, a room for massive and imposing enterprises. It is the room in which Montesquieu wrote *L'Esprit des Lois*.

The masterpiece of Charles Louis de Secondat, Baron de La Brède et de Montesquieu was nearly twenty years in the making. It is a long, slow, thoughtful book, the sort of book that should be done in a land where time and space mean little, the unchanging and featureless part of France beyond Bordeaux. The great, vaulted guardroom-made-library, the ancient moat outside, the vineyards that were the particular pride of the baron whose walking stick was a vine prop, beyond them the featureless *landes*—emptiness and distance were the proper setting for abstract thoughts, long pondered, tentatively expressed, revised, and revised again. Slowly *The Spirit of the Laws* grew until, in 1748, it was ready for the press.

Probably it is true that *The Spirit of the Laws* is the least read of the French masterpieces. Time has long since passed by the kind of writing that Montesquieu did, and where time has not passed him by, scientific knowledge has superseded him. But Montesquieu has a primacy which can never be denied, and an importance derived from it which cannot be diminished. Hume had seen the importance of the historic approach, but Montesquieu created the historical method. The proper approach to the study of society and its institutions is in terms of place and circumstance. Hobbes, Filmer, Locke, Bolingbroke, Hume, and the others had created in their several ways political systems in the abstract. But the baron of La Brède, who spent part of each day chatting in the local patois with the commoners of the village, who knew the soil and the vine, the dike and the ditch, the good earth from which the wines of Bordeaux are born, knew that man does not live in the abstract. The long hours of meditation in the vaulted library are important, but so are the leisurely, curious walks around the estate. Countries differ, climates differ, and the men and manners of countries differ profoundly. Much of Montesquieu is abstract, but his abstractions are turrets of thought that soar above what he always intends, at least, to be a solid structure of objective fact.

The Spirit of the Laws contains thirty-one books grouped in six parts. The first part contains a general consideration of laws and governmental forms, the second part a study of military matters, taxation policy, and related subjects. The third part is the best known and, in its implication to learning, perhaps the most important; it deals with the influence of climate on manners and customs. The fourth part is economic, the fifth religious, and the sixth part comprising the last five books deals with Roman, French, and feudal law.

Montesquieu is never more metaphysical than in his opening chapter. He presents the reader with a definition of law staggering to the eighteenth century and requiring at least some mental readjustment in the twentieth. Laws are "the necessary relationships that derive from the nature of things." He goes on to say that in this sense all beings have their own laws. God has His laws, the material world has its laws, intelligences superior to man have their laws, as do men and beasts. God is related to the universe as Creator and Preserver; the relationship is codified by the laws according to which He created and preserves the universe. The laws of God are related to His wisdom and power; they are the ordainments which His wisdom and power require.

The mental adjustment is necessary, but not too difficult. We speak of the law of gravitation. The law of gravitation is one manifestation of the nature of things. Montesquieu starts with the concept of the scientific law, and couples with it a concept with which we are by now familiar, the concept that the wisdom and goodness of God are limitations on His ominipotence. Once one realizes that Montesquieu does not ground his concept of law on the concepts held by jurists but on those beginning to be held by scientists, then the difficulty disappears.

It does not follow, however, that Montesquieu discarded the traditional concept of natural law. In the same opening chapter he states: "Before laws were made, relationships based on justice were possible. To say that there is nothing just or unjust except what positive laws ordain or prohibit is to say that the radii of a circle are not equal before one has drawn the circle."[1] Montesquieu repeatedly expresses his belief in a natural moral law entirely consistent with the definition of Grotius: "A dictate of right reason, indicating for any act, from its consistency or inconsistency with rational nature itself, the presence of moral

turpitude or moral compulsion, and hence as forbidden or commanded as such an act by the author of nature, God Himself."[2]

On the other hand, Montesquieu is not interested in speculation about the state of nature. He dismisses the entire business
with dispatch, and with it he dismisses speculation about the
social contract. Society is a fact, and man is to be studied in
terms of society. But society lends itself to study by the scientific
method, and speculation about man's state prior to the formation of society or about the means that brought society into being is not scientific. The terms are those of the twentieth century, but the pattern of thinking is that of Montesquieu. It is
important that Montesquieu belongs to the rationalistic eighteenth century in terms of his scientific interests but not in terms
of such seventeenth- and eighteenth-century preoccupations as
the state of nature and the contract which so engaged Hobbes,
Locke, and Rousseau.

Montesquieu is equally original in his analysis of governmental patterns. The traditional approach had been that of Aristotle,
with his division into monarchy, aristocracy, and democracy.
Montesquieu treats aristocracy and democracy as subdivisions
of one pattern, the others being monarchy and despotism.
Despotism is totally bad from its very nature; the other patterns
are capable of being good or bad according to tangible practice.
Each pattern has a motivating passion: the motivating passion of
the republic, which may be an aristocracy or a democracy, is
virtue; that of the monarchy is honor; that of the despotism,
fear. Fear needs no definition. Honor is perhaps best defined in
French: *noblesse oblige*. Virtue means patriotism, the placing
of country before self. Of the concepts met so far, the one closest
to it is the general benevolence of Shaftesbury and Hume.
Patriotism of this sort is characteristic of republics at their best;
it is not to be found in monarchies and of course is utterly
foreign to despotisms. Montesquieu does not openly align himself with those who favored the republic over the monarchy, and
indeed there is a broad conservative streak in the baron of La
Brède, but understandably those who favored republics took
him to their bosom. The Americans adopted him, and in France
the proposal that his bust should stand opposite that of Brutus
came before the *Conseil des Anciens* in the fourth year of the

Republic. The general principle, that any potentially good form of government can return to actual goodness by cultivating its characteristic passion, is implicit throughout. A monarchy is kept good or made good by cultivating honor, a republic by cultivating virtue. Montesquieu is logical and ironical enough to add that a despotism is kept in prime condition by cultivating fear.

From the viewpoint of the development of thought in the English-speaking world nothing in the book is more important than the part which deals with the English constitution. Montesquieu's interest in England was natural and lifelong. His mother was half English. He spent eighteen months in England in 1729–1731. He had shown an interest in the English concept of liberty in *Lettres persanes* (1721). He knew the English diplomats at Paris, was friendly with Chesterfield, and had dealings with the English wine merchants who purchased at Bordeaux. He had some knowledge of English, having taken language lessons from an Irishman in Rome. He knew Bolingbroke, apparently was friendly with him for a time and then drifted away from him, but Montesquieu read *The Craftsman* closely and derived many of his ideas of English liberty from it. Not much is known of the details of Montesquieu's period in England, but he certainly moved in aristocratic circles and satisfied in every way possible his avid and sympathetic interest in everything English. It is a commonplace of French criticism, which fails to find in Montesquieu the limpid clarity of arrangement so cherished by the Gaul, that he wrote like an Englishman.

THE SEPARATION OF POWERS

The very title of his masterpiece is instructive: *On the Spirit of the Laws: or, On the Relationship Which the Laws Should Have with the Constitution of Each Government, Its Customs, Climate, Religion, Commerce etc.* As Robert Shackleton points out in his excellent study of Montesquieu,[3] the word *Constitution* unmodified applied in Montesquieu's day to the papal bull *Unigenitus*. Use in the political sense was an Anglicism which did not enter the Academy dictionary until 1798. Montesquieu appears to have written an essay on the English constitution by

the end of 1733, after his return from England. He then revised
it for inclusion in *L'Esprit des Lois* as Chapter VI of Book XI.[4]
Chapter VI is entitled "On the English Constitution," but it opens
with a statement that in each state there are three kinds of
power, the legislative, the executive which deals with foreign
affairs, and the executive which deals with matters of civil law.
The division is essentially that of Locke in the *Second Treatise
of Civil Government*, with Montesquieu's first kind of executive
power corresponding to Locke's federative power but his second
kind, the judicial power in modern terminology, without an exact
parallel to Locke. As a matter of fact it is Montesquieu and not
Locke who formulates the classical division into the executive,
the legislative, and the judicial powers, and Shackleton presents
the evidence[5] to indicate that Montesquieu had worked out the
division before he read Locke.

If the three powers are concentrated in the same hands, the
government is a despotism. This is always and essentially evil.
Two of the three powers may be concentrated in the same hands
and the government characterized as moderate, but liberty demands the separation of the three powers. Most governments of
Europe, says Montesquieu, are moderate, but in the republics of
Italy where the three powers are united there is less liberty
than in the European monarchies. As for the meaning of liberty,
Montesquieu defines it as follows: "Political liberty does not consist of doing what one wishes to do. In a State, that is to say in
a society where there are laws, liberty can only consist of being
able to do what one should wish to do, and not being forced to
do what one should not wish to do. . . . Liberty is the right to
do all that the laws allow, and if a citizen could do what they
forbid, he would not have more liberty because others would
have the same power."[6]

Montesquieu devotes little space to the judicial system, his
most significant statement being approval of trial by jury. He
concentrates his attention on the legislative and executive,
the aspects of the English government which most interested
him. To understand his analysis, one must bear in mind that in
Montesquieu balance of power means one thing, and separation
of powers another. The balance of power was something maintained among the three orders, Crown, Lords, and Commons;

the separation of powers had to do with the functioning of departments of state which in turn implied participation by all three orders. There is an interesting touch of utilitarianism in his chapter on the principle of monarchy: "Honor motivates all parts of the body politic; it likewise binds them by its action; and it reveals that everyone acts for the common welfare when he thinks that he is acting in his own interests."[7] It was Montesquieu's belief that freedom for the exercise of self-interest in English society promoted the balance of power among the orders. As Fletcher points out in his study of Montesquieu's influence on English politics, the interpreters of Montesquieu to England—Blackstone, Delolme, Paley, and Burke—accepted his concept of the balance of powers without substantial change.[8]

The doctrine of the separation of powers is historically more important and is more intimately connected with the name of Montesquieu. It is to be found before him in Locke as a derivative of the contract theory, in a number of anti-Walpole works issued in the 1730s which defend the doctrine against Walpole's absolutism (Lyttelton's *Letters from a Persian*, 1733, is typical of them and has the debt to *Lettres persanes* which the title suggests), and in Bolingbroke. But it remained for Montesquieu to sense the link between liberty and separation of powers, and yet to see that in the practical realm of government the separation of powers had to be reconciled with a fair measure of interaction and a degree of interdependence. The executive should convoke the legislature, determine the period for which it would be in session, and have a certain veto power over its acts. The legislative should have the right of investigating the administration by the executive of the laws which it had passed and of intervening when the law is too rigorously applied by the judiciary. On the other hand, the essential freedom of the judiciary was to be achieved paradoxically by being attached to no definite order or profession and, in a sense, by being invisible and nonexistent. The paradox is resolved when Montesquieu says: "The power of judging should not be given to a permanent senate, but exercised by individuals drawn from the ranks of the people at certain times of the year and in the manner prescribed by law, to form a tribunal which would continue to exist no longer than necessity requires."[9] He has in mind, of course, trial by jury. That trial by jury is possible only within a permanent judicial system is omitted from Montesquieu's discussion of the British constitution, an omission which could well have resulted from the feeling that one can safely omit the obvious. The essential point is that Montesquieu saw through the interdependence and the interaction of the three powers to the basic independence which must be theirs if the liberty of the people is to be preserved. The American Constitution was written on the fundamental principle first enunciated by Montesquieu.

Montesquieu's discussion of the effect of climate upon the customs and so upon the laws of a people is less trite than it would appear at first glance. Implicit in all the studies of the human order we have met has been the supposition that all men are always the same everywhere. Hence there is a certain intangibility about the development of the social order in Hobbes, Filmer, Locke, Hume, and the rest. The life of man in the state of nature is nasty, brutish, and short always and everywhere to Hobbes; the contract is evolved without regard to time and place according to Locke; society comes into being on the principle of utility, but it may have done it east o' the sun or west o' the moon so far as Hume is concerned. Underlying the constant and wearisome citing of classical sources by writers of a century steeped in Latin and at least dipped in Greek is the concept that since man is always and everywhere the same, principles drawn from classical life are automatically valid for life in eighteenth-century England or France. This Montesquieu did not believe.

For one thing, Montesquieu was fascinated by the Orient, and especially by China. He owned a translation of the Koran; he used the voyages of Chardin and Tavernier to provide local color for *Lettres persanes;* like all France he had read *Arabian Nights* in Galland's translation; he knew Malebranche's *Conversations of a Christian and a Chinese Philosopher;* he was friendly with Nicolas Fréret, whose chosen field of study was Chinese; and he actually knew a Chinese, one Arcadio Hoange, who took charge of the Chinese books at the Bibliothèque du Roi.[10] Montesquieu's conclusion was that men are not always the same everywhere, but that they are almost always different

and the Chinese are the most different of all. On this thesis
he wrote the third part of *L'Esprit des Lois*, "The Relationship
between the Laws and the Nature of the Climate." Much of
what Montesquieu believed about that relationship has been disproved, many of his opinions superseded, and not a few of them
now are quaint, but the fact remains that Montesquieu was the
first to make it clear that the customs and the laws of any people
are to be judged in terms of their environment. After Montesquieu such abstractions as the state of nature and the contract
were obsolete. The skeptic Hume may have held that the only
foundation for knowledge is experience, but it was Montesquieu
who applied the principle to the study of the human order.

There is always a sense in which one's attitude toward religion determines one's position in the history of thought. Montesquieu had evolved as a logical corollary to his belief in the
influence of environment upon society, a concept of a common
character which each society develops from a multitude of
causes, a character observable in its individual members. In
Book XIX, Chapter IV, of *L'Esprit des Lois* he analyzes this
esprit général: "Many things govern men: climate, religion,
laws, maxims of government, examples of the past, morals, manners; from these as a result there is formed an *esprit général.*"
Religion, then, is a factor in the common character of a society.
He lists seven reasons for adherence to Christianity: a sense of
elevation above idolatry, its tangible nature (a feeling stronger
in Catholics than in Protestants), a sense that one belongs to
the church of God, the regularity and frequency of its services,
its promise of a future life, the purity of its moral code, and the
splendor of its churches and the wealth of its clergy.[11] The
author of the *Lettres persanes* is by no means dead in *L'Esprit
des Lois*. The last reason cited attests to this, as does the closing
sentence of the chapter: "Thus the very wretchedness of the
people is a motive that attaches them to this religion, which has
served as a pretext to those who have caused their wretchedness."
Montesquieu is a forerunner of the American Revolution. He is
also a forerunner of the French Revolution.

There are also local causes for the choice of religion, including
local political patterns and local customs. A free country like
England will have a large number of competing sects. Chapter V

of Book XXIV bears the title "How the Catholic Religion Better Fits a Monarchy and the Protestant a Republic." He treats in considerable detail the influence of climate on religious beliefs and practices, concluding that "humanly speaking, it is climate that has prescribed the boundaries of the Christian and Mohammedan religions."[12] He believed that if a state was satisfied with the religion which it had, it would be well advised not to permit the introduction of another. Few statements in the book received more bitter attack than this, since it was interpreted as justifying the princes of pagan lands in closing their boundaries to Christian missionaries. Typical of the desire of Montesquieu to remain on good terms with the Church even as he perversely wrote things calculated to raise ecclesiastical ire is the footnote he added in the 1757 edition. "I certainly do not speak in this chapter of the Christian religion because, as I have said elsewhere, the Christian religion is the primary good. See the end of chapter one of the preceding book, and the *Defense of the Spirit of the Laws*, part two."[13]

Montesquieu unhesitatingly elevated morality above dogma. In doing so, however, he explicitly avoids the sort of position taken by Hume. The position of Hume had been essentially the position of Pierre Bayle, Montesquieu's real opponent. Bayle had argued in *Pensées diverses sur la comète* that moral principles exist independently of religion. Montesquieu rejects this position totally, devoting Book XXIV to the relationship between religion and the laws as revealed in local practices. He holds that the study of the comparative worth of religions can be more effectively pursued in terms of moral codes than in terms of dogmatic beliefs. As a logical consequence of this elevation of morality above dogma he believed that it was the role of the State to issue precepts, the role of the Church to give guidance. "Human laws, designed to speak to the understanding, should give precepts and not advice; religion, designed to speak to the heart, should give much advice, few precepts."[14]

DEIST OR NOT?

To sum up the attitude of Montesquieu toward religion, one must start with the external and objective facts. He was born a Catholic, into a family that had given many sons and daughters to the Church. A brother was a priest, two of his sisters were nuns. He was formally a Catholic all his life. He repeatedly avows his belief in God and in a divinely created moral order. He was a man of changing moods, but Montesquieu the believer is just as truly Montesquieu as the son of the Enlightenment with the mocking smile. There is one of his *Pensées* that could have been written by St. Theresa. Regretting his inability to revise *L'Esprit des Lois,* he writes: "My reading has weakened my eyes and it seems that what light I still have left is merely the dawn of the day when they will close forever. I approach the moment when I am to commence and to end, to the moment which unveils and covers all, to the moment of mingled grief and joy, to the moment when I shall lose even my weaknesses. . . . Immortal God! The human race is your noblest work. To love is to love You, and as I end my life I consecrate that love to You."[15] St. Theresa could have written those lines, but David Hume could not.

What is of supreme importance is the attitude that Shackleton, in a nicely selected phrase, calls the "Ecumenical outlook" of Montesquieu. To him the religion of each nation is the tribute it renders to God; the nature of the tribute varies by time and place and for reasons to be verified by scientific inquiry, but the meaning of the tribute does not vary. That such a man should believe in religious toleration follows inevitably. Liberty of conscience was a vital part of liberty itself, and liberty was enshrined in the very heart of Montesquieu.

Was Montesquieu a deist? The statement has frequently been made, and at least on occasion has been denied. If not to conform to rigid orthodoxy, not merely of belief but of attitude, was to be a deist, then of course he was. If to believe that religion is more a way of life than a body of belief is to be a deist, then he certainly was one—and could point to many a gospel passage to substantiate his attitude. If to retain a belief in God and a divinely created moral order and yet to subject to scathing satire the Church, its pompous prelates and the wealth and worldly power so strangely foreign to the spirit of its Founder was to be a deist, his guilt is certain. The point is of no essential importance. Labeling, whether simple labeling or disguised namecalling, seldom is.

Deist or not, Montesquieu ended the stagnation in thought to which the dead-end street of English deism led. He also was concerned with the man-made order, but it was the order man has made on earth. After him such abstractions as the state of nature and the social contract are thin and insubstantial ghosts. After him, human society is never again the simple thing, human nature never the uniform entity they had been in those who wrote before *L'Esprit des Lois*. He laid the foundation for the scientific study of society, and however much others have exceeded his achievement it has been on the foundation which he laid. He sensed the ideal of liberty beneath the balance of power and the division of powers which characterized that British constitution which he considered the most admirable in human history. Across the ocean British colonists, more aware than Europeans ever could be of the differences that life in a new land with the wilderness at one's back makes in the patterns of society, more avid of liberty than Europeans ever could be who could not know the need for freedom when a new people must create a new life in a new land, read Montesquieu. A few read him directly, more read him indirectly in those who wrote in the tradition he created; almost all absorbed some of his ideas even if they did not suspect the source. Montesquieu, whose interest in America as evidenced in *L'Esprit des Lois* was limited to its economic possibilities and its Spanish iniquities and who never dreamed that it would be the most glorious justification in history of his essential thought, was in a sense a Founding Father. This is true not only because Montesquieu wrote but also because what he wrote brought into being what might be called the school of Montesquieu.

EDMUND BURKE

A number of now forgotten writers wrote under the influence of Montesquieu. They were read avidly then, however forgotten they are today. They introduced the reading public to the key concepts of Montesquieu: there is a moral order antecedent to statute law, the state of nature and the social contract are figments of the historical imagination, the ideal of liberty is the inspiring force that permeates the balance of power and the

division of powers in the British constitution, the right approach
to the study of social institutions is through the physical setting
in which institutions have developed, a new race in a new world
may be expected to develop new institutions and new customs.
The age of stagnation was over in the world of the intellect, if
it was to linger for a time in the world of politics. A new vitality
had been given to old concepts, some of them in Locke and
other earlier theorists of the social order. The proper study of
mankind might still be man, but the study is far more complex
than those in the Bolingbroke-Shaftesbury-Pope tradition thought.
Except in the most recondite and metaphysical sense, no one
could say that whatever is, is right. The world had passed by
Hutcheson and Hume, for a time. The immediate future belonged
to Burke and the *Federalist*. The immediate future belonged to
those who believed in the natural law and its concomitant, the
natural rights of man.

For thirty years Edmund Burke was a member of Parliament.
His achievement is unique in the annals of English politics and
of English literature; out of the issues of current political life
and within the framework of party politics he molded a profound and enduring philosophy of society and enshrined it in as
masterful prose as English literature possesses. Almost everything in Burke is topical, yet very much in Burke is permanent;
Burke is uniquely of his age and of the ages.

Burke argued and fought for five "great, just, and honourable
causes": the restoration of the balance of power in the public life
of England by the freeing of Commons from the domination of
George III; the restoration of the American colonies to their
traditional and proper relationship to England by freeing them
from imposts equally unprecedented and unjust; the restoration
of the Irish people to their proper place in the society of Europe
by freeing their Church, their Parliament, and their economy
from the iron hand of theological, political, and economic op-
pression; the restoration of justice to the people of India by
freeing them from the unjust tyranny of the East India Company; and the restoration of law, order, justice, and freedom to a
world threatened by the man-made order gone mad in France.
They were great, just, and honorable causes; there is no more

honorable name in the history of English thought than Edmund Burke.

To call a man of Burke's imposing stature a member of the school of Montesquieu would be a pointless belittling. His work, however, is the culmination of the work of that school, so towering above everything else in it as to obscure its origins. Burke never expends his rhetoric more lavishly than in praise of Montesquieu: "Think of a genius not born in every country, of every time; a man gifted by nature with a penetrating, aquiline eye; with a judgment prepared with the most extensive erudition; with a herculean robustness of mind, and nerves not to be broken with labour; a man who could spend twenty years in one pursuit . . . a man capable of placing in review, after having brought together from the east, the west, the north, and the south, from the coarseness of the rudest barbarism to the most refined and subtle civilization, all the schemes of government which had ever prevailed amongst mankind, weighing, measuring, collating, and comparing them all, joining fact with theory, and calling into council, upon all this infinite assemblage of things, all the speculations which have fatigued the understandings of profound reasoners in all times."[16] That was what Burke thought of Montesquieu, and Montesquieu was a challenge to Burke as well as an inspiration.

Like the thought of Montesquieu, the thought of Burke is grounded on the concrete. The laws and institutions of a country must be appraised in terms of the milieus in which they evolved; they are to be evaluated in terms of the service they render to the people who have created them. These laws can never be inconsistent with the fundamental natural law of which they are specific codifications, designed for specific times and places. Speculation about the state of nature and the original contract is of little value, and Burke evolved a concept of the contract which he reasonably considered far closer to reality than the abstractions of Hobbes, Locke, and Rousseau. Liberty is an ultimate ideal, best achieved and maintained in Britain by the maintenance of the division of powers and the balance of power which are the glories of the British constitution. We cannot say that Burke derived such concepts from Montesquieu merely because Montesquieu had them earlier than Burke. We can say

that Burke read Montesquieu closely and thoughtfully in the
early years when he was working out the theories of man and
society to which he held tenaciously all his days.

Like Montesquieu, Burke had a scientific concept of law;
but for Burke, with his organic concept, the analogy to the
science of biology is closer, the analogy to the science of physics
not so close. Burke thought of the gradual evolution of society
itself and its institutions, from the very simple and primitive to
the intricate and complex, as the true contract. Montesquieu
is less interested in problems of organic growth than Burke.
There is at least something of the deist in Montesquieu, nothing
of the deist in Burke; the concept of general providence is more
consistent with the thought of Montesquieu than with that of
Burke. Burke did not share Montesquieu's interest in remote
lands and their manners; Montesquieu is far more detached
from current issues than Burke, in whom they were present in
the blood and bones. There is much of the upper-class attitude
in both men, but as seems inevitable it is less visible in Montesquieu, who was born securely to the purple, than in Burke,
whose claims were less exalted. Otherwise they differed as
Frenchmen differ from Irishmen. Burke reverenced Montesquieu; there can be no doubt that if their ages were reversed,
Montesquieu would have reverenced Burke. The two men never
met. When Montesquieu died, Burke, twenty-five years old, was
preparing for his wedding.

Burke began his writing career in 1756 with *A Vindication of
Natural Society*. The essay taught him a lesson that he might
have learned from the experience of Swift and Defoe: satire is
often misunderstood, parody often not suspected. Bolingbroke
had written to vindicate natural religion. His vindication had
taken the form of an attack on "artificial" religion, the religion
of the organized churches. Burke, writing in the same spirit and
in a magnificent replica of Bolingbroke's spread-eagle style,
proceeds to parody him by an attack on "artificial" society, on
government and all other formal social institutions. Following
Montesquieu's division, he examines the three forms of artificial
society and shows that all have led to tyranny and war. Artificial
society is as bad as artificial religion. If Bolingbroke was right
in maintaining that the road to salvation lay through the domain

of natural religion, then man's hope of earthly salvation was a
return to the state of natural society, to the state of nature.
"We are indebted for all our miseries to our distrust of that
guide which Providence thought sufficient for our condition,
our own natural reason, which rejecting both in human and
divine things, we have given our necks to the yoke of political
and theological slavery."[17] Mankind should cast off alike the
yoke of religion and government, and enter the paradise of
total liberty and hence of total virtue.

The result was instructive. The style was that of Bolingbroke,
but Bolingbroke was dead. Was this essay by "A Late Noble
Writer" the work of a protégé, or was it a posthumous work of
the master himself? Bolingbroke's editor Mallet disowned it as
authentic Bolingbroke, but Chesterfield and Bishop Warburton
were certain that the master's hand had penned it. To Godwin
it was as effective an attack on the evils of society as ever had
been written; to Dr. Johnson it was a piece of bad judgment
that might hurt Burke in an election. Satire and parody are
dangerous weapons, with the curious propensity of the boomer-
ang. A literal-minded English generation, inexperienced in Irish
wit and its ways, could easily read the *Vindication* as an oblique
plea for deism. Merciful providence sheltered them from the
knowledge that the day was coming when Godwin could read
it as a direct plea for anarchy.

FIVE GREAT, JUST, AND HONORABLE CAUSES

Otherwise the major writings of Burke concern his "five great,
just, and honorable causes": America, Ireland, India, France,
and Britain. To them he gave the finest of his thought and
action for three decades. Burke never wrote a *Spirit of the Laws*
and there is a sense in which it would have been profoundly
illogical for him to have attempted it. It is of the essence of
Burke's thinking that it deal with the tangible and concrete,
that it be directed to specific issues, that his philosophy find
expression in moral judgments about the particular. Burke had
a contempt for theory, which grew into a fear and hatred as
he watched it loose a blood bath in France and threaten the
Western world with chaos. John MacCunn, in his very useful

Political Philosophy of Burke,[18] has gathered on his first page a florilegium of epithets that Burke hurled at the theorists: "refined speculatists, smugglers of adulterated metaphysics, atheistical fathers, metaphysical knights of the sorrowful countenance, political aeronauts, modern philosophers which when you say of them you express everything that is ignoble, savage, and hardhearted." To his constituents at Bristol he voiced the most fundamental conviction that he had: for a nation to resort to theories is "one sure symptom of an ill-conducted state."

It is obvious, then, that when we abstract the political philosophy of Burke from its proper setting in his speeches, essays, and books, and then attribute to Edmund Burke this, that, and the other theory of man, life, law, and society, we are doing precisely what he fulminated against all his life. But commentators have done exactly that for two centuries, and man, life, law, and society have been the richer and the wiser for it. Philosophy is certainly not the less secure for being grounded on the bedrock of experience and the concrete rather than floated over the abyss of theoretical speculation. The political philosophy of Burke can be abstracted from its tangible setting, because it exists. It might even be plausibly argued that Burke the political philosopher deserves to be separated from Burke the politician. The latter was an honorable man, but there was not always in his actions the farsighted wisdom of Burke the political philosopher.

There are axioms in the thinking of Burke, as there must be even in the most inductive of reasoners. Burke believed in a personal God and in a divinely instituted moral code. Hence he believed in the natural law and in that concept of natural rights which makes them inevitable corollaries to the natural law. He expresses these beliefs many times, perhaps never more eloquently than in his "Draft of Letter to the Bishop of Chester" (1771): "My principles enable me to form my judgment upon men and actions in history, just as they do in common life, and are not formed out of events and characters, either present or past. History is a preceptor of prudence, not of principles. The principles of true politics are those of morality enlarged; and I neither now do, nor ever will admit of any other. . . . The principles that guide us in public and private, as they are not of our devising, but moulded into the nature and essence of things, will endure with the sun and moon,——long, very long after whig and tory, Stuart and Brunswick, and all such miserable bubbles and playthings of the hour, are vanished from existence and from memory."[19]

The term "prudence" above is of considerable importance in the thought of Burke. Professors Bredvold and Ross, in their philosophic anthology of Burke, devote an entire chapter to illustrations of its meaning.[20] *Prudence* is the *prudentia* of Cicero, "the necessity of intimate knowledge of a situation in its concreteness, and an insight into its potentialities, before an attempt is made to apply general principles or abstract theories to it."[21] Burke waged a lifelong war against the a priori theorists, a war that only increased in intensity and even fury as the perils of the high a priori road became ever clearer in France. Burke saw clearly into the fundamental cleavage between the thinking of those who based their belief in natural rights upon natural law and those who thought only in terms of rights, never in terms of obligations. He saw clearly that the inevitable terminus of the latter thinking is the bloody aphorism "Might makes right." He lived to see that aphorism made reality in France, and he dreaded its extension to the rest of Europe. As he puts it in his *Reflections on the Revolution in France* (1790), "By these theorists the right of the people is almost always sophistically confounded with their power. The body of the community, whenever it can come to act, can meet with no effectual resistance; but till power and right are the same, the whole body of them has no right inconsistent with virtue, and the first of all virtues, prudence. Men have no right to what is not reasonable, and to what is not for their benefit."[22]

"MADE FOR THE ADVANTAGE OF MEN"

The state of nature interested Burke very little, the social contract hardly more. Both were a priori concepts. Speculation about the historical reality of the social contract seemed to him as pointless as it did to Montesquieu and for the same reason: it could not be verified by historical evidence. To Burke with his organic concept of society the contract is society itself, slowly evolving from relatively simple stages to more complex ones, slowly developing an ever more intricate set of ties among its members, slowly working out a better pattern of life by applying the virtue of prudence, or failing to do so by ignoring that virtue. Society is at once natural and man-made, natural because it is a part of the immutable order of things that God created, man-made because its institutions and ordainments are of human making. "Each contract of each particular state is but a clause in the great primeval contract of eternal society, linking the power with the higher natures, connecting the visible and invisible world, according to a fixed compact sanctioned by the inviolable oath which holds all physical and all moral natures each in their appointed place. This law is not subject to the will of those who, by an obligation above them, and infinitely superior, are bound to submit their will to that law."[23] Undisturbed by theories of the origin of society, undiverted by abstruse speculations of the a priori sort, believing that society is a natural organism which may be studied like any other organism, Burke was in a far better position to bring an objective and uncommitted viewpoint to the study of social institutions than those who carried the onus of a priori theory.

In similar fashion he was unhampered in his concept of human rights. Burke believed quite as sincerely and as deeply in natural rights as did Rousseau and Paine. It is even possible to read Burke and to read Rousseau, and to say with Annie M. Osborn, ". . . there was no important divergence of opinion on the question of fundamental principles. Indeed, when on occasion Burke presents a statement of abstract principle, he gives the best possible phrasing of Rousseau's doctrine."[24] Yet the divergence exists and is profound. In part it lies in Burke's conviction that duty precedes right and is its justification for being. Before natural rights is the natural law; one must have the right to obey the law. If the law is eternal and immutable, so are the rights. In part it lies in Burke's conviction that the only thing that really matters about an abstract doctrine is its practical application. Burke was not interested in abstract theories about natural rights; he was profoundly interested in their implementation in the legal structure of society. It was the tangible rights of man in society that were his concern. Civil society, in his view, did not exist to realize the rights of man; it existed to improve their application. Society to Burke was an institution of beneficence, "made for the advantage of man."

This in turn brings us to another fundamental in the thinking of Burke. There is a sense in which Burke thinks of a right as an advantage, an opportunity to utilize the beneficent action of society for one's spiritual and physical betterment. He thought in these terms of individuals and of nations. England might well have the abstract right to tax the American colonies, but to insist upon the retention of a right when the price is the loss of a continent is folly. England should have utilized the right to its advantage. If it was more advantageous to forego the right, England should have waived it. There is much of the utilitarian in Burke, without the dogmatism of Bentham. But if a right is to be equated with an advantage, one can see the point to his statement in the *Reflections*: "All men have equal rights, but not to equal things." Burke believed that the natural right of man to equality envisaged as opportunity is consistent with the lesson of history; to destroy the existing social structure in the name of equality is an outrage to ultimate truth. The people of America, Ireland, France, and India were being denied in their several ways their natural rights to equality and hence to opportunity. They were four of Burke's five "great, just, and honorable causes," and he fought for them all. The fifth cause was that of the people of England. He was their devoted public servant.

Thus the school of Montesquieu taught a new lesson to England and to America, and to those elsewhere who would listen. Such abstractions as the state of nature and the social contract might provide speculative interest to theorists but were of no practical consequence. God exists, He has ordained a moral order, His concepts are embodied in the natural law, and natural rights are its logical corollaries. Thus the ancient foundation of the Judaeo-Christian tradition and that other tradition which stems from Stoicism and Roman legal concepts were reaffirmed. Beyond that, the proper study of mankind is man. Montesquieu makes far more solid than ever before the foundation of social studies by investigating the influence of climate and other geographical factors upon social institutions. His

English followers carried out this work within their several capacities. Burke enormously expanded it by developing the historical method and creating that most fruitful of approaches, the organic. Both Montesquieu and Burke demonstrated, the one with his pen and the other with his pen and his every act, that one can believe in the divinely created order and yet believe in progress and reform. It is of the essence of the organism that it grow, develop, evolve. It is of the essence of good government to aid and expedite the process.

Montesquieu and Burke had the present and the future partly as their ally, partly as their enemy. Two of the three great revolutions of the modern world soon would come to pass, the American Revolution and the French Revolution. The American Revolution was fought in the name of the divinely created order, the French Revolution in the name of the man-made order. Montesquieu and Burke are part of the American Revolution. The French Revolution belonged to their enemies.

VII
THE SCHOOL OF
ROUSSEAU

To trace the background of the French Revolution is an undertaking far beyond the scope of this book. The call for Liberty, Equality, Fraternity was voiced all through the eighteenth century; it is a natural battle cry, as natural a battle cry for the oppressed who would be oppressors in their turn as for the sincere liberators. But whatever the sincerity of the call, it is at least an affirmative and optimistic call. The world can be made better, if man will make it so. Skepticism was universal in eighteenth-century France, but there was a world of difference between the languid skepticism of the aristocrat who had lost faith, and with it hope and charity, and the skepticism of the philosophe who was skeptical about the past but pinned his faith and hope on the future and at least pledged his charity to it. The philosophe might be skeptical about the Church and the Crown, but he was not skeptical about Man. He was not skeptical about the intelligence of the average man, about his good will, about his capacity, if free to use his reason and his will, to achieve a better life on earth. Liberty and equality were the prime requisites for the betterment of man; when free and equal, men might achieve their earthly paradise in a spirit of fraternity.

For all its surface elegance and sophistication, there is always something simple and even naïve about eighteenth-century thought. It conceived of an essentially orderly universe. Galileo has explained its constitution and Newton has outlined its operational principle. Man is an orderly being, orderly constituted and orderly in his thought processes. Granted freedom to do so, he can achieve his own redemption. Reason is sovereign, and man controls his reason and is controlled by it. It is the old, simple, comforting doctrine of deism, just as simple and comforting in French as it is in English. Shaftesbury may or may not have had the influence on French deism that some have claimed, but there is a similarity to Shaftesbury and the other English deists that runs through Diderot and Holbach, and is not absent from Voltaire and Rousseau. It is the spirit of the age, of course, not the spirit of Shaftesbury. By comparison Montesquieu and Burke are complex and disquieting. They think that the earthly paradise may not be quite so easy to achieve.

In determining, therefore, what that group of thinkers and writers of the French Enlightenment known collectively as the philosophes thought and wrote, one may find the thought and writing of Shaftesbury a useful touchstone. The inference should not be that Shaftesbury is the source of their thought, or more than one of the many influences that went to make up eighteenth-century concepts in France, but in Shaftesbury, better than in any other English deist, one can see both the points of origin and the logical conclusions of deism. The point can be illustrated in Diderot.

DIDEROT

Denis Diderot (1713–1784) was a dramatist and critic as well as principal director of the *Encyclopedia;* it was the boast of the philosophes that they were not philosophers, by which they meant ivory-tower speculatists. Diderot had the belief in natural religion which was a common denominator of deism. The constant tendency in Diderot, however, is to break away from deism and go in the direction of materialism. Both Shaftesbury and Diderot consider the problem of the maintenance of the human identity in light of the constant changes in the human cells. Shaftesbury suggests that it is the presence of God within His creatures that produces the continuity;[1] Diderot suggests in his *Letter on the Blind* that matter itself may be God. Indeed Diderot presents a hypothesis of evolution, grounded on what from one viewpoint is materialism and from another pantheism, in his *Thoughts on the Interpretation of Nature* (1754). Shaftesbury believed in the unity of creation, but never believed that the creative force was within matter itself. As Diderot moved toward materialism, he moved away from the concept of the moral sense. In *Rameau's Nephew* (1762) he rejects totally the concepts of the moral sense and universal benevolence. Heredity, environment, and chance determine all in a materialistic universe. His disciple Holbach went the entire distance.

Baron Paul Henri d'Holbach (1723–1789) developed a universe the gods of which were the laws of matter. In his *System of Nature* (1770) he finds in the material universe all the attributes traditionally conceived of as belonging to the Deity: matter is infinite, independent, incomprehensible, and eternal. One of the common denominators in the thinking of the philosophes is the necessary existence of a moral code. Holbach, who held to a concept of the universe more materialistic than that of Diderot and very similar to that of Lucretius, of necessity denied any moral code that was not man-made. He believed that man has an instinct to seek his well-being, experience shows him that his well-being is promoted by pleasing others, he pleases others by acting toward them on the principle of mutual well-being. In Holbach materialism leads to utilitarianism rather than the other way around, but the road traveled is the same. Oddly enough, Holbach equates truth and beauty, the two forming a trinity with utility. He travels a very different road, but he reaches a conclusion in this respect not too different from that of Shaftesbury. Perhaps quite as important to the development of eighteenth-century thought as his beliefs were the circumstances under which Holbach preached them. The baron's dinner parties were the favorite rendezvous of radical France. In his Paris establishment, the "Café de l'Europe" as the philosophes called it, gathered as guests of the "Maître d'Hôtel de Philosophie" one might find Turgot and Condorcet, Englishmen like Hume and Priestley, and possibly Benjamin Franklin.[2]

VOLTAIRE

Like the others Voltaire started with certain concepts that may be found in Shaftesbury, and have their most celebrated expression in English literature in Pope's *Essay on Man*. He started with a belief in the Great Chain of Being which links in a series, that to the eye of man at least seems infinite, every entity from God to the last and least bit of inorganic matter. The Great Chain is constructed on the principle of plenitude, that every possible entity exists in a universe created by an omnipotent and infinite God. Closely related to these concepts, as we have seen, is the aphorism "Whatever is, is right." Then came the Lisbon earthquake (1756). Thereafter Voltaire never trusted Shaftesbury's kind of optimism. He slipped easily, as a deist does, into utilitarianism. Behind the familiar injunction of Candide to cultivate one's garden, lie two principles, utilitarianism and skepticism. The Lisbon earthquake promoted Voltaire from the school of Shaftesbury to the school of Hume.

In general, the philosophes are more skeptical than the English deists, more materialistic in their thinking and possibly more utilitarian in their ethics. They held far more consciously than the English deists to the concept of the man-made order; among the English deists there is, rather than a conscious avowal, a subconscious tendency in the direction of belief in the man-made order. Yet it was the very belief of the philosophes in the man-made order which saved them from the stagnation of skepticism. The Church, in their view, could no longer give spiritual direction. They would build a new church of humanity, a new religion founded on human values; they would build, as Professor Becker has it, "the heavenly city of the eighteenth-century philosophers," but they would build it here on earth.[3]

It is precisely at this point that the great difference appears between the English deists and the French philosophes. There is an ivory-tower aspect to English deism. The Cambridge Platonists were academicians, and the English deists for the most part were in no position to be other than theorists. Bolingbroke does not become a philosopher until he is finally finished as a politician, and Shaftesbury had neither the health nor the desire for public life. Hence there was no possibility of the English deists actively influencing the course of English life. But this is dwarfed in importance by the fact that deism was really seized upon in England because it provided a convenient moral foundation for the compromise of 1660. If English deism did not exist, it would have had to be invented.

The situation was quite different in France, although, as the outcome proved, these matters were certainly not better ordered there. It was the boast of the philosophes that they were not philosophers but men of action, although the justice of the claim is open to the widest question. They did strive to influence public action by molding public thought, and they did ultimately provide at least a rationale for the French Revolution. Fundamentally the philosophes worked to change an intolerable situation, not to justify a comfortable one. The purpose for which English deism was manipulated was to justify a generally desired state of affairs; the purpose toward which French philosophism (to borrow without overtones Carlyle's pejorative) was directed was to change a generally resented one. In the very nature of things English deism had to glorify the here and now; French philosophism had to glorify the future. The deists thought in terms of today, the philosophes in terms of tomorrow.

From this fact arises the most striking aspect of the entire movement in France, the aspect that Professor Becker treats in his central lecture "The Uses of Posterity."[4] "For the philosophe," said Diderot, "posterity is the other world of the man of religion." The philosophes are as one in thinking, working, dreaming about that glorious tomorrow when the human race will be transfigured out of the recognition of the present generation. Burke and his followers might look to the past, the deists might look to the present, but the philosophes looked to the future. The future was the land of opportunity for eighteenth-century France, as it was for the few in eighteenth-century England who thought like the philosophes. Joseph Priestley spoke for these Englishmen when he wrote: "Whatever was the beginning of this world, the end will be glorious and paradisiacal, beyond what our imaginations can now conceive. Extravagant as some may suppose these views to be, I think I could show them to be fairly suggested by the true theory of human nature, and to arise from the natural course of human affairs."[5]

The contrast between the thinking of Priestley and of Burke is instructive. One must have in abundance that virtue which

Burke calls *prudence,* and one must combine with it much knowledge and human understanding, to put into execution the concepts of society and government in which he believed. The Founding Fathers of America were men of prudence, knowledge, and human understanding, and so in a broadly philosophic sense they belonged to the school of Montesquieu and Burke. But anyone can dream of the future, and when those dreams are coupled with the conviction that the entire order is man-made, then one can be brought to the determination to "shatter it to bits, and then remould it nearer to the heart's desire." Such was the promise that the philosophes held out to France, and later the revolutionists held out to England. All that was necessary was the appearance of that figure so graphically described by Leslie Stephen: "Suddenly there has entered a man stained with the filth of the streets, his utterance choked with passion, a savage menace lurking in every phrase, and announcing himself as the herald of a furious multitude, ready to tear to pieces all the beautiful theories and formulas which may stand between them and their wants."[6] English deism led to stagnation, American political philosophy led to the Constitutional Convention, but French philosophism led to the guillotine. Behind the frenzy that with the Jacobins passed for thinking was the thought of Jean Jacques Rousseau.

ROUSSEAU

"Man is born free; and everywhere he is in chains." Rousseau's *The Social Contract* has the most famous first sentence in French literature, and one of the most effective first sentences in world literature. Man is by nature free, Rousseau meant; he was certainly not born free in Rousseau's France. It was not so much the logic of Rousseau—for he has little logic—that made his book the bible of insurrection and vengeful violence; it was the inexorable logic of events. The deluge had been predicted, and the deluge came. The order that the Sun King had made and his successors had tried to preserve was swept by the deluge to oblivion, but another man-made order ultimately was imposed on the chaotic disorder that followed. The word of Rousseau inspired the deluge, and the word of Napoleon stemmed the raging current. The word of Montesquieu might be heard in Philadelphia, but the word of Rousseau was heard in Paris. Montesquieu had his school and his greatest student was Edmund Burke. Rousseau had his school and his greatest contemporary student was Robespierre. As we turn to the school of Rousseau we turn from the salons to the streets, from Versailles to the wilderness, from the philosophe to the sans-culotte.

Rousseau commits himself to the man-made order in the first chapter of *The Social Contract:* ". . . the social order is a sacred right which is the basis of all other rights. Nevertheless, this right does not come from nature, and must therefore be founded on conventions."[7] Implicit in these two sentences are three of the tenets fundamental to the concept of the man-made order: one starts with a human right and this implies that will and not law is one's starting point; this human right is not founded on the natural order; it is founded on conventions which are made by man. The central problem for Rousseau, the central theme of his book, is the establishment of a line of reasoning which permits rights to be deemed inalienable and yet to be founded on the man-made order. Rousseau has no greater glory than his ability to see the problems that are really central.

Like many who accept the concept of the man-made order Rousseau employs the hypothesis of the contract. He is highly dubious about its historic nature, and no more concerned about that aspect of it than was Hume. He is immensely concerned with the problem of individual freedom within the contract. "The problem is to find a form of association which will defend and protect with the whole common force the person and goods of each associate, and in which each, while uniting himself with all, may still obey himself alone, and remain as free as before. This is the fundamental problem of which the Social Contract provides the solution."[8] To Rousseau the contract is neither more nor less than society itself. He reduces it to these terms: "Each of us puts his person and all his power in common under the supreme direction of the general will, and in our corporate capacity, we receive each member as an indivisible part of the whole. At once, in place of the individual personality of each contracting party, this act of association creates a moral and collective body, composed of as many members as the assembly contains voters, and receiving from this act its unity, its common identity, its life, and its will."[9] This public person was once called a city and is now called a republic; in a passive sense it is a State, in an active sense it is the Sovereign, and it is called Power when compared to other societies similar in nature.

Rousseau's concept of the contract is neither obscure nor unconvincing, nor particularly important. It is the two related concepts, that of the Sovereign and that of the Common Will, which are metaphysical in the less desirable sense of the word and formidable in their impact upon history. The body politic is the Sovereign. It draws its being from the sanctity of the contract. It can never bind itself to do anything contrary to the original act which brought it into being. Since its members comprise one body, it is impossible to offend against one of its members without attacking the body. There is no possibility of a conflict of interest between the Sovereign and its member. "[Again], the Sovereign, being formed wholly of the individuals who compose it, neither has nor can have any interest contrary to theirs; and consequently the sovereign power need give no guarantee to its subjects, because it is impossible for the body to wish to hurt all its members. We shall see later on that it cannot hurt any in particular. The Sovereign, merely by virtue of what it is, is always what it should be."[10] This is not true of the individual in relation to the Sovereign since the individual may have a will contrary to the general will. Hence whoever refuses to obey the general will must be forced to do so by the whole body.

In Book I Rousseau establishes his theoretical foundation for human liberty. He conceives of the state as that multitude of individuals united for mutual protection and well-being which Hobbes envisaged. He parts company from Hobbes in the concept of the Sovereign. Viscount Morley, Rousseau's biographer, puts it excellently: "Strike the crowned head from that monstrous figure which is the frontispiece of the Leviathan, and you have a frontispiece that will do excellently well for the Social Contract."[11] To Hobbes the Sovereign is an individual to whom the people surrender sovereignty in return for protection. To Rousseau the Sovereign is the embodiment of the individuals who comprise the state; sovereignty is the embodiment of their collective power. Hobbes's thought leads logically to the despotism of the individual; Rousseau's thought leads logically, and led historically, to the despotism of the proletariat. Rousseau's Sovereign is omnipotent and infallible in its realm. Omnipotence and infallibility are attributes of the Deity. Rousseau believed in the absentee God of deism, but the deity he really worshiped was that abstraction, the People.

The concept of the Sovereign is metaphysical, but it is sharply etched when contrasted with the other and equally important concept, the General Will. Sovereignty is the embodiment of the General Will, and cannot be divided because the General Will cannot be divided. What, then, is the General Will? In the literal sense the question can be simply answered: the General Will is the will of the Sovereign and the Sovereign is the body politic. Hence the General Will is the will of the body politic.

The difficulty starts when Rousseau tries to draw a distinction between the will of all and the General Will. The former is merely the sum total of the wills of individuals; "but take away from these same wills the pluses and minuses that cancel one another, and the general will remains as the sum of the differences. If, when the people, being furnished with adequate information, held its deliberations, the citizens had no communication one with another, the grand total of the small differences would always give the general will, and the decision would always be good."[12] The difficulty cannot be entirely eliminated, nor indeed does Rousseau himself, who recognized its existence, entirely eliminate it. He certainly did not think that the will of the majority was the General Will and hence infallible, although he did think that a majority was more likely to express the General Will than was a minority group. The haze can be thinned out a bit, perhaps, if one returns to Viscount Morley's symbol of Leviathan with the crowned head removed. The headless Leviathan is Rousseau's Sovereign. Each tiny human being included in the Sovereign always wills his own good. Each human being is an entity possessed of human freedom. But the Sovereign, the composite of all these human beings, is also the composite of their individual wills which are always and infallibly oriented to their individual good. Hence the composite being, the Sovereign, also has a General Will always and infallibly oriented to the good of the body politic.

The problem is to determine what that will is, to distinguish it
from the sum of particular wills or the particular wills of groups
within the body politic. The difficulty, one should observe, is in
determining what it is, not in proving that it exists. The foundation of the individual will is human freedom; the foundation of
the General Will is the freedom of the body politic. The General
Will always is directed to the preservation of individual freedom
and hence the omnipotence of the Sovereign offers no threat in
terms of the General Will. The Sovereign must respect the
freedom and equality of its every member or it ceases to be the
Sovereign. As Rousseau's translator G. D. H. Cole well puts it
in the Introduction to the Everyman's Library edition of *The
Social Contract*, "Thus the justification of Rousseau's theory of
liberty returns to the point from which it set out—the omnipotence of the *real will* in State and individual. It is in this sense
that he speaks of man in the State as 'forced to be free' by the
General Will, much as Kant might speak of a man's lower nature as forced to be free by the universal mandate of his higher,
more real, and more rational will. It is in this recognition of the
State as a moral being, with powers of determination similar
to the powers of the individual mind, that the significance of
the General Will ultimately lies."[13] We must obey the General
Will because it is inside us, not outside, and we necessarily will
our own good.

Everything else in *The Social Contract* is subordinate to these
central concepts of the Sovereign and the General Will. Society
itself is really the natural state. Man is a social being and, having
the benevolence which Shaftesbury proclaimed and Hobbes
denied, he really wills the welfare of his fellow man. The natural
goodness of man is implicit in *The Social Contract* and not explicit as in *Émile*, but in the very nature of the concept it underlies the General Will. The practical question, which form of
government best expresses the General Will, Rousseau resolves
in favor of an elected aristocracy. "Were there a people of gods,
their government would be democratic. So perfect a government
is not for men."[14]

Behind the thinking of Rousseau is Locke's concept of the
contract and Hobbes's concept of sovereignty. But it is an
obvious and complete misunderstanding of Rousseau to imagine

that he is in any sense an amalgam of Locke and Hobbes; at the most their thinking produced in him a chemical compound of the mind entirely different from its constituent elements. Hobbes had the pragmatic turn of mind; man had to enter society for self-protection. Locke had the legalistic turn of mind; man entered society under definite conditions and limitations for his self-betterment. Rousseau has the mystic turn of mind; man and society fuse and are one. "Man is born free." That is true, not in the state of France but in the state of nature. In the state of nature man is born free and equal to his fellow man. Man is a social being, and his fellow man is his brother. Liberty, Equality, Fraternity; society is social brotherhood. The concept came to the Jacobins as formulated by Rousseau. Even the term *citizen,* originally applied in Rousseau's native Geneva to the two classes eligible to hold magisterial office, came to the Revolution from the pages of Rousseau. Man and society fuse and are one. Now the entire concept of the man-made order takes a new and portentous turn. Heads will tumble and blood will pour on the streets of Paris in the name of that headless Leviathan, the People. Robespierre and the Jacobins are of the school of Rousseau.

We must now turn to the English thinkers who may, with varying degrees of accuracy, be considered members of the school of Rousseau. One, Thomas Paine, is remembered. Another, William Godwin, is known to students of the romantic movement in literature. A third, Joseph Priestley, is known to scientists. A fourth, Richard Price, once celebrated, is now unknown. We may start with Priestley, since in his *An Essay on the First Principles of Government* (1768) the first English reflection of *The Social Contract* may be observed.

JOSEPH PRIESTLEY

Joseph Priestley (1733–1804) was a theologian, philosopher, psychologist, historian, classicist, and chemist. In theology he ran the gamut from a strict Calvinism to a Unitarianism barely recognizable as such. His theological views in the later stages were most incongruously affected by the vestigial remains of his previous beliefs. For example, he came to believe that the soul was material and to reject the inspiration of the Apostles, but not to reject his earlier conviction that the Second Coming would occur within twenty years. As a philosopher he was the student of David Hartley, simplifying the thought of the master in a work which reproduced Hartley's rejection of the moral sense and his foundation of morals on the association of pleasure or pain with specific actions. As a historian his chief effort, *History of the Corruptions of Christianity* (1782), was directed at proving that the teaching of the primitive Church was Unitarian. A resulting debate with a slightly better informed opponent, Samuel Horsley, led to his writing in the same cause a monumental and deservedly neglected work of four volumes, *History of Early Opinions concerning Christ* (1786). A man of roving and dissatisfied mind, capable of concentration intense but not prolonged, one who dabbled with total seriousness in matters that require a lifetime of study to master, yet a man of complete good will who commanded the respect of the advanced minds of the age, Joseph Priestley was entitled to make one solid and permanent contribution to the body of human knowledge. The theologian, philosopher, and political theorist who reflected Rousseau, sympathized with the French revolutionists, who celebrated the anniversary of Bastille Day in 1794, had his house destroyed over his head by an infuriated mob, and at the age of sixty-one had to seek a new life in Pennsylvania, lives in the history of science as the discoverer of oxygen.

Our concern is with his *An Essay on the First Principles of Government*. He opens by avowing his debt to Rousseau and by modifying slightly Rousseau's distinction between natural and civil liberty into a distinction between civil and political liberty. Man, according to Priestley, relinquishes some of his civil, i.e. natural, liberty for some political liberty, i.e. share in the government.[15] He then proceeds to give the argument from Rousseau what will be its characteristic English form, the argument from utility. The social contract exists to promote the greatest good of the greatest number: "the good and happiness of the members, that is the majority of the members of any state, is the great standard by which everything relating to that state must finally be determined."[16] He then proceeds to voice his belief that this principle, which he considers the foundation of politics, is also the foundation of morals and theology.

Priestley makes two contributions of significance to the development of English thought. Arguing that governmental interference in education would be inexpedient because it would run counter to that variety which is native to human nature and because it would interfere with parental rights, Priestley expresses a viewpoint clearly anticipatory of *laissez faire*. He does so in terms of education and not of economics, but the basis on which he does it would admit of that expansion which the doctrine took in one of the most characteristic developments of thought in the century ahead. The other contribution, his emphasis upon progress, has already been illustrated. No characteristic of nineteenth-century thought is more striking than the nearly universal acceptance of the idea of progress. The idea has many roots, and one of them certainly grows out of the devotion of the philosophes to the realization of their dreams in a glorious posterity. Optimism of that sort was congenial to Priestley, and he is among the first to voice in his period what would be the universal conviction of the English revolutionists. Indeed, his fervid conviction that the French Revolution was the dawn of the millennium cost him his house and his country.

Priestley is too undisciplined a thinker, too given to enthusiasm in the modern sense of the word, to be a figure of major importance in the development of the concept of the man-made order. His importance is in chemistry. But in him and the other minor figures of the school of Rousseau, we can see characteristic developments of the concept, once thought has turned from the dead-end street of deism. In Priestley the one significant development is the fusion of Rousseau's concepts of the contract, sovereignty, the General Will, and human rights into the native English concept of utility. For France that soul-stirring triad: Liberty, Equality, Fraternity. For England that cautious monad: Utility. Priestley was an enthusiast, a visionary, a passionate pursuer of the new idea—but before all else, in his kind-hearted, idealistic, muddled confusion he was an Englishman. Not for England the soul-stirring slogans—but not for England the Reign of Terror.

WILLIAM GODWIN

When we come to William Godwin (1756–1836), first a dissenting minister, then an anarchist and atheist, later father-in-law to Shelley, and ultimately author of books for children, we come to a man whose importance in the life of one of England's greatest poets inevitably dwarfs and distorts his significance to our field of interest. Just as the immigrant's first view of New York used to be its topless towers looming through the mist as he came up the harbor, so the college student first meets Godwin as an apparition rising from the foam of Shelley's perilous seas of poetry. The apparition tends to resemble a monster, a resemblance which does not disappear since the apparition remains to the student a figure of hearsay. In the name of cold and prosaic reality, there is much to be said for meeting Godwin by himself, apart from Shelley and, for that matter, apart from young Wordsworth and Coleridge. There is much to be said for meeting him in his proper company, a now-forgotten company including such names as Thomas Cooper, Joshua Toulmin, John Thelwall, and Thomas Holcroft. This was England's revolutionary generation, along with Priestley and Paine. It is Godwin's proper company.

Godwin, like Priestley, started as a dissenting minister. In the most radical pages of his *Enquiry concerning Political Justice*, the pages in which he discards government, marriage, and the other social bonds and shackles, there is mirrored with strange distortion the face of John Calvin. Book II, chapter five, is a key passage in the work; its title is "Rights of Man." Godwin believes in the reality, not of rights but of duties. He rejects all forms of the man-made order which start with a concept of the primacy of the human will and hence of rights. He also rejects the argument for the divinely created order which holds that rights are necessary corollaries of duties, but his starting point is certainly closer to it than to the axioms of the man-made order. Political society, he holds, is founded on morality and justice. Both require the performance of duty. We have duties toward our fellow men and duties toward society. We can have no rights that conflict with those of our fellow men or society. One man's rights cannot conflict with another's; both are bound by duty. At the most, men might be said to have rights to do things of total indifference, and the latter are very few. "In reality nothing can appear more wonderful to a careful enquirer than that two ideas so incompatible as man and rights should ever have been associated together. Certain it is that one of them must be utterly exclusive and annihilatory of the other."[17] Man must have freedom, of course, for the performance of duty, but Godwin does not equate that freedom with human rights. At the very least he betrays his Calvinistic starting point in his emphasis on duty.

Godwin also shows the influence of his earlier background in his concept of justice. Probably the best-known passage of *Political Justice* is Book II, chapter two, the passage for which Charles Lamb refers to Godwin as "counsel for Archbishop Fénelon versus my own mother." Godwin wrote, "In a loose and general view I and my neighbour are both of us men, and of consequence entitled to equal attention. But in reality it is probable that one of us is a being of more worth and importance than the other. . . . In the same manner the illustrious archbishop of Cambrai was of more worth than his chambermaid, and there are few of us that would hesitate to pronounce, if his palace were in flames and the life of only one of them could be preserved, which of the two ought to be preferred. . . . Supposing I had been myself the chambermaid, I ought to have chosen to die rather than that Fénelon should have died. . . . Supposing the chambermaid had been my wife, my mother or my benefactor. This would not alter the truth of the proposition."[18] In the subsequent editions, the chambermaid became Fénelon's valet and was Godwin's hypothetical father and not his mother. It is, presumably, less austere to let your father burn in the name of justice than your mother. The real point to be established, assuming that Godwin's lack of humor and dauntless courage in the face of absurdity are self-apparent, is that justice is something objective, something existing apart from one's emotional reactions and personal scale of values. As Godwin puts it, "The inference most clearly afforded by the preceding reasonings is the competence of justice as a principle of deduction in all cases of moral enquiry."[19]

Godwin continues in his next chapter, "Of Duty," to consider the difference between concrete justice and one's subjective idea of justice. If one does his duty according to the latter, is the act virtuous? Godwin says no, since morality is something fixed and immutable. One's disposition may be virtuous without one's act being virtuous. Virtue lies in the act, not in the disposition. It is wrong to think that one is virtuous because he had done what he deems his duty, unless what he has done is itself objectively virtuous. "In reality the most essential part of virtue consists in the incessantly seeking to inform ourselves more accurately upon the subject of utility and right. . . . Since absolute virtue may be out of the power of a human being, it becomes us in the meantime to lay the greatest stress upon a virtuous disposition, which is not attended with the same ambiguity."[20]

It is clear, then, that Godwin does not start with a concept of human rights nor with a subjective concept of morality. His starting point is equidistant from the viewpoint of Rousseau and the human rights theorists and from Hume and the utilitarians. It is quite understandable, however, from the viewpoint of Calvinism if by no means consistent with its development. The point is worth stressing, because the revolutionary school in England, for all its debt to Rousseau and the philosophes, also learned lessons from the Dissenter churches. The really important common denominator which the English revolutionists shared with the French was the belief in human perfectibility. One can never hope to understand Godwin, to understand why intelligent people read him with respect, why young Wordsworth may have listened to him in a London underground in days perilous for English revolutionists and why young Shelley turned Godwin into verse crudely in *Queen Mab* and gloriously in *Prometheus Unbound*, if one does not start with the understanding that Godwin wrote about man as a perfectible being, not as a perfected one.

Godwin's *Political Justice* is the ultimate expression of the revolutionary spirit in England during the age of revolution. Man is a rational being. Let right reason be his guide and right action will necessarily follow. Vice originates in false judgment caused by the lack of right reason. The vicious must be given the instruction they so patently need; punishment does nothing for them. Although Godwin rejects subjective morality, he by no means rejects the utilitarian conclusions of Hume and the utilitarian school. The most moral act is the one which produces the maximum of human happiness. The promotion of human happiness is better achieved by saving Fénelon than by saving his chambermaid. The vital thing is so to perfect the human reason that man will inevitably act rationally in the way calculated to produce the maximum of human happiness without being influenced by emotional considerations and personal factors. Man obviously is not perfected to this point. Godwin never claims that he is. Man is perfectible, however, and presumably can reach this point.

When the point of perfection is reached, the human institutions which exist to promote the rule of right reason will be obsolete. Government will not be necessary to make men act rationally. Government, as a force restrictive by its very nature, will no longer have a cause for being. The Church is another institution that exists to promote the rule of right reason. In the millennium there will be no Church, for there will be no need for a Church. When right reason prevails, there will be no excessive concentration of material wealth in individual hands, but a natural equality perpetuated by right reason will prevail. So obviously tyrannical an institution as marriage will be obsolete in that happy day, although it is not on record that Godwin's own right reason had perfected itself to the point of equanimity when Shelley abandoned Harriet and eloped with Godwin's daughter Mary. In short, when man is rationally perfected, he will have a mind and will necessitated to right conduct by right reason. For man in that state, the institutions of varying degrees of necessity required during his period of perfectibility will no longer be needed and will wither on the vine. Radicalism also can have its orthodoxy: that government will become obsolete when human perfection is an accomplished fact is an orthodox radical dogma. It is Godwinian orthodoxy, accepted by Godwin's disciples, just as it is Marxian orthodoxy that government will become obsolete in the final stage of true Communism. It is perhaps something a shade more pronounced than coincidence that theologians also talk of the mind and will necessitated to what is right and incapable of error. Unlike the

Godwinians and the Communists, however, they place that state
of man in heaven, not on earth. One who would seek out the
concept in pages less austere than the theologians' and more
attractive than Godwin's may find it in Book IV of Swift's
Gulliver's Travels, where he describes the perfected rationality
of the Houyhnhnms.

There was probably a reason sounder than the improbability
of a three-guinea book coming into proletarian hands that
prompted Pitt to oppose proceedings against Godwin. Pitt
well knew that one of the most effective ways of combating
extremism is by letting it exhibit itself at its illogical extreme,
and Pitt, a man experienced in political techniques, was more
than willing to give Godwin and his kind all the rope they
desired. Godwin, furthermore, was an extremist without being
a revolutionist. He called for the storming of no Bastilles except
the Bastilles of the mind, and they were not to be stormed by
violence but taken by the slow, sapping force of reason. Indeed,
improbable as it may appear to those who know Godwin's
conclusions without having had the experience of reading him,
there is a certain persuasiveness to Godwin, a certain impressive
show of logic and reason that carries the reader along and could
quite easily carry such a reader as Shelley away. Nothing can
be quite so illogical as undiluted logic, but it can be persuasive.

There are few of Rousseau's ideas in Godwin, and nothing of
the revolutionary fervor of such a man as Paine. On the other
hand, nowhere in English literature can one find a man more
totally dedicated to the concept of the man-made order than
William Godwin. Every consideration of human history, every
facet of human nature except the mind, every impulse and
instinct and experience of human record he banishes to limbo.
Man is a perfectible being, reason is his all-sufficient guide, and
when he is perfected he will have that total freedom in which he
will be incapable of doing anything but his total duty. All human
institutions are outgrowths of man's imperfect state and thus
evils varying in their degrees of necessity. Again we see illustrated the phenomenon: in these revolutionists are the seeds
of *laissez faire.* When perfected, man will be in the state of
nature once more, without an institution to curb him, ruled by
the sovereign intellect, necessitated by mind to the performance

of duty. It is the Calvinist heaven on earth for which future generations are predestined. Godwin the anarchist, Godwin the Communist, Godwin the advocate of free love goes on in the strangest of ways being Godwin the dissenting minister. The difference is that he now believes in the man-made order.

THOMAS PAINE

Thomas Paine (1737–1809) illustrates as well as anyone in the period the truth of Cicero's adage, one so acceptable to the Age of Revolution, that natural ability is worth more than formal training. Paine had virtually no formal training, yet no Englishman of letters in the Age of Revolution had a natural ability that even approached that of Paine, if one limits the statement to those who wrote in the revolutionary cause. The philosophic depth of Burke surpasses that of Paine as depth surpasses shallows, but it is no inconsequential light that shines through Paine's rhetoric. The light was kindled by sincerity, fervor, courage, and endurance, and above all by a total, absolutely unquestioning faith that it was a light in the final sense divinely kindled. It is not without importance that Paine was brought up a Quaker.

Paine had reason to trust his inspiration, if it is largely the tragedy of his life that he trusted it overmuch. To the son of a corset maker, apprenticed to another at the age of thirteen, driven from pillar to post as teacher, tobacco dealer, grocer and tax collector by the time he was thirty, life seemed to offer nothing but an uneasy, unhappy drifting through its economic lower depths. Even his inspiration, at the age of thirty, did not tell him that before he was forty he would play a major part in dealing to the British Empire the gravest defeat in all its history.

While lobbying for higher wages for the excisemen, he met Benjamin Franklin. Franklin made it possible for him to move to America and to find in Philadelphia employment for the pen which the shrewd Franklin knew was richly gifted. The rest belongs to the familiar story of the American War of Independence. On January 10, 1776, Paine published at Philadelphia the pamphlet *Common Sense*, the first call for the Declaration of Independence which would be proclaimed six months later.

Within two months 100,000 copies had been sold, as Americans pondered the solemn decision. Passage from one state of mind to another was necessary before the Declaration of Independence could be a possibility. In the first state of mind the Americans were British subjects demanding their rights. In the second state of mind they were American citizens fighting for their freedom. Passage from the one to the other demanded agonizing searching of the soul, and many Americans who were completely sincere in the first frame of mind never achieved the second. Enough did to make possible the Declaration of Independence and the winning of the Revolution. No document did as much as Paine's *Common Sense* to make possible the passage from the first frame of mind to the second.

The winter of 1776–1777 marked the lowest depths to which American fortunes sank during the entire war. On November 20 Washington was surprised at Fort Lee. On November 22 his army retreated to Newark. During the retreat Thomas Paine, who had resigned his position with the *Pennsylvania Magazine* to enlist in Washington's army, started the first pamphlet of *The American Crisis.* A few days after entering Newark, Washington's army fled from one end of the city as the British entered the other. Washington retreated to the Delaware, able to muster only five thousand men against Howe's entire army. On December 19 Paine had his first pamphlet in print. Washington had it read to every regiment. Two weeks later Washington crossed the Delaware and won the victories of Trenton and Princeton. The Americans had fought their way back from the valley of the shadow of defeat, a shadow deeper even than the terrible shadow which was to lie across Valley Forge. Paine's pen fought beside Washington's sword.

Everything that is best in Paine, as a writer and as a man, is in the magnificent first paragraph of *The Crisis.* "These are the times that try men's souls. The summer soldier and the sunshine patriot will, in this crisis, shrink from the service of his country; but he that stands it now, deserves the love and thanks of man and woman. Tyranny, like hell, is not easily conquered; yet we have this consolation with us, that the harder the conflict the more glorious the triumph: what we obtain too cheap we esteem too lightly; 'tis dearness only that gives everything its value. Heaven knows how to put a proper price upon its goods; and it would be strange indeed if so celestial an article as Freedom should not be highly rated." If one would know why in 1791 England feared the pen of Thomas Paine, a reading of this first pamphlet will make it clear. Paine's style is oratory at its most eloquent and most moving. It is emotional but the emotion wells up from profound sincerity and conviction, and from an unassailable sense of eternal truth and righteousness. Never does there enter the mind of Thomas Paine a scintilla of doubt that his cause is right and his viewpoint just. He believed that in America in 1776, in England in 1791, and in France in 1793. Utter sincerity and utter obliviousness of any viewpoint other than the one Paine holds and passionately expresses inspire *The Crisis, The Rights of Man,* and *The Age of Reason.*

There is a final simplicity to Paine that makes him hard to describe, hard to sense unless one does the right thing and reads his own words. He is remembered for his two great contributions to the American Revolution, *Common Sense* and *The Crisis;* for his treatise on government, *The Rights of Man;* and for his venture into deism, *The Age of Reason.* The first two were written in his hour of glory; the third brought upon him exile from his native land; and the fourth was written partly in a French jail to which he was condemned as the moderate cause to which he had dedicated his last fight for freedom gave way to the incipient Terror. For all the differences in subject matter, there is a certain pattern of thought that joins eloquence of utterance in linking the four.

As Leslie Stephen points out,[21] his deism and his democracy have much in common. Paine believes in God, arguing in *The Age of Reason* for God's existence by the time-tried arguments of causality and design. Man has the moral duty to hear the word of God transmitted to him through the wonders of creation, and to obey it. That word has been stifled by the churches, those "human institutions set up to terrify and enslave mankind, and monopolize power and profit." As for Scripture, it is a hodge-podge of contradictions and absurdities. All is so simple, so obvious, except one nagging point. If this is the Age of Reason and man is a rational being—and this is a cardinal principle of the school of Bolingbroke to which Paine unconsciously belonged

—why has it taken man so long to see through priestly imposture and Scriptural hocus-pocus? Why, for that matter, if it is all so clear, has it taken man, born a democrat, so long to see through kingly imposture and monarchical hocus-pocus? If the question ever occurred to Paine, he concealed it thoroughly.

There is little in *The Age of Reason* that calls for analysis, little that is not present in the earlier deists, but the date of publication is important. Collins, Woolston and the others wrote when deism was welcome, when it offered a pietistic justification for the compromise of 1660. But when Paine wrote, the shadow of the guillotine lay across the land of France and priests waited, in resignation or in despair, within its shadow. Might not that shadow extend to England, might it not extend even to America, if the hateful viewpoint of this godless infidel, this blasphemous enemy of all things sacred were to prevail? It was not an age of reason but an age of terror. Hence the last sad, lonely years of poverty and ostracism at New Rochelle where the body of a simple, God-fearing man with a closed mind was denied burial in consecrated ground.

There is the same simplicity and directness, and a great, telling force of sincerity and fervor, in *The Rights of Man*. The book is more a cento of revolutionary commonplaces than a reasoned refutation of Burke's *Reflections on the Revolution in France*. Paine, writing in a spirit much more reverent than he would show in *The Age of Reason*, starts with human rights maintaining that they come from God. Thus in Paine, as in all the followers of Rousseau, a right is not contingent upon a duty but is an absolute, to be exercised not under the guidance of the human conscience but under the impulse of the human will. Paine does have a concept of duty, to be sure, with a simplicity that betrays its obvious Biblical origin. "The duty of man is not a wilderness of turnpike gates, through which he is to pass by tickets from one to the other. It is plain and simple, and consists but of two points. His duty to God, which every man must feel; and with respect to his neighbour, to do as he would be done by."[22] The duty of man is always plain and simple to the school of Rousseau, never to the school of Montesquieu.

Paine divides human rights into the natural and the civil. The former arise from man's nature, the latter from his membership in society. But every civil right is founded on a natural right: "Every civil right has for its foundation some natural right pre-existing in the individual, but to the enjoyment of which his individual power is not, in all cases, sufficiently competent. Of this kind are all those which relate to security and protection."[23] In short, man retains the natural rights which he can make effective, but resigns to society those which he cannot. It is the contract concept, somewhat modified, as one finds it in Hobbes. Paine is as doctrinaire about the contract, both as a historic fact and as a principle of society, as he is about everything else. "The fact . . . must be that the individuals themselves, each in his own personal and sovereign right, entered into a compact with each other to produce a Government: and this is the only mode in which Governments have a right to arise, and the only principle on which they have a right to exist."[24]

Paine accepts Rousseau's concept of sovereignty and couples with it the thought, important to his purpose, that each generation has rights equal to those of its predecessors. Sovereignty always resides in the present majority which expresses the common will; the contract is, in a sense, re-enacted in every generation. No generation can bind its successor; each generation has the right to work out its own destiny in the form acceptable to itself. "Sovereignty, as a matter of right, appertains to the Nation only, and not to any individual; and a Nation has at all times an inherent, indefeasible right to abolish any form of Government it finds inconvenient, and to establish such as accords with its interest, disposition, and happiness."[25] At this point comes the direct conflict in ideology between Paine and Burke.

The immediate cause of Burke's *Reflections on the Revolution in France* was Richard Price's sermon of November, 1789. Price had maintained the right of the English people to remove the king for misconduct, the right Paine also proclaimed. Burke denies that the Revolution of 1688 established this doctrine and maintains that the right of hereditary succession is fully established in English law. But fundamentally Burke was concerned with that organic growth of society and social institutions which he considered the only sound and healthy form that social growth can take. He wrote: "Our political system is placed in a just correspondence and symmetry with the order of the world, and with the mode of existence decreed to a permanent body composed of transitory parts; wherein by the disposition of a stupendous wisdom, moulding together the great mysterious incorporation of the human race, the whole at one time is never old, or middle aged, or young, but in a condition of unchangeable constancy moved on through the varied tenor of perpetual decay, fall, renovation and progression. Thus by preserving the method of nature in the conduct of the State, in what we improve, we are never wholly new; in what we retain we are never wholly obsolete.[26]

Burke's concept has a subtlety far beyond the grasp of Thomas Paine. Human action can influence organic growth for better or for worse, but it cannot control it. Organic growth has an origin still beyond man's ken and control. The application by metaphor to those who believe in the divinely created order is obvious, but the metaphor is completely inapplicable to those who believe in the man-made order. The school of Rousseau starts with the axiom of human rights, carrying as its corollary the absolute equality of man. Denying the organic nature of society, the school of Rousseau would return by political action to a state of natural equality achieved within a new framework of society constructed on a priori grounds. The old order is shattered to bits, in the confidence that the new order can be easily and quickly achieved. Between the honest expectations of Thomas Paine and the cloud-cuckoo-land dream of Shelley that if the oppressive institutions of society were abolished the golden age would return automatically and immediately, the difference is one of degree and not of kind. There is a naïveté to this belief, appealing in the English revolutionists, appalling in the French aftermath. The school of Montesquieu, wiser and more experienced, never deceived itself about the distance of the millennium and the difficulty of achieving it. "The nature of man is intricate," says Burke, "the objects of society are of the greatest possible complexity; and therefore no simple disposition or direction of power can be suitable either to man's nature or to the quality of his affairs."[27] The American Revolution organized itself when victory was won, because the Founding Fathers never lost sight of the organic concept of society. The French Revolution had order imposed upon it by Napoleon, because it denied the organic nature of society and affirmed the man-made order. Leslie Stephen sums it up with a finality beyond improvement: "In fact, the revolutionary ideas embodied the formal contradictory to that truth, the full appreciation of which was Burke's greatest title to speculative eminence, and which guided his wisest reflections. To him a nation was a living organism, of infinitely complex structure, of intimate dependence upon the parts, and to be treated by politicians in obedience to a careful observation of the laws of its healthy development. To them a nation was an aggregate of independent units, to be regulated by a set of absolute a priori maxims. In Burke's own language, the 'people' is an 'Artificial idea.' It is, he means to say, a complex body whose will is to be determined from its recognised organs, and not a mere mass of individuals, whose will is to be discovered by counting heads."[28]

Perhaps as important as any other fact about them is the fact that the English revolutionists of the school of Rousseau were men of humble origin. Priestley was the son of a cloth dresser who went bankrupt in 1777, Price was the son of one Calvinist minister, Godwin of another who never received more than sixty pounds a year, and Paine of a corset maker. The same was true of other English revolutionists not considered here. Thomas Cooper was an unsuccessful bleacher and calico printer, John Thelwall was the son of a silk mercer, and Thomas Holcroft's father was an itinerant peddler. Like Paine, Thelwall and Holcroft went to work at the age of thirteen. These were the men who assailed the sturdy ramparts of the established order, the champions of the personal rights that they had so sadly lacked, the champions of the liberty which was theirs so imperfectly and the equality which was not theirs at all. Their adherence to the a priori doctrine of human rights—their right to liberty they had established and their equality in the things that are fundamental they had proved—was natural and human. Everything else in their thinking rests on this simple, natural, human fact. That there was more opportunity for men of their stamp in the nineteenth century than in the eighteenth, and far more in America, Canada, and Australia than in England proves that they were not entirely wrong. Most of them were idealistic, God-fearing men who took the tenets of deism in a spirit of simple faith. English materialists or atheists like the later Diderot and Holbach were all but unknown. As revolutionists they belonged to the school of Rousseau, since they accepted his concept of the people as the Sovereign, and the Common Will as the motivating force in the state. As believers in the omnipotence of human reason they are followers of Bolingbroke; adherence to the Shaftesbury-Hutcheson doctrine of the moral sense is uncommon among them. Belief in the perfectibility of man by the light of reason linked them to the philosophes. They were ardent, idealistic, often uninformed, frequently undisciplined minds, but their natural ability frequently was great. Priestley and Paine achieved renown in their several ways; the others deserved to live in a century more hospitable than the eighteenth. They were suppressed after war broke out with France on February 1, 1793, but to the great glory of England there were fair trials, usually acquittals, and no Terror. There was a maturity to England, even in hours of peril, that testifies to the profound truth of Burke's concept of society and governmental responsibility. The same maturity is to be observed in the United States at its very hour of birth, and for the same reason. We may now turn to the American Founding Fathers.

VIII

THE FOUNDING FATHERS

THERE IS no more impressive paradox in all American history, and none more firmly rooted in the truth, than this: never since the United States came into being has it been as experienced and mature as it was at the hour of its birth. It was the unique good fortune of the United States to have presiding over its foundation an extraordinarily wise, experienced, dedicated, and unselfish group of statesmen. Among themselves their differences were often deep and bitter, but the quality of their devoted patriotism was constant and exalted. General Washington was their military genius and by unanimous choice their first President. He was a man of action and an inspiring presence; he lived a philosophy, but he did not formulate one. That was the work chiefly of Jefferson and Madison, Franklin and Adams, Hamilton and Jay.

The temptation is always present to let the differences among the six men named obscure their fundamental philosophic pattern. Books have been written about the differences, and more books need to be written about them. Our concern is the fundamental philosophic pattern and the inner harmony from which the discords surged and died again. That there was an inner harmony is a fact, just as the fact of an island proves the existence of an unseen land mass beneath the unbroken surface of the waters. If that inner harmony had not existed, the United States of America could not have existed. The proof is the contrast of what happened in France a generation after the American Revolution.

We have spoken of the school of Montesquieu and the school of Rousseau. Both terms, of course, are metaphors, but the concrete metaphor can be a useful device. Did the Founding Fathers study at the school of Montesquieu or at the school of Rousseau? Did they believe that society is an organism steadily developing by laws unique to its nature although modified by time and place, or did they believe that society is a mechanism contrived by the mind of man and by the human will? Our thesis is that the Founding Fathers were of the school of Montesquieu, that they believed in the organic concept of society, and that they believed society and all other organisms to be part of a divinely created order. Such beliefs are usually implicit in their thinking, but the explicit aspects of their thought develop from them.

We do not have in mind, of course, anything so literal and obvious as the direct influence of Montesquieu, or the absence of a direct influence wielded by Rousseau. It is true that Montesquieu is often cited in the writings of the Founding Fathers, but that the works of Rousseau and the philosophes in general were not imported in numbers until the 1780s and not widely read until the 1790s. The truth is that a close reading of the works of the extraordinarily well-read men whom we have named, and especially the best-read of them—Jefferson, Madison, and Adams —will prove that they knew the works of the philosophes but found themselves more often than not in disagreement with them, that they knew the Latin classics and the Roman concept of a republic and were more than a little influenced by them, that they knew the Continental political theorists but that they studied chiefly the political philosophers of England, and in them and in their kindred who speculated on moral and religious themes found the major part of their inspiration which did not come from life itself. The major portion of their inspiration did come from life itself.

BENJAMIN FRANKLIN

Certainly the major inspiration of Benjamin Franklin came from life itself, although to label Franklin a pragmatist and nothing more is gravely to misunderstand a most unusually gifted man and original thinker. Franklin as a boy showed that he was not one to take easily to intellectual trammels. He had been reading some books against deism. "It happened that they wrought an effect on me quite contrary to what was intended by them," he tells us in the *Autobiography;* "for the arguments of the Deists, which were quoted to be refuted, appeared to me much stronger than the refutations; in short, I soon became a thorough Deist."[1] At the age of nineteen he had his fling at formal philosophy, in "A Dissertation on Liberty and Necessity, Pleasure and Pain." He had been setting type for William Wollaston's *The Religion of Nature Delineated* and found himself arguing with the author's contention that virtue may be deduced by a quasi-mathematical process from natural religion and found to be consistent with the moral principles taught by the orthodox churches. Franklin, letting go the intellectual reins and following his theological fancy where it led him, reached the conclusion that there can be no evil in a universe created by an all-good God, that free will is an illusion, that man has neither merit nor demerit in the eyes of God, and that no values are valid but those provided by the pleasure and pain calculus of utilitarianism.

The conclusion would have appalled him if he had taken it seriously. Benjamin Franklin, age nineteen, had an awareness that there is no surer road to fantasy land than the high road of untrammeled logic, and the logic of his conclusion that there are no moral principles but the ersatz ones of pleasure and pain was to him self-evident proof of its illogicality. Experience eschews the high road, but leads to a realistic conclusion. He says in the *Autobiography:* "I grew convinc'd that *truth, sincerity* and *integrity* in dealings between man and man were of the utmost importance to the felicity of life; and I form'd written resolutions, which still remain in my journal book, to practice them ever while I lived. Revelation had indeed no weight with me, as such; but I entertain'd an opinion that, though certain actions might not be bad *because* they were forbidden by it, or good *because* it commanded them, yet probably these actions might be forbidden *because* they were bad for us, or commanded *because* they were beneficial to us, in their own natures, all the circumstances of things considered."[2] In short, Franklin was a theoretical deist who on occasion identified himself as such, but in reality was a pragmatist of a sort. The important question to ask is, a pragmatist of what sort?

Certainly not a pragmatist in the materialistic sense. He was brought up in the Presbyterian Church and in his later years attended the Episcopal Church. He believed in the moral tenets of both churches, but he believed in them because they worked. He did believe that such moral principles as truth, sincerity, and integrity are sound, because the experience of a long, active, extraordinarily diversified lifetime convinced him that when the relationships of men and of nations are conducted with truth, sincerity, and integrity, happiness results. Perhaps these principles worked because they were true; that question is a metaphysical one and Franklin was finished with metaphysical questions when, at the age of nineteen, he had finished analyzing liberty and necessity, pleasure and pain. He was satisfied to say that these principles were true because they worked. But never did he dream of denying that they are religious principles, that they are expounded by the churches, that they are of divine ordainment and bear the weight of divine sanctions. He says in the *Autobiography*, ". . . I never was without some religious principles. I never doubted, for instance, the existence of the Deity; that he made the world, and govern'd it by his Providence; that the most acceptable service of God was the doing good to man; that our souls are immortal; and that all crime will be punished, and virtue rewarded, either here or hereafter. These I esteem'd the essentials of every religion; and, being to be found in all the religions we had in our country, I respected them all, tho' with different degrees of respect, as I found them more or less mix'd with other articles, which, without any tendency to inspire, promote, or confirm morality, serv'd principally to divide us, and make us unfriendly to one another."[3]

This passage could have been written by Shaftesbury, or by Bolingbroke in his more genial mood. In this fact lies something of fundamental importance where Franklin is concerned. He belongs to an earlier generation than the other Founding Fathers; Franklin was twenty-six years old when the next oldest of them, George Washington, was born. Franklin was old enough to be grandfather to Hamilton and, with a little violence to likelihood, to Madison. Franklin was of the generation to which Pope's

Essay on Man was the customary introduction to deism, the generation that cut its intellectual eyeteeth on Shaftesbury, that in its profounder moments talked of the Newtonian universe and the Great Chain of Being. Chronologically he was of the generation that produced the Age of Stagnation, although clearly he was of it in no other sense. Franklin had known poverty too intimately, was too ambitious and too aware that talents are no respecters of social position to think that "whatever is, is right." Franklin was just such a deist as he would have been if born in England instead of Boston, and he was subject to precisely the same influences.

He met Mandeville, as he records in the *Autobiography*, but there is no evidence that Mandeville influenced him. On the other hand, it is crystal clear that Shaftesbury influenced him greatly. Franklin reprinted two of the lesser dialogues of Shaftesbury in the *Pennsylvania Gazette*, and until recently they passed detection as original writings of Franklin.[4] As Alfred O. Aldridge, who detected them, points out, "By reprinting them, Franklin registered himself as a Shaftesburian, and he confirmed this intellectual affiliation by later composing and printing the two essays which are described in his autobiography."[5] Franklin, a man far more experienced in public affairs than Shaftesbury, and a far shrewder judge of the limitations of his fellow man, is a Shaftesburian very much restrained in his estimate of human perfectibility, but a Shaftesburian in his deistic outlook. As for the effusive optimism of the school of Rousseau, compared, for example, to the enthusiasm of Priestley on the subject of human perfectibility the outlook of Franklin is rather like that of Mark Twain.

Franklin rejected completely, as it were by instinct, the Rousseauistic concept of the General Will. He believed that few people work for the welfare of their country, fewer still for the welfare of mankind, and that there is no such thing as a general will for the general good. There is no real inconsistency between this viewpoint and his opposition to a bicameral legislature and his support of the unicameral principle. Logically one would expect that a man of Franklin's somewhat jaundiced view of his fellow man would favor the system of checks and balances provided by a bicameral legislature. John Adams did, bewailing the advocates of the unicameral legislature as students at "the school of folly, but alas, Franklin, Turgot, Rouchefoucauld, and Condorcet, under Tom Paine, were the great masters of that Academy."[6] Franklin's opposition to the bicameral legislature did not arise from a mystic trust in common man but from a vigorous opposition to an upper house controlled by the wealthy and influential. Franklin had a strong instinct for equalitarianism, but no mystical belief in the corporate wisdom of the people. His democracy stems from the former, not the latter. There is no evidence that Franklin was ever too much concerned about the specific form that government took, and he clearly believed that the people have more equalitarianism under a monarchy than under an aristocracy.

It would seem that two facts best explain the attitude of Franklin before and after 1775. The first is the experience of the self-made man. Franklin had exactly the same sort of background as the English members of the school of Rousseau whom we cited in the last chapter. Unlike the members of that school, however, Franklin was a complete success in an amazing variety of roles: publisher, writer, inventor, scientist, political philosopher, shirt-sleeve philosopher, ambassador. No man could possibly have a greater belief in the superiority of natural ability to formal training than Franklin, but no man of his achievements could belittle formal training. Such a man instinctively believes in equality of opportunity coupled with freedom for achievement.

The second is the naturally pragmatic bent of his mind. He had his fling at metaphysical theory in his youth, and found that it led him up a dead-end street. Thereafter he retained just enough metaphysics on which to found a pragmatic philosophy of life. He retained a belief in God and in the traditional moral order, in the former because He existed and in the latter because it worked. He believed that man can be improved and he worked hard at improving himself, but he had no illusions about the natural goodness of man or about the degree of human perfectibility. He was not really concerned about such questions as the divinely created order versus the man-made order, although he gave his intellectual consent to the former. To Franklin the important thing was the properly conducted order, based on a recognition of human equality and a maximum of human opportunity. As long as he could he hoped for it under the king of England; later he hoped for it under the Constitution of the United States. The private philosophy of Benjamin Franklin was a blend of deism and pragmatism, the pragmatism his own, the deism characteristic of the early eighteenth century into which Franklin was born and during which his thinking was formulated. He never expressed it more thoroughly than in a letter written to President Ezra Stiles of Yale on March 9, 1790.

You desire to know something of my religion. It is the first time I have been questioned upon it. But I cannot take your curiosity amiss, and shall endeavor in a few words to gratify it. Here is my creed. I believe in one God, creator of the Universe. That he governs it by his providence. That he ought to be worshipped. That the most acceptable service we render to him is doing good to his other children. That the soul of Man is immortal, and will be treated with justice in another life respecting its conduct in this. These I take to be the fundamental principles of all sound religion, and I regard them as you do in whatever sect I meet with them.

As to Jesus of Nazareth, my opinion of whom you particularly desire, I think the system of morals and his religion, as he left them to us, the best the world ever saw or is likely to see; but I apprehend it has received various corrupting changes, and I have, with most of the present dissenters in England, some doubts as to his divinity; though it is a question I do not dogmatize upon, never having studied it, and think it needless to busy myself with it now, when I expect soon an opportunity of knowing the truth with less trouble. I see no harm, however, in its being believed, if that belief has the good consequence, as probably it has, of making his doctrines more respected and better observed; especially as I do not perceive that the Supreme takes it amiss, by distinguishing the unbelievers in his government of the world with any peculiar marks of his displeasure.

I shall only add, respecting myself, that having experienced the goodness of that being in conducting me prosperously through a long life, I have no doubt of its continuance in the next, though without the smallest conceit of meriting such goodness.[7]

One hardly looks for the fervor of piety in Benjamin Franklin, and one hardly finds it. It is unwise to look for it in any of the Founding Fathers, and it should be suspect when it is found. They were sons of the eighteenth century and insofar as there was a common denominator of religious attitude among them, it is the earlier pattern of English deism better illustrated by

Shaftesbury, perhaps, than by anyone else of the period. The important point is that it was not the deism of Hume nor of Condorcet. It was a native English deism transported to the colonies in its earlier form and blended with a native pragmatism unmistakably American. The blend is transparently clear in Franklin, and it is present even in Jefferson, by instinct the most philosophic of them all. Even the Sage of Monticello had a broad streak of practicality in his make-up, and more than a little of that annoyance with abstract philosophy which is typically American.

THOMAS JEFFERSON

Like Franklin, Jefferson abandoned the formal faith in which he was reared, a distinctly easier thing to do in Virginia than in Massachusetts. Like Franklin, Jefferson dabbled in pure philosophy in his intellectual salad days, and with no more substantial results. Unlike Franklin, however, Jefferson was under a substantial debt to the ancient classics. Indeed, the starting point of Jefferson's philosophy is at least two parts ancient Epicureanism to one part deism, a not unprecedented blend in eighteenth-century thought. Pierre Gassendi had achieved a certain synthesis between the deistic tenets of the ancient Epicureans and Christian fortitude. Wollaston, in his *Religion of Nature Delineated,* had identified the happiness of the contented mind which Epicureanism predicates with the performance of one's moral duty. The result was a philosophic attitude quite acceptable to young Thomas Jefferson, who desired to reject institutional Christianity but not its moral code.[8] But Jefferson was impatient with purely abstract thought, and his impatience tends to betray itself in a certain fuzziness that is present in his more abstract flights.

Jefferson felt the same need for ethical reassurance that Shaftesbury had felt when he cast off the mooring of institutional Christianity, and he found it in the same way. Jefferson's moral sense is the familiar one of Shaftesbury, with a direct debt indicated to Henry Home, Lord Kames, whose *Essays on the Principles of Morality and Natural Religion* Jefferson carefully annotated. But the moral sense works out some saliences in

Jefferson not to be expected in an English thinker. It blends with a sort of native Rousseauism in Jefferson, who accounts for the superior morality of the American Indian and the American farmer over that of city dwellers by the smoother functioning of moral sense in God's cathedral of the open air. Considerably more important in practical terms is its implications for Jefferson's political theory. Believing as he did in the universality of the moral sense and its perfectibility, and believing also in that universal benevolence which is so important a tenet of Shaftesbury and his school, he believed that everyone is competent morally, intellectually, and emotionally to assume his share of ordering the affairs of state. Among the unforeseen and far-reaching consequences of the teachings of the school of Shaftesbury is an important argument for Jeffersonian democracy. Hence his recognition of the full equality of such minority groups as the Negroes and the Indians; his unwavering opposition to the entrenched position of the feudal aristocracy of Virginia; his belief that a Bill of Rights has a natural priority to a Constitution and should serve as its preamble; hence to some degree all the hallmarks of Jefferson's thought, which slowly, painfully, and at times imperfectly has established itself as the abiding pattern of American thought and has made Thomas Jefferson, intellectually speaking, the foremost Founding Father.

So far removed was Jefferson from hostility to what he deemed essential Christianity that one of his long-cherished and never-completed projects was a compilation of the moral principles of Jesus. With an assurance that more subtle theologians might have envied, he felt capable of detecting the true statements of Jesus amidst the welter of apocrypha. Total purity and simplicity he took to be their hallmarks, and the Christ who emerges in his *The Life and Morals of Jesus of Nazareth extracted Textually from the Gospels in Greek, Latin, French, and English* is a splendidly inspired human being. As so often in eighteenth-century literature and thought, a certain naïveté lies just below the surface: Jefferson shared to the full the conviction of the early English deists that Christianity is essentially clear, the message of salvation basically simple, mystery the hocus-pocus of priestcraft. The Jefferson who emerges from the work is a typical early English, religion-oriented deist with a morality that is es-

sentially social, a morality grounded on a personal selection of
the sayings of Jesus whom he, like all deists of his sort, regarded
as an inspired man. There is nothing whatever in his moral and
religious theory to suggest the empiricism of Hobbes, the skepticism of Hume, or for that matter the mockery of Mandeville and
Bolingbroke.

The interpretation of Jefferson which finds him starting with
a concept of rights lacks an essential distinction. He starts with
a concept of "inherent and inalienable rights." They are inherent
and inalienable because everyone has the duty, revealed to him
by his moral sense, and founded on the principle of universal
benevolence, to do justice always and everywhere to his fellow
man. Jefferson conceives a divinely instituted moral order. God
created man and endowed him with certain inalienable rights.
He has these rights because he has his duties to his fellow man.
The framework is that of early English deism rather than of
institutional Christianity, but the moral order contained within
the framework is divinely ordered and not of man's making. The
ultimate foundations of the political ideals of Thomas Jefferson
is Shaftesbury's doctrine of the moral sense.

The moral principles which Jefferson felt binding upon individuals he felt to be binding upon states, and for the same reasons. He wrote: "The law of nations . . . is composed of three
branches. 1. The moral law of our nature. 2. The usages of
nations. 3. Their special conventions. The first of these only concerns this question, that is to say the moral law to which man
has been subjected by his creator, and of which his feelings or
conscience, as it is sometimes called, are the evidence with
which his creator has furnished him. The moral duties which
exist between individual and individual in a state of nature,
accompany them into a state of society, and the aggregate of the
duties of all the individuals composing the society constitutes
the duties of that society towards any other; so that between
society and society the same moral duties exist as did between
the individuals composing them, while in an unassociated state,
and their maker not having released them from those duties on
their forming themselves into a nation. Compacts, then, between
nation and nation, are obligatory on them by the same moral
law which obliges individuals to observe their compacts."[9] The

obvious conclusion is that Jefferson believed the moral law for nations to be identical with the moral law for individuals, and to rest on the same ideological foundation. The usages of nations and their special conventions are, of course, matters of a different sort. They rest upon formal law, not upon the law of nature.

The logical conclusion is that the philosophic foundation of Jefferson's thought does not differ fundamentally from that of Franklin. It is more formally philosophic than that of the more pragmatic Franklin, but its foundation is the same. In their theory both men inherit from Grotius and Pufendorf, inherit substantially from Locke, and in the specialized sense in which we have used the term are of the school of Montesquieu. Both men have a more important inheritance from the earlier English deists, especially Shaftesbury, and the framework within which both formulate their thinking is that framework which early English deism abstracted from Christianity, with the institutional part left out but the moral part left in. Otherwise they differ as two vivid, original, forthright, active minds of the very highest quality are bound to differ. All the Founding Fathers differ among themselves in that way, and for the same reason: they all had vivid, original, forthright, active minds of the most excellent quality. The person who thinks that Madison was the shadow of Jefferson knows little about Jefferson and nothing about Madison.

It has been Madison's fate, however, to remain for nearly two centuries in the shadow of Thomas Jefferson. Jefferson was a tall, strikingly handsome man; Madison looked more like Chaucer's Clerk. Jefferson was the brilliant writer, the eloquent orator, the commanding presence; "Poor Jemmy Madison," says Washington Irving, "but a withered little applejohn." He was something of a withered applejohn, this little man soberly dressed with more than a suggestion of the threadbare to the clothing. It was said that Madison never owned more than one suit at a time, that each suit's predecessor went to an indigent relative. Those who knew Madison very well knew how generous he was; others he kept from suspecting. People could be surprised by Madison. When the room was warm and the drinks were frequent, it was Madison who was the center of attention, not Jefferson. People then found that the vivacious and commanding Jefferson was really a humorless man, that the dry wit and the fund of stories were at the command of Madison. Quiet and retiring, ready to rest in the shadow of the man he always honored and nearly adored but whom he never followed slavishly, Madison had a benignity of temper and a gentleness of heart that won him friends. Madison was close to the three most imposing figures among the Founding Fathers, Washington, Jefferson, and Hamilton. No one of them really dwarfed him.

MADISON

Madison was Jefferson's complement, not his reflection. Jefferson was the brilliant writer and speculative thinker, but Madison was the deeper scholar and more adroit politician. When Jefferson was in danger of getting beyond his philosophic depths over the principles of government, the relationship of Church and State, and the rationale of an agricultural state as he composed his *Notes on Virginia*, it was Madison to whom he turned for philosophic guidance.[10] Not Jefferson alone but all his associates had a respect verging on awe for the scholarship of Madison. No one of them rivaled him in theoretical knowledge of what comprises the good society, and few could match him in practical experience with the legislative process. Madison had far less trust of the common people and their judgment than did Jefferson, a far stronger feeling for the necessity of a strong centralized government to insure the reign of justice. He once summed up his viewpoint in a letter to Jefferson: "The great desideratum in Government is so to modify the sovereignty as that it may be sufficiently neutral between different parts of the society to control one part from invading the rights of another, and at the same time sufficiently controlled itself from setting up an interest adverse to that of the entire society."[11] Jefferson, with his mystic faith in the people, never had the distrust of majorities that Madison had, nor the fear that local majorities would trample on minority rights. In 1788 Madison told the Virginia ratifying convention that the great destroyer of republics is the hatred and strife resulting from majority tyranny over minority rights. It is characteristic of the two men that Jefferson belittled Shays's Rebellion, whereas Madison was appalled by it.

Out of his conviction that majority tyranny is particularly a danger in small republics, for which the American equivalent would be individual states, grew the pattern of thinking which made it logical that Madison join Hamilton, always Jefferson's ideological enemy and later his political foe, in the composition of *The Federalist*. Madison and Hamilton were no more in complete agreement about the pattern of the central government than were Madison and Jefferson about its powers, but that fundamental philosophic pattern which we referred to at the outset was shared by Madison and Hamilton as truly as it was shared by Madison and Jefferson, and so their differences could be reconciled in a joint undertaking. Madison believed that the preservation of justice and equality demanded a strong central government, but a government that was limited and balanced to prevent its generating the tyranny within itself which it was created to prevent in the separate states. Hamilton believed that the preservation of efficiency and solvency demanded a strong central government, guided by the nation's financial and industrial leaders but conducted in the interests of the people as a whole. There are two common denominators in the thinking of the two men: both believed in the political principle of a strong central government and both believed in it as a means to protect the divinely created moral principle of justice in society. There was much of the practical politician in Madison, much of the instinctive aristocrat in Hamilton. Beneath both attitudes was a moral code that both men shared, which allowed them for all their differences to collaborate on *The Federalist*. When allowance is made for all their deeper and more nearly fundamental differences, the same code was shared by Hamilton and Jefferson. By that code Hamilton made his portentous choice of his inveterate political and ideological foe, Jefferson, over the man toward whom he harbored no grudge but the man who did not share the code, Aaron Burr. It was one of the noblest acts in American political history, and it cost Hamilton his life.

The clearest indication of Madison's fundamental philosophy is to be found in his *Memorial and Remonstrance against Religious Assessments* (1785). The Church of England had been established in Virginia from the foundation of the colony. The first crack in its entrenched position came in 1779 when the requirement that all Virginians pay taxes for its support was abolished. Demand for the abolition of the establishment mounted, as more and more Virginians worshiped at Presbyterian and Methodist churches and felt less and less inclination to contribute to an Anglican establishment. At the time that the taxation requirement was abolished, however, Jefferson's more radical bill for the abolition of the establishment itself was defeated. In 1780 a bill was introduced to the General Assembly which provided for a tax to be applied to the support of all Christian denominations, with the taxpayer indicating the church of his choice. This bill, which had its parallel in other states, was in effect a falling back upon a second line of defense, an attempt to establish Christianity in the United States. The term "establish" in this connection carries, of course, its connotation in the eighteenth century and earlier, the integration of the Church into the State as part of its fabric. The defeat of the establishment in this sense was largely the work of Madison.

In November, 1784, the bill to establish Christianity was reintroduced and passed by a 47 to 32 vote. Madison delivered in opposition a meticulously prepared speech, steadily protecting himself against innocent, or less than innocent, misinterpretation. He was not raising the question, Is religion necessary; he was raising the question, Is a religious establishment necessary. He answered in the negative, buttressing his philosophic arguments with an abundance of historical evidence. He lost, but Madison seldom lost totally and finally. The incorporation part of the bill got through the Assembly, but not the assessment part. Madison was disappointed, but had the politician's moderate reaction to disappointment. His own instinct told him that the people of Virginia shared his conviction. He proceeded to draw up his *Memorial and Remonstrance against Religious Assessments*, which was printed in Alexandria, circulated about the state, and signed by thousands of Virginians.

The *Memorial and Remonstrance* opens with a ringing affirmation of the inviolability of the human conscience. "We remonstrate against the said Bill because we hold it for a fundamental and undeniable truth, 'that Religion or the duty which we owe to our Creator and the manner of discharging it, can be directed only by reason and conviction, not by force or violence.'

The Religion then of every man must be left to the conviction and conscience of every man; and it is the right of every man to exercise it as these may dictate. This right is in its nature an unalienable right. It is unalienable; because the opinions of men, depending only on the evidence contemplated by their own minds, cannot follow the dictates of other men: it is unalienable also; because what is here a right towards men, is a duty towards the Creator. It is the duty of every man to render to the Creator such homage, and such only as he believes to be acceptable to him. This duty is precedent both in order of time and degree of obligation, to the claims of Civil Society. Before any man can be considered as a member of Civil Society, he must be considered as a subject of the Governor of the Universe: And if a member of Civil Society, who enters into any subordinate Association, must always do it with a reservation of his duty to the general authority; much more must every man who becomes a member of any particular Civil Society, do it with a saving of his allegiance to the Universal Sovereign. We maintain therefore that in matters of Religion, no man's right is abridged by the institution of Civil Society, and that Religion is wholly exempt from its cognizance."[12]

This is Madison's most explicit and nearly complete exposition of fundamental philosophy. Upon it depends everything else in whole or in part from his pen up to and including the Constitution of the United States. Madison expresses explicitly his belief in the divinely created order. God exists, God created man, man's primal duty antecedent to everything else in his existence and the existence of the universe is the worship of God. Out of this primal duty arises his unalienable right to religious freedom, a right antecedent to society and its ordainments. In the thinking of Madison as in the thinking of Jefferson and the other Founding Fathers, upon this primal duty of man to God rests the unalienable rights of man. The division between the school of Rousseau and the school of Montesquieu crossed the Atlantic. The Founding Fathers belonged to the latter school, not of course as followers fundamentally of the much quoted Montesquieu but as followers of the Christian tradition.

Everything in the *Memorial and Remonstrance* depends upon this primal duty and unalienable right. Religion is not subject

to the authority of legislative bodies. The establishment of one
sect may connote the barring of others, with the obvious injury
to the free exercise of conscience. To deny another man the free
exercise of his conscience because its dictates do not coincide
with those of our own is "an offence against God, not against
man: To God, therefore, not to men must an account of it be
rendered."[13] Christianity need not be buttressed by a human
establishment; indeed, human establishment implies a questioning of its divine origin and support. Religious establishments
have not made for purity of religion nor are they necessary for
the soundness of civil government. They make merely for unnecessary dissension and tend to weaken and not to strengthen
the states in which they exist.

At the conclusion of the document, Madison returns to his
initial point, this time not only affirming his belief in the divinely
created order but his disbelief in the man-made order. His
fifteenth and last remonstrance is: "Because, finally, the equal
right of every citizen to the free exercise of his Religion according to the dictates of conscience is held by the same tenure with
all our other rights. If we recur to its origin, it is equally the gift
of nature; if we weigh its importance, it cannot be less dear to
us; if we consult the Declaration of those rights which pertain to
the good people of Virginia, as the basis and foundation of
Government, it is enumerated with equal solemnity, or rather
studied emphasis. Either then, we must say, that the will of the
Legislature is the only measure of their authority; and that in the
plenitude of this authority, they may sweep away all our
fundamental rights; or, that they are bound to leave this particular right untouched and sacred: Either we must say, that
they may controul the freedom of the press, may abolish the trial
by jury, may swallow up the Executive and Judiciary Powers of
the State; nay that they may despoil us of our very right of
suffrage, and erect themselves into an independent and hereditary assembly; or we must say, that they have no authority to
enact into law the Bill under consideration. We the subscribers
say, that the General Assembly of this Commonwealth have no
such authority."[14]

It is difficult to find in the writings of the Founding Fathers
detailed and explicit avowals of fundamental philosophy such

as this. The reasons are many, but one is paramount above the others. When axioms are generally accepted and unchallenged, they are seldom voiced. Belief in the divinely created order was a generally accepted and unchallenged axiom among the Americans of the revolutionary generation. Madison, Jefferson's rival as the most philosophic of all the Founding Fathers (Saul K. Padover, editor of *The Complete Madison*, well calls him the exegete of American democracy, Jefferson the poet), voices his basic axiom only once. It was his axiom, however, as it was the axiom of Washington, Franklin, Jefferson, Adams, Hamilton, and the rest. If it were not the axiom of them all, it would have been voiced by those who held it. It would have to be voiced, because the Founding Fathers were by nature thinkers as well as men of action. It can happen, however, that when an axiom is not voiced, its existence may later be questioned by those who do not believe in its validity. This has been the fate of Madison and Jefferson. Both were sons of the Enlightenment, neither was a son of infidelity.

HAMILTON

That it was the fundamental axiom of Alexander Hamilton can be demonstrated on about the same sort of evidence available for its demonstration in the works of his associate on *The Federalist*, James Madison. The need to demonstrate it in the case of Hamilton is more peremptory, perhaps, than in any other case except that of Jefferson, and for reasons that go far beyond the confines of this book. The thought of no one of the Founding Fathers is more in need of basic re-examination than that of Alexander Hamilton, the one Founding Father whose claims to paternity have been grudgingly acknowledged by the American people. Such a re-examination would undoubtedly reveal that there is a far larger area of agreement between the instinctive aristocrat Hamilton and his instinctively democratic colleagues than is generally imagined. The starting point of re-examination could well be his concept of the implications of the divinely created order.

In 1774 an Anglican clergyman named Samuel Seabury attacked the Continental Congress in four pamphlets signed

"Westchester Farmer." Hamilton replied in *A Full Vindication of the Measures of the Congress from the Calumnies of Their Enemies* (New York, 1774). The Westchester Farmer took his rebuttal; and in February, 1775, Hamilton answered him in *The Farmer Refuted; Or, A More Impartial and Comprehensive View of the Dispute between Great Britain and the Colonies, Intended as a Further Vindication of the Congress* (New York, 1775). *The Farmer Refuted* is the most fundamental statement of philosophy that we have from the pen of Hamilton.

In part it is an outline of the military tactics best suited to the American forces. This part is not our concern. The rest is a statement of Hamilton's basic philosophy of life. The Farmer had demanded that Hamilton spell out his ideas about the natural rights of man. In his reply Hamilton accused the Farmer of upholding Hobbes's view of the origin of society, and adds: "Good and wise men, in all ages, have embraced a very dissimilar theory. They have supposed that the Deity, from the relations we stand in to Himself and to each other, has constituted an eternal and immutable law, which is indispensibly obligatory upon all mankind, prior to any human institution whatever.

"This is what is called the law of nature, 'which, being coeval with mankind, and dictated by God Himself, is, of course, superior in obligations to any other. It is binding over all the globe, in all countries, and at all times. No human laws are of any validity, if contrary to this; and such of them as are valid derive all their authority, mediately, or immediately, from this original.'— BLACKSTONE.

"Upon this law depend the natural rights of mankind: the Supreme Being gave existence to man, together with the means of preserving and beautifying that existence. He endowed him with rational faculties, by the help of which, to discern and pursue such things as were consistent with his duty and interest; and invested him with an inviolable right to personal liberty and personal safety.

"Hence, in a state of nature, no man has any *moral* power to deprive another of his life, limbs, property, or liberty; nor the least authority to command or exact obedience from him, except that which arose from the ties of consanguinity.

"Hence, also, the origin of all civil government, justly established, must be a voluntary compact between the rulers and the ruled; and must be liable to such limitations as are necessary for the security of the *absolute rights* of the latter: for what original title can any man, or set of men, have to govern others, except their own consent? To usurp dominion over a people, in their own despite; or to grasp at a more extensive power than they are willing to intrust, is to violate that law of nature, which gives every man a right to his personal liberty; and can, therefore, confer no obligation to obedience.

"'The principal aim of society is to protect individuals in the enjoyment of those absolute rights which were vested in them by the immutable laws of nature; but which could not be preserved, in peace, without that mutual assistance and intercourse, which is gained by the institution of friendly and social communities. Hence it follows, that the first and primary end of human laws is to maintain and regulate these *absolute rights* of individuals.'—BLACKSTONE."[15]

It would be difficult to find a more explicit, clear, and succinct exposition of the philosophy of the divinely instituted order and its concrete expression in the thinking behind the American Declaration of Independence and the Constitution of the United States than this statement by Alexander Hamilton, buttressed as it is with liberal quotations from Blackstone. Hamilton's church membership is a different matter. He seems to have had a period of religious enthusiasm as a youth, a period which passed and was not followed by any other period of religious emotionalism until his indignation was aroused by the attacks made on religion by the French revolutionists. Hamilton favored that attempt to establish Christianity which Jefferson and Madison opposed, proposing the establishment of a Christian Constitutional Society for "the support of the Christian Religion" when the Anglican establishment in the South began to crumble and the Congregational establishment in New England began to develop fissures. Hamilton's close friend Oliver Wolcott said that in his late years he expressed his belief in the truths of Christianity and at his request was attended by a clergyman on his deathbed. In the lack of positive evidence we cannot even say that the deism which is clearly the foundation of the religious thought of Franklin, Jefferson, Madison, and Adams—and indeed of all the political philosophers of the American Revolution except the stalwart Huguenot Jay—was the substructure of Hamilton's religious beliefs. We can say that he had religious beliefs, that they included belief in the divinely instituted order, and that his tangible political convictions arose naturally from them.

Hamilton, for all his aristocratic instincts, regarded human equality as a corollary to his belief in the natural order. His view that government can exist morally only with the consent of the governed was applied in the practical forum of politics when he eloquently and successfully defended the claim of Vermont to be considered a sovereign state over the objection of New York.

From Hamilton's belief that government exists to defend the rights of individuals, developed logically his belief that the judiciary must be independent of the administrative and legislative branches. The former, as he says in *Federalist* no. 78 of May, 1788, controls the sword of state, the latter controls the purse strings. The courts control neither and hence cannot threaten the freedom of the people which they exist to safeguard. It follows that the courts must be free. Indeed Hamilton carries this conviction beyond what seemed to Madison its logical limit. Madison believed that the American people would give their consent to the federal government through the states, a form of consent which would make it a truly federal rather than a national government. Hamilton believed that the national government was truly national, resting directly on the consent of the people.

One aspect of Hamilton's thought has come to have a new and vital application in the mid-twentieth century. The charge of an antidemocratic bias so often leveled at Hamilton probably would not stand up under a totally fresh re-examination of his thought. What would certainly stand up is the belief less frequently voiced that Hamilton's real fear was never of the people as the people, nor of the states as states, but of the political machines which he feared could manipulate the people in the limited geographic and population confines of the states. He believed that a national government would be too large and too diversified to be subject to these localized pressures and controls, and hence a strong national government would be a natural champion and protector of the rights of the people. Madison shared this conviction, which is repeatedly voiced in *The Federalist*. It is noteworthy that this essentially Hamiltonian philosophy underlies the federal civil rights movement of the mid-twentieth century and that many twentieth-century liberals who advocate a strong civil rights stand by the national government, in what they consider to be the spirit of Jeffersonian democracy, actually are using one of the arguments for a strong federal government which weighed most heavily with Alexander Hamilton. America's greatest debt to Hamilton is in the realm of sound finance, but the often amazingly prophetic Hamilton foresaw the nullification of the pre-Civil War period and the approach to nullification which has hamstrung the civil rights movement of the mid-twentieth century. A thorough re-examination of Hamilton's thought should pay full attention to this aspect of it, and to the basic philosophy on which it rests. Alexander Hamilton, the trusted friend and brilliant aide to General Washington and something not far removed in spirit from prime minister to President Washington, is just as truly a Founding Father as Jefferson and Madison and one whose paternal guidance has at least as much significance for the twentieth century as theirs; generations to come may even say that it had more.

JOHN JAY

If Hamilton is the Founding Father never fully accepted as orthodox, John Jay is the unknown Father. This is strange, nor does the strangeness lessen when one reads his name linked in nineteenth-century Federalist histories with those of Washington and Hamilton as the trio who presided over America in its birth. It deepens, if anything, as one reads the subtitle of the standard biography of John Jay: "Defender of Liberty against Kings and Peoples; Author of the Constitution and Governor of New York; President of the Continental Congress; Co-Author of the *Federalist;* Negotiator of the Peace of 1783 and the Jay Treaty of 1794; First Chief Justice of the United States." Such is the rotund yet accurate subtitle that Frank Monaghan gave his life of John Jay.[16] John Jay was all of this, yet today his name stirs the embers of recognition only in connection with a treaty

the terms of which even the well informed would be perplexed
to spell out. That is what it means to lack color when your
associates are as colorful as Washington and Hamilton. Jay is far
deeper in their shadows than Madison is in the shadow of Jefferson.

John Jay was a precise man, somewhat bilious in temperament
as well as physiology, yet not without his share of wit and a bent
toward the smoking-room story when the shades were securely
drawn. He was a man of deep and sincere conviction, deep and
sincere probity, a conservative in every fiber of his being yet
one of the makers of this utterly new country in a New World.
He was a less simple man, perhaps, than he seemed to be even
to himself. Nothing but ill health kept him from being the full
and equal partner of Hamilton and Madison in the composition
of the *Federalist*. Jay was capable of being a philosopher, yet
even more perhaps than his eminently practical-minded colleagues he had an instinct for the practical and tangible.

John Jay was born into a church and a tradition, and he never
budged an inch from either. A native New Yorker of Huguenot
stock, he was educated at a Huguenot school in a community
then nearly as French in language and tradition as its name,
New Rochelle. Religion was not taken lightly there. Professor
Monaghan in his life of John Jay, a life based in large measure
upon a wealth of unpublished manuscript material, states: "Although in America the Huguenots took life a little more cheerfully than did many of the Puritans to the northward, they still
worshipped the God of John Calvin. Before a church had been
erected in New Rochelle many of the Huguenots had walked
each Sunday to worship in the French church in New York: this
meant a trip of forty miles, but they walked it cheerfully, singing
psalms as they went."[17] It may be questioned if there was any
Puritan Geneva in New England that kept pristine Calvinism
quite as pure and unsullied as did the Huguenots of New
Rochelle. John Jay had in his veins the blood of the Jays, the
Bayards, and the Philipses, all refugees from persecution, and
his instinct for the Huguenot tradition was immeasurably
strengthened by his formative years in a Huguenot settlement.
A total acceptance of Calvinism, a total dedication to its pattern of life, a deep-seated abhorrence of everything Catholic but

also a deep-seated abhorrence of everything deistic, skeptical, or materialistic marked John Jay as boy and man. He never changed. Once he stalked from the room in Franklin's house in France when a visitor questioned the divinity of Jesus. Once when his physician questioned the Resurrection, Jay chilled him: "Sir, I pay you for your medical knowledge, and not for your distorted views of the Christian religion."

The views of John Jay on the matter of the man-made order need hardly be investigated. Actually they can hardly be discovered, except by obvious inference. Jay never questioned the Calvinistic interpretation of the universe, but he never felt called upon to expound it. Of all the Founding Fathers he was the one most removed from the influence of the Enlightenment. Yet the occasional expression of fundamental philosophy by a dedicated Calvinist like Jay has its own interest; its fundamental identity with the philosophy of Franklin, Jefferson, and Madison shows that however far the latter had strayed from the gospel according to Luther or Calvin, they had not abandoned the concept of a divinely created order on which that gospel rests. Jay opposed slavery on precisely the same grounds as Jefferson and Madison: not that it was uneconomic, not that it was wasteful, not that it was degrading to slave and slave owner alike; like the Virginians, he opposed it because it was fundamentally contrary to the natural law. For Americans to pray for freedom he considered impious until Americans granted freedom: "I believe God governs this world, and I believe it to be a maxim in his as in our court, that those who ask for equity ought to do it."[18]

Like the Virginians, he believed that ultimate sovereignty resided with the people. As Chief Justice he expounded in *Chisholm v. Georgia* the principle to which Chief Justice Marshall would give the classic expression years later in *McCulloch v. Maryland:* "From the crown of Great Britain the sovereignty of their country [the United States] passed to the people of it. . . . then the people, in their collective and national capacity, established the present Constitution. It is remarkable that, in establishing it, the people exercised their own rights and their own proper sovereignty; and conscious of the plenitude of it, they declared, with becoming dignity, 'We, the *people* of the

United States, do ordain and establish the present Constitution.' Here we see the people acting as sovereigns of the whole country, and, in the language of sovereignty, establishing a Constitution, by which it was their will that the State governments should be bound, and to which the State constitutions should be made to conform . . . the sovereignty of the nation is in the people of the nation, and the residual sovereignty of each State in the people of each State. . . ."19

There is little in the writing of John Jay on which to base a detailed presentation of his philosophic thought. It wasn't that he lacked philosophic convictions; if anything, his were excessively incrusted. They were incrusted because they were contained within the framework of an ancient tradition, that of Calvinism. But those whose convictions are contained within ancient framework of tradition seldom expound them; the fathers have done that already, for all time. So with John Jay. As a Calvinist he believed that duty was paramount. He believed that the existence of a right is essential to the performance of a duty. He believed that duties to the Almighty are antecedent to all human obligations, and hence the rights which are their correlatives are inalienable rights. He believed, therefore, in the principles of the Declaration of Independence and it was his consistent effort, acting as a Federalist in politics and a conservative in instinct, to implement these principles in the basic law of the land. His theological convictions were far removed from those of Franklin, Jefferson, and Madison, but his basic philosophy was not. The basic philosophy of this belated Calvinist and the basic philosophy of the three reputed sons of the Enlightenment rested upon a belief in the divinely created order. So did the basic philosophy of that New England son of the Enlightenment, John Adams.

JOHN ADAMS

In many ways the most difficult of the Founding Fathers to analyze in terms of philosophic thought is Adams. It is not that the materials are lacking; they are present in overpowering abundance. The trouble is a certain mistiness of expression, a certain tendency to mount to what old Sir Thomas Browne

called an *O Altitudo!* of phraseology that overtakes Adams
when he enters the holy precincts of metaphysics. He is at once
a religious believer and not a believer, or a believer in something
a little intangible and difficult to express. His was the fate that
so often befell those of the New England Calvinist tradition who
had strayed from the fold in search of another fold, the site of
which they did not know. It is always essential to their thinking
that they are in search of a fold.

"God has infinite wisdom, goodness, and power," Adams assured Thomas Jefferson, who was apt to be Adams' chosen
recipient for such confidences; "he created the universe; his
duration is eternal, *a parte ante* and *a parte post*. His presence
is as extensive as space. What is space? An infinite spherical
vacuum. He created this speck of dirt and the human species
for his glory; and with the deliberate design of making nine
tenths of our species miserable for ever for his glory. This is the
doctrine of Christian theologians, in general, ten to one. Now, my
friend, can prophecies or miracles convince you or me that
infinite benevolence, wisdom, and power, created, and preserves for a time, innumerable millions, to make them miserable
for ever, for his own glory? Wretch! What is his glory? Is he
ambitious? Does he want promotion? Is he vain, tickled with
adulation, exulting and triumphing in his power and the sweetness of his vengeance? Pardon me, my Maker, for these awful
questions. My answer to them is always ready. I believe no such
things. My adoration of the author of the universe is too profound and too sincere. The love of God and his creation—delight,
joy, triumph, exultation in my own existence—though but an
atom, a *molecule organique* in the universe—are my religion."[20]
Three months later Jefferson got a similar if more astronomical
definition: "Allegiance to the Creator and the Governor of the
Milky Way, and the Nebulae, and benevolence to all His
creatures, is my Religion."[21]

The thought and phraseology are familiar to those familiar
with the thought and phraseology of New Englanders in the
days when the one-hoss shay of Puritanism was developing
alarming creaks and groans, the thought and phraseology to be
expressed most memorably a generation later by Emerson and
Thoreau. New England Calvinism was melting into New Eng-

land Unitarianism. Men like John Adams had liberated themselves from the austere creed of their forefathers but had no intention of liberating themselves from a belief in God and in a divinely created moral order. When they were reading men like Adams, they tended to turn to the English deists for confirmation of their instinctive belief in Christianity as a moral system. Adams did so, as many volumes in his library with their rich marginal annotations testify.[22] The thought in his letters about religion is Unitarian, but the poetic phraseology is distinctively of New England for a reason that can be pondered but, by the writer at least, cannot be determined. Its unmistakable flavor can be detected in the whole school of New England Unitarianism, from John Adams to the present day.

In details the social and political thought of Adams differs from the social and political thought of his favored correspondent of the twilight years, Thomas Jefferson, as the natural cast of thought of the prudent, cautious, instinctively conservative Bay Stater differs from the natural cast of thought of the open-handed, expansive, instinctively liberal Virginian. Adams wrote a monumental work on government, perhaps the most detailed from an American pen. His three-volume *A Defence of the Constitutions of Government of the United States of America* was written as the federal Constitution was on the drafting table, such popular insurrections as Shays's Rebellion were in men's thoughts, and there was an ominous cloud to the east, hanging over the land of France. In the heart of Adams, as in the heart of Hamilton and Madison, was the haunting dread that the American experiment might be frustrated, that a stable government of laws might crumble beneath the uncontrolled passions of men. Here is the key to Adams' conservatism. He dreaded the possibility that sectional factions and rivalries might destroy the new and still untested union. There is a second key. Adams had an undeviating dread of tyranny, and he knew that tyranny can be quite as truly the result of mob rule as of despotic. Hence his fear of "simple democracy," whether it be fathered by Franklin, Jefferson, or Turgot; hence his opposition to a unicameral legislature, which he feared as a potential center of tyranny; hence his devotion to a government of checks and balances, in which an aristocratic Senate and a popular House would be mediated by a powerful chief executive.

Adams always believed that ultimate sovereignty resides in the people. On April 18, 1790, he wrote to his friend Benjamin Rush, "My friend Dr. Rush will excuse me if I caution him against a fraudulent use of the words *monarchy* and *republic*. I am a mortal and irreconciliable enemy to monarchy. I am no friend to *hereditary limited* monarchy in America. This I know can never be admitted without an hereditary Senate to control it, and a hereditary nobility or Senate in America I know to be unattainable and impracticable. I should scarcely be for it if it were. Do not, therefore, my friend, misunderstand me and misrepresent me to posterity. I am for a balance between the legislative and executive powers, and I am for enabling the executive to be at all times capable of maintaining the balance between the Senate and House, or, in other words, between the aristocratical and democratical interests. Yet I am for having all three branches elected at stated periods, and these elections, I hope, will continue until the people shall be convinced that fortune, providence, or chance, call it which you will, is better than election."[23] His views on human equality and its foundation in the divinely instituted order he made equally clear in a letter to John Taylor dated April 15, 1814. "That all men are born to equal rights is true. Every being has a right to his own, as clear, as moral, as sacred, as any other being has. This is as indubitable as a moral government in the universe."[24]

Behind Adams' political theory were the usual sources for an American of his generation: Locke, Bolingbroke, Montesquieu. Bolingbroke was probably his first and most influential mentor, one who could lead him equally down the paths to organized republicanism and away from organized religion; in 1813 Adams said that he had read Bolingbroke more than five times, starting fifty years before. In Bolingbroke he could find the concept of mixed government and balance of power, a concept that solidified in the mind of Adams as he saw its wisdom repeatedly confirmed in actual practice. Delolme was another influence upon his thinking; Adams always considered Delolme the most intelligible interpreter of the British constitution. The influence of Blackstone reinforced that of Delolme, and Montesquieu is present always and everywhere as a tutelary genius benign toward the Founding Fathers. Consequently Adams had the habitual beliefs of a Founding Father: belief in the divinely instituted order, in the consequent inalienable rights of man, in government as something dependent on the consent of the governed. He was among the first to call for a break with England, but also among the first in his admiration of the English mixed government of balanced powers and separate departments. He wanted an independent America, with a government modeled upon that of England.

Adams' *Diary* has many an echo of the English deists; and to them is undoubtedly due his concept of Christianity as a system of moral idealism. "The good of the governed is the end, and rewards and punishments are the means, of all government," he wrote in his *Diary* late in 1770 or early in 1771. "The government of the supreme and all-perfect Mind, over all his intellectual creation, is by proportioning rewards to piety and virtue, and punishments to disobedience and vice. Virtue, by the constitution of nature, carries in general its own reward, and vice its own punishment, even in this world. But, as many exceptions to this rule take place upon earth, the joys of heaven are prepared, and the horrors of hell in a future state, to render the moral government of the universe perfect and complete. Human government is more or less perfect as it approaches nearer or diverges further from an imitation of this perfect plan of divine and moral government."[25] Adrienne Koch and William Peden put it well: "Adams never wholly freed himself of Puritan righteousness. The moralism that had led him to crusade against drinking and local taverns in his early days as a lawyer accounts also for that moral virtuousness which at times approximated obsession. Born too late to exercise the managerial rights of Puritan theocrats, both John and John Quincy regarded statesmanship as a spiritual mission."[26] The conclusion is obvious: neither father nor son believed in the man-made order.

Another conclusion that suggests itself is that John Adams would have felt less than perfervid enthusiasm for the French Revolution. This is correct. What is considerably more to the point is the fact that all the Founding Fathers here considered

were either benignly unaware of the true nature of that cata-
clysm, or took a stand beside Edmund Burke. Franklin and Jefferson are typical of the first attitude, Hamilton and Adams of
the second.

THE AMERICAN AND THE FRENCH REVOLUTIONS

One must start with an understanding that America, even at
its most literate and intellectually alert, had very little knowledge of the philosophes until the 1780s. Professor Howard Mumford Jones, who has investigated the matter painstakingly, has
made it clear that their works were not brought into the United
States in substantial numbers until after the American Revolution.[27] But that lack of awareness of the philosophy behind
the tumultuous events of the Revolution did not preclude a
most enthusiastic American welcoming of them. Americans of
all rank and station hailed the French Revolution as the dawn
of a human freedom in Europe which the American Revolution
had heralded less than two decades before. France had been the
noble ally in America's dark hour of need. Now the chains were
being struck off France, and the nation that had nursed the
infant America into being could go confidently hand in hand
with the thriving youngster across the sea down the glory road
to man's exalted destiny. America's reaction was the reaction
of young liberals everywhere. Wordsworth gave it the accepted
formulation in *The Prelude:*

> Bliss was it that dawn to be alive,
> But to be young was very Heaven!

That reaction was the starting point for America's reaction to the
French Revolution.

There were those in America, like Franklin and Jefferson,
who never really came to see that the French Revolution was not
merely the American Revolution carried across the sea. Both
men had lived in France, and had come to love France. Franklin
had struck his pose in Paris, and had convinced the people
that this urbane, sophisticated, worldly-wise publisher, inventor,
and master of statescraft was a simple son of nature out of the
gospel according to Jean Jacques. Franklin totally fooled France,

but perhaps France inadvertently fooled Franklin at the same time. Franklin had been admitted in 1777 to the French Masonic lodge of the Nine Sisters. The Nine Sisters, among whom were Danton, Condorcet, and the Abbé Sieyès, were moderate reformers. They did look to America as the model of liberty, and they were, except the Abbé, among the first victims of the Terror. Franklin saw to it that they had copies of the American Constitution in La Rochefoucauld's translation, bestowing it benignly as the needed political nostrum. After the Revolution broke out he wrote to Benjamin Vaughan: "The Revolution in France is truly surprising; I sincerely wish it may end in establishing a good constitution for that country. The mischiefs and troubles it suffers in the operation, however, give me great concern."[28] There is not a vestige of reason to think that Franklin, shrewd though he was in his advanced years, ever thought of the French Revolution as other than the American Revolution transferred to France, or expected any other outcome for it than the ones the Americans achieved at the Philadelphia Constitutional Convention. Franklin had done much studying at the school of Montesquieu, vastly less at the school of Rousseau.

Jefferson's attitude was fundamentally the same. He had associated only with moderate Girondists, ones kin to the Nine Sisters. To think that Jefferson was infected with Jacobinism and returned to America to spread the infection is totally to misunderstand the Girondists, the Jacobins, and Thomas Jefferson. Jefferson never advocated force as a means of social or economic reform; he never thought of class society as necessary nor of class warfare as inevitable; he believed that good will and gradual legislation would cure all social and economic ills, and he hoped that they would in France. Jefferson always had a passion for Bills of Rights and when the French adopted their Declaration of the Rights of Man and the Citizen, he felt they had done the one thing vital. Jefferson believed in the French Revolution, much as Franklin did. To them both it was a philosophical reformation in the pattern of French society and French government; there is no evidence that either man had an inkling of the forces behind it that were so clear to Edmund Burke. Dumas Malone, Jefferson's brilliant biographer, well describes him as a statesman who preferred a path a bit left of center and hence one who seemed a conservative in revolutionary France, if he seemed a dangerous radical to many in America during the conservative reaction.[29] Until the Reign of Terror, the viewpoint of Franklin and Jefferson was the viewpoint of the United States. Thereafter American enthusiasm for the Revolution collapsed, even the enthusiasm of the Jeffersonians. Americans had seen the French Revolution as the American Revolution in France, and now they saw that they had been wrong.

The viewpoint of Hamilton and Adams was a different matter. The first reaction of Hamilton to it was the ordinary American reaction, the reaction of Franklin and Jefferson. Like them, Hamilton saw it as the American Revolution transferred to France, the dawn of human freedom in Europe. By April, 1793, like other thinking Americans Hamilton saw the implications of the Reign of Terror. He wrote to Washington his generalizations about the spirit of a revolution and the methods it might employ, concluding: "It appears, thus far, but too probable, that the pending revolution of France has sustained some serious blemishes. There is too much ground to anticipate that a sentence uncommonly severe will be passed upon it if it fails. . . ."[30]

A month later he wrote to an unidentified correspondent: "The cause of France is compared with that of America during its late revolution. Would to Heaven that the comparison were just. Would to Heaven we could discern in the mirror of French affairs the same humanity, the same decorum, the same gravity, the same order, the same dignity, the same solemnity, which distinguished the cause of the American Revolution. Clouds and darkness would not then rest upon the issue as they now do. I own I do not like the comparison."[31]

By July his disillusionment was complete. He wrote in a draft of *Pacificus* No. 2: "Whatever partiality may be entertained for the general object of the French Revolution, it is impossible for any well-informed or sober-minded man not to condemn the proceedings which have been stated, as repugnant to the rights of nations, to the true principles of liberty, to the freedom of opinion of mankind; or not to acknowledge as a consequence of this, that the justice of the war on the part of France, with regard to some of the Powers with which she is engaged, is from those causes questionable enough to free the United States from

all embarrassment on that score, if it be at all incumbent upon
them to go into the inquiry."[32] Thereafter the expression of this
viewpoint merely grows stronger as more heads topple and more
blood flows down the gutters of Paris.

Hamilton's final viewpoint is very close indeed to that of
Edmund Burke. In or about 1796 he wrote a "Fragment on the
French Revolution." In it he recognized the profoundly radical
nature of the French Revolution, the intensely antireligious spirit
that permeated it, and the fundamentally secular viewpoint of
those of the school of Rousseau who believed in the man-made
order. "As a corollary from these premises, it is a favorite tenet
of the sect that religious opinion of any sort is unnecessary to
society; that the maxims of a genuine morality and the authority
of the magistracy and the laws are a sufficient and ought to be
the only security for civil rights and private happiness."[33] Hamilton came to see by 1796 what Burke had seen so much earlier
and with equal clarity, that the essential difference between the
American Revolution and the French Revolution is the difference between belief in the divinely created order and belief in
the man-made order, and that the difference is an ideological
Grand Canyon.

No one of the Founding Fathers was disillusioned with the
French Revolution so quickly as John Adams. As early as April,
1790, he wrote to Richard Price: "The Revolution in France
could not be indifferent to me; but I have learned by awful
experience, to rejoice with trembling. I know that encyclopedists
and economists, Diderot and d'Alembert, Voltaire and Rousseau,
have contributed to this great event more than Sidney, Locke,
or Hoadly, perhaps more than the American Revolution; and I
own to you, I know not what to make of a republic of thirty
million atheists."[34]

Before long Adams had ceased to rejoice, but not to tremble.
He trembled at the fatal combination of arrogance and ignorance
which he saw present in the philosophes. To their character he
paid the tribute he felt that they deserved, but he deplored
much of what they did. Again and again he testified to the purity
of motive characteristic of them, shaking his head sadly as he
testified. Purity of motive cannot overcome ignorance of the
practicalities of life. The philosophes, in his view, were theorists,

dogmatists, closet philosophers dealing with abstractions. Some of their abstractions were ungrounded: their failure to found the doctrine of natural rights upon moral duties, their failure to recognize a moral order not of man's making, their thought that man could shatter the existing order to bits and then create a better order by sheer rationalizing about what life ought to be. He argues with them and their supporters steadily in the margins of his books. In Mary Wollstonecraft's *French Revolution* alone he wrote some twelve thousand words on some five hundred passages, the whole comprising John Adams' account of the French Revolution, an account that differs from Mary Wollstonecraft's at every turn. Adams saw in the Reign of Terror the inevitable outcome of the thinking of the philosophes. His stand on this point was never shaken.

One conclusion and one only can come from a study of the thought of the Founding Fathers: all believed, in one sense or another and with varying emphasis on its aspects, in a divinely created order. All believed in God and divine providence; all believed in a moral imperative of divine ordainment; all believed in rights inalienable because they must exist if man is to obey the divine ordainment; hence all believed in human freedom and in a human equality derived ultimately from man's equality before the tribunal of Omnipotence. That much is philosophy; the rest is politics. Jefferson and Hamilton might be poles apart in the ways that they would implement the philosophy that they shared; Franklin and Adams might wonder, each of them, how the colony of Massachusetts could produce the other; Madison might strive to be the human gyroscope that would level the Ship of State as it slipped out of the ways into the turbulent waters of independence; Jay might hold to a set of religious beliefs at which his friends of the Enlightenment would stand aghast, and then stand in wonderment as they sensed beneath his rigid Calvinism a philosophy fundamentally at one with their own. They were not of one church, and the whole matter of churches had to be muted if America were ever to become one nation. If they had any religious common denominator it tended to be a deism of the earlier English sort, the kind produced in the school of Shaftesbury rather than the school of Bolingbroke, although Jefferson at least had his share of the latter. With all the risks of a broad generalization, one may say that their graduate study was done at the school of Montesquieu, not the school of Rousseau. The American Revolution was profoundly different from the French Revolution, different in its basic axioms, its fundamental philosophy, its ethical ideals, its practical implementation. The American Revolution was grounded upon the concept of natural law, the concept of the divinely created order; and the history of the United States is the history of the success of the Revolution. The French Revolution was grounded on the concept that society is a mechanism, created, operated, modified, changed, and abolished by the human will; and the history of France has been, ever since—the history of France.

IX

"THE GREATEST HAPPINESS OF THE GREATEST NUMBER"

THE EXPLICIT FORMULATION of the utilitarian objective into the phrase "the greatest happiness of the greatest number" seems to have been the work of Joseph Priestley, and its systematic development into something like a philosophy was the work of Jeremy Bentham, but the concept itself is virtually inseparable from the concept of the man-made order. If the proponent of the man-made order is an idealist, if justice and the reign of order are his goals and a cornerstone of ethical principles underlies the structure he would erect, what other objective can take its place in his philosophy? The selfish man can believe in the man-made order and not believe that the greatest happiness of the greatest number should be its objective. It is difficult, however, to accept the philosophy and reject its objective if one is an idealist and a believer in justice and order, and one who would see the affairs of men ordered on ethical principles. The sincere and disinterested believer in the man-made order has to be a utilitarian. Jeremy Bentham, who could depart from his usual atheism when it was to his forensic advantage, made God Himself a utilitarian. ". . . if we presume that God wills anything, we must suppose that he has a reason for so doing, a reason worthy of himself, which can only be the greatest happiness of his creatures. In this point of view, therefore, the divine will cannot require anything inconsistent with general utility. If it can be pretended that God can have any will not consistent with utility, his will becomes a fantastic and delusive principle, in which the ravings of enthusiasm, and the extravagences of superstition, will find sanction and authority."[1]

It follows that all the believers in the man-made order whom we have met have been to some degree utilitarians, with their sincerity to be measured by the sincerity of their idealism and protestations of brotherhood. Hobbes discusses the dimensions of pleasure and pain, maintaining that the good which benefits the larger number is greater than the good which benefits the smaller number, "for the more extended and the more limited good differ as the greater and the less."[2] Locke can find no "innate practical principles" except a desire of happiness and an aversion to misery: "Good or evil are nothing but pleasure and pain, or that which occasions pleasure or pain to us."[3] Morality to Hume is based upon experience and hence is induced by scientific observation, later to be systematized by the deductive process. We learn morals as we learn chemistry and physics, by experimentation, observation, and then generalization. Morality as a science is founded on psychology, and psychology is based on experience alone. If an act is useful it is good; its usefulness makes it good, its goodness does not make it useful.

There is utilitarianism in all these men, but they are not in the full sense utilitarians. Utilitarianism in Hobbes is limited by an ideal of society quite inconsistent with its objective; utilitarianism in Locke is blurred by his acceptance of a divinely created order based on the divine will but not on immutable justice; utilitarianism in Hume is hamstrung by a skepticism which keeps him from achieving a consistent philosophy of man as a social being. Hutcheson comes perhaps a little closer than they to the utilitarian ideal; indeed, the magic words themselves are to be found in Hutcheson. "That action is best, which procures the greatest Happiness for the greatest Numbers; and that, worst, which, in like manner, occasions Misery."[4] To make of Hutcheson a utilitarian, however, would be to deny him his major inheritance. One cannot be a follower of Shaftesbury and believe in the moral sense and yet be a utilitarian, no matter how much incidental utilitarianism there may be in one's thought. Hutcheson approaches a belief in the man-made order, but by a different route.

JEREMY BENTHAM—THE FIRST UTILITARIAN

Utilitarianism, then, by no means starts with Jeremy Bentham, but one can reasonably maintain that Jeremy Bentham is the first utilitarian. In Jeremy Bentham as in old Thomas Hobbes, we see illustrated how mild and benign the earth-shaker is apt to be. Bentham was born to a family of great wealth, and enjoyed all his life the peaceful leisure of the scholar and the retirement of the speculative thinker. When three and breeched he began his Latin, reading Rapin's *History* for relaxation. When five he played the violin and spoke French. When thirteen he entered Queen's College, Oxford; at fifteen he sat as a law student in the Queen's Bench, but he returned to Oxford to hear Blackstone lecture, quietly noting the fallacies in his reasoning. In 1776 he ventured into print with a powerful attack on Blackstone, an anonymous work called *Fragment on Government* that was honored by being fathered on the leading jurists of the age. Bentham never quite abandoned the dream of his youth, that some day some country (in the more roseate hours of the dream it was his own) would let him write its code of laws. The day never dawned, although France made him an honorary citizen in 1792 and other honors flowed to him from the four corners of the world. But the materials for the Bentham-made order are present in overflowing abundance for the new-born nation that would have him for its legal obstetrician; his collected works fill eleven octavo volumes, double column. He lived a quiet life of unostentatious luxury, enjoyed the best foods, best wines, best music, and best friends; harbored the limited strength of a small, frail body and the cheerful simplicity of a goodhearted boy; did his best to promote the greatest happiness of the greatest number; and died. His will ordered that his body be dissected, then reassembled, embalmed, given a wax mask, dressed in its usual clothes, and permanently displayed by London University. There it still is, just like the pea of Hans Andersen's story "The Real Princess," which was put into the museum—but perhaps we should add Andersen's cautious proviso, "where it may still be seen if no one has stolen it." (For parentheses as for footnotes, only a dead factual calm is per-

missible. Bentham's mummy was injured during an air raid in
1940 and placed, logically enough, in the Egyptian department
for repairs. Perhaps they are completed, perhaps the exhibit is
still "closed for repairs"; deponent knoweth not.)

The chief repository of Bentham's utilitarian thought is his
Introduction to the Principles of Morals and Legislation (1789).
The title should be illuminating, and the light is necessary if
justice is to be done to Bentham. Bentham's life work was the
logical reordering of the principles of legislation; any dogmatic
views he had on private morals were subsidiary to this primary
interest. He believed, and with a good measure of justice,
that the time had come for a systematic reorganization of the
machinery of government, a fundamental re-examination of the
principles and procedures of the civil and the criminal law;
that the time had come for a reunion of law and equity, for an
infusion of the spirit of justice into the institutions of the British
Isles. It is to this end that the book was written, and by far
the larger part of it is devoted to human misdeeds, their consequences, implications, motivations, and appropriate punishments. Much of Bentham is the mere application of common
sense to the problems of society, but few men have been less
sensible than Bentham in the way they handle common sense.
Bentham could "distinguish and divide/A hair twixt south and
southwest side," and he does so in *Principles of Morals and
Legislation*. He divides pleasure into fourteen simple types and
pain into twelve simple types. There are nine pleasures of sense,
all subdivisions of one of the fourteen simple pleasures. Coin-
cidentally there are nine pains of sense, similar subdivisions of
a simple pain. "Of all these several sorts of pleasures and pains,
there is scarce one which is not liable, on more accounts than
one, to come under the consideration of the law," is his ominous
conclusion.[5] One who has assimilated these distinctions is at
least emotionally prepared for the thirteen rules of proportion
between punishments and offenses, the eleven properties of
punishment, the five classes of offenses with their divisions and
subdivisions, including the twenty-three genera of class one, and
the other distinctions and divisions that are as the sands of the
sea. In a word, even the dedicated reader soon bogs down,
comforting himself with the assurance that in this imperfect

world he has done his duty by Bentham when he has assimilated his principle of utility. Perhaps he has, but the duty does not imply full justice.

"Nature has placed mankind under the governance of two sovereign masters, pain and pleasure. It is for them alone to point out what we ought to do, as well as to determine what we shall do. On the one hand the standard of right and wrong, on the other the chain of causes and effects, are fastened to their throne. They govern us in all we do, in all we say, in all we think: every effort we can make to throw off our subjection, will serve but to demonstrate and confirm it. In words a man may pretend to abjure their empire: but in reality he will remain subject to it all the time. The principle of utility recognises this subjection, and assumes it for the foundation of that system, the object of which is to rear the fabric of felicity by the hands of reason and of law. Systems which attempt to question it, deal in sounds instead of sense, in caprice instead of reason, in darkness instead of light."[6] Such is Bentham's opening paragraph, one of the celebrated opening paragraphs of English literature. It is far from containing all one needs to know about Bentham, but it is the heart of what one needs to know.

Nature has placed mankind under the governance of two sovereign masters, pain and pleasure. The first question to be answered is, how does one determine the maximum pleasure to which human felicity can aspire? Some computer of felicity is obviously necessary, and Bentham concludes that the greatest happiness of the greatest number will be recorded in the computer when each individual does all in his power to achieve his personal maximum of genuine and enduring happiness. In 1817 he published his *Table of the Springs of Action,* the closest he came to the computer that would capture and record in verifiable arithmetic those evanescent phantoms, pleasure and pain. There are many fallacies in the concept, fallacies that will be obvious to everyone, but on one fallacy attention may be concentrated. Bentham saw all mankind in his own image and likeness, and all his calculations of human motives, interests, emotions, and passions were based on what he read in his own heart, a fundamentally simple, honest heart, a well-intentioned heart, and one that beat its rather lonely rhythm remote from the pulsating rhythm of human life in general. Let the symbol of it be the name of Bentham's estate, the Hermitage. Carlyle summed up the fallacy in his own sardonic way: "Given a world of knaves, to evolve honesty out of their united action." The fallacy would never have occurred to Bentham.

At this point we should recall that neither Bentham's interest nor our own is in the doctrine of utility for its own sake. To Bentham it was an axiom on which he could ground his concepts of jurisprudence, his concepts of usury laws and poor laws, laws of real estate and banking, his concepts of criminal law, prison discipline, and prison reform. The concept of utility may provide a very practical basis for legal reform, acceptable to many who would never accept it as a philosophic doctrine. Like many another concept, it works far better in practice than it promises to in theory; it is far from synonymous with the theory of democracy, but it is tangent to it. But it is totally and inescapably inconsistent with belief in the divinely created order, totally and inescapably dependent upon belief in the man-made order. It is not illogical that Bentham should always have longed for the country that would let him write its laws. Every believer in the man-made order wants that.

Chapters two and three of Bentham's *Principles of Morals and Legislation* present what is in general his views on natural law. He does not say so, but it is obvious that he considers the concept of the divinely created order an illusion. "The will of God here meant cannot be his revealed will, as contained in the sacred writings: for that is a system which nobody ever thinks of recurring to at this time of day, for the details of political administration: and even before it can be applied to the details of private conduct, it is universally allowed, by the most eminent divines of all persuasions, to stand in need of pretty ample interpretations; else to what use are the works of those divines? And for the guidance of these interpretations, it is also allowed, that some other standard must be assumed. The will then which is meant on this occasion, is that which may be called the presumptive will: that is to say, that which is presumed to be his will on account of the conformity of its dictates to those of some other principle. What then may be this other principle? it must be one or other of the three mentioned above: for there cannot, as we have seen, be any more. It is plain, therefore, that, setting revelation out of the question, no light can ever be thrown upon the standard of right and wrong, by any thing that can be said upon the question, what is God's will. We may be perfectly sure, indeed, that whatever is right is conformable to the will of God: but so far is that from answering the purpose of showing us what is right, that it is necessary to know first whether a thing is right, in order to know from thence whether it be conformable to the will of God."[7]

"In God's will is our peace," says Dante. "In our will is God's peace," Jeremy Bentham comes close to saying. If it produces happiness, it is good. If it is good, it conforms to the will of God. If it produces the greatest happiness of the greatest number it is the supreme good. The supreme good is achieved, or at least envisaged, upon earth; it is ratified in heaven. The greatest number is as much a part of the formula as the greatest good; God is on the side with the heavier artillery. At the risk of tedious repetition, one repeats that Bentham's primary interest everywhere and always was sound and sensible legislation. The basic axiom of utilitarianism can often light the way to its realization in the realm of practical politics, even if it is a will-o'-the-wisp to lure the believer in the man-made order into a philosophic quagmire. But Jeremy Bentham, at the most, stands just one stage farther down the road that English thought had been traveling since the dawn of deism. Hume was at least an agnostic where the will of God was concerned. Bentham could see the will of God revealed in the effective will of man: "Whatever is right is conformable to the will of God." Into that salience few speculative thinkers have cared to follow him. But many thinkers, and many men of action, and many men far less gifted than Bentham with the fruits of the Holy Ghost have gleefully followed in his footsteps, and run ahead of him, down the primrose path he painstakingly trod, the path to the conviction that what gives one pleasure is good, and morals are as simple as that. It isn't in reality the gospel of Jeremy Bentham, nor of James Mill, and most decidedly not of John Stuart Mill, but it was the gospel that many of their followers heard. The principles of utility and *laissez faire* are two sides of the same coin; political reaction and economic injustice lie ahead. The principle of utility will lead, in the name of progress and enlightenment, to another era of stagnation, just as the principle of deism did.

JAMES MILL

The fusion of utility and *laissez faire* is even more explicit in James Mill than in Jeremy Bentham, and the passage of time combined with the growth of the "dismal science" to make the fusion more significant. But before we can consider it, our attention must be concentrated on the psychology of James Mill and its implications for utilitarianism specifically and in general for the concept of the man-made order.

Jeremy Bentham started with a private fortune, James Mill with a grim determination. Mill's father was a shoemaker, his mother a farmer's daughter. But his talents were rich and manifest, and he became the protégé of the local great man and his lady, Sir John and Lady Jane Stuart, who made young James Mill the tutor of their daughter Wilhelmina while he was still a student at Montrose Academy. Later they made it possible for him to attend Edinburgh University. Still later he immortalized their name in the name of the oldest of his nine children, John Stuart Mill.

Mill emerged from the university a clergyman, but his days in the Church of Scotland were numbered by an intellectual uneasiness that grew as he found increasingly unsatisfactory the answer of deism, "Whatever is, is right." "He found it impossible to believe that a world so full of evil was the work of an Author combining infinite power with perfect goodness and righteousness," says John Stuart Mill of his father.[8] From the disbelief that whatever is, is right grew a disbelief in formal religion of any sort. James Mill came to feel that formal religion provided a moralistic protection for abuses that could and should be remedied, and that morality must be founded not on traditional church dogma but on some objective principle. A dour man, he is vividly described by the son who knew his father only too intimately and too well. "In his views of life he partook of the character of the Stoic, the Epicurean, and the Cynic, not in the modern, but the ancient sense of the word. In his personal qualities the Stoic predominated. His standard of morals was Epicurean, inasmuch as it was Utilitarian, taking as the exclusive text of right and wrong, the tendency of actions to produce pleasure or pain. But he had (and this was the Cynic element) scarcely any belief in pleasure. . . . He thought human life a poor thing at best, after the freshness of youth and unsatisfied curiosity had gone by. . . . He would sometimes say, that if life were made what it might be, by good government and good education, it would be worth having: but he never spoke with anything like enthusiasm even of that possibility."[9]

James Mill was not an atheist, as was Bentham except when it suited his convenience to be otherwise, or George Grote the historian of Greece and the close friend of them both. In Mill one does not find the bitter attacks on religion one finds in Bentham, who maintained that religion was one of the foremost causes of the major human evils. Mill was, in Huxley's later coinage, an agnostic, but not one who inclined in the direction of belief in a good and intelligent Creator. But the agnostic, quite as truly as the atheist, must pour his own cement if he is to erect his structure of morality. James Mill was by instinct a moralist in rebellion against the fire-and-brimstone Calvinism in which he had been reared. Being a moralist and a man of good will, he was by necessity a utilitarian.

At this point a necessary and vital distinction must be drawn between what might be termed utilitarians of the school of Bentham, although John Stuart Mill specifically denied that there was such a school, and other believers in the man-made order who incline to the utilitarian concepts. It is of the essence of Benthamite utilitarianism that it reject the moral sense just as completely as it rejects dogmatic morals. Morals, to the Benthamite, cannot be grounded on a subjective reaction any more than they can be grounded on an authoritarian utterance or a traditional code. Morals to a Benthamite are part of the Newtonian universe, which is governed by ascertainable, objective, mathematical laws. There is nothing subjective about gravitation, and there is nothing subjective about the perception of right and wrong. At this point Shaftesbury and the moral sense school depart the scene. Right and wrong are inseparably linked with pleasure and pain, and even the qualitative distinction is merged with the quantitative: the greatest good is the one which produces the greatest happiness of the greatest number. At this point the shadow of tradition melts away and the voice of religious authority grows still. Because the Benthamite utilitarians were reformers who wanted and needed allies, they did not parade their antireligious views, but their views were fundamentally and inescapably antireligious.

James Mill made two contributions of fundamental importance to the utilitarian cause. He gave it a psychology and he linked it with classical economics. He did the former primarily in his *Analysis of the Phenomena of the Human Mind* (1829), in which he made the ancient concept of associationism form an ethical mold for utilitarianism. The associationist school comes to full development in the work of David Hartley (1705–1757), whose *Observations on Man, his Frame, his Duty, and his Expectations* (1749) was the chief guide for James Mill in the formulation of his psychology. Hartley rejects the moral sense concept, traces the evolution of ideas of pleasure and pain from sense reactions, follows the development of the higher pleasures out of the lower into a realm where James Mill and the utilitarians would never follow him, a realm in which the ultimate pleasure is the love of God. Hartley, who was a physician and interested in the physical apparatus of the human mind, also worked out a theory of vibrations in the "medullary substance" of the human mind as the physical principle of human thought. In fairness to Hartley it should be pointed out that he never made his doctrine of associationism dependent on his much-ridiculed theory of vibrations.

It was the achievement of James Mill to work out of the theory of associationism a psychology which in turn provides a system of ethics. He accepted, as did all utilitarians, the non-existence of innate ideas. He held that all ideas came through sense impressions, with man's entire complex of ideas and feelings traceable ultimately to association among sense impressions. Without rejecting the analyses of associationism of his predecessors, he inclined to the belief that all forms of associationism might be reducible ultimately to contiguity. In passing, one might note an inference of very substantial importance that can be drawn from the theory of associationism: since one blank mind is the same as as another blank mind, and whatever is in the mind enters through sense impressions, it follows that all men are created mentally equal and differ after birth as environment makes them differ. Associationism goes hand in hand with a touching faith in the powers of education.

All ideas come through sense impressions, including what are considered to be concepts of morality. We seek pleasure and avoid pain. We become aware of pleasurable sensations, which thereafter we seek and deem good; and painful sensations, which thereafter we shun and deem bad. The virtues are the means to the pleasurable sensations, the means of warding off the painful sensations. The primary personal virtues are prudence and fortitude, the primary social virtues are justice and benevolence. Since man always and inevitably seeks his own well-being, the social virtues are harder to establish than the personal ones. Mill relies basically on the principle of reciprocity. Out of the primary personal virtues, prudence and fortitude, arise the pleasurable sensations provided by wealth, power, and dignity; and there follows the elevation of these pleasurable sensations into virtues. Out of the primary social virtues, justice and benevolence, arise the pleasurable sensations caused by family, friend, country, party, and mankind; and there follows the elevation of these pleasurable sensations into the virtues.

"Virtue is the name of Prudence, Fortitude, Justice, and Beneficence, all taken together. It is also, like the name of each of the species included under it, at once the name of the Affection, the Motive, and the Disposition. The man who has the Disposition toward all the four, Prudence, Fortitude, Justice, Beneficence, in full strength; that is, who has acquired, from habit, the facility of associating with those acts the pleasures which result from them, in other words, a habit of obeying the motives, is perfectly virtuous."[10] This is the final statement of morality in the work of James Mill, and it is the foundation of morality in the entire utilitarian school. The moral sense of the utilitarians is a capacity to distinguish between pleasurable and painful sensations acquired through experience and developed through habit. Virtue is obedience to the dictates of the moral sense. The test of its reality is its applicability to others, whether on the principle of reciprocity or on more elevated and disinterested grounds. In an extensive note to Chapter XXIII, the central chapter of a long, leisurely, minutely detailed and painstakingly methodical book, the author's son John Stuart Mill commented for the 1869 edition: ". . . it is undoubtedly true that the foundation of the moral feeling is the adoption of the pleasures and pains of others as our own: whether this takes place by the natural force of sympathy, or by the association which has grown up in our mind between our own good or evil and theirs. The moral feeling rests upon this identification of the feelings of others with our own, but it is not the same thing with it. To constitute the moral feeling, not only must the good of others have become in itself a pleasure to us, and their suffering a pain, but this pleasure or pain must be associated with our own acts as producing it, and must in this manner have become a motive, prompting us to the one sort of acts, and restraining us from the other sort. And this is, in brief, the author's theory of the Moral Sentiments."[11]

James Mill is even more explicit and detailed in his founding of the moral sense upon the principle of associationism in his *Fragment on Mackintosh* (1835). Sir James Mackintosh (1765–1832) had attacked utilitarian ethics in his *Dissertation on the Progress of Ethical Philosophy* (1830). In a rejoinder that is spirited to the point of being bellicose, Mill reaffirms the theory of morals that he presents in the *Analysis*. After distinguishing between the acts which we perform because they are to our personal interest and those that we perform for other reasons, Mill points out that unless some artificial reason were created for the performance of these altruistic acts, they would seldom be performed. "And here we clearly perceive the origin of that important case of classification. . . . the classification of acts as moral and immoral. The acts which it was important to other men that each individual should perform, but in which the individual had not a sufficient interest to secure the performance of them, were constituted one class. The acts, which it was important to other men that each individual should abstain from, but in regard to which he had not a personal interest sufficiently strong to secure his abstaining from them, were constituted another class. The first class were distinguished by the name moral acts; the second by the name immoral. . . . The whole business of the moral sentiments, moral approbation, and disapprobation, has this for its object, the distribution of the good and evil we have at command, for the production of acts of the useful sort, the prevention of acts of the contrary sort. Can there be a nobler object?"[12] He goes on to state that there was a distinction between the acts that society could sponsor or prevent and those which had to be left to the individual. "The first portion was placed under the control of what is called law; the other remained under the control of the moral sentiments; that is, the distribution of good and evil, made by individuals in their individual capacity. No sooner was the class made, than the rule followed. Moral acts are to be performed; immoral acts are to be abstained from."[13]

Thus we see a totally new and at least quasi-scientific foundation laid for morality and the man-made order in the work of James Mill and the associationists to whom he is indebted. In one way Mill denies the existence of a moral sense, but in another way he explains its existence. The moral sense is not a sense but a very complex network of sensations, some pleasurable and therefore good, others painful and therefore bad. It rests on a physiological basis and so can be objectively verified. Upon this complex network of sensations Mill constructs his system of ethics: pleasurable sensations give rise to ideas of the good and hence the virtuous; painful sensations give rise to ideas of the bad and hence the vicious. Paradoxically, even as James Mill rejects Shaftesbury and the moral sense concept he presents what is the entirely logical extension and conclusion of that very concept. An act is good if I feel that it is good. The good and the beautiful coalesce,[14] and the man-made order is a fusion of the subjectively aesthetic and moral. Utilitarianism now has its psychology and its ethics.

A psychology and an ethics were not enough. One loses sight of the basic meaning of utilitarianism if one forgets that fundamentally it was a movement of reform, and that everything else —be it psychology, ethics, economics, or sociology—was to provide an ideological basis for a movement of reform. Hence from the start the utilitarians were in league with the economists and the sociologists. The names of Bentham and both Mills cannot be dissociated from the names of Adam Smith, Malthus, and Ricardo. They cannot be dissociated from the concepts of *laissez faire*, the food-population ratio, the wage fund, and the unearned increment of land value. Smith, Malthus, and Ricardo were not in a primary sense exponents of the man-made order, but what they thought in the realms of economics and sociology affected what the utilitarians thought in the realms of ethics and natural theology.

ADAM SMITH AND *LAISSEZ FAIRE*

Adam Smith followed the lead of the French economists down the road to *laissez faire*. They started with the thesis that all is for the best in the best possible of worlds—except man. Civilized man and the monkey wrench he throws into the smooth working of the natural order are the sole disturbances in that order. But the disturbances can be eliminated. If man returns to the natural order, regains the wisdom of his primitive ancestors, and lives naturally, the universal harmony will be restored. It is a program of simple living, plain thinking, and lower taxes. Under it government has no function but to protect life and property. When the French coined the phrase *laissez faire*, they had in mind nothing beyond the elimination of undue and injurious governmental interference with the ordinary operation of industry. By its companion phrase *laissez passer* they advocated merely free trade inside France. François Quesnay (1694–1774) and the other physiocrats saw the possibility that the best hope for individual freedom might well be a powerful monarch, just as John Adams saw it many years later. The very fact that they suggested China as a model confirms the point.

It was in England and not France that *laissez faire* took on the meaning habitually associated with it. The theory that government exists only to protect life and property accorded well with the individualism of Locke in the *Treatise on Government*. To Quesnay the following of nature meant the living by laws that could be induced from the study of nature. To Adam Smith the following of nature meant the granting of the maximum liberty to individual impulses and the fulfillment of individual desires consistent with the preservation of law and order. He accepted the thesis that the proper standard for economic action is the self-interest of the individual involved, and with it the other thesis that if all men have the maximum freedom to pursue their self-interest, the greatest happiness of the greatest number will be achieved. The phrase belongs to the utilitarians, but they must share it as an objective with the classical economists. Thus *laissez faire*, which to Quesnay and the physiocrats meant the following of an objective norm set by nature, to Adam Smith and his followers meant the following of a subjective norm set by one's own desires.

The relationship of Jeremy Bentham to the thinking of Adam Smith is a subtle one. He accepted, as in logic he had to, the concept of *laissez faire* held by Adam Smith. One must have the maximum freedom to attain one's maximum happiness, and the greatest happiness of the greatest number depends on the greatest number having the maximum freedom. But Jeremy Bentham's lifework was legal and penal reform. Law is to curb those whose actions interfere with the happiness of others, prison supposedly is to reform them. Hence in theory Jeremy Bentham supported *laissez faire* as Adam Smith conceived it, but in practice he was concerned with suppressing *laissez faire* among those whose actions would interfere with the greatest happiness of the greatest number. He accepted the theory that man should have the maximum freedom to pursue his self-interest, but the practical concerns of his life centered about the control of those whose pursuit of self-interest brought them into collision with society. In theory Bentham was committed to a drastic limitation of the functions of government, but in practice he was committed to an extension of them. Again we see illustrated the paradox which has so often beset the believer in the man-made order: total freedom tends to mean no freedom at all. The believer in the divinely created order is theoretically limited in his interference with the freedom of others by his acceptance of the principle of inalienable rights. Quesnay and the physiocrats who believed in a natural order were limited by their rather physiological but at least objective concept of natural law. But Bentham in theory was limited by nothing. Hence the paradox that he can simultaneously accept the theory of *laissez faire* and the practice of close legalistic supervision of human activities. There is no provision in Benthamism for the observance of minority rights. There never is in utilitarianism, until John Stuart Mill tries to justify it on pragmatic grounds.

THOMAS MALTHUS

The fusion of utilitarianism with the theory of *laissez faire* which Bentham achieved was accepted and extended by James Mill. Far more than Bentham, James Mill was a man of action, and he had a keener awareness of the ways in which economic and sociological theories could be translated into modes of action. Hence he added to the theoretical arsenal of utilitarianism tangible weapons from the store of Thomas Malthus and David Ricardo. Thomas Malthus (1766–1834) was another of those quiet men who have a way of shaking the world. He was born to a good family and a good fortune. His father was an independent thinker literally of the school of Rousseau; he was one of Rousseau's executors. He brought up his son in secluded comfort, had him trained by private tutors, sent him to Cambridge, and saw that as a clergyman he got the right sort of living in the right sort of parish in Surrey. Thomas Malthus was happy as a clergyman, happy as a husband, and for many years happy as professor of modern history and political economy in the East India Company's college at Haileybury. He died a happy death in 1834, leaving an unhappy legacy of confusion and misrepresentation. Malthus never desired anything but the happiness of his fellow man; no utilitarian could have desired it more fervently, no believer in *laissez faire* more ardently. But his legacy was one of confusion and misrepresentation.

The first edition of his work on population appeared in 1798, the second and mature edition in 1803. The title of the 1803 edition is instructive: *An Essay on the Principle of Population: or, A View of Its Past and Present Effect on Human Happiness.* Human happiness was his genuine concern. He was devoted to it both by instinct and by profession. He saw as the greatest barrier to human happiness on earth two inexorable, diametrically opposed, implacable mathematical factors in a single equation.

Human population tends to increase by geometric ratio (2, 4, 8, 16, etc.), food tends to increase by arithmetic ratio (2, 4, 6, 8, etc.). The two are kept in balance by human misery, kept in balance by war, plague, and famine, kept in balance by vice and crime. That implacable equation is the great earthly barrier on the path to human happiness.

Malthus had done his work when he described the barrier. He did not advocate birth control. He did urge people not to marry until they could support a family. But his fundamental purpose in writing was to present what seemed to him a profound economic truth, and one which revealed for the cloud-cuckoo-land fantasies which he deemed them to be the theories of human perfectibility held by his father's idols, Condorcet and Rousseau. Thomas Malthus was no believer in the man-made order. He was a sincere lover of truth and a sincere preacher of the Word in the Church of England. Yet he added a vital weapon to the arsenal of utilitarianism, and he aided Charles Darwin immeasurably in working out the principle of natural selection. He had no solutions for the problem that he exposed beyond the obvious ones of improved agriculture, more emigration, and prudent marriage. The solutions others would advocate for the problem he exposed would have shocked him to the depth of his simple, well-meaning, benevolent, and pious soul.

Although his name on the issue of rent is soon eclipsed by that of David Ricardo, Malthus was an inciting force in Ricardo's work as well as in that of the group known quite inappropriately as the Malthusians. In 1815 Malthus published his *An Inquiry into the Nature and Progress of Rent*. It is a by-product, in a sense, of his famous book on population. Malthus saw that the increase in population caused an increased demand for agricultural products and hence a rise in their market cost. Better land produced better revenue than poorer land; and Malthus, who was always concerned with the nature of things and not with their alteration, accepted this as a matter of fact, calling this excess of profits "differential rent." He recognized it as a fact without moral significance, and he recognized as another fact the possession by other countries of better farm land than the best in England. Hence he believed that a tariff against foreign agricultural products was justified as a protection to the differential rent from the better English farm and a protection from extinction for the worse ones. Malthus had a country background, not a city one.

DAVID RICARDO

David Ricardo (1772–1823), on the other hand, had a city background. He was the son of a Dutch Jew who had lived successively in Portugal and England, and had achieved very substantial success on the London Stock Exchange. Ricardo was educated in Holland but at the age of fourteen entered his father's business. He entered matrimony and the Church of England in 1793, both steps separating him from his family but neither impairing his native skills. Before he was twenty-five he had become a rich man and had the leisure for the intellectual pursuits that attracted his capacious, fertile, and inquisitive mind. Economics came first, but mathematics and mineralogy were others. In 1811 he met James Mill, and thereafter the influence of the one man on the other was very great. Bentham called Ricardo Mill's disciple, Mill called himself Ricardo's follower. The deduction that intellectually they walked side-by-side is justified. Encouraged by Mill, in 1817 he published his *Principles of Political Economy and Taxation.*

Ricardo took the stand that a food tariff would force more of the bad land into cultivation and, by raising prices, further enrich the owners of the good land. His conclusion, "the interest of the landlord is necessarily opposed to the interest of every other class in the community,"[15] is one of the celebrated and influential conclusions of English economic thought. It was the sort of thinking present in Malthus, however, and not that of Ricardo which currently prevailed. Parliament proceeded to sow the seeds of disaster before the year 1815 was out by passing the Corn Laws, which forbade the importation of foreign grain until domestic grain had skyrocketed to 80 shillings a quarter. Ricardo wrote his *Principles* in the vain attempt to undo the evil implicit in the Corn Laws.

Ricardo divided England roughly into landlords, capitalists, and workers. He believed that Malthus' principle of population increase explained the fact that the profit of the landlords tended to rise at the expense of the profit of the capitalists, and that the wages of the worker tended to sink to the subsistence level. As for moral desserts, Ricardo gave the palm to the capitalist for his brains and second award to the worker for his brawn. Since most land was inherited, luck had done enough for the landlord. To balance things, Ricardo would increase substantially the tax on land and by a policy of free trade increase the profits of capital and the working opportunities of labor. His primary concern, however, was for capital. No one ever held more fervently to the doctrine "What is good for General Motors is good for the country" than David Ricardo.

THE UTILITARIAN CAUSE

Closely related to his theory of rent is his theory of wages and profits, the celebrated wage-fund theory. Ricardo held that there is a fund in a business from which come both profits and wages. As wages rise, profits fall; as profits rise, wages fall, since the wage fund itself remains unchanged. In the total picture of society, however, the size of the wage fund is determined by the cost of producing food. Hence the cost of food is the ultimate determinant of both profits and wages. It is a mechanical view of society, a view so rigidly mechanical as to have been suspect even by some of those who accepted its practical applications. To call Ricardo a conscious believer in the man-made order would be absurd. Philosophic issues were unknown to him. It may even be questioned if he was an unconscious believer in the man-made order. The entire economic order that Ricardo envisages is too mechanical, too automatic, too remote from human control to be considered a man-made order. What we begin to see in David Ricardo is the unconscious foreshadowing of a new kind of natural order, not one of divine making but one that evolves out of the nature of things. Even as we reach the nineteenth-century peak of belief in the man-made order, it begins unconsciously to be undermined by those who might be deemed its conscious adherents. We have seen the same thing happen to belief in the divinely created order in the writings of the deists.

Thus, behind James Mill and the later utilitarians is a body of economic and sociological belief associated with the names of Adam Smith, Thomas Malthus, and David Ricardo. A utilitarian may be assumed to believe in *laissez faire*, in the population-food ratio, in the iniquity of unearned rent, and in the wage-fund concept. By the 1820s the so-called school of Bentham was a reality. James Mill and David Ricardo were its outstanding members; others were Francis Place, J. R. McCulloch, Thomas Tooke, and, with reservations, Henry Brougham. Still others, younger men whose powers and names were crescent, were George Grote, Eyton Tooke, George Graham, William Ellis, John Roebuck, and first and foremost by a margin so great as to be beyond calculation, John Stuart Mill.[16]

Granted that there was a school of Bentham; the question naturally arises, was there a utilitarian cause? There is a sense in which there was, and a sense in which there wasn't, just as it is both true and false that there was a school of Bentham. All those who belonged to what, with a begging of the question, may be termed the school of Bentham accepted the fundamental felicific calculus with its grounding of morality on perceptions of pleasure and pain. Hence all were believers in the man-made order and all were dedicated to the improvement of that order. In that sense there was a utilitarian cause and there was a school of Bentham. The phrases cease to be valid when one seeks among them a single program of reform, but this must not obscure the fact that they were all reformers. The dedication of the Benthamites to diversified good causes is the dedication that Matthew Arnold lampoons under the name of Liberalism in the mischievous last chapter of his *Culture and Anarchy*. But there was a certain unity underlying that diversification. However varied the specific good causes to which individual utilitarians dedicated themselves, they all sought within the limitations of the Benthamite dialectic to better the condition of the common man.

In terms of that fundamental objective, there is a basic utilitarian program into which the specific good causes the utilitarians advanced may be fitted. With all the risks that inaccuracy in details invites, one might say that a member of the school of Bentham was likely to be an active proponent of plans for secular education, with a leaning to the cooperative venture

associated with the name of Joseph Lancaster; he had an awareness of the legal liabilities of the common people and the
way that these legal liabilities made worse their economic handi-
caps, and so he opposed the laws forbidding combinations of
workmen and he favored the Reform Bill, the People's Charter,
and the Anti-Corn Law League; he took his fundamental economics from Adam Smith, Thomas Malthus, and David Ricardo
and therefore believed in *laissez faire*, free trade, the wage fund,
the food-population ratio, and might even believe in birth control; above all he pinned his faith upon the education of the
masses, and so institutes for mechanics and that Oxford for the
common man, London University, were among his most cherished benefactions.

He was a man of good will with all his limitations, a reformer
by instinct and in practice, one who had a philosophy but who
believed that the philosophy was not truly one until it was
translated into action. Hence utilitarianism was far more a course
of action than a pattern of thinking. Since there was no more
fundamental unifying principle in it than a confident belief in
human perfectibility under the felicific calculus, no definite
program ever developed from it. For the same reason no definite
philosophy ever developed from it either; John Stuart Mill is
simultaneously the disciple of Jeremy Bentham and the answer
to him. But when Queen Victoria assumed the throne in 1837
there was in England a group of reformers analogous to the
philosophes, insofar as things English can be analogous to
things French, and equally dedicated to the perfectibility of
the generations by the managed improvement of the man-made
order. In France it led to the guillotine; in England, and
America, it led to a frustration equally complete but unbloody.
The banner bore a strange device, *Laissez faire;* the youth who
bore it would be succeeded by later standard-bearers whose
destination would not be Alpine heights but murky depths.

X

UTILITARIANISM
IN PRACTICE

UTILITARIANISM was a movement of reform, and reformers are men of good will. But reformers can be imprisoned in shackles of their own fashioning, and the utilitarians had beaten out upon the forge of abstract thought a particularly rigid set of intellectual shackles. The early years of utilitarianism were years of hope and promise, but the intellectual rigidity that marked the founders of utilitarianism petrified in the epigoni, as the Germans call the economists who followed Smith, Malthus, Ricardo, Bentham, and Mill. Mr. Gradgrind, of Dickens' *Hard Times*, was a utilitarian of this second generation. He could see the utilitarian heavenly vision, but he could not see what that heavenly vision would be changed to by those in a position to manipulate the utilitarian Utopia. "Did he see himself," Dickens asks, "a white-haired decrepit man, bending his hitherto inflexible theories to appointed circumstances; making his facts and figures subservient to Faith, Hope, and Charity; and no longer trying to grind that Heavenly trio in his dusty little mills? Did he catch sight of himself, therefore much despised by his late political associates? Did he see them, in the era of its being quite settled that the national dustmen have only to do with one another, and owe no duty to an abstraction called a People, 'taunting the honourable gentleman' with this and with that and with what not, five nights a week, until the small hours of the morning." Mr. Gradgrind was an innocent man, a cold, hard, repellent, unattractive, innocent man. He never understood Bounderby. That was the great tragedy of the epigoni. Bounderby understood them, and knew how to manipulate them, but they did not understand Bounderby. Bounderby was a utilitarian devoted to the greatest happiness of Bounderby.

THE REFORM ACT OF 1832

The first great cause of the utilitarians was the Reform Act of 1832. The Reform Act in one sense attained its goal, and in another fell far short of it. It did disfranchise certain minor and minuscule boroughs and it did give many additional seats to the counties and to cities and boroughs not franchised before. Thus it made Commons a much more nearly representative body than it had been. On the other hand it did not make Commons a more democratic body, and it may well be said to have made it less so. There were few workingmen entitled to the franchise as ten-pound householders. It did have the advantage of making the politicians aware of great segments of the English people that they could safely ignore before, and it did break the ice jam behind which were piled up the frustrated forces that would ultimately carry England into universal male suffrage. And the Reform Parliament acted in the spirt of reform; it emancipated slaves in the British dominions, passed an act regulating the labor of factory children, and provided a tiny, token payment for the support of elementary education. The real test of utilitarianism, however, a test alike of the will to reform and of the shackles that checked the will, came in the Poor Law Act of 1834.

The Poor Law Act was largely a utilitarian measure. The Bishop of London was chairman of the commission which studied the problem prior to the writing of the Act, but the most important member of the commission was the utilitarian Nassau Senior. An assistant commissioner more important than his lesser rank suggests was Jeremy Bentham's quondam private secretary Edwin Chadwick. It may or may not be unfair to the commission to point out that amidst all the abuses which it found in the administration of poor relief, and they were there to be discovered, the one that it excoriated most was the practice of feeding people on relief better than independent farmers were able to feed themselves. One link in the chain of utilitarian reasoning was that under no circumstances was the lot of the person on relief to be happier than the lot of the self-employed or self-supporting.

This in itself was not unreasonable. We live in a generation when such Spartan pronouncements are gravely out of fashion, but it could be reasonably argued that one on relief should not live even so modestly high on the hog as do the least of those who pay their own way. But there were other links in the chain of utilitarian reasoning to be considered. There was the wage-fund theory of Ricardo, which was part of the utilitarian credo: wages by nature tended and should tend to the minimum of subsistence. If those on relief were to have a lower living standard than the last and least of those who were self-support-ing, then that standard had to be lower than the iron level of subsistence. There was the food-population theory of Malthus, which was also part of the utilitarian credo: poverty and deg-radation were the inescapable consequences of a birth rate increasing the population by geometric ratio while food produc-tivity increased at a reluctant arithmetic ratio. If the welfare costs were not to swamp the national capacity to meet them, the number of welfare recipients must be cut back at the source.

The Poor Law Amendment Act of 1834 was written by men who saw what no one could deny, manifold corruptions and inequities in poor-law administration. Their motivation was fun-damentally sound, to provide a means of sustenance for those incapable of providing for themselves in a fashion just to both the recipients and the taxpayers who made it possible. But coupled with their motivation was the utilitarian economic creed: no one on relief must fare better than anyone self-supporting, those self-supporting supported themselves at the bare level of subsistence by inexorable economic laws, the trend was from bad to worse as the population rose faster than the food supply. Hence the utilitarian solution: the workhouse in which men and women were rigidly separated. That rigid separation would help to solve the Malthusian problem. Add workhouse cuisine, with oatmeal gruel as its unvarying foundation. That unvarying foun-dation was even more watery than the stewpot in the Lancashire kitchen. Gradgrind had, or thought he had, the facts and figures

on his side; hence Faith, Hope, and Charity were subservient
to them. But Faith, Hope, and Charity cannot be subservient
and survive. There was no Charity, and so Faith dwindled and
disappeared, and then Hope, which always outlasts Faith, also
dwindled and disappeared. Those in the workhouse called it
the Bastille; the oatmeal and gruel was "hell broth"; the Chartists
published *The Murder Book, by Marcus, One of the Three.*
It purported to be the work of one of the commissioners, a
Malthusian, and it called for a national benevolent and protective association of bachelors and old maids commissioned
by law to strangle the newborn children of the paupers. But
the final symbol of that institution, with its case buttressed by
facts and figures, its philosophy founded on principles of Bentham, Malthus, and Ricardo, that instrumentality of utilitarian
reform, the workhouse, was a little boy, a workhouse child,
Oliver Twist asking for more. It was all so simple as Jeremy
Bentham reasoned it out in the Hermitage; it was all so clear
on the pages of Malthus and Ricardo; it was all so logical as
John Stuart Mill and the other earnest young men debated it
pro and con in George Grote's banking rooms early in the
morning, before the heavy doors were opened and properly
attired clerks attended to the fiscal transactions of Englishmen
who were exempt from the economic laws of Malthus and
Ricardo. It was all so different in the workhouse, where the
guardian of the poor was not a "cautious, statistical Christ"
operating the establishment on Benthamite principles but rather
Mr. Bumble, and the final fact was Oliver Twist finally asking
for more. The theory is in Bentham, but the reality was in
Bumble. The workhouse was an instrumentality of reform; the
entire history of the man-made order contains no fact more
ironic than that. Yet the devastating failure of the workhouse
should not obscure the success of other Benthamite causes. One
successful good cause with considerable Benthamite backing was
the Anti-Corn Law League.

The first corn laws (the word *corn* has its English meaning,
the small grains) were passed to lower the price of corn; they
were prohibitions on the exportation of food. Then agricultural
England discovered that the sword had two edges, and the
granting of bounties and a heavy tax on imports were used to

raise the price of corn. In 1773 Edmund Burke tried to stabilize the situation by imposing a nominal import duty of sixpence when the domestic price of wheat reached 48s. a quarter, and stopping both the freedom to export and the bounty on export when it fell to 44s. a quarter. The difficulty with Burke's Act of 1773 was that it threatened to work, an outcome viewed dimly both by those who wanted more expensive wheat and those who wanted less expensive. The political atmosphere engendered in England by the French Revolution and intensified by the Napoleonic Wars favored those who wanted more expensive wheat, and in 1815 a law was passed forbidding importation until domestic wheat reached 80s. a quarter.

This bit of pious protectionism failed only because the domestic price obstinately refused to rise that high, and so a sliding scale of duties was devised. But the days of the Corn Law concept were numbered by the Reform Bill of 1832, now that the industrial cities had a voice in Parliament. In 1839 the Anti-Corn Law League was formed at Manchester, with its inspiring genius Richard Cobden and his right bower John Bright. Cobden, not a utilitarian himself, was a master of that fusion of moralistic and economic argumentation for which the English have a racial aptitude, and there was a nice blend of moral denunciation and economic rationalization in his eloquent propaganda. This is precisely the blend that is native utilitarianism, and such prominent utilitarians as Joseph Hume and Sir John Bowring served in the ranks of the Anti-Corn Law League and on occasion carried its banners to high place. Logic and justice were on their side, and all they needed was votes. Logic, justice, the conversion to the cause of Robert Peel, and the devastating famine of 1845 gave them the votes, and in 1846 the corn laws passed into oblivion. To call it a utilitarian victory would be to put things out of focus, but it was a victory to which utilitarian reasoning and action contributed.

THE CHARTIST MOVEMENT

On the other hand the utilitarian position where the Chartist movement was concerned was by its nature intellectually precarious if not utterly untenable. The Chartist movement started in 1838, reached its climax in 1848, and in one sense collapsed the same year. In another sense, it was perpetuated in the trade union movement and made its contribution to the ideology of the Labour Party. The Reform Bill of 1832, as we have seen, by no means enfranchised a larger percentage of working-class England than had enjoyed the vote before; it extended the franchise more widely geographically speaking, but not sociologically speaking. The resultant disillusionment and dissatisfaction in working ranks gave rise to the Chartist movement with its celebrated six points: annual parliaments, universal male suffrage, the ballot, abolition of a property proviso for membership in Commons, equal electoral districts, and payment of members of Parliament. It came to its climax in 1848, the year of revolution. There had been rumblings in Glasgow, Edinburgh, and Manchester, but the main thrust was reserved by the Chartists for London. Half a million people were to assemble on Kennington Common on April 10, to march on Parliament with a petition for the People's Charter bearing six million names. The procession was forbidden, the militia was called out to foil the projected march, public buildings were put under a state of siege, and some 170,000 special constables were sworn in. If it was to be an English Revolution, it was a revolution to be handled English-style.

It was a revolution, English-style. Not half a million but about fifty thousand met on Kennington Common. No one really wanted to take the initiative and start a march on Parliament. And so the tumbrils rolled, English-style, as a dignified procession of hansom cabs moved in battle formation to Parliament, bearing the petition that bore six million names. But it didn't bear six million names, and many of the names it did bear were clearly forged. It was a fiasco, distressing anyone who would prefer a revolution French-style to a fiasco English-style. Thereafter the Chartist movement quietly evaporated. The cause was lost but not the specific causes. All the provisos of the People's Charter have long since been the unquestioned law of the land except the equal electoral districts, an Elysian condition more apt to be realized in the kingdom of Heaven than in any earthly realm, England included.

To such a movement as Chartism the utilitarian position had

to be equivocal. On the one hand the specific points of the People's Charter were well within the scope of utilitarian desiderata; on the other hand, the utilitarian dedication to classical economics very thoroughly tempered any utilitarian dedication to Chartist aims. To be both a utilitarian and believer in classical economics, and to be a friend of the workingman and a supporter of his economic and social advancement required a capacity for ideological straddling beyond the powers of the most dexterous. Hence in practice the utilitarians who devoted themselves to the Chartist cause simply forgot their utilitarian tenets for the duration.

FRANCIS PLACE

Involved in the Chartist movement, indeed the author of the Charter itself, is a figure who for the intriguing aspects of his career as well as for the way he illustrates the truth that utilitarianism was less a philosophy than a plan of action deserves to be resurrected from the oblivion which has engulfed him and most of his contemporaries. Francis Place (1771–1854) was another man like Priestley and Paine born in a class-conscious society far below the level to which his native talents would lead him to aspire. Such men are the natural recruits for revolutions, and it is perhaps the highest tribute to the fundamental soundness of Francis Place that he had his chance to be a revolutionist and rejected it. His father had run a sponging house where men were held for debt. Young Francis was apprenticed to a maker of leather breeches and in time became a maker of leather breeches himself and an organizer of those in the craft. For this abortive venture into what might by anticipation be called trade unionism he was blacklisted by the masters and suffered severely as a result. At the age of twenty-three he joined the radical London Corresponding Society, the secretary of which, Thomas Hardy, was the defendant in one of the most famous treason trials of English history. Francis Place could have joined Hardy, Thelwall, Godwin, and the others of the school of Rousseau, but he chose not to do so.

In 1799 he opened a tailor's shop in Charing Cross and prospered mightily. As time went on and his prosperity increased, he became interested in public affairs. About 1812 he became friendly with James Mill, and through him met Jeremy Bentham. Thereafter his career is the typical career of the utilitarian in active life. With the other utilitarians he sided with Joseph Lancaster in the rivalry between his school system and that of Bell, helping Lancaster organize the West London Lancasterian Society. His greatest political triumph came in 1824, when he led the fight for the repeal of the laws against combinations of workmen, the anti-labor union statutes that came in with the post-Napoleonic period of reaction. Place was a practical politician who knew that his role was behind the scenes. He became a mighty supplier of facts and arguments for those who mounted the hustings; in 1826 an article in the *European Magazine* called him the true power behind the throne among the electors of Westminster. He threw all his oblique and hidden strength to the support of the Reform Bill, and was satisfied that others have the honor for its passage. In 1838 he drafted the People's Charter, although personal unpopularity with its working-class backers kept him from an active part in the early struggle of Chartism. Workingman England is also conservative England, and his highly unorthodox ideas made him suspect even among those for whose interests he worked with single-minded energy for decades. His worst offense would seem to have been his espousal of what was known politely as neo-Malthusianism; support of birth control was something far beyond the imaginative powers of working-class England, and in simple justice something must be said for its perplexity at Place's advocacy of birth control. The most conservative estimate makes him the father of fifteen children, and some say seventeen.

His last days were worthy of the rest, spent in active support of the Anti-Corn Law League until protracted illness struck him down. Francis Place is typical of the utilitarian in action: support for the Reform Bill, the People's Charter, the Anti-Corn League. Thus utilitarianism is never understood until one realizes that it is not so much a philosophy as a plan of action. What Place supported were the typical utilitarian causes; the roster becomes familiar as one goes through the utilitarians and their activities. He was a man of action, but also a man of words.

It is tragic but true that an all-encompassing dullness shrouds his writings. Hence the bookshelves contain one book from his pen, *The Principles of Population* (1822), and the shelves of the British Museum are reported to groan beneath seventy-one of his unprinted manuscripts.

When Francis Place dedicated himself to the Chartist cause, he did so as a workingman himself and the son of a workingman. The fact that he was also a utilitarian simply was not a factor in the situation. Similarly, the parliamentarian and scholar of Greek history, George Grote, devoted himself to the specific cause of the ballot, one of the primary Chartist objectives, but he did it as a matter of intellectual conviction, not as a follower of Chartist thought on the one hand or of utilitarian thought on the other. John Arthur Roebuck was another strong advocate of the ballot, and an advocate of a more democratic spirit in the ordering of public affairs. In general, the contributions of the utilitarians to the Chartist cause and in the broader sense to the advancement of the working classes were limited in scope and individual in nature. They tended to center about the desirability of the ballot, a limited and specific cause to which a utilitarian could readily devote himself without impairing his dedication to classical economics.

THE LANCASTERIAN SCHOOLS

There is no area of reform in which the contributions of the utilitarians were so valuable or so lasting as education. It is true that some of them chased an impossible pedagogic will-o'-the-wisp in the Lancasterian schools, but this failure cannot obscure their very real success elsewhere. And even the Lancasterian schools were not total failures, if a charitable view is taken of the inevitable gap between the aspirations of their founder and the possibilities of his methods, and then extended to what they actually did achieve. Joseph Lancaster (1778–1838) was a poor boy of unusual seriousness and aspiration toward learning. He got the rudiments, and he wished to extend them to others. At the age of twenty he was running his own free school under his father's roof, supported by a pittance from parents able and willing to pay it. He had an idea that was systematic, economical, and theoretically productive of the greatest educational good of the greatest possible number, an idea with all the utilitarian virtues and one calculated to enlist utilitarian support.

Lancaster's idea was to train the brightest children first, to inspire them with a sense of *noblesse oblige*, and to set them to work teaching the others. Before long he had a thousand students, and before much longer there were Lancasterian schools in many industrial towns. Joseph Lancaster was even honored by an interview with his gracious and semi-enlightened Majesty George III, who expressed the pious hope that every child in his realm might be taught to read the Bible and the confident belief that the Lancasterian schools were the places in which they might attain this Utopian ideal. The *Edinburgh Review*, with that rapturous enthusiasm for cut-rate education which is one of the most reliable hallmarks of the economic conservative, hailed the Lancasterian device as "a beautiful and inestimable discovery, a plan now brought very near to perfection, by which education could be placed within the reach of all classes." If ever a device was designed to spread the light of learning, one utilitarian objective, within the framework of classical economics, a utilitarian shibboleth, it was the Lancasterian school. Understandably, Francis Place helped Lancaster establish the West London Lancasterian Society, William Ellis devoted himself to mass education, and other utilitarians saw in Lancaster's schools a solution to the problem of mass education. Furthermore, since the Bible was the basic textbook of the Lancasterian schools, unsupported by any catechism of any church, there was a natural attraction in Lancaster's system for deists, ultraliberal churchmen, and such Whigs and nonconformists as had by instinct a bias in the utilitarian direction.

Difficulties arose from the improvident, extravagant, and unreliable character of Lancaster himself, a man of good will but austerely limited prudence and common sense. The basic trouble, however, was that the system did not work. Children who had just learned something, or partly learned it, or had met it in the classroom, were incapable of going into another classroom and teaching it to their equals. The children in the Lancasterian schools were able to stumble through parts of the

Bible, but to read nothing else, and their educations ended with a very partial realization of the pious ideal of their gracious sovereign George III. Yet at their worst the Lancasterian schools did bring under the roof of schools children to whom schooling would otherwise have been totally unknown. They did teach quite a bit to the bright little monitors who were the teachers, since no form of learning is nearly so effective as being forced to teach what one barely knows himself. The teachers certainly learned more than the taught, and perhaps in some vague and half-formed way all learned that a school is a place of mutual endeavor and that scholarship is a community enterprise. Not much can be said for the Lancasterian schools, nor can support of them be called a utilitarian triumph, but perhaps they were not total failures.

The other contributions of the utilitarians to education were sound and constructive. The workingmen's institutes, the institutes for mechanics, the vocational institutions of one sort or another that appeared in Victorian England did so with steady and dedicated utilitarian support. This was the sort of thing that Dr. Gradgrind could understand and do, and he did it very well. Above the workingmen's institutes was that institution which was, at least in aspiration, the workingmen's college. The University of London was a prime benefaction of George Grote and other utilitarians, and one of the great educational institutions of twentieth-century England owes an incalculable debt to the utilitarians who could see that the need for higher education could not be met entirely within the storied Gothic of Oxford and that a secular age required also a secular education. One may at least hope that repairs have been completed on the mummy of Jeremy Bentham and that the father of utilitarianism looks benignly on the institution that owes so much of its being to those who followed in his train, just as one may hope that the spirit of Thomas Jefferson looks down from Monticello upon the American university which he brought into being.

All in all, the record of the utilitarians in reform is not what they dreamed it might be, but neither is it a record to be read with contempt. The Reform Act of 1832, which had much utilitarian support, did not do everything its proponents hoped of it, but it did free the slaves, help the factory children, and make the politicians aware that disfranchised England was not quite so helpless as it had been before. The Poor Law Act was the supreme utilitarian failure, and a failure for reasons implicit in the utilitarian rationale. Malthusianism, Ricardian economics, and the approach through caution and statistics are incompatible with Faith, Hope, and Charity, and it was these three that the poor of England needed. On the other hand the Corn Laws were scandalous survivals of what was always a dubious economic theory, and the utilitarians at least made a contribution to their abolishment. The position of the utilitarians in the Chartist movement could not avoid being equivocal; just as Faith, Hope, and Charity are incompatible with Malthusianism and Ricardian economics, so classical economics in general was inconsistent with the economic objectives of the Chartists. Hence individual utilitarians could support such specific and noneconomic Chartist objectives as the ballot and the annual Parliament, but the fundamental philosophy of Chartism and the fundamental philosophy of utilitarianism could not be reconciled. Finally, there remains the most important fact of all. Men of good will, ranging from economic ultraconservatives like Carlyle to philosophic liberals like John Stuart Mill, saw, proclaimed, and strove to advance the cause of education. Here the record of the utilitarians is entirely honorable and marked by very substantial success. The Lancasterian schools were conducted on a fallacy, but the workingmen's institutes were not, nor were the institutes for mechanics or the University of London. The utilitarians did achieve notable triumphs in the world of education.

It is very important to attempt justice to the constructive and disinterested side of utilitarianism, because the manipulation of utilitarian concepts in the mid-nineteenth century and later could easily lead one to think, and indeed has led many to think, that it had no constructive and disinterested side. Not without reason did Viscount Morley write in 1870 that Victorian England was "a paradise for the well-to-do, a purgatory for the able, and a hell for the poor." It was not that the economic blessed in paradise enjoyed the spectacle of the tortured striving of the impecunious able and the apathetic degradation of the

hopeless poor. It was simply that the blinders of utilitarian thinking protected them from the appalling vision. "Laissez-faire and
Devil take the hindmost" was Carlyle's way of putting it. If
the poor suffered it was part of the inexorable order of things.
The person who so reasoned, even if his conscious viewpoint
were fashioned in the very sanctuary at Canterbury itself, had
a subconscious and real viewpoint based upon classical economics
and utilitarian ethics. The greatest good of the greatest number
is achieved by the unimpeded action of free economic forces.
The greatest good of the greatest number is the reality achieved
by *laissez faire;* all the rest, the sorrow and the suffering, the
degradation, the degeneration, the despair, must somehow be an
illusion. In any case, it will pass away since progress is the
inevitable rule of life. Observe the progress we have had already.

MACAULAY

No one observed it more acutely and recorded it with greater
certainty and vigor than that supremely endowed representative
of the economic blessed, Baron Macaulay of Rothley. There can
be no doubt that Macaulay was on the side of the angels or, to
put it more accurately, that the angels were on the side of
Macaulay. His father, Zachary Macaulay, was a sincere and
energetic reformer, a tireless foe of the slave trade, a prominent
evangelical churchman, editor of the *Christian Observer.* Macaulay breathed the air of humanitarianism from the day of
his birth, was suckled on the milk of reform and waxed strong
on food of the spirit. Since Macaulay never doubted anything,
least of all his own convictions, he never doubted that he was a
humanitarian, a reformer, a man of spiritual outlook and even
vision. Every fiber of his being recoiled in horror at the thought
of worshiping a golden calf, but the economic blessed of
Macaulay's stamp never suspected that a steam engine might
be a golden calf. It was certainly Macaulay's intent to hear the
still, small voice, but the still, small voice Macaulay heard was
that of Adam Smith. And so Macaulay, who could and did
speak with the tongue of angels and never suspected that his
message was other than angelic, preached the gospel according
to St. Jeremy Bentham and St. Adam Smith. That government

is best which governs least; government exists to protect person and property; the greatest good of the greatest number is achieved by *laissez faire;* England is earth's fairest province and the nineteenth is the greatest of centuries, although the twentieth will be greater; there are no real values but pragmatic values. "An acre of Middlesex is better than a principality in Utopia" is his own concise summary. Baron Macaulay, who thought that he believed sincerely and even fervently in the divinely created order, really believed in nothing of the sort. He was the totally innocent Philistine of Matthew Arnold, with his cloak of Dissenter Protestantism flung over his head protecting his vision from what Matthew Arnold and Thomas Carlyle could see with crystal clarity, the fundamental materialism on which his entire fabric of thinking rested. The paradox must remain.

There was in England only one Macaulay, but the followers of Macaulay were legion. In theory they were still churchmen. In practice they were still churchgoers. In their consciously held beliefs they were still supporters of the divinely created order. But they had accepted as the foundation of their effective beliefs the sheer materialism of Jeremy Bentham and his school and the classical economics which dovetailed with it with such devastating perfection. It would never occur to Macaulay to suspect a scintilla of inconsistency between his protestations of religious faith and his statement in a review of Robert Southey's *Colloquies:* "It is true that the Christian religion sanctions government, as it sanctions everything which promotes the happiness and virtue of our species. But we are at a loss to conceive in what sense religion can be said to be the basis of government, in which religion is not also the basis of the practices of eating, drinking, and lighting fires in cold weather."[1] It is entirely in keeping with his viewpoint as one of the economic blessed that he be quietly unmoved by protestations of suffering from the depths, and somewhat bored by them. "We must take into the account the liberty of discussion, and the strong interest which the opponents of a ministry always have to exaggerate the extent of the public disasters. . . . In the old world we must confess ourselves unable to find any satisfactory record of any great nation, past or present, in which the working classes have been in a more comfortable situation than in England during the last thirty years."[2]

It is totally within the pattern of his thought that he trust the greatest happiness of the greatest number to the mystical effectiveness of *laissez faire*. "Our rulers will best promote the improvement of the nation by strictly confining themselves to their own legitimate duties, by leaving capital to find its most lucrative course, commodities their fair price, industry and intelligence their natural reward, idleness and folly their natural punishment, by maintaining peace, by defending property, by diminishing the price of law, and by observing strict economy in every department of the State. Let the Government do this: the People will assuredly do the rest."[3]

Macaulay was to his generation what Alexander Pope had been to his. His was the voice of authority, in both senses of the word. The absolute clarity of his style, the absolute tone of his utterance, the absolute quality of his dogmatism made his message one that no man could mistake and no man could dispute with impunity. Macaulay, with one of the most inconceivably capacious memories in human record, with one of the most extraordinary powers for marshaling facts and arraying evidence in the annals of rhetoric, could and did blast his opponents with thermonuclear completeness. The upper classes could bask in the sunlight of his utterance, a sunlight that soothed and quieted consciences that might have disturbed their owners if Macaulay did not assure them that there was nothing to be disturbed about, or very little, or nothing that would not be righted soon by the natural play of natural economic forces operating for the greatest happiness of the greatest number. And as for the lower classes, very little sunlight penetrated to them. Very little sunlight penetrated to women and children who went to work in the mills before sunrise, worked through the livelong day in the phantasmagoria of whirling machines and shrieking engines, worked with throbbing heads in the half-light that sifted through the grime-stained little windows high on the blackened walls, and staggered into the fetid streets long after sunset. Very little sunlight sifted into the narrow alleys with the roofs that almost met above their filthy depths, the abodes of such practitioners of *laissez faire* as Bill

Sikes and the Artful Dodger, and what was worse, the abodes of the innocent and helpless ones, the abode of Oliver Twist and Little Jo the crossing sweep. Macaulay spoke with the tongue of an upper-class angel, but Charles Dickens with the tongue of an avenging angel.

The point to note is that Macaulay, the churchman, the Whig, or may we now say the Liberal, the unconscious believer in the man-made order, preached the gospel of Jeremy Bentham fused with the gospel of Adam Smith. Dickens, who did not go to church, whose politics are not a matter of record, who never pretended to anything so dignified as a philosophy, preached the gospel of Christ. Technically Macaulay, who inherited the Dissenter tradition, was reared in the Clapham sect, and became publicist for the viewpoint which had started with an instinct for reform, should have been the spokesman for reform. But utilitarianism, just as truly as deism, degenerated with amazing suddenness from a reform movement to something very different. The utilitarian objective, the greatest happiness of the greatest number, became fused with *laissez faire*, with the food-population ratio and the wage-fund theory. When it did, it ceased to be a movement of reform and became a palliative for those whose private interests favored the *status quo*. It may never have occurred to Macaulay that he was really in the tradition of Jeremy Bentham and James Mill, but he was. That tradition had become the moralistic adjunct to the tradition of Adam Smith. D. C. Somervell puts it very well indeed: "Politically Macaulay was a Whig rather than a Benthamite. He was the kind of reformer who approved the reforms already enacted without demanding any more."[4]

THE EVANGELICAL UTILITARIANS

Macaulay was unique among his kind only in the quality of his utterance. By no test of logic or philosophic consistency should a product of the Clapham sect be even a subconscious Benthamite, unless of course he disowned his religious birthright. But devotion to logic and philosophic consistency are not common human virtues, and perhaps they are a little less common in England than in some other countries. Be this true or false, a surprising number of evangelicals managed to be utilitarians as well, managing the logical and philosophical straddle by a blessed unawareness of its existence. There was, of course, a common denominator for the two in devotion to reform. It was not entirely illogical for a devout evangelical who opposed human slavery, who opposed pluralism of holdings in the Church, who favored the repeal of the Corn Laws and the expansion of educational opportunity, to see a brother in the Benthamite who favored the same good causes. But there was a deeper link between the two than devotion to specific good causes. Utilitarianism is atomistic in the very nature of its basic thesis: the greatest happiness of the greatest number is achieved where there is the maximum of individual liberty, and Government exists to make it more easily attainable. Evangelicalism is similarly atomistic: the greatest opportunity for salvation rests in the direct relationship of the individual soul with the Infinite, and the Church exists to make it more easily attainable. Tradition did not enter the calculations of either the utilitarian or the evangelical, but a very doctrinaire and narrow *Weltanschauung* did. In the last analysis they pursued respectively prosperity and piety in much the same spirit, and it is not surprising that sometimes the scent of the one was confused with the scent of the other. To distinguish the evangelical from the utilitarian in Matthew Arnold's Philistine is not always a simple task. One should recall that Jeremy Bentham made God a utilitarian.

On the other hand it was next to unknown for an Anglo-Catholic to be a utilitarian. For one thing, the common denominator of reform was hardly present. Individual Anglo-Catholics were devoted to individual good causes, sometimes in a most admirable spirit of dedication and self-sacrifice, but reform and progress were not High Church watchwords. For another thing, Anglo-Catholicism was the opposite of atomistic and indeed had an instinctive bias in the direction of socialism rather than of utilitarianism, as the emergence of Christian Socialism proved. In its good and bad days alike there has been a comfortable latitude to the Church of England, a comfortable breadth and depth to its outlook which may keep it from being spiritually inflammatory but also keeps it from being doctrinaire. A well-bred High Churchman might not confuse charity with religion, but neither would he confuse religion with economics. When there appeared what Somervell calls "a body of thought which challenged, on religious grounds, the whole organization of industrial society, and denied, in the name of the Gospels, the principles of orthodox economics, *laissez-faire,* and competitive marketing,"[5] it was expounded from Anglo-Catholic and not from evangelical pulpits. Thomas Arnold, Frederick Denison Maurice, and Arthur Stanley were Broad Churchmen, but they had more in common with Newman and Pusey than they had with the evangelicals, and infinitely more than they had with the utilitarians.

The legislation of the era, however, was utilitarian legislation passed with Evangelical backing. It was Liberal in the only historic meaning of the word: it was founded on the principle that the free man should have the maximum of individual freedom for self-advancement. It carried as its corollary that such freedom promoted the greatest happiness of the greatest number. The Reform Acts, Corn Law repeal, the Poor Law Act, and the Act of 1870 which established state schools were such acts. But the Factory Acts were not Liberal. They impinged on the freedom of women and children to work the fourteen-hour day. The Health of Towns Act was not Liberal; it impinged on the freedom of local communities to disregard health menaces. Not without good reason did the London *Times* rejoice when it was defeated. "We prefer to take our chance of cholera and the rest, rather than to be bullied into health," The Thunderer editorially proclaimed. Self-help was the ideal of the day, as Somervell points out; and Samuel Smiles, who wrote *Self-Help* and followed it with *Thrift, Character, Duty,* and a series of biographies illustrating what in America is known as the Horatio Alger story, sold his volumes by the tens of thousands. It was anti-Liberals like Shaftesbury (the seventh of that notable and diversified line) who found help for others who needed help a nobler cause, and so devoted himself to the women and children in the mills. Anthony Ashley Cooper, seventh Earl of Shaftesbury, with the assurance of one who has had earth-shakers in his ancestry from the days of bonny Prince Charles, called down all the brimstone of heaven upon the utilitarians, their works and pomps. Today, from the vantage point of just about a century, it is Shaftesbury who appears the reformer, the progressive, the advanced thinker, the humanitarian, dare we say the Liberal, and not his utilitarian foes.

The melancholy truth is that utilitarianism had gone precisely the same way that deism had gone a century before. It began as a reform movement, an adjustment to the new age. It did achieve a respectable measure of reform. But it was grounded on the concept of the man-made order and so entered an instinctive and probably inevitable alliance with an economics similarly grounded. Before long the reform motive was gone and nothing remained of it but a sort of moralistic protective coloration for the economics. In the literal sense the Liberal Party was the product of a fusion of the Whigs and Radicals in the 1830s, but the family tree of Liberalism shows that it was the child of utilitarianism and *laissez faire*. Blood will tell, and the blood of Liberalism soon told. Reform in the real sense was left to an ill-assorted group with nothing much in common but a love of their fellow man. Shaftesbury bore one of the proudest titles in English history, and bore it proudly for the sake of the nameless women and children in the factories. Dickens moved from a blacking factory into immortality, but he remembered the David Copperfield he left behind in the factory. Elizabeth Barrett in her darkened sickroom could hear "The Cry of the Children." John Ruskin, sheltered aesthete and heir to a massive fortune, spent half his life and all his fortune on the welfare of the nameless people of the island. Anglo-Catholic priests whose names are now only of heavenly record went into the place Dickens called Tom-All-Alone's, the ultimate slums where Jo the crossing sweep existed. They had no common denominator except the love of their fellow man, and the belief that the order which existed in nineteenth-century England was not His order. They served Christ, but not the cautious, statistical Christ of the Liberals.

XI

ETHICS
BY NATURAL SELECTION

IT MAY reasonably be questioned if the English-speaking world
has ever been asked in one century to revise and reject so much
of its previously unquestioned thinking as it was in the nineteenth. The century opened with very few people directly and
explicitly questioning the divinely created order, and relatively
few questioning it even in the unsensed tenor of their reasoning.
Most Englishmen and Americans accepted a literal reading of
the opening chapters of Genesis as part of their religious belief.
This reading was clear and neither required interpretation nor
admitted of it: God created the universe and all the creatures
in it, including man, in six days, and the species were fixed and
unchangeable from the moment of creation. John Milton conceived the act of creation as a miraculous growth from the earth
itself, in a nice blend of poetic fantasy and religious dogma.
God spoke:

> The earth obeyed, and straight
> Opening her fertile womb teemed at a birth
> Innumerous living creatures, perfect forms
> Limbed and full grown: out of the ground uprose
> As from his lair the wild beast where he wonns. . . .
> The grassy clods now calved, now half appeared
> The tawny lion, pawing to get free
> His hinder parts, then springs as broke from bonds,
> And rampant shakes his brinded mane; the ounce,
> The libbard, and the tiger, as the mole
> Rising, the crumbled earth above them threw
> In hillocks; the swift stag from under ground
> Bore up his branching head. . . .[1]

Thus John Milton conceived the divinely created order in the hour of creation, and in some such sense men continued to regard it in the year 1800.

Allied with this poetic concept of creation as a miraculous bringing into being of the divinely created order was the concept of the golden age, a concept partly the product of the Garden of Eden in Genesis and partly a product of classical mythology. We have already met the state of nature as a sort of golden age, although not in Hobbes and his ilk. "The first age was the golden age" is the opening half-line of Ovid's *Metamorphoses,* and the statement of the Latin poet accords with Genesis and the description of the Garden of Eden and the innocence of man before the Fall. Man's present depraved state is the result of Adam's sin, and any progress that the optimistic may perceive in society is but a painful and very incomplete clambering back to where Adam stood. Even when Christianity itself was rejected, the concept of the golden age tended to survive. It is at the very heart of Rousseau's thinking, with its doctrine that man is good by nature but made evil by society. The concept of the goodness of man in the state of nature had its obvious appeal to the primitivism which is one aspect of the romantic movement. Wordsworth believed fully that nature can teach moral lessons beyond the ken of saint and sage, when he wrote:

> One impulse from a vernal wood
> May teach you more of man,
> Of moral evil and of good
> Than all the sages can.

Later, to be sure, he changed his view.

To these fundamental and, in the main, unquestioned concepts of the direct and separate creation by God of the species as they now exist and the golden age of primitive innocence, whether one conceives it as a state of nature in Biblical terms or in the pseudohistorical terms of Rousseau, must be added a third concept. Bishop James Ussher (1581–1656) had worked out in his *Annals of the Old and New Testament* a chronological history of the world from the six days of creation to the age of Vespasian. He had determined the year of creation to be 4004 B.C. and this and the other dates of his chronology were habitually printed in the margins of English Bibles.

THE AGE OF CHARLES DARWIN

Thus we reach the year 1800 with the overwhelming majority of Englishmen and Americans believing that God created the world in 4004 B.C., in six days; that he created the species as they now exist, in permanent and unchangeable form; that he created man in a state of innocence and that the first age was indeed the golden age, but man sinned and fell and Adam's sin brought to mankind its trials and tribulations. Even those who rejected the entire Judaeo-Christian tradition took refuge in a golden age concept of their own, a state of nature clearly indebted to the golden age concept of the ancients. When we reached the year 1860, people are being asked to believe that the world was not created in 4004 B.C. but has existed for unmeasured epochs, that species are not fixed but constantly changing with next to infinite slowness into other species, and that the original state of man upon the earth was considerably closer to that of the apes in the trees than of Adam and Eve in Paradise.

The last concept was, of course, the most earth-shaking of all. It was one thing, even if a hard thing, to change one's belief to the conviction that God did not create the plants and animals each after his kind but that they slowly differentiate into a multiplicity of species through the operation of impersonal natural laws. The last concept to be shaken, the last to be relinquished, the one in which relinquishment would seem relinquishment of all that mattered, was the concept that God had created man after His image and likeness. Perhaps man started in neither the Garden of Eden of Genesis nor the state of nature of Rousseau. Perhaps he started in the branches of the trees, or perhaps that is far too lofty a state for his primordial condition. Perhaps he started in the slime, in the bottom of the sea. Perhaps he started as an animalcule, something one can see through a powerful microscope, or perhaps as vaguely waving antennae swayed by the stream of ocean. It should, of course, have bred the sort of profound humility that paradoxically gives birth to an upsurge of the spirit. The English-speaking peoples, however, are mysteriously protected from that kind of humility. It actually bred in those who accepted the animalcule hypothesis the thrill of superiority that only the scientist knows as he contemplates the uninitiated. It produced thinkers of the breed of Herbert Spencer, whose brow no wrinkles furrowed despite the incessant nature of his thinking. "I suppose it is because I am never puzzled," Spencer told George Eliot, who was puzzled.[2]

We can scarcely undertake an outline of the scientific advances of the nineteenth century, to which the English-speaking peoples contributed more than any other people of the earth. The Victorian age was the age of the chemists Dalton and Faraday, the anatomist Owen, the botanist Hooker. It was the age of Simpson and Lister in surgery, of Lyell in geology, and preeminently from both our viewpoint and the viewpoint of greatest historic importance it was the age of Charles Darwin. These men tore down and then rebuilt much of the framework of scientific thought. When their work was done, insofar as it is done, some ideas persisted, some were modified, some developed new and unexpected mutations, and some disappeared. Perhaps the most important intellectual result of the new science was a substantial disappearance of the old dichotomy between man and nature, the appearance of a new concept of natural law, to be differentiated as an explanation of the conditions of human life from both the concept of the divinely created order and the concept of the man-made order. Belief in progress persisted, but now it was belief in progress by evolution, belief in progress as a necessary and inevitable part of a world order that had come into its present state from lower forms by evolution and was destined to evolve with nearly infinite slowness into higher forms. Darwin, after viewing the vista down time's interminable corridor of the past, had taken the view down time's other corridor and made the promise: "Hence we may look with some confidence to a secure future of equally inappreciable length. And as natural selection works solely by and for the good of each being, all corporeal and mental endowments will tend to progress toward perfection."[3] The new thought has its roots extending securely into the old soil. There is determinism in Darwin, as the above statement indicates, but there is utilitarianism as well. There is a viewpoint, one which Darwin himself held, from which evolution guarantees the attainment of the utilitarian objective.

THOMAS HENRY HUXLEY

But not all the Darwinians believed this, not even the most important Darwinian of them all, Thomas Henry Huxley (1825–1895). Huxley could not see that evolution automatically made for perfection; he saw natural selection—or survival of the fittest, to use the more graphic and less pleasant phrase—as the method of elimination that the jungle employs. The state of nature was a state of Hobbesian war, and the history of civilization is the history of man's attempts to escape from the state of nature. "The ideal of the ethical man is to limit his freedom of action to a sphere in which he does not interfere with the freedom of others; he seeks the commonweal as much as his own; and, indeed, as an essential part of his own welfare. Peace is both end and means with him; and he founds his life on a more or less complete self-restraint, which is the negation of the unlimited struggle for existence. He tries to escape from his place in the animal kingdom, founded on the free development of the principle of nonmoral evolution, and to establish a kingdom of Man, governed upon the principle of moral evolution. For society not only has a moral end, but in its perfection, social life, is embodied morality."[4]

Huxley, then, is a Darwinian with a difference, even if he proclaimed himself Darwin's bulldog and tried valiantly and successfully to fit the part. Huxley was an evolutionist without being a moral determinist. He believed that "much can be done to change the nature of man himself." Huxley believed that ethics are man-made, and thus that ethical progress differs in its fundamentals from cosmic progress. Henceforth, as we trace the development of the concept of the man-made order, we must be aware of those who deny its fundamentals from two starkly contrasting points of view. One is the familiar point of view, the historic concept of natural law held by believers in the divinely created order. The other is the new viewpoint, not the creation of Charles Darwin to be sure, but a viewpoint enormously advanced by the inferences to be drawn either legitimately or illegitimately from *The Origin of Species*. This is the new concept of natural law, the deterministic concept of morals as some-

thing automatically and unalterably evolved by natural processes. Between the two is the believer in the man-made order,
but henceforth his thinking will be influenced by the trains of
thought that operate now to the left as well as to the right of his
own. Since Huxley, as Frederick Roe well puts it in the Preface to
his admirable anthology, *Victorian Prose,* "the ethical process is
itself a human creation and thus, like all else in man, a product
of nature and nature's evolutionary method, one may say that
those Victorians were not mistaken who assumed that the survival
of the fittest in the struggle for existence at long last must mean
the survival of the ethically strongest and best."[5] The true believer in the man-made order henceforth must walk a tightrope.
On the one hand he can lapse from secular grace and fall into
the camp of the religious believers, on the other hand he can
slip into determinism and forfeit his birthright of free will. His
thought has always to some extent borne the hallmarks of the
older natural law concepts; henceforth it will bear also the hallmarks of the newer natural law. Unadulterated utilitarianism has
disappeared. The utilitarians who survive will either try to
salvage the old creed by blending it with values proper to the
natural law creed, as did John Stuart Mill, or they will gradually
coalesce with the new scientific generation and emerge as social
Darwinians. No man better illustrates the earlier stage of the latter transition, in both the characteristics of his thinking and the
quality, than Thomas Henry Huxley, for reasons that the facts of
his life reveal.

Huxley was born at Ealing in 1825, son of the local schoolmaster. His formal education was limited except in the field of
medicine; Huxley was self-taught with a seldom-attained pre-
cision. The undirected but intensive reading of his youth was
followed by the study of medicine at London University, where
he graduated in 1845 with his medical degree. There followed
the cruise on the *Rattlesnake,* on which he held the post of assistant surgeon and filled unofficially and sometimes secretly
the role that Charles Darwin filled on the more celebrated but
not dissimilar voyage of the *Beagle.* Darwin had embarked on
the *Beagle* in 1831, for five rapturous years of absorption in the
study of natural phenomena. Huxley embarked on the *Rattlesnake* in 1846, for four years as medical officer and enraptured

student of natural phenomena in the service of that insatiable curiosity and will to know that comprise the vital spirit of the scholar. The expedition, headed by Captain Owen Stanley, who was the son of a celebrated bishop and brother of a more celebrated dean, was given for its surveying cruise of the waters between Australia and the Great Barrier Reef a distinguished crew and a vessel from the mothball fleet. The captain even understood what Huxley was about in his leisure hours, as he strove to find the principle of order that he knew lurked somewhere in the chaos of the invertebrates. Yet in the day when modern biology was struggling within the cocoon and at best had only fitful glimpses of the light of day, even to a selected crew of technicians and geographers the researches of Huxley were the senseless aberrations of a crank. Specifically, he could not leave his specimens to dry on deck without the risk of their being swept overboard by scientifically minded associates—and they were scientifically minded—who could not see Her Majesty's decks strewn to Huxley's senseless and smelly whim. But it was a day when Huxley could write to his sister, "There is no chance of living by science. I have been loth to believe it, but it is so. There are not more than four or five offices in London which a Zoologist or Comparative Anatomist can hold and live by. Owen, who has a European reputation, second only to that of Cuvier, gets as Hunterian Professor £300 a year! which is less than the salary of many a bank clerk."[6] Perhaps it was just as well that Huxley brought with him on the *Rattlesnake* Carlyle's *Sartor Resartus*. More than once he was to know a depth of despair about his life and future as deep and as dark as Carlyle's alter ego, Herr Teufelsdrockh, ever knew. He was also to have his revelation in Sydney, Australia, as Teufelsdrockh had his in Paris and Carlyle his creator had his in Leith Walk, Edinburgh. But appropriately to Huxley as a man, the revelation came through love.

Her name was Henrietta Heathorn and she was sister-in-law of a leading merchant of Sydney. With Huxley it was love at first sight, an achievement as easily within the capacity of the reticent Victorians as it was within the capacity of the lovers of Shakespeare's comedies. It was love at first sight for her also, but the simple, direct, Shakespearian avowal was not part of the Victorian pattern. It was not long, however, before she slipped on a bit of wood upon the path and he removed it with winged words: "So would I remove all hindrances from your path in life." Seven years later he could afford to marry her, and they lived happily forever after.

It is to Huxley and not to Darwin that one should look for the clear-cut effect of the fusion of the utilitarian tradition with the new theory of evolution. Yet the fusion is there in Darwin to a certain degree. Darwin was not primarily concerned with the moral order and he tended to take his moral concepts ready-made, but he tended to take them from the utilitarian tradition and the tradition of classical economics. Without concerning himself particularly with the pleasure-pain calculus, he founded his concept of morals upon the utilitarian thesis. He had read Shaftesbury, accepted the concept of the moral sense, and held that conscience evolves from the moral sense into that extension of the moral sense which should govern one's relations with others, in its more rudimentary form because public opinion dictates as much, in its more developed form because *noblesse oblige* dictates it. He believed that the same process of moral elevation by evolution takes place in society as a whole, partly because the successful have more children than the unsuccessful and partly because the social tendency to imitate the successful expedites the acceptance of their patterns of behavior. Implicit in this, of course, is an acceptance of that concept of classical economics which stems ultimately from the Calvinistic tradition, that the successful are the Lord's anointed and hence the good. Most important of all is the thesis that as civilization progresses, natural evolution is superseded by ethical evolution in human society. A reading of *The Descent of Man* directed toward determining the often implicit ethical attitudes of Darwin will justify the statement of William Irvine in his *Apes, Angels, and Victorians,* a book as readable as its title is promising: "Darwin was no crude leveler down to origins. He may more readily be accused of making animals too human, than of making men too animal."[7]

This is the precise distinction that lies at the heart of Huxley's ethical theory and justifies the interpretation of his work as that of a believer in the man-made order. Had Huxley been born in the generation of James Mill, he probably would have been one of the epigoni if, indeed, his scientific preoccupations left him leisure for ethical and economic speculation. But life could never be the same again for Huxley after the year of *The Origin of Species*. Thereafter he had to accommodate his ethical beliefs to his belief in evolution. He had rejected belief in the divinely created order, even coining for his attitude that convenient neologism *agnostic*, which is now so firmly implanted in the language that one would imagine its ancestry considerably more extended than a single century. When Huxley read *The Origin of Species*, a form at last appeared on the face of the waters. Darwin had the answer to the problem that had vexed Huxley all his adult life, and never for an instant thereafter did Huxley doubt the essential correctness of Darwin's answer. But neither did he relinquish his basic belief in free will, the belief that everyone must always maintain who believes in the man-made order. Now, it is not simple to maintain simultaneously belief in evolution, which always has a tug in the direction of naturalism, with belief in free will. Consequently one should expect and will find a division in Huxley's thinking that at times leaves him open to the charge of serious inconsistency. It also leaves the one who quotes Huxley open to the danger of misrepresenting him in either of two directions if the choice of quotation is injudiciously made.

The title of one address which sent the spiritual seismographs of Britain into wild gyrations invites misrepresentation in one form; it was "The Physical Basis of Life," which he delivered in that citadel of faith, Edinburgh, in 1868 and then delivered to John Morley for publication in the *Fortnightly Review*. In it Huxley maintains that protoplasm is the physical basis of life, and the basis as well of nonlife if the molecules are rearranged a bit. Man is cousin to the ape, more remotely to the amoeba, and is a family connection of the molecule and atom. Mind is not the final earthly mystery; matter is. What is matter but "the name for the unknown and hypothetical cause of states of our own consciousness"?[8] Matter is the unknowable which underlies what can be known. It obeys laws; but, in a way that harkens back to Hume and at least parallels if not anticipates John Stuart Mill, these laws are merely observed reactions which are not contradicted. Mind is neither over matter nor under matter but in some unknowable sense is one with matter. One might easily prove the total determinism of Huxley's thought by judicious quotation from "The Physical Basis of Life."

On the other hand, it would not be too difficult to make Huxley out to be nothing but a utilitarian with a scientific bias. In his study of Hume which he did for the English Men of Letters Series he attempts the straddle between utilitarianism and determinism by maintaining that the choices men make are dictated by nature and cannot rest on a freedom to choose what is incompatible with nature. Man chooses pleasure and avoids pain because it is his nature to do so; thus put, the element of free will is lessened in the equation and the factor of determinism is increased. Yet the materialistic foundation of Hume's thinking he accepts in terms entirely consistent with orthodox utilitarianism. "The moral approbation, therefore, with which we regard acts of justice or benevolence rests upon their utility to society, because the perception of that utility or, in other words, of the pleasure which they give to other men, arouses a feeling of sympathetic pleasure in ourselves. The feeling of obligation to be just, or of the duty of justice, arises out of that association of moral approbation or disapprobation with one's own actions, which is what we call conscience."[9] The distinction, of course, is that Huxley sees in Hume something lacking from the orthodox utilitarians, a recognition of the material basis of the nature which underlies the pleasure-pain calculus. The nub of the problem is the reconciliation of nature in this sense with the free will which is essential to the utilitarian and to every believer in the man-made order as the operational principle in human life.

MAN'S FREEDOM TO CHOOSE

Huxley grappled with this problem repeatedly, swaying sometimes in the direction of determinism and sometimes in the direction of free will. Insofar as he can be said to have solved it, his solution took the form that Darwin's solution took, the concept that man is not really one with the rest of the material universe from which he sprung since in man natural evolution has progressed to the point at which it has been superseded by ethical evolution. So long as man was subject to the processes of natural evolution, he was not master of his ethical destiny. In that state he was Hobbesian man. But when natural evolution had carried him to the point of civilization, he passed into another state of being, and the processes of ethical evolution began. Rationality and free will play a part in this state of being, because man has evolved to the point at which rationality is part of his nature and therefore the exercise of free will is also part of his nature. Man has, so to speak, evolved all the way out of the natural order as the rigid evolutionists understand it into an order which is of his own making. The man-made order is the state above the natural order, ethical evolution the stage beyond natural evolution. Thus Huxley salvages both his evolutionary and his utilitarian convictions, and in the process refutes what he considers the pretensions of Auguste Comte to scientific competence.[10] His final and most nearly explicit expression of the distinction between natural and ethical evolution is to be found in his Romanes lecture of 1893, and its Prolegomena.

The Romanes lectures had been established at Oxford in 1891 by George Romanes (1848–1894), Canadian-born scientist, friend of Darwin and author of *Darwin and after Darwin* (1892), professor at Edinburgh and at the Royal Institution. Gladstone inaugurated the series in 1892 with a safe-and-sane lecture on the *Odyssey*, attended by a distinguished audience better attuned perhaps to Homer than to Huxley. Huxley received the invitation to give the 1893 lecture. He announced his subject to be "Evolution and Ethics," worked on his talk intermittently through 1892, cleared it with Romanes, and in it presented his matured and final views on the relationship of nature to morality. After the Romanes lecture there remained in his career only a triumphal appearance at the meeting of the British Association; the editing of his *Collected Essays* in nine volumes; the winning of the Darwin Medal; a last mounting of the barricades of debate in a rebuttal to A. J. Balfour's *The Foundations of Belief;* another of his increasingly frequent attacks of influenza, this the final one; and death on June 29, 1895, at the age of sixty. The Romanes lecture and the Prolegomena which he wrote for its published form was his last significant statement.

Huxley does not rule out the possibility of a Creator of the cosmic process and hence of all its products; he maintains, however, that evolution as a natural process is free from supernatural intervention just as the tree is in its development from the seed, or the fowl from the egg. Even if the earth itself evolved out of a nebulous cosmic magma, as he thinks likely, there was order in its disordered beginnings. "The faith which is born of knowledge, finds its object in an eternal order, bringing forth ceaseless change, through endless time, in endless space; the manifestations of the cosmic energy alternating between phases of potentiality and phases of explication."[11]

He then proceeds to his dominant metaphor. The state of nature is hostile to the state of a garden. The former is characterized by a relentless struggle for existence, the latter by the elimination of that struggle. The cosmic process adjusts the forms of plant life to the conditions needed for survival, the horticultural process adjusts the growing conditions to the forms of plant life the gardener chooses to grow. The dwellers in a beehive, from the moment that they begin to work, do the labor required for survival in terms of the cosmic process, and it may well be that human society also came into being as a similar product of organic necessity. But this is no longer true in human society, because human society functions by a process more nearly analogous to the horticultural than to the cosmic. Man in society is motivated, not by the struggle for survival but the desire for approval. "Every forward step of social progress brings men into closer relations with their fellows, and increases the importance of the pleasures and pains derived from sympathy. We judge the acts of others by our own sympathies, and we judge our own acts by the sympathies of others, every day and all day long, from childhood upwards, until associations, as indissoluble as those of language, are formed between certain acts and the feelings of approbation or disapprobation. It becomes impossible to imagine some acts without disapprobation, or others without approbation of the actor, whether he be one's self, or any one else. We come to think in the acquired dialect of morals. An artificial personality, the 'man within,' as Adam Smith calls conscience, is built up beside the natural personality. He is the watchman of society, charged to restrain the anti-social tendencies of the natural man within the limits required by social welfare."[12]

Such is the ethical process, one that cooperates with the cosmic process insofar as it makes human society more efficient in the struggle with the state of nature, one that is antagonistic to the cosmic process insofar as it suppresses the self-seeking qualities which make for the survival of the fittest. Common sense indicates the limitations to its application; the malefactor can hardly be protected by the golden rule. "What would become of the garden if the gardener treated all the weeds and slugs and birds and trespassers as he would like to be treated, if he were in their place?"[13] In short, when man has reached the social state the struggle for existence is over; cosmic evolution has been replaced by ethical evolution. The struggle is no longer for the means of existence, but for the means of enjoyment.

In the struggle for the means of enjoyment, energy, industry, intellectual capacity, tenacity of purpose, but also sympathy, are the qualities that make for success. But the men who possess these qualities are the men who tend to acquire wealth and influence, and it is good for society that they should do so provided they are not devoid of sympathetic humanity. The process is not one that resembles natural selection in the state of nature, and obviously *laissez faire* bears no resemblance to the artificial selection of the horticulturist. The resemblance to the latter does exist in the fact that just as the horticulturist produces conditions more favorable to the survival of the desired species than does the state of nature, so society produces conditions more favorable to the survival and development of the qualities that make for its advancement than does the cosmic process. Once man is in the state of society, he is out of the state of nature and the cosmic process has been replaced by the ethical process. But in one respect Huxley is false to his Victorian heritage of optimism; life is a cycle and not an ascent. "That which lies before the human race is a constant struggle to maintain and improve, in opposition to the State of Nature, the State of Art of an organized polity; in which, and by which, man may develop a worthy civilization, capable of maintaining and constantly improving itself, until the evolution of our globe shall have entered so far upon its downward course that the cosmic process resumes its sway; and, once more, the State of Nature prevails over the surface of our planet."[14] So far removed, then, is the injunction to "live according to nature" from the desirable reality that if nature is used in the sense consistent with the meaning of the cosmic process, the proper injunction is precisely the opposite. "Social progress means a checking of the cosmic process at every step and the substitution for it of another, which may be called the ethical process; the end of which is not the survival of those who happen to be the fittest, in respect of the whole of the conditions which obtain, but of those who are ethically the best."[15] It is in direct violation of this principle that the fanatical individualists of the age try to apply to human society, by false analogy, the principle of the cosmic process. "Let us understand, once for all, that the ethical progress of society depends, not on imitating the cosmic process, still less in running away from it, but in combating it."[16]

Thus Huxley's concept of the man-made order, in its definitive form, contains very much that is by now familiar, not uncomfortably adjusted to the new science. His agnosticism continues to be a sort of truce requested by Huxley of his religion-oriented adversaries and by 1892 ordinarily granted by them. He does not start with the golden age, but at least he starts with order in the cosmos. He distinguishes the state of society from the state of nature in the fundamental principle of its operation. He holds to a moral sense theory quite consistent with that of Shaftesbury as developed by Hutcheson, even if he fathers it on Adam Smith. He reconciles ethical evolution with *laissez faire*, but each time with a carefully inserted insistence upon human sympathy in the individual. He holds that the ethical process is the diametric opposite of the cosmic process, and in every stage of his argument he manifests an implicit faith in the reality of free will and in the responsibility of the individual to the moral code which has evolved from the twin principles of human sympathy and social cooperation. Huxley's final position is that of Darwin in *The Descent of Man*, and in both there is an easy fusion of evolutionary thought with the older concepts of deism and the newer concepts of utilitarianism. In Huxley as in Darwin, the tradition of the man-made order has received a new foundation stone in the form of evolutionary theory, but the structure itself remains unchanged.

HERBERT SPENCER

If one could substitute for the utilitarian cornerstone on which was erected the edifice of thought reared by John Stuart Mill a cornerstone hewed out of evolutionary theory, one would have the approximate foundation of the thought of Huxley. The reverse is, of course, equally true; Mill approximates Huxley without the evolutionary bias. In similar fashion Herbert Spencer is like a Lord Macaulay who made evolution the foundation of his thinking. He had in his day a following like that of Macaulay and composed in large measure of the same people, and today the dust of oblivion has sifted over his work and buried it even as it has buried the work of Macaulay. The Macaulay who was the high priest of *laissez faire* in the halls of Parliament and who lent his eloquence and his prestige to the tenets of classical economics is paralleled in the world of speculative thought by the once prestigious Herbert Spencer who did the same. Macaulay is remembered today as a prose stylist and a man of preternatural powers of memory; Spencer does not have even that sort of muted renown. Yet in his day he was a potent force in English thinking, and in the history of the man-made order the very facts that have so quickly elicited oblivion are the facts that made him once a name to conjure with. Perhaps his once celebrated ear stoppers are his proper symbol. Spencer was plagued all his life with bad nerves, and if the conversation took a turn he found unpleasant it could mean for him a sleepless night as he turned and twisted in silent debate with an imaginary adversary whom he could pulverize in his mind but not eradicate from it. So he had a pair of ear stoppers which he plugged in his ears when that unpleasant turn of conversation threatened, and a peaceful oblivion to disturbing ideas came upon him. Spencer always traveled in his mind the high a priori road, and a detour was a torture to him. Huxley once said, "Spencer's idea of a tragedy is a deduction killed by a fact."[17]

Francis Bacon once took all learning to be his province. That frequently ridiculed claim is not at all ridiculous when taken in the sense that Bacon intended, the creation of an encyclopedic pattern into which the knowledge available in his day and discoverable in the future might be fitted. Herbert Spencer also undertook something analogous to Bacon's *Instauratio Magna*. He called it his *Synthetic Philosophy* and he carried it through ten volumes. The *Synthetic Philosophy* comprises a volume devoted to *First Principles*, and successive volumes that present the principles of biology, psychology, sociology, and morality. The conclusion of the whole is not fundamentally different from the initial pronouncement of his basic belief, which appeared in 1851 in his first book, *Social Statics:* "Every man has freedom to do all that he wills, provided he infringes not the equal freedom of any other man."

Spencer's fundamental achievement is the fusion of *laissez faire* as an economic and political doctrine with evolution as a biological and even sociological concept. Like all stouthearted Liberals of the nineteenth century he would limit the powers of government to the performance of police duties at home and the maintenance of an army and navy for protection from aggression abroad. All other governmental services and functions—educational services, health services, welfare services—he deemed excrescences to be lopped off, to the economic well-being of the individual thus freed from the compulsion to aid his fellow man. As we have seen, the doctrine of *laissez faire* first begins to emerge in the thinking of the radicals of the generation of revolution. It becomes the foundation of the thinking of the classical economists, and is fused with the utilitarian creed by the early utilitarians. It still fitted the thinking of the philosophic radicals of Spencer's day, and *Social Statics* won the favorable attention of George Henry Lewes and the lady known to social theory as Marian Evans and to literature as George Eliot. So favorable did the attention of the latter become that those with ears nicely attuned to tintinnabulations fancied they heard the bells proclaiming the nuptials of Herbert Spencer and George Eliot. Nothing came of it except an article for *The Leader* of March, 1852, called "Development Hypothesis," in which Spencer advanced a theory of evolution seven years before Darwin published *The Origin of Species*. It had the merit of priority but like so much of Spencer's scientific writing, the demerit of fallacy.

Anything like an analysis of Spencer's *Synthetic Philosophy* would be a labor from which Hercules would shrink, and would be such a stirring of quiescent dust as to becloud an already sufficiently complicated theme. We might tear a metaphorical page from Spencer's book, however, and proclaim a Synthetic Abridgment of the *Synthetic Philosophy* of Herbert Spencer. This Abridgment will present, usually without benefit of chapter and verse and with many a debt to Hugh Elliot's study of Spencer,[18] the thought of Spencer under the following heads: his theory of evolution, his theory of the origin of religion, his theory of the origin and content of ethics, his theory of the nature of government, and his theory of the duties of the state. The result, one entertains the pious if not entirely confident hope, will comprise something like Herbert Spencer's view of the man-made order, a view of far greater importance when considered in its impact upon nineteenth-century thought than when considered in terms of its permanent plausibility. One should never lose sight of the validity of Elliot's statement: ". . . in the main, Spencer formed his theories *first,* and established them by induction *afterwards.*"[19]

Spencer had happened upon the statement that animals in the embryo develop from the homogeneous to the heterogeneous. Out of this statement he constructed his theory of evolution. With the wonderful capacity he had for getting the last inch of mileage from an idea, he extended this idea into an evolutionary explanation of the universe and all the life that is within it, as everything steadily evolves from the simple into the complex, until the ultimate product of evolution is the coherent and definite individual. On a slightly less metaphysical plane he found the operating principle of evolution to be the transmissibility of acquired characteristics, writing an article in support of his concept seven years before the publication of *The Origin of Species.* In this matter as in many others, Spencer was helped along what was essentially the scientific wrong road by the painstaking researches of Darwin, who plodded along the pathway of induction which roughly parallels the glamorous a priori road that Spencer traveled. The result—and it was a result that often occurred in Spencer's career and aided greatly in establishing his contemporary reputation—was the illusion that Spencer traveled the same road as Darwin but was ahead of him

upon it. It is the same illusion that often exists today in the area
of atomic science: there was a school of atomic scientists among
the ancient Greeks and so the ancient Greeks anticipated this
area of modern science. Democritus and his followers had the
right word, *atom*, and nothing more. Spencer had the right word,
evolution.

Spencer's theory of the origin of religion has little more to
recommend it than his theory of evolution. Technically he was
an agnostic, but the sort of agnostic who verges on deism. The
first part of *First Principles*, the introductory volume to his
Synthetic Philosophy, is devoted to "The Unknowable." He discusses "The Unknowable" in more than one hundred pages, an
achievement even for an a priorist of Spencer's caliber. Between
the Unknowable, a Being presumably infinite and eternal and
hence possessed of attributes beyond human understanding, and
the human institution called religion Spencer saw no connecting
link. Religion he believed to have developed from the worship
of dead ancestors, a sort of ghost worship in which the spirits
worshiped were disembodied replicas of living men. Ghost worship also demanded its professional practitioners, and so there
arose medicine men professionally capable of frightening spirits,
and priests professionally skilled at placating them. The function was so important among primitive societies that the priest
and the ruler tended to be the same man; at first the Church
and State were one. But in accordance with his parent theory
of evolution from the confused homogeneous to the definite
heterogeneous, out of the confused homogeneity of religion and
government evolved the separation of the two and the assumption by each of its definite function and pattern.

Ethics had its origin in obedience to the priestly caste, but as
society grew in complexity, and hence in heterogeneity and
definite form, this foundation for ethics ceased to be valid. Priests
might continue to inculcate ethical codes, but their objective
was obedience and not morality. As society continued to evolve
always in the direction of concrete individuality, the ethical
principle came to reside in the individual. It was nothing other
than the very familiar principle of utilitarianism, the pleasure-
pain calculus, but Spencer insisted as strongly as did John Stuart
Mill upon the presence of a qualitative distinction among plea-

sures. Indeed he believed that moral consciousness really grows by an always developing moral discrimination among the qualitative values of various pleasures. As always, that moral discrimination develops on the twin principles of heterogeneity and concreteness by which Spencerian evolution operates. The final achievement of moral evolution is the individual moral conscience, possessed of a high power of discrimination among the several pleasures and a highly concrete concept of their several values.

ETHICS AND GOVERNMENT

At this point emerges the one significant difference between the ethical concept of Spencer and those who followed him, and the ethical concept of the entire moral sense school of Shaftesbury, Hutcheson, and the utilitarians. The logical consequence of the utilitarian principle is to place altruism on the pedestal; he who best serves the greatest happiness of the greatest number is the best man. The logical consequence of Spencer's thought is to place egoism on the pedestal; he who best serves his own ends makes his maximum contribution to the greatest happiness of the greater number. As Elliot sums it up, "If, therefore, everyone were to abandon the pursuit of his own happiness, and give up his time to promoting the happiness of others, the result would be a smaller general happiness than might be. For each citizen would have his needs fulfilled less perfectly than if he himself had attended to them. The true course, therefore, is a rational egoism, modified by altruism. Each citizen should be free to pursue his own ends, so long as the similar freedom of other citizens is not interfered with."[20]

The passage from Spencer's theory of ethics to his theory of government is a short and simple one. Some government is necessary, to preserve internal order and to protect people from external aggression. Spencer felt that the traditional division of governments into monarchies, oligarchies, and democracies concerned only the form of government and was not the fundamental division. The true division concerned the substance of government, and in this regard he believed that there was a fundamental division between war-oriented governments and peace-oriented governments. In the former the needs of the state are paramount, and individual freedom is curbed. In the latter the needs of the individuals are paramount, and governmental power is curbed. Men work best when working for themselves with the minimum of interference from the state. Spencer held that the fundamental fallacy of socialism is that it operates on the principle of the war-oriented government by making paramount the needs of the state and curbing the freedom of the individual, even as it proclaims the objectives of the peace-oriented government. He believed that the representative form of government is the most effective for the government that is peace-oriented, and hence is the form under which individuals will have the maximum of freedom for self-realization and for that operation of rational egoism which produces the maximum of human happiness. The state, then, should maintain an army and navy to protect its citizens from external aggression; it should provide police protection against internal disturbance and crime; beyond that, it has no function. Spencer's basic principle never altered: "Every man is free to do that which he wills, provided he infringes not the equal freedom of any other man." Let private enterprise build the roads, run the schools, operate the postal service, determine health standards; in a word, do all the constructive work of society. Government exists only to preserve a free milieu in which private enterprise may do it.

It is difficult today to recapture the spirit of a generation which found in Herbert Spencer the scientist who satisfactorily reconciled the principles of evolution with the principles of classical economics. It is relatively easy to see in Huxley, and even for one with a bias toward belief in the divinely created order to accept, a fusion of evolutionary thought with the utilitarian spirit of reform and a judicious selection from the principles of classical economics. Huxley was a solid, careful thinker and a man of humane character. Herbert Spencer seems to have been a kindly man in his personal relations, yet his single-mindedness and arbitrary dogmatism kept him from seeing any goal to evolution but unfettered individualism, let him hold that no moral evolution would ever render obsolete the

literal and physical survival of the fittest, and even let him
proclaim in *The Man versus the State* (1884) that the derelicts
of London should not be kept alive by charity since their elimination is the law of nature. It was Spencer and not the far more
thoughtful and better-balanced Huxley who really gave the apostles of *laissez faire* the scientific blessing and sent them upon
their unfettered way to contribute to the maximum happiness
by self-aggrandizement. The fusion of evolution and classical
economics is complete in Spencer, and somehow the reform
motive, which is always the saving grace of utilitarianism, has
disappeared. The man-made order, in a way philosophically mysterious but abundantly clear in a practical sense, is buttressed
by evolutionary principles really evolved from the fertile brain
of Herbert Spencer.

It was not England, however, that listened most eagerly to
the message of Herbert Spencer and found most appealing the
protective cloak of righteousness he threw over the bony shoul-
ders of rapacity. In America there was a generation eager to
crack open a continent and ransack its riches. The Civil War
had been won, righteousness had triumphed, and the time had
come, not to forget righteousness, of course, since the cloak of
righteousness is always needed, but to make money. Once the
destiny of America was in the hands of Washington, Jefferson,
Adams, Hamilton, and Madison. More recently it was in the
hands of Lincoln. But now it would pass to the hands of Fisk
and Gould, Morgan and Carnegie and Rockefeller. These men
studied not at the school of Montesquieu but at the school of
Mammon. But they would not be Anglo-Saxons, or near Anglo-
Saxons, if they did not always feel the need for that protective
cloak of righteousness which Matthew Arnold assures us is the
inevitable garment of the Anglo-Philistine. Herbert Spencer had
woven the cloth, and all it needed was an American tailor. He
presently appeared, out of the Episcopal Church by way of
Darwinism into Yale University. His name was William Graham
Sumner, and he was an ideological John the Baptist for such
saviors of society as Fisk and Gould, Morgan and Carnegie and
Rockefeller. But before we can listen to his message, it may
be well to see what had happened to the message of Thomas
Jefferson, James Madison, and John Adams.

XII

SURVIVAL OF
THE FITTEST AMERICANS

THE FUSION of utilitarianism and classical economics which took place in England was imported to the United States as an accomplished fact. Consequently there has never been in American history a reform movement motivated by utilitarian principles, and what in England was in the nineteenth century largely the program of the Liberal party, in America has been called conservatism in the most reprehensible sense of the term.

In the post-Revolutionary period, belief persisted in that concept of natural law which rests upon belief in a divinely created order, but it gradually tended to become an implicit belief, an unvoiced axiom on which rested appeals to the reality of natural rights. It is such in the addresses of John Quincy Adams, who appealed from "the inflammatory principles of Paine to the sober and correct principles of our own declaration of independence." In a Fourth of July address at Quincy, Massachusetts, in 1831 he affirmed, "The pretence of an absolute, irresistible, despotic power . . . in every government somewhere is incompatible with the first principle of natural right."[1] Adams pleaded eloquently for abolition of human slavery before the House of Representatives, contending that to deny the principle of natural rights would be to deny the moral justification of the Revolution itself. That he based his concept of natural rights upon a concept of natural law is evidenced in his *Lecture on the Social Compact—Exemplified in the Constitution of Massachusetts,* in which he maintains that there is an inevitable limitation upon man's freedom imposed by "a law of nature, or in more proper words, a law of God, the author of nature."[2]

Benjamin Fletcher Wright, whose *American Interpretations of Natural Law* is the standard study of the subject from the colonial period to 1931, the date of publication, carefully traces the process by which belief in the natural law gradually becomes an unvoiced axiom underlying American political thought in the earlier nineteenth century. Andrew Jackson was not a philosopher and philosophic concepts are not to be sought in his public statements, but there were many nonphilosophic spokesmen of the Revolutionary generation whose statements are studded with political philosophy at second hand. Jackson at the most referred from time to time, and in passing, to natural rights. The phrase was hardly in the vocabulary of Henry Clay, as Wright notes, and Daniel Webster could give a Fourth of July address without using the term. More significant, in the naturally philosophic Abraham Lincoln the emphasis is on government by the people rather than on the rights of the people. Indeed the Bill of Rights concept, which seemed to Jefferson more important than a constitution itself, dwindled to a pious convention. State constitutions adopted in the nineteenth century usually have Bill of Rights, but they merely parrot what the political philosophers of the eighteenth century hammered out. The concept of natural law had become an unvoiced axiom; and even its corollary, the concept of natural rights, had become a conventional assumption. They underlay the tangible provisions of the state constitutions, but they were no longer living issues in the minds of men.

What we see illustrated is a pattern of human thought so common as to approach itself something like a law of nature. The eighteenth century saw conceived two basically different formulations of natural law, the one which we have designated as the teaching of the school of Montesquieu and the other taught in the school of Rousseau. With a few exceptions, of whom Paine is the most important, the spokesmen of the generation of revolution in America accepted the viewpoint of the school of Montesquieu. They founded a nation and it prospered. Their concepts stood the test of practice. But when a concept, radical at its hour of origin, stands the test of practice, imperceptibly but steadily it ceases to be radical and becomes conservative. There is more radicalism in Thomas Jefferson and James Madison, in the sense of a questioning of the root assumptions of contemporary society, than in Karl Marx and Friedrich Engels. But the radicalism of Jefferson and Madison worked when translated into practice. It became accepted, and then unquestioned, and finally unvoiced. It is not that Andrew Jackson, Henry Clay, Daniel Webster, and the men who wrote the state constitutions did not accept the concept of natural law and its concomitant, natural rights; they accepted them so completely, and could rely so totally on their acceptance by their fellow Americans, that they took them for granted. The very fact, however, that they took them for granted facilitated the distortion of such concepts by many who came after them. As the nineteenth century progressed, the image of Thomas Jefferson slowly faded and the image of Herbert Spencer gradually assumed its place. The abolitionists were the last important group in the nineteenth century to plead for the rights of man on the principle of the natural law. It may yet be one of the ironic judgments of history that the first important group to do so in the twentieth century are the civil rights advocates. The hundred years belong to the social Darwinians and the pragmatists.

SOCIAL DARWINIANS

The social Darwinian generation owed its hour of triumph to many causes, some of them extremely remote from the thinking of Charles Darwin. The very fact that social Darwinism was never so strong in England as in the United States throws some light on the nature of these causes. The American concept of society had stood the test of practice and the newly created nation had flourished. A tremendous test of national unity had been successfully passed, and the blackest moral blot on the national scutcheon had been erased. There was a continent to be opened, an industrial revolution to facilitate the process, and wealth that dwarfed the riches of Cathay for him with the enterprise and skill to make them his own. The entire order had been reformed in the glamorous New World, and the American mind could rest from its ideological labors and reap the rewards of reform.

The term "reform" has a pleasant sound in all but cynical ears. If one can be a reformer and still avoid the stigma of being deemed naïve, the achievement is a pleasing one. But the reformer who applauds the reform already accomplished and in hardheaded fashion holds to what is now the tried and true has the best of two worlds. He has the inner satisfaction of being at heart a reformer, the outer satisfaction of being acclaimed such by those who admire reform (all right-thinking men do, of course), and yet he has the reality which really attracts him, the *status quo*. America teemed with such reformers in the post-Civil War period, and the spread-eagle eloquence with which they neatly fused the radicalism of the Founding Fathers with their own complacent conservatism in their Fourth of July addresses and similar public utterances is still impressive in those printed orations which the nineteenth century stored with loving care in public libraries and which now are slowly oxidizing into oblivion. But the breed was not American alone. Macaulay was that kind of reformer. He was in favor of reform, and he was glad that it was finished. Now we can get about the real business of life, making the most of what we have achieved. Macaulay was the type of Englishman produced by the fusion of utilitarianism and classical economics, and he was the prototype of the American Fourth of July orator.

THE AMERICAN PHILISTINE

The fusion mentioned of utilitarianism and classical economics was imported to the United States. In this country there took place a further fusion, as the old Calvinist tradition and the philosophy of the Founding Fathers were added to the combination. The protective cloak of Dissenter Protestantism which Matthew Arnold called the garb of English Philistines was worn at least as much by American Philistines as by English, and perhaps worn more. But the American Philistine was a reformer satisfied with a different set of reforms than his English compeer. The English Philistine was satisfied with the set of reforms effected under the banners of Jeremy Bentham; the American

Philistine was satisfied with the set of reforms effected under the banners of George Washington. The English Philistine had assimilated the doctrine of the greatest happiness of the greatest number, and then gone about his real concern in life, the greatest happiness of himself. The American Philistine had assimilated the doctrine of natural rights and human equality, and then gone about his real concern in life, the entire exploitation of his own rights. The English Philistine gave to his kind of self-aggrandizement a protective coloration of moralism culled from Jeremy Bentham and James Mill; the American Philistine gave to his a similar protective coloration culled from Benjamin Franklin and Thomas Jefferson. If the American Philistine had been a philosopher, a role which would have bewildered him, he would have recognized that in his heart he believed in the man-made order, even if he took refuge in his citadel of moral rectitude and proclaimed the divinely created order, partly in terms appropriate to John Calvin and partly in terms appropriate to John Adams. Like Macaulay, who could not conceive what religion had to do with government, the American Philistine could not conceive what religion had to do with business. The English Philistine, if he happened to be Anglican, believed in the union of Church and State, but he did not believe in the union of religion and government. The American Philistine believed in both religion and business, but hardly in their union. A chemical analysis of the American Philistine of the nineteenth century would reveal in his thinking, molecules of utilitarianism fused with molecules of classical economics, coalescing with carefully selected molecules of the Calvinistic creed and molecules from the Declaration of Independence and other documents from the Age of Reform carefully and completely wrenched out of context.

The American Philistine, however, achieved his full development at a date late enough for a further fusion to take place in him, a fusion of social Darwinism with everything else that went into his ideological composition. As a utilitarian whose explicit utilitarianism is by now rather submerged by everything piled on top of it, he will continue to believe in the greatest happiness of the greatest number as the proper objective of the social order. As an American he will believe that the greatest happiness will be achieved by the greatest number when they pursue happiness, along with life and liberty, after the philosophy enunciated in the Declaration of Independence. As inheritor of the Calvinist tradition, aided by his conviction that Calvinism included among its tenets the manifest favor of the Almighty to His elect upon earth, he will believe that his success in achieving material wealth and the happiness that goes with it will give witness to the fact that he is one of the anointed. As a believer in social Darwinism he will believe that the *laissez faire* to which he subscribes as a utilitarian is part of an inexorable and unalterable law of nature leading mankind onward and upward on the evolutionary principle, but leading individuals onward and upward at varying speeds and to varying heights which are determined by their individual abilities. Thus the greatest happiness of the greatest number will be achieved under the liberty guaranteed by the American Constitution, to the degree that God wills that the individual achieve it, by an automatic process evolutionary in nature written into the very operating principle of the universe itself. "A vast stride," Henry Adams called it. "Unbroken evolution under uniform conditions pleased everyone —except curates and bishops; it was the very best substitute for religion; a safe, conservative, practical, thoroughly Common-Law deity."[3] Robert Green McCloskey well puts it in his expertly conceived *American Conservatism in the Age of Enterprise:* "As the conservatives employed it, the Darwinian revelation supported all their traditional premises. In nature, the fittest rise to positions of dominance, the less fit are eliminated. Thus the species slowly improves through natural selection, so long as no extraneous influence interferes. At a blow then, the timeworn presumptions of American conservatism were given new confirmation. 'Fitness' was defined in terms of material success, because nature is incapable of recognizing another standard. The elite, the saints of the new religion, therefore, were those who had proved their native superiority by their survival value. This will be recognized as the Puritan idea of 'election' in modern dress; the supporting rationale was different, but the implications were almost indistinguishable."[4]

A protesting voice might inquire, What has become of the "greatest happiness of the greatest number" principle? The answer must be that it has been sublimated into something grandiose and incalculably remote, into the far future of the human race. The survival of the fittest in society produces by the evolutionary process the finer and the happier society; it will be all for the best in the best possible of worlds when the evolutionary process has done its final work. Then whatever will be, will be right. The idea will be developed fanatically by Nietzsche in *Thus Spake Zarathustra* and elsewhere, thoughtfully by Bergson in *Creative Evolution*, playfully by Shaw in *Man and Superman*. But in the process the greatest happiness of the greatest number somehow changes into the greatest happiness of the selected few. To pinpoint the precise time when the change really took place in the United States is not easy, but 1870 might by rule of thumb be considered a plausible date. By that date the last spark of the reform spirit lingering from utilitarianism may be considered dead ash. The old liberalism had become the new conservatism, a conservatism profoundly and totally different from that of Edmund Burke. Once more the man-made order had ground to a dead halt, just as it did in the days of deism.

WILLIAM GRAHAM SUMNER

It remains to illustrate the fact from the thought of one who embodies at their clearest the thought patterns of the post-Civil War American Philistine. William Graham Sumner, professor of political and social science at Yale University from 1872 until his death in 1910, does so. Sumner had the sort of academic mind not always recognized as such; the mind that follows lines of thought right to the last thin strand, because it is not forced to stop short of the conclusion by practical considerations. There can be a haziness to the academic mind, but there can also be an uncompromising clarity; both effects are aided by the circumstances of the academic life which shelters its children from the compromises of the market place.

No paradigm can be a paragon of illustrative perfection, and Sumner is no exception. In several respects he is not quite the paradigm of post-Civil War American Philistinism, but in very many respects he is and to a certain extent he was its creator. His ancestry was English, his father an intelligent and hard-working but formally uneducated workman from Lancastershire

who settled in Hartford and worked in the local repair shop of
the New Haven Railroad. In many respects William Graham
Sumner was his father with a Yale education. The son was industrious to an awesome degree; sober, serious, and reserved;
marked for the ministry if ever a young man was. He entered the
ministry after European study, being ordained a priest of the
Episcopal Church in 1869. His inclinations were Broad Church.
About the time that he was introduced into the Church he was
introduced to Herbert Spencer, and Spencer conquered. Out of
the articles that were to comprise Spencer's *The Study of Sociology* he fashioned his own philosophy of life, abandoning the
dogma of Anglicanism for a dogma compounded out of social
Darwinism in part and in part out of his own interpretation of
the American tradition. As Stow Persons puts it, "The Spencerian
world view that Sumner embroidered in his own fashion was a
form of evolutionary naturalism."[5]

In 1872 Sumner left his clerical post to become professor of
political and social science at Yale. The rest of his incredibly
industrious life was devoted to teaching, writing, lecturing, and
propagandizing for what he deemed the solid principles of
society and government. No Yale man for the next thirty years
really thought his degree valid if it was not earned in part in
one of Sumner's courses. His influence permeated in that way
which is as difficult to trace as it is impossible to deny, the
burgeoning influence of a dominating and revered academic
figure at a great university attended by capable and privileged
young men at the most impressionable period of their lives. He
wrote and lectured without respite; of the bibliography in his
Essays collected in two volumes in 1940 the editors say with
proper prudence, "The following bibliography is as nearly ex-
haustive as we have been able to make it. There are doubtless
other articles which have not come to our attention."[6] Indeed
this bibliography occupies twenty-six pages and contains 313
entries. He wrote for newspapers and magazines, did books in
one volume and multiple volumes, did enough essays to fill two
large volumes, wrote four volumes on banking, three biographies
(Jackson, Hamilton, and Morris), gradually turned his primary
attention from economics and political science to society in the
deeper and more philosophic sense, and produced in *Folkways*

(1907) a classical study of the influence of custom upon the mores of society. He was a man of protean intellect, tireless capacity for work, indomitable confidence in his personal rectitude and the rectitude of his thought, and as encrusted a set of a priori convictions and antecedent axioms as can ever be found in that peculiar but not uncommon sort of dogmatist who fancies himself an open-minded scientist. Such men as Sumner are the massive dinosaurs of thought, at the mighty proportions of whose intellectual skeletons later generations gape. But the dinosaur does not survive the change in climate, and the Sumners do not survive when the intellectual climate changes. If a date must be set for the change in climate which transformed Sumner from a living influence to a museum piece, the stock market crash of 1929 will do.

We stated that in several respects Sumner was not quite the paradigm of post-Civil War American Philistinism. For one thing, he never accepted fully the comfortable doctrine of inevitable progress which comes so close to being the common denominator of Victorian thought. Sumner was an evolutionist, but not a believer in quick and simple evolution. For another, Sumner never abandoned the old utilitarian doctrine of free trade; the perfect paradigm would have been a protectionist. But probably the most important differentiation was an instinct for the glorification of the ordinary man which may be traceable in the main to his personal background but is certainly in keeping with the spirit of Jeffersonian democracy. It was not the plutocrat but the small businessman, who made his own living without fear or favor, brought up his family and educated it, kept society going with the money he paid in taxes and the services he rendered to its institutions, that Sumner considered the mainstay of America. One of the most delightful ironies of American semantics for those who remember Franklin D. Roosevelt's use of the phrase lies in the name Sumner invented for this bulwark of the nation. Sumner called him "the Forgotten Man."

It may be a sobering reflection that today Sumner seems best justified in those aspects of his thought which depart from the post-Civil War Philistine norm. Our present concern, however, is with the basic key of his thinking. Sumner left the Church in both senses of the word. His religious faith weakened, waned, and petered out. He was left, as was many a nineteenth-century materialist, with a sense of order but not a sense of divinely created order. The fundamental work of Sumner's lifetime was to determine the origin and significance of that sense of order. It was certainly not something that existed in the state of nature. In words that could be Thomas Hobbes translated into nineteenth-century English, he wrote: "We look in vain for any physical or metaphysical endowment with which men started the life of the race on earth. We look in vain for any facts to sustain the notion of a state of primitive simplicity and blessedness, or natural rights, or a boon of material goods. All the facts open to us show that man has won on earth everything which he has here by toil, sacrifice, and blood; all the civilization we possess has been wrought out by work and pain. All the rights, freedom and social power which we have inherited are products of history."[7] Nothing could be farther in his view from the historic truth than the illusion that the state of nature was a state of liberty. "No conception of the primitive man could well be more false to history than that which thinks of him as free in any sense of the word. The notion does not fit him at all. It is in the highest degree incongruous, because the whole conception of liberty in any sense is a product of civilization, and what little unrestrainedness of action men now enjoy they owe to the conquests of civilization."[8]

Sumner disbelieved in God, in the divinely created order, in the state of nature, in natural rights. Whatever is, is man-made to the degree that its making is within human control. But Sumner is an American Philistine. He has an instinct for seeing things within a moralistic framework, and although he never was a Calvinist he has a tendency to equate at least moderate prosperity with the favor of (to beg the question) God. He recognizes that men believe in rights, and indeed he believes in rights himself, and basically the subject matter of his later and more philosophic writing is the way in which folk beliefs and practices have developed into the mores of society, the observance of rights included. Like Hobbes four centuries before him, he believed that the state of nature was a state of war. "The question of right or rights can arise only in the in-group. All questions with outsiders are settled by War."[9] The "in-group," which is the family in its simplest form, the clan in a more developed form, and the society in a sophisticated form, evolves such concepts as law, order, duties, and rights. Law and order, he held, evolved out of the taboos of primitive society. So did duties. Rights were also implicit in the taboos, but they were contained within that framework of law, order, and duty which resulted from the taboos. "Rights have come to be expressions of the rules of the game in the competition of life."[10] But the game itself is the creation of man, and so are the rules of the game. Rights are subject to change as the rules of the game are subject to change; beneath Sumner the sociologist and anthropologist always lurks Sumner the utilitarian. To him the concept of inalienable rights is repugnant, as repugnant as any concept of the social order which does not view it as a thing of man's making. "It is certainly far wiser to think of rights as rules of the game of social competition which are current now and here. They are not absolute. They are not antecedent to civilization. They are a product of civilization, or of the art of living as men have practised it and experimented on it, through the whole course of history. They must be enjoyed under existing circumstances, that is, subject to limitations of tradition, custom, and fact. To be real they must be recognized in laws and provided for by institutions, but a great many of them, being inchoate, unsettled, partial, and limited, are still in the mores, and therefore vague and in need of further study and completion by courts and legislatures. This further work will be largely guided by the mores as to cognate matters, and by the conceptions of right and social welfare which the mores produce."[11]

GOD'S ANOINTED ARE THE PROSPEROUS

Thus the cornerstone of Sumner's thinking is belief in the man-made order, a belief grounded upon utilitarian concepts with a patina of sociology and anthropology. There remains to be constructed the social order which Sumner, as a spokesman for post-Civil War American Philistinism, believed to be the order best calculated to produce the greatest happiness of the greatest number. The key to his concept lies in his fundamentally simple and in a curious way Calvinistic sort of materialism. God's anointed are the prosperous. The sound social order is the fiscally sound social order. Every stage in the development of civilization has been made possible by capital. Hence it is the capitalist who carries the torch of civilization. Treasure will not rust nor will moth corrupt it if it is invested in productive enterprise. Not the truth but the savings account shall make you free. "It may be said, then, that liberty is to be found at the summit of civilization, and that those who have the resources of civilization at their command are the only ones who are free. But the resources of civilization are capital; and so it follows that the capitalists are free, or, to avoid ambiguities in the word capitalist, that the rich are free. Popular language, which speaks of the rich as independent, has long carried an affirmation upon this point. In reality the thirst for wealth is a thirst for this independence of the ills of life, and the interdependence of wealth on civilization and civilization on wealth is the reason why the science of wealth is concerned with the prime conditions of human welfare, and why all denunciations of desire to increase or to win wealth are worse than childish."[12]

The contributions of all the saints and sages to human welfare are dwarfed by the contributions of the entrepreneur; the greatest happiness of the greatest number is achieved by the greatest freedom to amass the greatest wealth. The pillar of society is that hard-working, independent, capital-accumulating Forgotten Man. "The next time that you are tempted to subscribe a dollar to a charity, I do not tell you not to do it, because after you have fairly considered the matter, you may think it right to do it, but I do ask you to stop and remember the Forgotten Man and understand that if you put your dollar in the savings bank it will go to swell the capital of the country which is available for division amongst those who, while they earn it, will reproduce it with increase."[13] Sumner remembered with crystal clarity from his theological days the parable of the talents, but it was the final shortcoming of Sumner that he could not conceive of talents as possibly anything but money.

The contribution of social Darwinism to this concept is the inevitable one. There is built into us all an emotional safety valve that gives us relief through the reflection that what is inevitable no doubt is right. The survival of the fittest, as social

Darwinism employed the term, was inevitable. "The truth is that the social order is fixed by laws of nature precisely analogous to those of the physical order. The most that man can do is by ignorance and self-conceit to mar the operation of social laws."[14] The survival of the fittest, which is guaranteed when these natural laws are granted free sway, means the uplift of civilization; the survival of the unfit, made possible by interference with their free operation, sets back the progress of civilization. Artificial attempts to set the rate of wages are simply "the old doctrine of spoliation." "If a man is forbidden to labor over eight hours a day (and the law has no sense or utility for the purposes of those who want it until it takes this form), he is forbidden to exercise so much industry as he may be willing to expend in order to accumulate capital for the improvement of his circumstances."[15] There is no wisdom in the state great enough to interfere with natural laws operating on the principles of social Darwinism in a way productive of human betterment; nothing but *laissez faire* can bring to civilization the final blessings of capitalism. "The truth is that liberty and property go together, and sustain each other in a glorious accord, but only in the highest and best civilization which men have yet attained. . . ."[16]

The full pattern of American Philistinism is thus revealed in Sumner. The utilitarian objective underlies all his argumentation and gives it an appropriate moral coloration; our only justifiable concern is the rise of civilization with the concomitant blessings that rise will confer on all its members. Civilization will rise so long as civilization is based upon classical economics; observes that the goal is a material one; recognizes that virtue is to be measured in terms of material gain; protects the enentrepreneur, who is the cornerstone of society, by strict observance of *laissez faire;* and never loses sight of the quasi-Calvinistic assurance that the rich man is God's anointed. There was something about Sumner, perhaps his personal inheritance and perhaps his inheritance as an American, that made him prefer the self-reliant small businessman to the blatant millionaire whom the system was producing so successfully in the post-Civil War era, but Sumner accepted the Fisks and Goulds as products of the system, reflecting that at the best we are on the road to perfection. Such concepts as natural rights and human equality are part of the outworn folklore of a romantic past; the scientific study of folkways reveals that all rights are man-made products of the mores of society, subject to change as society develops, and the entire tenor of social Darwinism rebuts the romantic fallacy of human equality. Liberty and property are one and inseparable, progress and the acquisitive instinct are Siamese twins. Government exists to protect one's liberty to exercise his acquisitive instinct in the accumulation of property and thus to forward the progress of civilization. All that really is needed is a properly educated and disciplined legislature to write this philosophy into law, and a properly educated and disciplined Supreme Court to read it in.

THE FOURTEENTH AMENDMENT

The Supreme Court began to show the requisite training and discipline about 1870, as the influence of the most dedicated social Darwinian in Court history, Stephen J. Field (1816–1899), began to make itself felt. Justice Field had an extraordinarily variegated background that included a clerical ancestry, a boyhood divided between Connecticut and Constantinople, a legal training in the rough-and-tumble of frontier justice in California, service on the California Supreme Court, and then service from 1863 until 1897 on the Supreme Court of the United States. Each and every aspect of his experience left its mark upon his judicial opinions and the philosophy which molded them. We have said that the American Philistine would take instinctive refuge in his citadel of moral rectitude and proclaim the divinely created order in terms appropriate to John Calvin and John Adams in their several ways, although it was the man-made order he was upholding. Justice Field did it with the eloquence of an Old Testament prophet, nor is there reason to doubt that when he proclaimed the doctrine of *laissez faire* in a phraseology indebted in part to Isaiah and in part to Thomas Jefferson he honestly believed that he was speaking in full accord with divine revelation. There was an instinct for liberty in the bone and marrow of Justice Field, an individualism rooted in his Calvinistic inheritance, strengthened by his boyhood experience with an

Oriental pattern of life and thought utterly foreign to the American, buttressed by the philosophy he learned at Williams College from Mark Hopkins, enormously increased by his experiences in the gold towns of frontier California where indeed it was root hog or die, and broadened into a comprehensive philosophy of the law partly by his own legal experience and partly by his reading in such social Darwinians as Spencer and Sumner. This was the philosophy of law that Stephen Field brought to the Supreme Court. At first it was the philosophy of one man, then the philosophy of a minority of the Court, and then the prevailing philosophy until it was successfully challenged by the philosophy of Justices Brandeis and Holmes. Field preached and practiced what one might term legal Darwinism, an outgrowth of which it was a part, social Darwinism.

The instrument Field chose to make effective his philosophy was the Fourteenth Amendment. The Fourteenth Amendment has always been the chameleon of Constitutional provisions, varying its shades of meaning as the philosophy of the Court and the nation has varied. The Amendment reads as follows: "No state shall make or enforce any law which shall abridge the privileges or immunities of citizens of the United States; nor shall any state deprive any person of life, liberty or property without due process of law; nor deny to any person within its jurisdiction the equal protection of the laws." Its broader purpose was to extend to the states the limitations imposed on the federal government by the Bill of Rights. Its specific purpose was to protect the civil rights of the freedmen of the former slaveholding states. To what extent the ratifying Congress and states had in mind the former, broader purpose and to what extent the latter, specific purpose has been subject to debate, but there is no serious debate about the fact that both motives were present in its passage. For many years a convenient test of the liberal and conservative attitudes of the justices of the Court was their attitude toward the intent of the Fourteenth Amendment. The conservative justices took the stand that the Amendment was designed to protect the civil rights of the former slaves; the liberal justices took the stand that the Amendment extended to the states all the limitations of the Bill of Rights. As an illustration of the semantic worthlessness of the terms *conservative* and *liberal* outside a limited framework of time and place, one must add that the liberal viewpoint was that of Justice Field and that it was directed at guaranteeing to corporations all the immunities guaranteed to citizens by the Bill of Rights. Field was a liberal, in the American tradition that approximately parallels the tradition that made Macaulay and Spencer liberals.

Field maintained that the passage of the Fourteenth Amendment made one a citizen of the United States and not a citizen of a specific state, and hence that personal rights do not come from state or local legislation and cannot be abridged or destroyed by state or local authority. He enunciated this thesis in 1870 in the celebrated Slaughterhouse Cases which concerned the rights of independent butchers to defy a legally created slaughterhouse monopoly in New Orleans; he lost, but his doctrine was enunciated. He lost again in 1876 in *Munn v. Illinois*, a case involving the validity of a law setting rates for grain elevators in the Chicago area. He lost again, but he lost proclaiming the meaning of *liberty* in the Fourteenth Amendment in terms that could easily be a conscious paraphase of Herbert Spencer: "freedom to go where one may choose, and to act in such manner, not inconsistent with the equal rights of others, as his judgment may dictate for the promotion of his happiness."[17] Significantly, the majority opinion in *Munn v. Illinois* conceded that "public interest" might set some sort of limitation on state laws affecting personal freedom.

Thereafter the ideological tide turned in Field's favor. In 1886 the Court decided in *Santa Clara County v. Southern Pacific Railroad* that a corporation was a person within the meaning of the Fourteenth Amendment. In 1887, in *Mugler v. Kansas*, it reversed the long-revered *McCulloch v. Maryland* doctrine, enunciated in 1819, that the wisdom of a regulative act is a question for the legislature's judgment. In 1905 it sounded what then seemed the death knell of *McCulloch v. Maryland* when it decided in *Lochner v. New York* that a law which limited working hours violated freedom of contract. In all these cases the due-process and the equal-protection-of-the-law clauses of the Fourteenth Amendment were applied to corporations in the guise of persons. Charles Warren, in his definitive *The Supreme Court in United States History*, reveals that between 1889 and

1918 there were 790 cases in which statutes were attacked under these two clauses, the great majority concerning the use of police power. There were fifty-three cases, however, in which the Court ruled a statute unconstitutional as a violation of the Fourteenth Amendment, and two-thirds of them involved the rates and regulations of public service corporations.

Thus the legal Darwinians found in the Fourteenth Amendment the instrument needed for their purpose. There is a vagueness to its phrasing that admits and even invites divergent interpretations, and as time passed and the spirit exemplified by Justice Field prevailed, a series of ever widening interpretations made of the Fourteenth Amendment a comprehensive Bill of Rights for corporations. Another series of decisions of an ever narrowing sort finally created a legal vortex into which were sucked most of the newly won rights of the former slaves. Their unimpeded right to vote, their rights of peaceable assembly and petition for redress of grievances, their right to the full and equal enjoyment of public accommodations and private accommodations that served the public were nullified by a series of eight Supreme Court decisions between 1876 and 1884 involving the rights of Negroes. Warren concludes that of the enforcement laws passed to implement the three liberation amendments only a small fraction remained even nominally in force. Of the forty-seven sections of the three amendments, forty-two were repealed or declared invalid. A corporation was a person, but a Negro was not. There were racist aspects to social Darwinism also—they are soundly treated by Richard Hofstadter in his *Social Darwinism in American Thought*[18]—but they lie outside the scope of this book.

"THE BUSINESS OF AMERICA IS BUSINESS"

Thus social Darwinism became the law of the land. Great was the rejoicing of the happy few, the Fittest Americans who survived. Chauncey Depew had a simple test for membership in the ranks of the Fittest Americans; was one at the head table when New York ran a banquet at Delmonico's? James J. Hill had one for railroadmen; does one's line absorb other lines? John D. Rockefeller, a Fittest American who found no difficulty in recon-

ciling his social Darwinism and his Baptist beliefs, assured a
Sunday-school audience, "The growth of a large business is
merely a survival of the fittest. . . . This is not an evil tendency
in business. It is merely the working-out of a law of nature and a
law of God."[19] Andrew Carnegie went the full course of William
Sumner, finding in social Darwinism a gospel entirely adequate to replace the creed of Moses and the evangelists. "I remember that light came as in a flood and all was clear," he
happily proclaimed after reading Darwin and Spencer. "Not
only had I got rid of theology and the supernatural, but I had
found the truth of evolution. 'All is well since all grows better,'
became my motto, my true source of comfort."[20] It might be
hard for the individual, Carnegie conceded as a Fittest American
if ever a man was and hence in a good position to make such
charitable nods, but it was best for the race. Social Darwinism
"insures the survival of the fittest in every department." Nor is
it at all accurate to say that the influence of Spencer and his
brand of social Darwinism failed to survive the economic up-
heavals of the 1890s. The shadow of oblivion did lie deep upon
Herbert Spencer while he still lived, and the philosophy of
social Darwinism was increasingly assailed from increasingly
diverse quarters, but in 1915 an edition of Spencer's essays with
a Republican party exegesis by such stalwarts as Nicholas Murray Butler and Charles Eliot for the world of scholarship,
Henry Cabot Lodge and Elihu Root for the halls of government,
and Harlan Fiske Stone for the judicial chambers was used to
combat Woodrow Wilson's New Freedom, and not without substantial impact. Nor does one have to be a graybeard to recall
the constant overtones of social Darwinism in the public utterances of the political generation that was nurtured under Warren
Harding, waxed mighty under Calvin Coolidge, and then felt
the bitter frost under Herbert Hoover. "The business of America
is business," remarked the cryptic Coolidge, a Massachusetts
politician and successful social Darwinian in that testing arena,
Bay State politics, who somehow kept people believing that he
was a Vermont farmer. The epigram had a meaning, even if it
tends to be lost upon the current generation. Business was the
most important thing in American life in the 1920s, to those who
were the fittest to share its rewards or to be its spokesmen, be-

cause the set of values the Fittest Americans of the age understood, respected, and sincerely considered valid were the values
of the man-made order as they had slowly evolved under the
deism of the eighteenth century and the utilitarianism and
social Darwinism of the nineteenth. Hofstadter quotes from the
Lynds's *Middletown in Transition:* "You can't make the world
all planned and soft," says the businessman of Middletown.
"The strongest and best survive—that's the law of nature after
all—always has been and always will be."[21] The businessman of
Middletown was hardly fittest by the standards of Hill, Rockefeller, and Carnegie, but he was by the standards of Middletown,
and that was what mattered.

We have found it necessary to trace in detail the difference between utilitarianism in theory and utilitarianism in practice.
John Stuart Mill, who represented utilitarianism in its most
highly developed and most socially responsible phase, was a
social thinker of the first order and a man of deep humanitarian
sensibility. But the utilitarianism that inspires his *Principles of
Political Economy* (1848), that finds its most thoughtful and
philosophic expression in *On Liberty* (1859), and its practical
application to problems of government in *Representative Government* (1861), is a continent away from the utilitarianism that
underlies the spread-eagle oratory of Macaulay, not to mention
the utilitarianism that inspires the fanatical single-mindedness
of Dickens' creation Gradgrind and the almost frightening rapacity of his other creation Bounderby. Mill accepted the principles of classical economics but he never accepted that blood-
less corollary, the economic man. He thought of man in social,
political, and ethical terms, another way of saying that he
thought of him in terms of flesh and blood. The consequence was
that Mill often found himself locked in ideological combat with
the members of the school his father had done so much to
found and which he himself represented at its finest, and the
Mill who is invariably the best exponent of utilitarianism is often
the most effective refuter of its developments.

In similar fashion it is necessary to draw a distinction between
social Darwinism in theory and social Darwinism in practice.
Charles Darwin, of course, was not a Darwinian; no germinal
thinker is really a member of his own school. Plato was not a

Platonist, nor was Aristotle an Aristotelian. Darwin was a biologist, and the metaphoric extension of his theory of evolution to the social, political, and economic realms was not of his doing. Darwin seldom allows himself the luxury of deductive speculation, but at the very end of *The Origin of Species* he does indulge in a sentence or two in which evolutionary theory inclines toward what came to be known as social Darwinism, with the utilitarian premise acting as philosophic catalyst: ". . . as natural selection works solely by and for the good of each being, all corporeal and mental endowments will tend to progress toward perfection."[22] A chain can be constructed between such a sentence as that and the doctrine of the survival of the economic fittest that appealed to Andrew Carnegie and John D. Rockefeller, but it would have to be a chain of many links and not all would be strong ones. In similar fashion Darwin's acceptance of the concept of the man-made order was tentative and intellectually too modest to represent a securely held philosophic belief. As good an expression of his attitude as exists can be found in a letter to the American botanist Asa Gray in which he writes, "I had no intention to write atheistically. But I own that I cannot see as plainly as others do, and as I should wish to do, evidence of design and beneficence on all sides of us. There seems to me too much misery in the world. I cannot persuade myself that a beneficent and omnipotent God would have designedly created the Ichneumonidae with the express intention of their feeding within the living bodies of Caterpillars, or that a cat should play with mice. Not believing this, I see no necessity in the belief that the eye was expressly designed. On the other hand, I cannot anyhow be contented to view this wonderful universe, and especially the nature of man, and to conclude that everything is the result of brute force. I am inclined to look at everything as resulting from designed laws, with the details, whether good or bad, left to the working out of what we may call chance. Not that this notion at all satisfies me. I feel deeply that the whole subject is too profound for the human intellect."[23] If philosophic labels must be attached to Darwin, a composite of deism of the Bolingbroke sort and the agnosticism which characterized his follower Huxley is fairly close, with at least a tincture of determinism added. What one never finds in Darwin is the social Darwinism of Spencer and Sumner.

In similar fashion Huxley was a Darwinian without being a social Darwinian of the Spencer-Sumner school. He drew a distinction between natural evolution and social evolution, as we have seen, maintaining that man had evolved beyond the deterministic sort of evolution that rules in the world of nature to a state of being in which he achieves his own progress by the proper exercise of his free will. In the state of social evolution he is dedicated to the improvement of the moral order by the twin principles of human sympathy and social cooperation. To be sure, Huxley does believe in what he terms the struggle for the means of enjoyment and he further believes that in that struggle the qualities dear to the social Darwinians—energy, industry, intellectual capacity, and tenacity of purpose—make for success. Again, a chain could be constructed between that belief and the concept of the survival of the fittest dinner guests and railroads held by Chauncey Depew and James J. Hill, but again it would be a chain of many links and more than one would be of doubtful holding strength.

Behind the rationale of Andrew Carnegie and John D. Rockefeller and behind the legal rationalizing of the liberal wing of the Supreme Court was the social Darwinism proclaimed by Herbert Spencer and William Graham Sumner. It was their extension by metaphor of the survival-of-the-fittest concept to the economic realm that fitted the thought patterns of the industrial titans of the post-Civil War period. Metaphor is the language of poetry, however, not of science, and the explanation of sociological facts in biological phraseology is a tricky and unconvincing business at best. Perhaps it is significant of the shallowness of the entire business that a literal application of the principle of natural selection of the realms of economics and sociology would be theoretically deterministic and therefore destructive of the very concept of free enterprise. This disturbing thought seems to have been entertained by neither Huxley, Spencer, nor Sumner. Logically or illogically, all the social Darwinians believed in the man-made order.

GONE BUT NOT FORGOTTEN

The social Darwinians had their day, and it has passed. But it is a reliable phenomenon of human nature that as ideas pass, they are passed down. What John D. Rockefeller said late in the nineteenth century, the businessman of Middletown would parrot half a century later, just as the debate over true Darwinism had its echo in the Scopes trial in Tennessee a half century after the dust of battle had settled over the English intellectual battlefields. Hofstadter is sound when he asserts[24] that Darwinian individualism has entered American political folklore and that its resurgence is always possible so long as predacity exists. Old Thomas Hobbes did not have the entire truth about human nature, but he had an important segment of the truth. There is something Hobbesian about the entire business of the survival of the fittest, and there is something not only Hobbesian but very definitely Marxist about the solution that only absolutism can combat it. There is a sense in which Hobbes was behind social Darwinism, and there is a sense in which social Darwinism is behind collectivism in the several forms it has assumed in the twentieth century. Social Darwinism has been behind fascism in its several forms. Karl Marx once declared, "Darwin's book is very important and serves me as a basis in natural science for the class struggle in history";[25] a literal interpretation of this sentence would make Marx a social Darwinian of a sort, and the interpretation would be justified. The man-made order has taken many forms, and our limitation to four specific forms— deism, utilitarianism, social Darwinism, and pragmatism—is a limitation self-imposed by considerations that are utilitarian, pragmatic, and practical. The common denominator is the ease with which the spirit of reform, which inspires each manifestation of the man-made order at its outset, is speedily snuffed out, and the speed with which reaction replaces it. Deism was not supposed to produce a Hoadley, utilitarianism a Macaulay, social Darwinism a Rockefeller, but so it worked out.

XIII

TRUTH IS

SUCCESSFUL EXPERIENCE

ONE of the fundamentals in the history of human thought is the fact that the intellectual tide is seldom at the same stage in separated harbors of the mind. Just as a midnight tide in New York does not connote a midnight tide in Boston, and certainly not in San Francisco, so there is no contradiction in the statement that a tide of thought is both advancing and receding at the same time. The tide of social Darwinism, in its Spencer-Sumner form, began to recede with professional economists in the mid-1880s; it continued to advance among American businessmen and therefore among American politicians, who have a keen sense of the progress of the tide and an educated ability to ride its current, until the late 1920s. One could still hear at the Harvard Business School, in 1925, economic doctrines that were being questioned in the Harvard Yard in 1885. In 1885 the American Economic Association declared the state "an agency whose positive assistance is one of the indispensable conditions of human progress."[1] Speculative economists talked in that vein at Harvard late in the 1880s; businessmen ruefully began to echo them when the Depression had well settled in, by the mid-1930s. We signal out Harvard, because the next major concept of the man-made order to appear in the English-speaking world, and the one concept native to the United States and not imported from England, had its birth at Harvard.

The ultimate progenitors of the next manifestation of the man-made order, however, were not the professional economists at Harvard but a group of philosophic academicians. Two of them,

Charles Peirce and Chauncey Wright, are unknown outside the
ranks of those who try to record the history of thought. Two
others, William James and John Dewey, by dint of personality
and attainments, moved beyond the academic circle to the larger
arena of American life. A fifth, the younger Oliver Wendell
Holmes, became America's brightest legal light of the twentieth
century, and probably the most important single progenitor of
the pattern of thinking that underlay the New Deal. There were
others, but these five are central to our purpose.

By 1880 America was ready to make its contribution to
original and imaginative human thought, and Harvard College
was the logical place for it to appear. In Van Wyck Brooks's
phrase, it was the New England Indian summer, the season of
mellow fruitfulness. The Calvinistic rigor which had stiffened
New England backbones for 250 years had been modified by
Unitarianism and transcendentalism, and by 1880 it had softened
to a moral earnestness. The claim of New England to intellectual
primacy in the new land had not yet been challenged, and the
claim of Harvard to intellectual primacy in New England has
never really been challenged. Perhaps the English visitor to
Cambridge who reported that there were enough brains along
the Charles to staff the universities of Great Britain let his
generosity sway his judiciousness, but like every exaggeration
the statement rested on a truth. There was an impressive concentration of intelligence at Harvard in the late nineteenth
century, at least as great as the later twentieth century knows
in these days when so much of the scientific intelligence of the
Western world is concentrated between Harvard Square and
Kendall Square, the subway stop for Massachusetts Institute of
Technology. Harvard of the 1880s was at once a very parochial
institution, very true to the essential spirit of its past even as it
broke the limited academic pattern which was its inheritance,
and a university with a worldwide outlook, especially aware of
the scholarship of Germany and aware as well of what lay
beyond the Western world. It was a day when Boston ships and
Boston men plied the seven seas, and it is by no means certain
that jet propulsion has broadened New England horizons quite
as effectively as did the clipper ships. Harvard was ready to
make an original and imaginative contribution.

CHARLES PEIRCE: BEGINNINGS OF PRAGMATISM

It started, as such contributions tend to start, in the thinking of two dedicated philosophers, professional philosophers if there be such a thing, Charles Peirce and Chauncey Wright. Charles Peirce was one of those unfortunate personalities denied more vital gifts but enormously gifted with the power of abstract thought, with a razor-blade mind that slashed unsparingly at those who lacked his crystal clarity of thought and expression, even when the bumbler was his truest, most forgiving, and endlessly attentive friend, William James. Peirce could follow a line of thought beyond the dim horizon, but he could not follow a line of action that would let him hold a job. Peirce had ties with Harvard that were so close that nothing short of his perversity could have cut them: his grandfather was the college librarian, his father was professor of mathematics at Harvard for forty-nine years, and his brother was successively dean of the graduate school and of the faculty of arts and sciences in the course of his forty-five years at the university. Yet President Eliot would not give Charles Peirce a university position despite the earnest pleading of that by no means inconsequential member of his faculty, William James, nor was it in James's heart to blame him. Consequently Peirce lived on the fringe of university life, giving series of lectures at Harvard on three occasions, working for the United States Coast and Geodetic Survey for thirty years, shocking Cambridge by divorcing his first wife, and ending his days in poverty and oblivion in 1914 at Milford, Pennsylvania. Only William James remembered, and strove to ease those tragic Milford days. The writings of the man who was too cantankerous and unreliable to hold his college classes on the intermittent occasions when he met them were brought out by the Harvard University Press long after his death.[2] Peirce is a Harvard luminary whose light was doomed to flicker fitfully in the antechapel of that cathedral of learning, but the fault was not that of Harvard.

William James maintained that pragmatism started with Charles Peirce in 1878, when he published in *Popular Science Monthly* a paper entitled "How to Make Our Ideas Clear."

Peirce came to grips in this paper with the problem presented by ideas which cannot be translated into mental images, ideas such as weight and free will. No one will maintain that because such ideas cannot be translated into sense images they do not correspond to realities. Peirce wrote, "Let us seek a clear idea of Weight. . . . To say that a body is heavy means simply that, in the absence of opposing force, it will fall. This (neglecting certain specifications of how it will fall, etc., which exist in the mind of the physicist who uses the word) is evidently the whole conception of weight."[3] Weight is conceived, not in terms of what it is but in terms of what in our experience it does. Thus we have a pragmatic knowledge of weight, a knowledge based upon experience with weight and the way in which it acts.

One of Peirce's most pregnant statements is that an idea is a plan of action. We can conjure up a mental picture of an illuminated bulb but not a mental picture of electricity. We conceive of electricity in terms of what it does, or in terms of a plan of action to make it do our will, such as illuminate a bulb. To the motorist the mental picture conjured up by red and green traffic lights are not mental pictures of colors; they are mental pictures of action, of stopping and starting the car. An idea that is a plan of action is good and true if it works to our advantage, worthless and false if it does not.

The next point to be considered is the significance of the word "works" in this statement. In the simplest form an idea works if it produces the advantageous result envisaged in it. There is in Boston an office building with a lighted weather beacon; blue means fair weather and red means rain. Granted the admirable accuracy of the Boston Weather Bureau, this beacon works for the Bostonian to whom blue and red in this instance are not colors but symbols of approaching weather. But there is said to be in Pittsburgh an office building with a lighted weather beacon on which red means fair weather. In Boston red "means" rain, in Pittsburgh red "means" clear skies. One might add that on the traffic beacons of both cities red "means" stop. Thus the body of truth changes and one's belief about the meaning of red in a weather beacon works only if adjusted to the idea which prevails in the city where one observes it. Therefore in such cases a belief works and so is good and true only if brought into coherence with another belief. In still more complicated matters beliefs work only if coherent with many related beliefs. Except in the simplest of cases it is not the belief that is true and therefore good, but the belief in its ideological setting. The body of truth continually changes, and only the pragmatic test reveals the truth. As Edward C. Moore puts it in *American Pragmatism,* "Pragmatism is an experiential or psychological meaning theory. It does not rest its criterion of meaning on logical or formal grounds—a proposition is not meaningful simply because it has a certain syntactical structure—but on psychological grounds. Pragmatism undertakes to explicate the psychological or cognitive content of a sentence in terms of volitions and sense-experiences, so that to say that a proposition (or a concept) is meaningless for a pragmatist is to say that it cannot be expressed in terms of psychological experiences."[4] "Red means stop" and "Purple means stop" are sentences with the same syntactical structure. The former has a meaning and the latter is meaningless. The latter is meaningless because in neither the volition of a traffic engineer constructing a system of traffic control nor in the psychological experience of any motorist driving with its assistance does purple ever mean stop.

The pragmatism of Charles Peirce obviously belongs to the realm of pure philosophy, and only those habituated to its attenuated air could breathe it, and Peirce was not the man to supply oxygen. He lived little known and he died forgotten, but he influenced men like John Dewey and Oliver Wendell Holmes who have had an enormous influence on American life and thought. "It was in the earliest seventies that a knot of us young men in Old Cambridge, calling ourselves, half-ironically, half defiantly, 'The Metaphysical Club,'—for agnosticism was then riding its high horse, and was frowning superbly upon all metaphysics—used to meet, sometimes in my study, sometimes in that of William James," Peirce wrote in or about 1906.[5] He lists as the other members Oliver Wendell Holmes, the celebrated Boston attorney Joseph Warner, another Boston attorney, Nicholas St. John Green, Chauncey Wright, the historian John Fiske, and on occasion a Unitarian minister of very advanced ideas, Francis Ellingwood Abbot. "Wright, James, and I were men of science," he continued, "rather scrutinizing the doctrines of the metaphysicians on their scientific side than regarding them as very momentous spiritually. The type of our thought was decidedly British. I, alone of our number, had come upon the threshing-floor of philosophy through the doorway of Kant, and even my ideas were acquiring the English accent."[6]

The significance of the British cast of thought we trust to develop shortly. As for the Metaphysical Club, which is never referred to by name by any pragmatist except Peirce, it was one of those tiny areas of fertility in which ideas germinate that are destined to grow to dimensions unconceived of by those who preside at their beginnings. Peirce was an obscure logician, but a mighty influence on American thought. William James dedicated to him his second book, *The Will to Believe* (1897), as one "to whom philosophic comradeship in old times and to whose writings in more recent years I owe more incitement and help than I can express or repay." Josiah Royce, in the Preface to *The Problem of Christianity* (1913), attributed to him a greater formative power over his own thinking than he did to the tradition of idealism or the doctrines of Hegel. John Dewey in his *Logic: The Theory of Inquiry* (1947) acknowledged his great indebtedness in logical theory to the long-dead and largely forgotten Peirce. Peirce, according to Catherine Drinker Bowen, was a yeasty figure in the intellectual ferment in which young Oliver Wendell Homes was reared.[7] Peirce was a philosopher's philosopher, a scholar's scholar, a man who did not bear fools easily. But on those with minds that would take a honing, and the Metaphysical Club was made up of such minds, his incisive wit and stark clarity of thought could help to produce the razor's edge. James, Royce, Dewey, and others gladly testified to their debt, and the fact that eight books about Peirce were published between 1939 and 1953, a quarter century and more after his death, reveals the slowly gathering and now fully developed awareness that this employee of the Coast and Geodetic Survey who occasionally returned to Harvard as a comet occasionally returns to the earth was one of the first begetters of modern American thought.

CHAUNCEY WRIGHT: PROTO-PRAGMATISM

The career of Charles Peirce was circumscribed severely by his own temperament; the career of Chauncey Wright was tragically foreshortened by his death of cerebral hemorrhage at the age of forty-five. Wright had a substantial and conventional New England country background. His father was a grocer of Northampton, conservative in his business dealings but advanced enough in his religious thought to be a Unitarian at a time when the newer church had made little headway on the banks of the Connecticut. His mother came from Connecticut and was a quiet, utterly humorless woman, on her son's testimony. Chauncey Wright records that when he was a youngster in the Northampton grammar school the teacher forced him, against his stubborn will, to his knees in the public prayer with which the school day was habitually opened, there and throughout New England. Wright was not easily forced to his knees, as a boy or as a man. He had a secondary-school training unusual for his time and place, attendance at Select High School where, in contemporary parlance, an enriched curriculum was offered the better students under the direction of a scientific-minded schoolmaster. This man introduced young Wright to pre-Darwinian concepts of evolution by having him read Robert Chambers' then notorious and now forgotten *Vestiges of the Natural History of Creation*. Wright had an instinct for science and mathematics, and apparently an instinct that rebelled at Latin and Greek. He went to Harvard, came under the influence of Charles Peirce's father the mathematician, and emerged from his bouts with the classics with his degree intact but his class standing battered. He also emerged with a conviction quite important in his evolutionary thought, a conviction that the difference in mental faculties between man and the animals is one of degree and not of kind. If there is any cornerstone on which his evolutionary convictions rested, it was this.

On graduation he got the job that fitted his independent spirit, with its native inclination for private research. He became a computer for the *Nautical Almanac*. He held the job for years, found ways and means of simplifying the mathematical calculations it required, managed thereby to cut down his work year to about three months, lived the simple life for most of his tragically few years, and, as a close student of his life and thought puts it, had "ample time for what turned out to be his real career, namely, being Socratic sage or scourge (depending on one's viewpoint) to the inhabitants of old Cambridge."[8] His career as such had its light and dark periods, but mainly it was dappled. Wright never married, and was never a man sufficiently independent to stand successfully the rigors of loneliness. His health was good and he did his work when he was watched and guarded, and the watcher's role was assumed in his earlier Cambridge years by a benefactor from Northampton and in his later years by Professor Charles Eliot Norton and his family. In between were the years of gall and old cigars, of brooding loneliness sadly and increasingly relieved by that melancholy companion of loneliness, the bottle. His health was undermined thereby, and not even the unremitting care of Norton could re-open to him the door to perfect health. It could open, however, the doors to the *Nation* and the *North American Review,* and the post of secretary of the American Academy of Arts and Science. He wrote for the former and worked for the latter and by the 1870s he was intellectually ready to be that mentor for Peirce's Metaphysical Club which its members admitted him to be. His years of close association with Peirce, James, Holmes, and the other metaphysicians, all his juniors in age, were also the years of his essays on evolution contributed to the *North American Review,* "Limits of Natural Selection" (1870), "The Genesis of Species" (1871), "Evolution by Natural Selection" (1872), and "Evolution of Self-Consciousness" (1873). The first three comprise his defense of Darwinism, but the last, which was written at the suggestion of Darwin himself, is the one of greatest significance in the development of pragmatism.

Wright did not live to formulate a comprehensive philosophy. Hence we can at the most single out tendencies in his thought, and trust to make it clear that the tendency is toward pragmatism. Behind Wright's evolutionary convictions was a conviction even more fundamental, a conviction of what has been termed the ethical neutrality of science. He states that "we are inclined to accept as the soundest and most catholic assumption, on grounds of scientific method, the too little regarded doctrine of Aristotle, which banishes cosmology from the realm of scientific inquiry, reducing natural phenomena in their cosmological relations to an infinite variety of manifestations (without a discoverable tendency on the whole) of causes and laws which are simple and constant in their ultimate elements."[9] His name for this infinite variety of manifestations with their separate governing laws but not their discoverable, all-encompassing, single law was "cosmical weather." The meteorologist also can reduce the weather to manifestations controlled by causes and even, to some degree, reducible to laws, but the all-encompassing, single law of weather escapes his comprehension, and presumably he is agnostic about its existence. In similar fashion Wright was a positivist and an agnostic where his "cosmical weather" was concerned, and both viewpoints fostered the conclusion that one should separate his ethical convictions from his scientific convictions, preserving at all times the ethical neutrality of science. It is probably unnecessary to look beyond this conviction for the cause of Wright's failure to receive an invitation to join the scientific faculty of Harvard, or even to lecture there until Eliot became president. Science was indeed a Harvard handmaid to theology during the evolutionary wars. But it in no sense follows that Wright was either a skeptic or a cynic about ethical values. "Religion and morality are both realized in the practical nature of man, in character, in the fashioning of his volitions and desires," he maintained; "religion and morality are definable and distinguishable independently of creeds and codes."[10] This, he added, is Mill's position, as indeed it is, and Huxley's too, and also that of William James.

Wright was, then, an evolutionist, a positivist of sorts, and a believer in the ethical neutrality of science. Beyond that he was a utilitarian. He believed that if the test of consequences is applied to moral judgments, they can be corrected and improved. This the utilitarian philosophy permits but not so any intuitive or moral sense philosophy. Hence as one of scientific bias and conviction Wright found that the utilitarian approach to ethics made one capable of an ethical growth and development impossible in a pattern in which ethical guidance came from the formal teachings of a church or from the moral dictates of the individual conscience. But observe that the superiority of utilitarianism, in Wright's view, arises from the fact that it admits of the improvement of moral concepts on the basis of experience. Wright never used the term "pragmatism" nor was there evolved a conscious philosophy of pragmatism before his death; but even if it be only by way of anticipation, there is evident the coming fusion of utilitarianism and pragmatism in his thinking. "The type of our thought was decidedly British," as Peirce put it.

Wright in his utilitarianism was very much of the school of John Stuart Mill in maintaining that the qualitative difference among pleasures is fundamental to a tenable utilitarianism. "It is a mistake," he maintained, ". . . to suppose that the measure of a pleasure in this philosophy is simply its intensity as a feeling, and not also its rank or preferability in kind, or a certain dignity it has in the spiritual hierarchy independent of and antecedent to its proper moral rank."[11] He is also very much of the school of Mill in maintaining that this spiritual hierarchy of pleasures is something acquired through experience and not derived from any a priori moral system. Again the coming fusion of utilitarianism and pragmatism is evident.

The letters of Wright show a very practical and specific bent to his utilitarianism and proto-pragmatism, and a decided opposition to social Darwinism of the Spencer-Sumner stamp. He believed in a drastic curtailment of the privileges of wealth, but without infringement on the fundamental principle of private property. He believed that private wealth is a public responsibility, and that the measure of its justification is the way that it is used. "Looked at rationally and from a utilitarian point of view, the rights of private ownership, the protection of the individual in the possession, accumulation, consumption, productive administration, and posthumous disposal of his surplus gain—is founded simply and solely in the motives they afford to his making such gains, and adding them, as he really does (in spite of his seeming private appropriation of them), to the store of public wealth."[12] For a third time, in his concept that wealth is intrinsically neither good nor bad but is good or bad in terms of its use as an instrument there can be seen in Wright the seeds of pragmatism.

That there are links between the utilitarianism of Chauncey Wright and what we have called his proto-pragmatism (one should not forget that Wright lived and died before pragmatism, and that the word was not in his philosophic vocabulary) seems clear enough. It is not nearly so clear that there are links between his proto-pragmatism and his evolutionary beliefs, although a certain kinship of concept at least can be traced. The relationship is established by Wright's insistence on the qualitative aspect of pleasure. What makes for pleasure makes for success, and what makes for success makes for survival. The higher forms of pleasure are those most conducive to lasting success and hence are the sure guarantors of survival. Consequently the evolutionary process is linked to the utilitarian rationale, since pleasure is the characteristic of the patterns of belief and action that make for survival and increase. Here, if anywhere, the thought of Wright and the thought of Spencer are tangent and Wright the utilitarian and Wright the evolutionist coalesce, but nowhere in Wright is there support for the planned economy or the planned society. He believed that since all men react alike to what causes unhappiness in the social and economic order but all men by no means agree as to what produces their happiness, it is simpler and more practical to weed out the evil growths from the social order than artificially to cultivate the useful ones.

To what extent was Chauncey Wright really the father of American pragmatism? He was more an ancestor in the direct line than a literal father. His concept of "cosmical weather," his positivism, his ethical neutrality in scientific speculation, the stress in his utilitarianism upon the element of experience, the way in which he tends to fuse his utilitarian and his evolutionary beliefs created the framework within which later thinkers— of whom three of the most important were his younger contemporaries and Harvard friends, Peirce, James, and Holmes—were to build pragmatism as a philosophy. To Wright as to Peirce, an idea is a plan of action; thinking is by its nature experimental and succeeds by the experimental method in determining and refining the bases of pleasure; man has slowly evolved from whatever were his beginnings to his present state. There is nothing more nearly central in Wright's work than the last of the *North*

American Review articles, the one written at the suggestion of Darwin, "Evolution of Self-Consciousness," in which he undertakes to demonstrate that human reason differs from animal instinct in degree but not in kind and emerged from it by the evolutionary process. Wright differs from the true pragmatists in that his proto-pragmatism is limited to the sphere of science and not the larger domain of general thought. He laid the groundwork, however, for those who would so extend it, and by fusing utilitarianism and evolutionary theory with his proto-pragmatism, he did much to predetermine the pattern that pragmatism would assume. When Wright said, "A theory which is utilized receives the highest possible certificate of truth," he was talking within the context of science, and hence was not a pragmatist. Let that context be extended to the realm of general thought and one has pragmatism. Peirce so extended it when he wrote: "In order to ascertain the meaning of an intellectual conception one should consider what practical consequences might conceivably result by necessity from the truth of that conception; and the sum of these consequences will constitute the entire meaning of the conception."[13] This is true pragmatism. James extended the concept farther by the contention that a conception has meaning if merely to believe in it has consequences that can be experienced. This is developed pragmatism.

WILLIAM JAMES

The influence of Wright on William James was partly affirmative and partly negative. It was affirmative to the extent that the older man was a formative influence upon James in his younger days, in the years 1865 to 1875 when Wright, a close family friend of the Jameses, as Ralph Barton Perry puts it, "held many a Socratic session with both father and son."[14] It was affirmative to the extent that James considered valid Wright's scientific bias toward the experimental approach and Wright's implied limitation upon the possibilities of scientific knowledge in his characterization of the phenomena of the universe as "cosmical weather," with specific patterns and laws that can be experientially determined but no all-embracing law within the comprehension of man. But no man is entirely the pupil of his master, and even when he accepted as valid Wright's pattern of thought James did not perfectly reflect it. There is a sharpness of division in Wright between scientific and ethical thought that is somewhat blurred in William James. For example, James writes in "Is Life Worth Living?": "The notion that this physical world of wind and water, where the sun rises and the moon sets, is absolutely and ultimately the divinely aimed-at and established thing, is one which we find only in very early religions, such as that of the most primitive Jews. It is this natural religion (primitive still, in spite of the fact that poets and men of science whose good-will exceeds their perspicacity keep publishing it in new editions tuned to our contemporary ears) that, as I said a while ago, has suffered definitive bankruptcy in the opinion of a circle of persons, among whom I must count myself, and who are growing more numerous every day. For such persons the physical order of nature, taken simply as science knows it, cannot be held to reveal any one harmonious spiritual intent. It is mere *weather*, as Chauncey Wright called it, doing and undoing without end."[15]

To this point James fairly well reflects the pattern of thinking one finds in Chauncey Wright, although Wright would probably be a shade more carefully agnostic in a similar statement. But James continues in a vein which reveals that Wright was his adversary in a sense at least as fundamental as the sense in which he was James's teacher. He says that "we have a right to believe the physical order to be only a partial order; . . . we have a right to supplement it by an unseen spiritual order which we assume on trust, if only thereby life may seem to us better worth living again."[16] At statements such as this Wright, who had no desires but the desire for the scientific truth, sadly shook his head. And although James was forced into a tactical retreat from his specific phrase, "the will to believe," he never really made that retreat in his heart. Later in the same lecture he assured his listeners of the Cambridge YMCA: "The inner need of believing that this world of nature is a sign of something more spiritual and eternal than itself is just as strong and authoritative in those who feel it, as the inner need of uniform laws of causation ever can be in a professionally scientific head. The toil of many generations has proved the latter need prophetic. Why *may* not the former one be prophetic, too? And if needs of ours outrun the visible universe, why *may* not that be a sign that an invisible universe is there."[17]

If the ultimate implication of the philosophic thought of William James can be summed up, it is a profound need to believe in God. William James was the son of the elder Henry James in every sense of the word. The elder James was a rebel against both the spiritual order of Calvinism in which he had been reared and the social order of which his own father had been so spectacular a beneficiary. At the age of thirty-three he suffered a sudden, severe, and prolonged nervous collapse from which he finally extricated himself with the aid of the writings of Swedenborg. The writings of the elder James are mainly an expression of his Swedenborgian version of what his son William later would castigate as the untenable concept of the Absolute, "the immanence of God in the unity of mankind." There was a neurasthenic side to the elder James, but the side that really mattered was his kindly, sympathetic, friendly, warmly human side, the side which he transmitted unaltered and unabridged to his eldest son, who built upon what he had inherited.

William James also had his neurasthenic side, and his nervous breakdown. In 1869–1870 this seizure took the form, as Perry puts it, of "the ebbing of the will to live, for lack of a philosophy to live by—a paralysis of action occasioned by a sense of moral impotence."[18] Perhaps it was not entirely different from the crisis through which Carlyle passed and which he describes so memorably in the central chapters of *Sartor Resartus*. Carlyle had lost his faith, and with it his hope. He emerged from his Leith Walk crisis as the first seedlings of that will to believe which Carlyle calls "the Everlasting Yea" took root and protruded from his then arid soul. There is a passage among the papers of William James, apparently some loose sheets cut from a notebook, in which he states, "A militant existence, in which the ego is posited as a monad, with the *good* as its end, and the final consolation only that of irreconcilable hatred—though evil slay me, she can't subdue me, or make me worship her. The brute force is all at her command, but the final protest of my soul as she squeezes me out of existence gives me still in a certain sense the superiority."[19] The words are those of William James, but with a very minor modification of the technical expression they could be those of Thomas Carlyle. Like Carlyle, William James felt a profound need to believe in God. The expression of that need is the final core of all his writing.

In William James, then, we find a man with a profound need for a religious faith who devotes his substantial philosophic powers to developing a pattern of belief to which he can give unqualified intellectual assent and a pattern which may be valid for other men as well. In his immediate, personal background are the pragmatism of Charles Peirce and the ethical neutrality of Chauncey Wright. Pragmatism opens the mind, Peirce assured James, but it does not furnish evidence. James found the assurance satisfying; faith does not require the closed mind, and one does not expect faith to gather evidence. Perhaps James had Peirce and Wright in mind when he established his well-known distinction between tough-minded and tender-minded thinkers. The tough-minded, he assured a Lowell Institute audience in 1906, are empiricist ("going by 'facts'"), sensationalistic, materialistic, pessimistic, irreligious, fatalistic, pluralistic, skeptical. The tender-minded are rationalistic ("going by 'principles'"), intellectualistic, idealistic, optimistic, religious, free-willist, monistic, dogmatical.[20] Peirce and Wright were tough-minded. It is the same sort of division of human types, James assures us, that shows itself in manners as the formal and the free-and-easy, in government as the authoritarians and the anarchists, in art as the classics and romantics. In philosophy the tender-minded are the rationalists, the lovers of abstract and eternal principles; the tough-minded are the empiricists, the lovers of facts in all their crude variety. "They have a low opinion of each other," he sadly adds, and he quietly abstracts himself from both their ranks and places himself with what he terms the philosophic amateurs.

The philosophic amateur wants facts, but he wants religion as well. He finds that the tough-minded are not religious enough and that the religion of the tender-minded is not factual enough. The tough-minded jest with Haeckel about God as a "gaseous vertebrate," or with Spencer reduce totality to matter and motion. The tender-minded climb above reality, through the clouds of abstraction, into the empyrean of the Absolute, where the God of deism dwells. "Absolutism," James concedes, "has a certain sweep and dash about it, while the usual theism is more insipid, but both are equally remote and vacuous. What you want is a philosophy that will not only exercise your powers of intellectual abstraction, but that will make some positive connexion with this actual world of finite human lives. You want a system that will combine both things, the scientific loyalty to facts and willingness to take account of them, the spirit of adaptation and accommodation, in short, but also the old confidence in human values and the resultant spontaneity, whether of the religious or of the romantic type. And that is then your dilemma: you find the two parts of your *quaesitum* hopelessly separated. You find empiricism with inhumanism and irreligion; or else you find a rationalistic philosophy that indeed may call itself religious, but that keeps out of all definite touch with concrete facts and joys and sorrows."[21]

The entire purpose of pragmatism, as William James conceived it, was to find a middle way between the sterile deism into which so much of Old England's Anglicanism and New England's Unitarianism had degenerated, and the sterile materialism which marked so much of *fin de siècle* thought. So far from being an advocate of the man-made order was William James that his fundamental purpose was to re-establish in empirical terms that would be intellectually and emotionally acceptable to a generation nurtured on science and reared in the scientific method, a belief in an order that is divinely created and, with limitations that are an integral and essential part of his thinking, divinely controlled. He would do this as a philosophic amateur whose mind was partly tough and partly tender. Hence James is, at least in intent, optimistic, religious, freewillist, empiricist, and pluralistic. So is his version of pragmatism.

James is optimistic in that he believes that will is capable of affecting outcome. To call him optimistic, however, is to use the layman's term. He certainly did not believe that the world is necessarily getting better, but he did believe that the world can be made better. His own term is *meliorism*, the belief that the world is neither getting better necessarily nor getting worse, that what it becomes lies partly within human control and hence the direction it assumes is in part a human responsibility. He recognizes that this can neither be proved nor disproved, but does not see in that fact a justification of skepticism. Skepticism, as he says in *The Will to Believe*, "is not avoidance of option; it is option of a certain particular kind of risk. Better risk loss of truth than chance of error,—that is your faith-vetoer's exact position."[22] James's concept of meliorism might be illustrated by his case of the man who innocently comes in a spirit of frank and open friendship to the man who harbors a grudge against him without his knowledge of it. Not infrequently such an approach blunts the edge of the grudge and may remove it entirely. In such a situation the will to believe in friendship has affected the outcome of the meeting. "Faith can move mountains" is more than an ancient adage; it is a formulation of meliorism and an aphoristic metaphor for pragmatism itself.

James was religious in that he believed in the Deity and in an order that is in some sense and to some degree of divine origin. The first major exposition of his religious thought is *The Varieties of Religious Experience* (1902), a lecture series given at the University of Edinburgh in 1901–1902. He writes from the viewpoint of a psychologist, not concerning himself with institutional religion, which he deems an external art comprising ritualistic acts, but with personal religion, "the inner dispositions of man himself." As a pragmatist his logical concern is with the effects of religion rather than with its sources or its content, and throughout the *Varieties* he concentrates upon the power of religion to comfort the afflicted, strengthen the healthy-minded, and lead to saintliness. "We have in the fact that the conscious person is continuous with a wider self through which saving experiences come, a positive content of religious experience which, it seems to me, is literally and objectively true as far as it goes,"[23] and James attributes these saving experiences to God. "I will call this higher part of the universe by the name of God. We and God have business with each other; and in opening ourselves to his influence our deepest destiny is fulfilled."[24] There are certain characteristics of pragmatism in James that set it apart from the pragmatism of the others. James is the disciple of Peirce insofar as he tends to define concepts in terms of their practical consequences; this is a sort of common denominator to pragmatism in any form. But there is also present in the pragmatism of James a certain tendency to define truth in terms of value. This we may with considerable confidence trace to the tender-minded James, the James who was religious.

James is free-willist as a logical consequence of his belief in meliorism and the reality of religion. The elder James was reared in the days when the battle was between Calvinism and Unitarianism; William James was reared in the days of the at least apparent and certainly most distressing battle between science and religion. His scientific bias, strengthened by the influence of Wright and even more by his natural interest in the human mind and its workings, brought him face to face with the problem of mechanism. Is man a mere machine and hence determinism the only tenable philosophy, or does he have free will? So central was this question to James that in a sense its resolution was the means of raising him from the Slough of Despond into which his nervous exhaustion had cast him. "I think that yesterday was a crisis in my life," he wrote in his notebook. "I finished the first part of Renouvier's second 'Essais' and see no reason why his definition of Free Will—'the sustaining of a thought because I choose to when I might have other thoughts'—need be the definition of an illusion. At any rate, I will assume for the present—until next year—that it is no illusion. My first act of free will shall be to believe in free will."[25] As we shall see, James's belief in free will is essential to his belief in pluralism and in radical empiricism. More to our immediate point, belief in free will is essential to James's concept of pragmatism. If an idea is a plan of action and truth is something we create, we must have free will; for the act of creation and indeed pragmatism is untenable as a philosophy unless free will implements it. But free will has to James an ethical importance at least as great as its psychological significance. The James who is meliorist and religious is the James who is free-willist and the James who is pragmatist. We make the world and ourselves better by the saving experiences of religion to which we open ourselves by the exercise of our free will—and we test the validity of our action by its results. As Julius Bixler puts it, "The whole pragmatic philosophy must indeed be understood in the light of its belief in the ability of the human individual to choose, and through choice to create."[26]

RADICAL EMPIRICISM

James was an empiricist, according to his own carefully defined radical empiricism. With this statement, of course, we reach the heart of his pragmatism, since by definition the empiricist believes that knowledge is derived from experience. Pragmatism of any sort conceives of the idea as a plan of action. If the emphasis is upon the plan of action itself, that is to say, upon the plan considered as a thought, one has the pragmatism of Charles Peirce. If the emphasis is upon the plan as a habitual form of action, one has the pragmatism of William James. By way of anticipation we might add that if the emphasis is upon the outcome of the action, one has the pragmatism of John Dewey. James called his form of empiricism, radical empiricism. James considered himself to some extent the follower of David Hume in his empiricism, and to some extent one who corrected the limiting fallacy that lies at the heart of Hume. Hume, as we indicated in Chapter IV, believed that experience and not reason leads us to pass from the idea of one object to the idea of another. Thus it is experience and not reason that gives us our ideas of cause and effect. But the skepticism of Hume, in James's view, with its concomitant sense that everything is dissociated from everything else, denied Hume the power of constructive thought. It is the same criticism that Leslie Stephen leveled at Hume when he accused him of "that stagnation which is the natural ideal of a skeptic." The limiting fallacy, James believed, was Hume's failure to recognize that life has its conjunctions as well as its disjunctions. "The conjunctions are as primordial elements of 'fact' as are the distinctions and disjunctions," James asserts.[27]

Radical empiricism admits of constructive thought because it does recognize conjunctions as well as disjunctions, and so admits all the experiences of life: "To be radical, an empiricism must neither admit into its constructions any element that is not directly experienced, nor exclude from them any element that is directly experienced. For such a philosophy the relations that connect experiences must themselves be experienced relations, and any kind of relation experienced must be accounted as 'real' as anything else in the system."[28] Consequently what one knows of an object is derived from every experience one has had of the object or, to use James's own term, the "practical consequences" of the object. As Moore puts it, "Thus pragmatism, for James as well as for Peirce, culminates in that principle which dominates twentieth-century philosophy. The abstract conception is only meaningful so far as it may be reduced to the concrete experience."[29]

Finally, James was pluralistic, rejecting the concept of the Absolute and viewing the central principle of the universe as diversity rather than unity. But on this point, as on so many points in the thought of William James, a careful distinction must be drawn. James rejected absolute pluralism, as a result of his concept of radical empiricism, just as entirely as he rejected absolute monism. "The world is One just so far as its parts hang together by any definite connection. It is many just so far as any definite connection fails to obtain."[30] The problem of understanding James's pluralism is considerably complicated by the difficulty of understanding what any philosopher means by pluralism. Dewey's definition in Baldwin's *Dictionary of Philosophy* is as succinct yet as comprehensive as any contrived: "The metaphysical doctrine that all existence is ultimately reducible to a multiplicity of distinct and independent beings or elements." James's pluralism began, it seems quite certain, as a revolt against absolutism in any form, as an instinct for independence that demanded expression. His radical empiricism made him recognize the reality of connections, but his pluralism made him view them as possible but not necessary. Shakespeare was an Englishman who wrote *Hamlet*. The connection is a fact, but not a necessary fact. A Frenchman might have written it. Bixler defines pluralism as follows, in his *Religion in the Philosophy of William James:* "It is specifically a theory of the additive nature of knowledge, of the disjunctive and external nature of relations, of the discreteness of parts of reality, of the finite numerical nature of bits of the universe."[31] As a pluralist, James shared the conviction of Carlyle that progress comes from the efforts of individuals. As another consequence, James had an instinct for democracy which made him denounce such ventures in imperialism, which had the blessing of the social Darwinians on the

survival-of-the-fittest-race thesis, as he deemed American occupation of the Philippines to be. It gave him an instinctive
sympathy for the individual, which could easily be translated
into a sympathy for the underdog. But most important of all, it
made religion for James a personal matter, a direct relationship
between Deity and the individual, and Deity appeared as somehow both more comprehensible and more approachable than
Deity conceived as the Absolute. Here, as so often in the thought
of William James, that fundamental and instinctive need for
religion seems to have affected the pattern of his religious
thought. Pluralism is fundamentally consistent with belief in free
will, and free will is essential for those saving experiences of
religion to which we open ourselves by its exercise.

Thus William James believed that man has the power and the
duty, within his limitations, to make the world better. He believed that the experiences of religion which make for increased
righteousness are essential to the process. He believed that man
has the free will without which an idea cannot be a plan of
action nor truth something we create. He rejected the skepticism
of Hume as fallacious on the gounds that life has its conjunctions
as well as its disjunctions, and that consequently the constructive
thought which conceives of ideas as plans of action is possible;
and the only meaningful conception, reduction to experience, is
attainable. He believed in a pluralistic universe and worked out
of that belief a set of corollaries: belief in individual effort, in
democracy, in a direct personal relationship with Deity. He
worked out his body of belief in a series of well-read books and
well-attended lectures. Peirce and Wright conceived pragmatism, but William James was its herald.

Very much of the strength and nearly all the weakness of
William James is visible in the way he wrote. He called himself
a philosophic amateur, and there is always something of the
brilliant amateur to his style. William James has been called the
psychologist who wrote like a novelist, his brother Henry James
the novelist who wrote like a psychologist. William James did
write with a clarity, directness, and simplicity not always visible
in his brother's prose style, and certainly not characteristic of
philosophic writing in general. He who runs can read William
James, a statement never made of Immanuel Kant or Hegel. But

the strength was also the weakness; the clarity, directness, and simplicity invited those who read as they run. Hence William James, like Berkeley, was often vanquished by coxcombs with a grin. *The Will to Believe* was an unfortunate title, inviting what it received, such parody versions as "the will to make-believe." James really meant, as he confessed, the right to believe but the rhetorical effect of the more striking title left him open, presumably among those who did not bother to read the essay, to the charge of deliberate self-deception. Similarly such statements in *The Meaning of Truth* as "the true . . . is only the expedient in the way of our thinking, just as the right is only the expedient in the way of our behaving" almost called aloud for misinterpretation, that is, for the interpretation of pragmatism as a philosophic defense of expediency. Even his Yankee phrase for the meaning an idea has in experience, its "cash-value," was taken to mean that the only value James considered valid was a monetary value. Little wonder that John Dewey later wrote ruefully, "It is easier to start a legend than to prevent its continued circulation. No misconception of the instrumental logic has been more persistent than the belief that it makes knowledge merely a means to a practical end, or to the satisfaction of practical needs —practical being taken to signify some quite definite utilities of a material or bread-and-butter type. Habitual associations aroused by the word 'pragmatic' have been stronger than the most explicit and emphatic statements which any pragmatist has been able to make."[32] On the other hand, it is the distortion of deism that produced a Bishop Hoadley, the distortion of utilitarianism that produced a Macaulay, the distortion of Darwinism that produced Herbert Spencer and William Graham Sumner. Pragmatism was destined to produce its apostles of distortion. Distortion is part of the history of thought, and it is not entirely cynical to say that very frequently it is the distortion that has the lasting effect and historically the important one rather than the original thought.

SUMMING UP PRAGMATISM

To sum up the original thought of pragmatism, even to the limited extent that we have seen it in Peirce, Wright, and James, is not simple. The following might be tentatively offered as a summary. Life requires belief in certain values, certain modes of action, certain objectives. If the values prove to have a genuine worth, the modes of action an established effectiveness, and the objectives a stable validity, then belief in them is good. They are true because they are good and they are good because they make for the better life. Hence that is true which makes for the better life; that is true which stands the test of practice. Pragmatism applies to truth the test of goodness in the form of experience, not the test of goodness in terms of conformity to some a priori standard of goodness. Pragmatism also suggests that the difficulty of achieving an a priori standard of goodness and the agnosticism that difficulty invites can be avoided by making the test of goodness the test of experience.

The relationship between utilitarianism and pragmatism is fundamental to the train of thought we are trying to establish. The initial tenets of the two philosophies have nothing in common, to be sure, nor is there any reason to find in utilitarianism the initial inspiration of Charles Peirce, whose *Popular Science Monthly* article "How to Make Our Ideas Clear" was acknowledged by William James to be the seedbed from which pragmatism grew.[33] But the pragmatist and the utilitarian have precisely the same attitude toward a priori and immutable standards. Both apply the test of experience: to be good, a thing must produce a good; the good and the true are determined by experience. The utilitarian did not have at his disposal a psychology comparable to the psychology that William James gave to pragmatism; between the mind chemistry of James Mill and the idea analysis of William James there is a difference equally striking from the viewpoint of content and the viewpoint of profundity. The utilitarian did not probe beneath the surface to the nature of the idea, but he did accept the experiential viewpoint that the good and the true are determined by experience. Chauncey Wright was both a utilitarian and a proto-pragmatist, and he was the teacher of William James.

There is a further link between utilitarianism and pragmatism that arises from the nature of the pragmatic test. Total individualism can only travel the road that David Hume took to skepticism, a fact that William James clearly recognized. Human experiences tend to be partly the same and partly different. Hence the truth induced by two men who have undergone similar ex-

periences will tend to be partly the same and partly different.
Truth will then be relative, and one man's entire truth will at the
best be his neighbor's partial truth and may not even be that. Individual pragmatism can result in nothing but skepticism. So, as
Professor Hocking puts it, "'individual pragmatism' tends to give
way to 'social pragmatism,' which holds that belief to be true
which works for the great majority of men, and ultimately for
all men, in the long run. The truth of a belief would then only be
determined by a long course of social experiment."[34] The true
belief is the one which produces the greatest happiness of the
greatest number, and social pragmatism and utilitarianism gently
merge.

When we turn from the relationship of pragmatism and utilitarianism to the relationship of pragmatism and social Darwinism, we meet a totally different situation. The only thing that
preserved social Darwinism from being deterministic was the
resolute failure of the social Darwinians to think their philosophy through. There is no logical connection whatever between
the "survival of the fittest" metaphor and *laissez faire,* between
the extension to the economic realm of the "natural selection"
concept and free enterprise. The fittest might quite readily prove
their right to survival by organizing to suppress *laissez faire* and
free enterprise; it could be plausibly argued that they have done
precisely that under Communism. But as a historic fact in the
United States, social Darwinism was linked with *laissez faire,*
free enterprise, and ultimately with economic and social standpattism.

Pragmatism, on the other hand, is inconsistent with standpattism. Of its nature it demands experimentation, the testing of
the new approach. It carries as an inevitable corollary the concept of free will and so is opposed to that sort of post-factum
determinism which made the Fittest Americans who survived
proclaim their survival as part of an inevitable law of nature.
Pragmatism is individualistic; by philosophic inclination, democratic; and by its bias toward the experimental, benign toward
experimentation in every realm, including the social and economic. One could be a social Darwinian and a reformer, provided the inclination of one's pattern of reform was socialistic.
One could be a pragmatist and a reformer within the American

pattern of individualism, democracy, and free enterprise. Peirce and Wright were the progenitors of the new philosophy and James its popularizer. They were not the men to transfer it from the realm of philosophic theory and personal application to the broader realm of American life. But John Dewey was the close student of William James, and Oliver Wendell Holmes was his close friend. With them pragmatism leaves the academic cloister and enters the forum, the place of action and also the place of distortion.

To what extent is the pragmatist a believer in the man-made order? To date we have considered the contributions of the three men who, in their several ways, were the creators of pragmatism. Peirce believed in the Deity, but in Deity conceived transcendentally as the Absolute into which every reality merges. But the transcendentalist believes in neither the divinely created order nor the man-made order; he believes that the order in its totality is the divine. Wright was an agnostic who held that rational proofs that God exists are illogical, that mystical intuition that God exists is inconsistent with knowledge, and hence that theism and atheism are alike untenable and that the only logical position is agnosticism. He did not believe, however, that the agnostic should ignore what he considers the religious motivation, but rather direct it toward the proper recipient of its benefactions, his fellow man. James was motivated, as we have seen, by an intense need to believe in God; and indeed the final motivation of all his writing is the philosophic justification of his grounds for belief. Yet, as part of his pluralism, he held to a concept of a finite God, denying to him the omnipotence and omniscience proper to the Absolute. "The line of least resistance . . . both in theology and in philosophy, is to accept, along with the superhuman consciousness, the notion that it is not all-embracing, the notion, in other words, that there is a God, but that he is finite, either in power or in knowledge, or in both at once."[35] Thus we observe in our three pragmatists the phenomenon observed in all the true deists and in many of the utilitarians: belief in the divinely created order does not suddenly and totally disappear, to be replaced instantly and totally by belief in the man-made order. These pragmatists of Cambridge were not instantly and totally false to their New England heritage. Rather there is the effort, which may be unconscious and therefore un-disturbing as in Peirce, or conscious and in some degree agoniz-ing as perhaps in Wright, to reconcile the one with the other. The effort, fully conscious and not really agonizing once he had determined the road to the goal, is present in William James.

It would probably be fairly close to the truth to say that all three lodged each in his intellectual part-way house to belief in the man-made order. Certainly their belief in it is not so un-qualified as that of Hume, who in a sense is the last of the deists, or of those social Darwinians who believed that Darwin's biological theories and discoveries had freed them from belief in God. However, the entire tenor of pragmatism is in the direction of belief in the man-made order. When the test of truth becomes experience, then the criterion of truth is man's experience. When man has also the free will to mold his pattern of life on utilitar-ian principles after he has appraised that experience, he is creating the man-made order. No apostle of true pragmatism ever intended to be an apostle of expediency, but false prophets will call man to the worship of false gods. That has been the fate of pragmatism, just as truly as it has been the fate of deism, utilitarianism, and Darwinism. The only difference is that prag-matism is a relatively new philosophy, and its destiny is still un-rolling.

XIV
INSTRUMENTALISM

WE HAVE SEEN that social Darwinism was an extension, by way of dubious metaphor, of Darwin's concept of natural selection into the realms of sociology and economics by such social Darwinians as Herbert Spencer and William Graham Sumner. We shall now see an extension of pragmatism, far more logical and far better reasoned, into the same realms. It was the work of many men, but none more important than John Dewey.

Charles Peirce had held that an idea is a plan of action and that a belief "established in our nature a rule of action, or, say for short, a habit."[1] James extended this concept: a belief is true if it establishes a worthwhile habit. Thus truth is successful experience. There is in the concept a generous measure of utilitarianism and possibly a dash of Darwinism. Utilitarianism also makes experience the test of truth, and it might be contended that the worthwhile habit is the one that makes for survival and hence that truth is determined on the principle of natural selection. An idea, then, is a plan of action; a belief establishes a habit of action; if it is a worthwhile habit of action the belief is true; truth is successful experience. To this point pragmatism was carried by Peirce and James.

JOHN DEWEY

Dewey's contribution was the concept that thought has as its object the development of life and not the discovery of truth. The starting point of Dewey's instrumentalism, as he called his form of pragmatism, was James's *Principles of Psychology*. Until he read it Dewey was a Hegelian, and taught Hegelianism at the University of Michigan.[2] After he read it Dewey was an instrumentalist, in some respects the follower of William James but in other respects one who traveled a far different road from the one taken by his relatively more cloistered predecessor. Dewey was far more strongly conscious of the social implications of pragmatism than was James, and vastly more possessed of a sense of mission. James recognized the necessity of what we termed in Chapter XIII social pragmatism, but he was not nearly so motivated by its implications as was John Dewey.

There is another basic difference between the thought of James and the thought of Dewey. Beyond social pragmatism lies an extension obviously logical in nature but abstruse as well. Beyond the single concept is the codification of a group of related concepts into a conceptual system. The conceptual system may be illustrated, in a rudimentary way, by the system of traffic lights. Green means *Go*, red means *Stop*, and amber warns of the change from the one to the other. Taken together, they comprise a sort of rudimentary conceptual system. Granted that a system of varying lights is the practical way to control traffic, then those colors which present the most striking contrast are the best colors to use. Experimentation presumably brought out the truth that green, red, and amber make the best conceptual system for traffic lights. But the more intricate and recondite the areas of human knowledge become, the more they tend to formulate themselves into conceptual systems and so the more nearly inevitable becomes the test of what has been called conceptual pragmatism. But is that test entirely inevitable? In a sense this is the great point of cleavage between William James and John Dewey. James would hardly cavil at the test of conceptual pragmatism as applied to traffic lights, but he would definitely cavil at its extension to ethics and religion. James, whose thinking was fundamentally theistic, held that a belief in God and some sort of divinely created order is essential to human happiness. He would not apply the test of conceptual pragmatism to "the things that are God's." John Dewey held that any sort of supernaturalism merely slowed down the rate of human progress. Hence, from his viewpoint, the test of conceptual pragmatism admits of universal application. We shall see illustrated in pragmatism as we did in deism, utilitarianism, and within its philosophic limitations in social Darwinism, the trend toward secularism which is inescapable in any philosophy grounded on the concept of the man-made order despite the efforts of those in the movement to prevent it.

John Dewey's life spanned nearly a century and spanned as well very nearly the entire development of American philosophic thought, a development to which he contributed at least as much as any other man. He was a native of Vermont, with a Vermonter's intellectual and physical heritage. He was totally dedicated to his lifework, totally convinced of its profound importance, and totally tireless in its performance. The bibliography of his writings is itself a book of substantial proportions—seventy-five pages long, to be exact. He entered what Coleridge called "the holy jungle of metaphysics" a Hegelian, but by the time he reached its first clearing he was a pragmatist, or to use his term, an instrumentalist. Four years as an undergraduate at the University of Vermont (faculty, in 1879, eight members) and then three years as a schoolteacher matured his naturally philosophic bias to the point at which he began to think of philosophy as his possible lifework. Encouragement from the editor of *The Journal of Speculative Philosophy*, to which he had submitted an article on the metaphysical assumptions of materialism, sent him to Johns Hopkins and the Hegelian camp. Oddly enough, a hook and eye really significant in the life of John Dewey did not mesh at that time; although he had two courses in logic with Charles Peirce, who was then in his teaching period at Johns Hopkins, he did not fall under the influence of his experiential concept of thought. Later the hook and eye would mesh and Dewey would be intellectually allied with Peirce, but it would be through the medium of William James and his psychology. The important Hopkins influence on Dewey was that of George S. Morris, a Hegelian, Dewey's favorite teacher and soon his fast friend. When Morris went to Ann Arbor to head the philosophy department at the University of Michigan, he offered Dewey a position on his staff. Dewey accepted, became a valued member of the department, and succeeded Morris as department chairman in 1889. He found in Michigan both his lifework and his life partner. Her maiden name was Alice Chipman, she was one of Michigan's first coeds, Dewey married her in 1886, and they had nine children, six by birth and three by adoption.

There is always a problem presented by the life and work of such a man as John Dewey, by a life that covers ninety-two years and a work that fills every minute of it. Justice cannot be done to either without an expenditure of space unjustified in terms of a subject that spans three centuries in its development and has more than its share of ramifications even after branches have been sternly pruned. Specifically, there is no aspect of Dewey's life and work more important or better known than his services to education. His interest in pedagogy was aroused at Michigan but flowered at Chicago. His years at Ann Arbor were followed by ten years at the University of Chicago, where Dewey headed the department of philosophy and psychology, a department which embraced pedagogy among its responsibilities. In 1896 he founded the University Elementary School, and in the succeeding years made world-famous the educational theories and practices worked out in that bustling laboratory for the teaching arts. Ten years at Chicago, where he resigned because of a difference of opinion with the university authorities over his educational experiments, were followed by twenty-four years at Columbia, and far greater renown in the field of pedagogic theory and practice. Dewey's contributions to pedagogic theory and his services to educational practice rank with anything in his abstract thought where importance is concerned, and immeasurably outrank it in public recognition. It is hardly an overstatement to maintain that everything good, bad, and indifferent in American public education has at some time or other been attributed to John Dewey and Columbia Teachers College, in terms that range from ecstatic reverence, through cautious appraisal of the pro and con, to the utter finality of total rejection. That he has been the *genius* of American public education, in the root meaning of the word, no one can deny; no one has established with finality whether he was the sort of genius inspired from on high or the sort of genius that eddies from a bottle. In tracing the history of the man-made order as a philosophic concept we face many a conundrum in composition, but at least we are spared the task of appraising John Dewey's contribution to American education. That is grist for another mill, and the mill needs the solidest of millstones.

On the other hand, the quality in John Dewey which let him bring a fresh approach to educational problems, to question root assumptions of the past and to establish experimentally new assumptions on which education might develop, is precisely the quality that characterizes him as an abstract thinker. Furthermore, the quality which makes him tangible, specific, intelligible, and practical in his pedagogic approach is equally present in his approach to the ancient problems of philosophy. His prose style hardly measures up to the very fine prose style of William James, but there is seldom any doubt as to what John Dewey means. If American philosophy has nothing else to its credit, it is not so formidable as English and very much less formidable than German. Dewey had a capacity unsurpassed by anyone in twentieth-century philosophy and equaled only by William James to say what he meant in direct and simple language, uncluttered by the technical jargon of the schools, and to say things that are fresh, fundamental, and provocative of thought.

THE QUEST FOR CERTAINTY

In many ways *The Quest for Certainty*[3] is a central book in the Dewey corpus of so many books, if anything can be central in their serried ranks. It starts with a Hobbesian thesis and proceeds in a pattern partly reminiscent of Hume and his views on natural religion, partly reminiscent of Comte and his three stages of human development. Yet it is sheer Dewey, original as Dewey is always original. "Man who lives in a world of hazards is compelled to seek for security. He has sought to attain it in two ways. One of them began with an attempt to propitiate the powers which environ him and determine his destiny. It expressed itself in supplication, sacrifice, ceremonial rite and magical cult. In time these crude methods were largely displaced. The sacrifice of a contrite heart was esteemed more pleasing than that of bulls and oxen; the inner attitude of reverence and devotion more desirable than external ceremonies. If man could not conquer destiny he could willingly ally himself with it; putting his will, even in sore affliction, on the side of the powers which dispense fortune, he could escape defeat and might triumph in the midst of destruction. The other course is to invent arts and by their means turn the powers of nature to account; man constructs a fortress out of the very conditions and forces which threaten him. He builds shelters, weaves garments, makes flame his friend instead of his enemy, and grows into the complicated arts of associated living. This is the method of changing the world through action, the other is the method of changing the self in emotion and idea."[4] Thus on the opening page of *The Quest for Certainty* can be seen certain axioms of John Dewey, and certain projected lines of development: man's central preoccupation has been his security, as Hobbes said; man has believed himself subject to supernatural and malevolent powers which must be placated by sacrifice and rite, as Comte said; out of this belief there has grown by refinement the advanced religions like Christianity, as Hume said; the true reality, however, is the natural order which man in his most advanced state manipulates in the interest of his own security, as Hobbes, Comte, and Hume said. There is nothing new in the axioms, nothing new in the projected lines of development. What is new is Dewey's concept of the objective of thought, a concept that is rationalistic but rationalistic in a very different way from the concepts of Hobbes, Comte, or Hume. To Dewey the objective of thought, as we have stated, is not the discovery of truth, as it was to his rationalistic predecessors, but the development of life.

Just as truly as William James, John Dewey saw the modern problem to be that of reconciling the lessons of science about the world in which we live with the "realm of ideal and spiritual qualities, which get no support from natural science. . . . This effect of modern science has, it is notorious, set the main problems of modern philosophy. How is science to be accepted and yet the realm of values to be conserved?"[5] Dewey begins his solution of the problem by an analysis of the process of knowing. What do we know? How do we know? He rejects the traditional view that what we know has an objective reality independent of the person who knows it. First we have an experience of the object, but experience is not knowledge. Experience has significance for thought, but knowledge is the product of thought and investigation. The process of scientific investigation illustrates what Dewey means. The astronomer starts with the sun, moon, and stars that we all see; the chemist begins with familiar acids, salts, and metals; the botanist studies the plants and trees with which we are all acquainted. We have "experienced" the sun, the metal, and the plant, but that does not mean we have knowledge of them. The scientific investigator proceeds by inductive observation and deductive reasoning, each process carefully differentiated in his mind from the other, to reach a knowledge of them. The man in the street experiences the sun, the metal, and the plant; the scientist knows them. But the man in the street is capable, within the limitations of his capacity for inductive observation and deductive reasoning, to acquire knowledge. He can lie in the hot sun, employ the metal in his daily tasks, and eat the plant, and thereby acquire knowledge of a sort about each. Dewey, of course, does not deny that the known object has an existence prior to one's experience of it; he maintains that the object as known is the result of the knowing process.

Dewey states the practical application of his concept of knowledge as follows: "The sum and substance of the present argument is that if we frame our conception of knowledge on the experimental model we find that it is a way of operating upon and with the things of ordinary experience so that we can frame our ideas of them in terms of the qualities they directly present, and that thereby our control of them, our ability to change them and direct their changes as we desire, is indefinitely increased. Knowing is itself a mode of practical action and is *the* way of interaction by which other natural interactions become subject to direction."[6]

When experience is thus regulated by the processes of scientific investigation, it can develop its own regulative ideas and standards. If this is true in the realm of natural science, may it not be true as well in the higher realm to which belong what Dewey himself called the higher values? May not what has traditionally been considered the subject matter of ethical and moral judgment be comparably refined and elevated by the scientific method? Dewey was optimist enough to believe that such was the case. "The conclusion is a good omen for the possibility of achieving in larger, more humane and liberal fields a similar transformation, so that a philosophy of experience may be empirical without either being false to actual experience or being compelled to explain away the values dearest to the heart of man."[7]

It is easier to take the man out of Vermont than Vermont out of the man. There is something hard to define in the English-speaking heritage that is always uneasy without some sort of moral justification for either a pattern of thought or a plan of action, and it is if anything uneasier in the United States than in England, and uneasier in Vermont than in the other states. John Dewey became a figure of world renown, but he never got away entirely from the heritage of Vermont. He had cast in his intellectual lot with empiricism, but it had to be an empirical philosophy that did not explain away the moral values, "the values dearest to the heart of man." But observe the difference of emphasis between the phrase "not explain away" and William James's phrase "the will to believe." The will to believe is a positive force, and indeed the strongest force behind the thinking of William James. He did achieve an empirical philosophy, and his concept that the belief which establishes a worthwhile habit in effect is a belief that creates a truth was a positive and important contribution to pragmatism. But the fundamental appeal of pragmatism to James lay in the fact that it permitted him the free exercise of the will to believe without the counter-irritants that other philosophies may present to the intellect. Religious belief was foremost with James; and, consequently, pragmatist though he was and a believer in the dictum that successful experience establishes truth, he never accepted in its entirety the concept of the man-made order.

The motivation that was central in William James was at best peripheral in John Dewey. His empiricism was not to explain away moral values, but neither was it to make them its objective. Consequently one finds in Dewey extended to the moral realm the concept already referred to, that thought has as its object the development of life. This, in Dewey's view, might be moral development as well as development of any other sort. As he puts it in *Reconstruction in Philosophy:* "The supposed fact that morals demand immutable, extra-temporal principles, standards, norms, ends, as the only assured protection against moral chaos can, however, no longer appeal to natural science for its support, nor expect to justify by science its exemption of morals (in practice and in theory) from considerations of time and place— that is, from processes of change. Emotional—or sentimental— reaction will doubtless continue to resist acknowledgment of this fact and refuse to use in morals the standpoint and outlook which have now made their way into natural science. But in any case, science and traditional morals have been at complete odds with one another as to the kinds of things which, according to one and the other, are immutable. Hence a deep and impassable gulf is set up between the *natural* subject matter of science and the *extra-* if not *supra-*natural subject matter of morals. There must be many thoughtful persons who are so dismayed by the inevitable consequences of this split that they will welcome that change in point of view which will render the methods and conclusions of natural science serviceable for moral theory and practice. All that is needed is acceptance of the view that moral subject matter is also spatially and temporally qualified."[8]

THOUGHT AS AN INSTRUMENT

To Dewey a thought is an instrument; if it will solve a problem, it is a practical instrument. The problem, be it noted, need not necessarily be a practical one; the instrumentality of thought may be directed at solving hypothetical problems as well as actual ones. Indeed much intellectual progress is the result of the solution of hypothetical problems, the sort that arise in the anticipatory imagination prior to the emergence of the actual and physical problem, and especially the emergence of the moral problem. Every instrument is predetermined by the problem it is designed to solve; the form of the screwdriver is predetermined by the screw. Put into the terms of instrumentalism, an idea starts in a fact and returns to the fact: "We estimate the import or significance of any present desire or impulse by forecasting what it will come or amount to if carried out; literally its consequences define its *consequence,* its meaning or import."[9]

Dewey drew a distinction between activity and conduct. Conduct he considered to be purposive activity, activity with an end in view. To throw a stone is an activity; to throw a stone at a neighbor's window is conduct. Ethics is the study of conduct, the study of the ends that man should strive to attain and the conduct he should employ to reach those ends. Thus Dewey avoided what he considered the dead-end street of traditional morals, which found moral justification in motive alone, and the other dead-end street of utilitarian morals, which found justification in consequences alone. Dewey believed that the possibility for improvement in moral concepts lay in a philosophy that took account of both motives and consequences, and a philosophy that never lost sight of the fact that specific conduct is always specifically performed under specific circumstances for a specific end. "Morals is not a catalogue of acts nor a set of rules to be applied like drugstore prescriptions or cook-book recipes,"[10] he assures us with that nonphilosophic directness which is one of his philosophic charms.

At the heart of Dewey's concept of ethics lies the concept of conduct cited above: conduct is always specifically performed under specific circumstances for a specific end; "moral conceptions and processes grow out of the very conditions of human life."[11] We do not know good and evil in terms of a decalogue or its equivalent, in Dewey's view, nor do we learn it by experience with pleasure and pain as the utilitarians have it, although Dewey in the nature of his concept has more respect for the utilitarian viewpoint than for the traditional concepts of natural law and revealed precepts. We learn good and evil, right and wrong by experience. "Action is always specific, concrete, individualized, unique. And consequently judgments as to acts to be performed must be similarly specific."[12] We thus return to the basic creed of pragmatism: an idea is a plan of action, a belief establishes a habit of action; if it is a worthwhile habit of action the belief is true. Conduct by definition has a motive and an end. Experience with the specific motives and ends of specific instances of conduct provide the experimental material on which one may exercise thought and reach moral judgment. It is an application to conduct of the scientific method, the one method of developing life since it is the one method of determining truth and truth is the development of life.

No Victorian weighed down by the apparent conflict between

science and religion viewed its baleful consequences more soberly than Dewey; Dewey's solution, however, was very much his own, the fusion of science and religion in terms of the only unity which he attributed to truth, the unity implicit in its objective, which is the development of life. "When physics, chemistry, biology, medicine contribute to the detection of concrete human woes and to the development of plans for remedying them and relieving the human estate, they become moral; they become part of the apparatus of moral inquiry or science. . . . When the consciousness of science is fully impregnated with the consciousness of human value, the greatest dualism which now weighs humanity down, the split between the material, the mechanical, the scientific and the moral and ideal will be destroyed. . . . At the same time that morals are made to focus in intelligence, things intellectual are moralized. The vexatious and wasteful conflict between naturalism and humanism is terminated."[13] And Dewey summed up the moral aspect of his concept that truth is the development of life in one of his best aphorisms: "The bad man is the man who no matter how good he *has* been is beginning to deteriorate, to grow less good. The good man is the man who no matter how morally unworthy he *has* been is moving to become better."[14] Implicit also in the aphorism is the foundation of Dewey's thought, the concept that life is not being but becoming.

MAN AND HIS ENVIRONMENT

Another element of prime importance in Dewey's concept of ethics is his concept of the interrelationship of the individual and his environment. One of Dewey's basic philosophic purposes was to eliminate the artificial dualism which had grown up in sociological thought between those whose preoccupation was human psychology and those whose preoccupation was human environment. The former was at least assisted in its growth by social Darwinism and its extension of the principle of natural selection, with a resultant emphasis on the study of heredity. The eugenics movement marched stride by stride with social Darwinism as they combined to assure the Fittest Americans, who were happily immune from poverty, and in a better position to control disease and conceal immorality than the less fit, that poverty, sickness, and immorality were the unfortunate and inevitable result of bad heredity. On the other hand all who opposed social Darwinism on a variety of grounds and with a multiplicity of arguments placed their primary emphasis on the effects of environment, with particular attention from the nature of their case to the bad effects of bad environment. Dewey strove to achieve the rational midpoint and indeed considered the achieving of that rational midpoint one of the jewels in the crown of instrumentalism. Man, in his view, is subject to his own nature and to his environment. His nature is manifested in the habits he has developed, habits which have resulted for better or for worse from the degree to which intelligence has controlled and directed the impulses of emotion. To the extent that man can better his habits he can contribute to the improvement of his environment. On the other hand the individual is himself a part of the environment; a neighborhood is people, not houses. Because conduct, in Dewey's concept of the term, affects others, conduct is social in its nature and hence conduct is a concern of society. The improvement of society, then, is not something to be effected in a way entirely subjective, the inner reform of the individual, although such reform is necessary for the production of better habits and the consequent improvement of conduct with the benefit it brings to society. Neither is the improvement of society to be effected in a way entirely external to the individuals who comprise it, by the improvement of social institutions and the betterment of the physical milieu, since in the real sense society is the individuals who make it up. Society is made better by improving the conduct of its members, by translating that improvement into an improvement of its social institutions and physical milieu, and, since life is not being but becoming, by accepting and acting on the principle that change to meet changing conditions is a primary hallmark of the healthy society. "Not perfection as a final goal, but the ever-enduring process of perfecting, maturing, refining is the aim in living. Honesty, industry, temperance, justice, like health, wealth, and learning, are not goods to be possessed as they would be if they expressed fixed ends to be attained. They are directions of change in the quality of experience. Growth itself is the only moral 'end.'"[15]

At this point a word of interpretation is perhaps in order. The doctrine that the final reality is change is nothing new with Dewey; it is as old as Heraclitus of Ephesus, whose *Concerning Nature* dates to about 500 B.C. Heraclitus also held that all things are in a state of change, and the sense of permanence is merely the false report given by the human senses. But the doctrine that nothing is fixed, everything changes, the only unchanging thing in life is change itself, necessarily negates all values and leads to final skepticism, a melancholy state that explains the identifying label the ancients gave to Heraclitus, "The Weeping Philosopher." Walter Pater revived the doctrine in the Conclusion to his *Studies in the History of the Renaissance* (1873), to the intense delight of the iconoclastic young men of Oxford and the great sorrow of their stable elders. But John Dewey, of course, never maintains that the final reality is change. He maintains that the final reality to which man should aspire is that creative activity which develops better habits and thus enriches personal life and betters the environment, and he further implies at least that to such growth there is no end. "Activity is creative in so far as it moves to its own enrichment as activity, that is bringing alone with itself a release of further activities. . . . While from the standpoint of what precedes it is a fulfillment, it is a liberative expansion with respect to what comes after."[16] Thus the final reality is not change but growth, and the creative activity is not directed toward some external end but is the end itself. Ethics exists to give man a steady growth, a deepening, expanding, and increasing vision in his perception of the meaning of life—and that is precisely what we live for.

> Then felt I like some watcher of the skies
> When a new planet swims into his ken;
> Or like stout Cortez when with eagle eyes
> He star'd at the Pacific. . . .

Growth is what John Keats experienced on first reading Chapman's Homer, and instrumentalism is the philosophy that explains its nature.

We said some pages ago that it is easier to take the man out of Vermont than Vermont out of the man. Behind John Dewey were those generations of Vermonters who preached the word of God and in their imperfect human ways practiced it. It is orthodox Christian belief, and nowhere preached more fervently than in the white-steepled churches that crown the Vermont hilltops, that all life is a moral striving upward toward a goal that never can be reached in mortal life. It is orthodox Christian belief that man's purpose in life is indeed creative change, the development of better habits, the deepening and expansion of his moral vision that his life on earth may be the richer and better, and the more deserving of its eternal reward. In the final analysis, John Dewey says the same thing without the promise of an eternal reward, or more exactly, says that creative change is itself the reward. "A clear and intense conception of a union of ideal ends with actual conditions is capable of arousing steady emotion. It may be fed by every experience, no matter what its material. In a distracted age, the need for such an idea is urgent. It can unify interests and energies now dispersed; it can direct action and generate the heat of emotion and the light of intelligence. Whether one gives the name 'God' to this union, operative in thought and action, is a matter for individual decision. But the *function* of such a working union of the ideal and actual seems to me to be identical with the force that has in fact been attached to the conception of God in all the religions that have a spiritual content; and a clear idea of that function seems to me urgently needed at the present time."[17]

Thus human experiences are both the source of moral values and the measure of their worth, a viewpoint that in some form or other must be held by everyone like Dewey who subscribes to ethical naturalism. But Dewey differs from many ethical naturalists, as truly as he does from William James and many other pragmatists, in his insistence on the social orientation of instrumentalism. To Dewey the measure of the moral worth of concepts is social, and there is always a sense in which Dewey is the counterpart among the ranks of the pragmatists of those in the Progressive movement who opposed social Darwinism in the name of the common man. In the last analysis Dewey always judged that belief to be true which in the long run was most beneficial to the greatest number of people. One may call it social pragmatism or democracy as one wishes, and one may make all that he desires out of the difference between utilitarianism with its insistence on the goal and pragmatism with its concept that creative activity is itself the goal, but the final truth is that once pragmatism is entirely posited on values determined by experience in this world, it merges with utilitarianism. Dewey puts it in the terms of instrumentalism when he writes: "A genuine idealism and one compatible with science will emerge as soon as philosophy accepts the teaching of science that ideas are statements not of what is or has been but of acts to be performed. For then mankind will learn that, intellectually (that is, save for the esthetic enjoyment they afford, which is of course a true value), ideas are worthless except as they pass into actions which rearrange and reconstruct in some way, be it little or large, the world in which we live."[18] The underlying principle of what he says is the greatest good of the greatest number. But that is not to deny to Dewey a very true originality of thought and a very genuine contribution to philosophy. As Professor Hocking presents the thesis of social pragmatism: "Experimental science shall not consist of mere common sense beliefs put in logical order, but rather of active rebuilding of the social environment through the instrumentality of ideas many of which are so technical as to be very far from common sense. As a result, our common sense beliefs become pliable and undergo indirect change by way of the progressive reconstruction of our environment."[19]

RIGHT COMES BEFORE EXPERIENCE

At the heart of pragmatism in any form is its final codification: truth is successful experience. If a proposition works, it is true. But as Professor Hocking points out,[20] there is a fallacy implicit in this conversion of the proposition, "a true proposition works." If *true* and *works* were identical, as they would be in an ideal world, then the conversion of the proposition would be valid. But this is not an ideal world, and even in an ideal world the proposition would work both ways only because the world was antecedently ideal. The point is not really recondite. In an ideal world of perfect virtue, the end would justify the means because there would be no evil means. But this is not an ideal world. If the ultimate test of pragmatism, *pace* the pragmatists, is really the old, familiar utilitarian test of the greatest happiness of the greatest number, so the ultimate operational principle of pragmatism is the justification of the means by the end, *pace* John Dewey in whose instrumentalism the terms "means" and "end" obviously have no meaning. But if there is a difference between the operational principle of pragmatism as applied in an ideal world and as applied in this world, it must be because there is a difference between the two worlds. In other words, the ideal is antecedent to pragmatism; right comes before experience. An idea is not right because it works; it works because it is right. Just as scientific thought and progress are made possible by the fact that there are natural laws unalterable by any act of man, so ethical progress is made possible by the antecedent existence of a belief in both ethical progress itself and the existence of a standard by which it can be measured. James held his pragmatism anchored to a belief in a final, objective truth, the existence of God.

Dewey cast off the anchor by identifying God with "a union of ideal ends with actual conditions." God to James was an objective reality, to Dewey a pattern of human life. But the theist will never accept as valid the thesis that man can be ethically self-sustaining. As Hocking graphically puts it, "God is nothing if not that on which we depend. But every chosen belief, every man-made idea of God too palpably depends on us. We cannot swing up a rope which is attached only to our own belt."[21] When all is said and done, John Dewey would have us climb an ethical rope ladder tied to our own belts. So would every believer in any form of the man-made order.

Even one who believes that the fundamental fallacy just outlined is present in pragmatism in its every form can recognize and should acknowledge the substantial and valuable contributions of John Dewey to American thought. If there is one lesson evident in the history of the man-made order among the English-speaking nations it is that the reform motivation, strong in the initial stages of the various aspects that the order takes, soon peters out and standpattism replaces it. Deism in its initial stages introduced a reform into English life so basic that England could hardly have survived without it, but deism before very long degenerated into skepticism in philosophy and opportunism in the Church. Utilitarianism in its initial stages was inspired by the reform motive and advanced a number of valuable and needed reforms, but utilitarianism soon degenerated into an apology for *laissez faire* and the *status quo*. Social Darwinism has a far less secure claim to the reform motive even in its initial stages although the devil's advocate might argue that a philosophy of progress is consistent with the spirit of reform. But social Darwinism practically from the start lent its support to selfish aggrandizement and unbridled rapacity. Far worse, social Darwinism paradoxically combined determinism with the spirit of free enterprise, and the former invariably operates against the spirit of reform.

Pragmatism has a far sounder claim to being grounded in science than has social Darwinism, and it made once more available to believers in the man-made order the reform motivation invariably present in the early supporters of a new form of ethical naturalism. Peirce and Wright did the intellectual pioneering for pragmatism, laying the groundwork for a new, experiential theory of knowledge. William James in turn laid the groundwork for the extension of pragmatic principles into the social arena by his thesis that the test of truth is success in practice. It was John Dewey, however, who achieved what would seem to be the successful welding of the pragmatic explanation of thought, life, and society to the spirit of reform in a social order made by man. His concept of life as becoming rather than being is the obvious antithesis of the concept of the *status quo*. His concept that creative activity is itself the goal of life is antithetical to any preconception of a fixed operating principle of society, whether it be *laissez faire* or anything else. Experience can hardly be separated from experiment, and the essence of Dewey's instrumentalism is the testing of experience by experiment and the application of the lessons thus learned to the attainment of more creative activity. The instrumentalist by the very nature of his philosophic convictions is an experimenter, a man ever eager to try the new thing, an ancient Athenian in the bone and marrow.

An instrumentalist might, like Thoreau, who belonged to a

very different school, find his world of experience in Concord
and let posterity glean what lessons it chose from his intellectual
rugged individualism. Dewey was as antithetical by instinct
to Thoreau as he was to Spencer or Sumner. His instincts were
social, his preoccupation the social order, his chosen field of
activity education, which not only should prepare the coming
generation for the social order but also prepare the better social
order for the coming generation. By the very nature of his thinking, Dewey was committed to no concept of the social order,
no concept of the powers, functions, limits of activity, or potentialities of service of the state or its institutions. The very interest
that he showed in socialism and other collectivist patterns is
more properly evidence of this intellectual receptivity to newer
concepts than evidence of a commitment to any one of them.
Hence a follower of Dewey logically should be an experimenter
on the social order, one without prior intellectual commitments
to either form or function in the state or its component parts.
A follower of Dewey logically should have the ideal ideology
for the reform motivation, and indeed the great service of
Dewey to the concept of the man-made order was to restore to
it that reform motivation which had been denied it by social
Darwinism.

On the other hand, John Dewey was not a follower of Heraclitus, and he knew as well as anyone that the interpretation
of life as mere change without purpose or direction led to nothing but blank pessimism and arid skepticism. Besides, he had
that Vermont background, and it told. Arthur Hugh Clough himself did not believe more completely in the conflict between
science and religion than did John Dewey; the difference between the melancholy English poet and the vigorous American
philosopher was that the latter tried to end the conflict by reconciling the two. Judgments of fact belong to the realm of
science, and judgments of value to the realm of ethics—but that
is precisely the trouble. There should be one realm, not two. A
basic aim of instrumentalism is to end the dualism between the
scientific and the ethical, to make the scientific method serve the
ethical purpose and to bring to the unending betterment of
ethical principles the experimental approach of science. "At the

same time that morals are made to focus in intelligence, things intellectual are moralized. The vexations and wasteful conflict between naturalism and humanism is terminated."[22] John Dewey was a naturalist, but very much an ethical naturalist.

DEWEY'S INFLUENCE

The influence of John Dewey is one of those pervasive and fundamental influences that one cannot escape yet neither can one measure. He became the high priest of American public education and his altars were erected in two of the nation's most imposing cathedrals of learning, the University of Chicago and Columbia. His apostles staffed the university departments which he graced, his disciples manned the teachers colleges of the country, and their disciples ran the schools of America. The gospel of John Dewey, however interpreted, expanded, contracted, distorted, applied and misapplied, pointed up or watered down, became the educational gospel of the United States; and for that matter, when all things are considered, it still is. His name is heard less often than it used to be, partly because those whose gospel is modernism and progressivism habitually drop the new name as well as run after the new thing and partly because his concepts have met stout opposition among those who have taken a sober look at American education since Russia launched the first sputnik. But the new name dropped is often the name of a disciple, immediate or derived, of John Dewey; the new thing sought after is apt to be a contemporary refurbishing of a Dewey idea, and what has been called the "educational establishment" still teaches the only gospel that it knows, the gospel as John Dewey taught it. John Dewey's influence is still the most important single influence operative in American education, with all that implies for American thought and life.

Beyond that is the less ponderable yet equally important fact that the philosophic thought of John Dewey was consonant with something instinctive in American thinking. Dewey defended himself and his predecessors and followers as best he could against the charge that pragmatism is a philosophy of material success, and the accusation, of course, is without foundation. The very fact, however, that the charge was so often made and so

instinctively accepted as true has its own significance. The truth
is that the American people are by nature experimenters, are
prone to try new ideas, are relatively uncommitted to the *status
quo* in any form, do tend to apply the yardstick of material
success in all their undertakings, in short are pragmatists in the
nonphilosophic sense of the word. But it isn't quite the nonphilosophic sense; call it rather the semiphilosophic sense. No
naturalist can free himself entirely from the charge of having
a material set of values. What other set can he have? Be this as
it may, there is something in pragmatism to which America by
nature responds. Those who admit that pragmatism has its
European sources yet maintain that pragmatism is nevertheless
the American philosophy are not without a historic case. Nor,
indeed, are they without a case in the absolute sense. The truth
often can be determined only by action. Where would medicine
be if doctors and surgeons could not conscientiously take calculated risks with untested procedures? And one kind of truth,
the factual kind, can be created by action. It is true that Spring-
field is the capital of Illinois because the people of the state
made it their capital. The real problem, of course, lies in that
no man's land which John Dewey tried to eliminate, the stretch
between the entrenchments of factual values and ethical values.
Dewey tried, as a naturalist must try if he believes in ethical
values, to eliminate the no man's land by making the scientific
method serve the ethical purpose. Truth is successful experience,
to John Dewey as to all pragmatists, but to John Dewey as to
William James ethical truth is part of truth. It had to be a part
of truth to James, who anchored his pragmatism to a final and
objective truth, the existence of God. It was merely a part of
truth to Dewey, who thought of God as a sort of spirit pervading
the pattern of human life. But the Dewey who believed that
there is no inaccessible truth, to use Professor Hocking's phrase,
invited the skepticism which is the bedrock upon which sheer
materialism always rests. The man-made order, however well
intentioned and expertly designed, always has within itself the
seed of its own destruction.

XV

THE LIFE OF THE LAW
IS EXPERIENCE

ONE of the celebrated first sentences of legal literature opens Justice Oliver Wendell Holmes's *The Common Law:* "The life of the law has not been logic; it has been experience."[1] In the sentence that follows Holmes expands his thematic sentence: "The felt necessities of the time, the prevalent moral and political theories, intuitions of public policy, avowed or unconscious, even the prejudices which judges share with their fellow men, have had a good deal more to do than the syllogism in determining the rules by which men should be governed."[2]

We have seen develop among the pragmatists the concept that the law of life is experience. It was the conviction of Justice Holmes that the life of the law is experience. A logical presentation of pragmatism—not the only logical one, to be sure—has called for a consideration first of Peirce and Wright, who evolved the pragmatic theory of meaning; then of William James, who made pragmatism a philosophy of life; then of John Dewey, who made it a philosophy of life in society; and now of Oliver Wendell Holmes, who found in pragmatism an approach to law and thus made pragmatism a philosophy of one aspect of life in society—a basic one, the legal aspect. But the transition from the professional philosophers hitherto considered to the professional jurist must be preceded by a transition in logic itself. Granted the premise of pragmatism that the law of life is experience, is Holmes's converse logical? Can it logically be held that the life of the law is experience? What follows is an attempt to see law and its operations as a pragmatist might be assumed to see them, a viewpoint which is neither universal in acceptance nor necessarily right.

There is a sense in which the outcome of every lawsuit is the resolution of a syllogism. The facts of the case comprise the minor premise, the law that applies constitutes the major premise, and the verdict is the outcome. This man is a murderer, murderers shall hang, this man shall hang. But the very expression of the legal process in syllogistic form reveals of how little value the expression is. What we have stated is a truism, not a truth. The real job is to determine the premises, a fact-finding job in which logic is of little help except in the sense that in any human undertaking it helps to be logical. In pure logic the major premise is a datum (murderers shall hang), the minor premise is discovered (this man is a murderer), and then the major premise is applied to it and a conclusion deduced (this man shall hang). But in the syllogism of the law neither premise is a datum, both must be discovered, and hence the process of discovery of both the facts and the law is not only antecedent in time but in a sense antecedent in significance to the final working out of the syllogism. The objective is not that the law fit the facts or that the facts fit the law, but that each fit each other.

If this is true in the individual law case, it is collectively true in the total experience of the law. Legal precedent, by its very nature, is not established on a priori principles but on legal experience. Actually the minor premise in law is not so much the discovery of the law that applies as it is an awareness of the developing significance of the law as it evolves through precedent. Law is in a state of becoming, not a state of being. It builds in the present for the future, on the foundation provided by the past.

The consistency of this concept of law with the instrumentalism of John Dewey should be self-evident. The legal theory holds that legal experiences are the source of legal principles and that their outcome is the measure of their worth. Dewey held that human experiences are both the source of moral values and the measure of their worth. The evolution of law is by its nature a continuing process and one destined not to end this side of the pearly gates. The same is true of Dewey's conception of life as a process of development. By its nature law is a cumulative science, and every legal decision depends at least implicitly on legal precedent. Instrumentalism teaches that the good life is a cumulative science, and that our whole conception of knowledge is framed within the experimental pattern. Any concept of law is based on the axiom that law exists to establish, improve, and perpetuate the orderly and just society. Instrumentalism advances precisely the same objective for human thought. Finally, the legal theory rejects legal a priorism of the traditional kind just as completely as Dewey rejects moralistic a priorism of the traditional kind. The haunting question is whether this instrumentalist concept of the law has deliberately cast off a needed anchor as philosophic instrumentalism may have.

OLIVER WENDELL HOLMES

So much for the theoretical kinship of pragmatism and the experiential concept of the law. Do the pair also meet the test of blood relationship? The question brings us back to the 1870s and the Metaphysical Club that remained so fondly in the memory of Charles Peirce. Peirce could not have been unaware of the mental caliber of that group of young men that met sometimes in his study, sometimes in that of William James. "Wright, James, and I were men of science," he says, which one may properly interpret as men dedicated to the reconciliation of science and metaphysics after their recent Darwinian quarrel. He does not pin a label upon Oliver Wendell Holmes, nor perhaps could a label have been pinned on him in the early 1870s. He had fought through the Civil War. He had gone to Harvard Law School, despite his father's assurance that a lawyer cannot be a great man. The elder Holmes had discovered a potential great man among his own medical students, and was vastly pleased when a close friendship developed between his son and this student whom he found not brilliant but original and imaginative, and whose name was William James. James found the younger Holmes brilliant, as well as original and imaginative. "The only fellow here I care anything about is Holmes. . . . He is perhaps too exclusively intellectual, but sees things so easily and clearly and talks so admirably that it's a treat to be with him," James assured his friend Thomas W. Ward.[3] But it was

neither the law nor medicine that Holmes and James argued so
easily, clearly, and admirably. It was the distinctions of Kant and
the reconciliation of Hegel that preoccupied the bright young lawyer and the bright young medico. Then Charles Peirce and
Chauncey Wright joined them and dispelled the metaphysical
moonshine partly by the sunshine of science and partly by the
searchlight of their own technically trained, incisive philosophic
intelligences.

There was one problem, however, that haunted William James
but never bothered Wendell Holmes. James, as we have seen,
had the will to believe because he had the need to believe. At
the heart of James's pragmatism is that desperate need to find
some middle zone where science and religion could meet and
the tabernacle of religion be erected on solid ground. Not so
Holmes. As Catherine Drinker Bowen puts it: "For Holmes the
core had been taken out of Christian theology a generation ago,
when the Unitarians disavowed the doctrine of original sin. Man
lost his fear of hell-fire—and on that day gave back Christian
doctrine to the preacher as irrelevant to life. After that, disbelief
in Genesis I was a small thing. Wendell Holmes had achieved it
without the least struggle. He was born to it. His father's frantic
efforts to free himself from Calvinism had never freed Dr.
Holmes. But they freed his son."[4]

James was a theist, in whom the will to believe found the way.
Dewey was a humanist, who found the concept of Deity embodied as a spirit in the developing pattern of human life. Holmes
was simply a man without religion. He tested many philosophies,
but his search was for temporal truth and not eternal. With an
instinct natural in an incipient pragmatist before the term was
coined, when he went to England in 1865 he sought out John
Stuart Mill and Leslie Stephen. Emerson had aided thought
down the icy descent from the mountaintops of theology to the
high and wind-swept plateau of transcendentalism, but Mill had
brought it down to the solid earth of practical morality, "the
greatest happiness of the greatest number." Holmes was not disappointed in Mill, nor in Stephen. He found in the utilitarians
the same sure grasp on realities that he had sensed in his science-
oriented philosophic associates of Cambridge, Peirce and Wright.

The facts of Holmes's life make clear that he was at the very heart of the intellectual ferment from which pragmatism was distilled. William James was one of his closest friends, not impossibly his closest friend in the formative years. Like James he listened to Peirce and Wright, tried to cross swords with them, and more than once learned what a skilled intellectual fencer can do with the Toledo blade of logic. He argued philosophy with James, fencing—perhaps by a joint preference understandable when men are young, ardent, and not fully home with the Toledo blade of logic—on the Kantian heights rather than the utilitarian plains. He attended Peirce's Cambridge lectures, cheerfully assuring his sister that he did not understand a word. But as time passed and the future began to make its peremptory demands of the present, not without reluctance he turned from philosophy to the law.

The year 1867 marked in Holmes's life the start of an all-absorbing and intense, even dangerously intense, concentration on legal studies. In December of that year he wrote to James, "For two or three months I debauched o' nights in philosophy. But now it is law—law—law."[5] Four months later he told James, "Since I wrote in December I have worked at nothing but the law. Philosophy has hibernated in torpid slumber, and I have lain 'sluttishly soaking and gurgling in the devil's pickle,' as Carlyle says. It has been necessary,—if a man chooses a profession he cannot forever content himself in picking out the plums with fastidious dilettantism and give the rest of the loaf to the poor, but must eat his way manfully through crust and crumb. . . . And the winter has been a success, I think, both for the simple discipline of the work and because I now go on with an ever increasing conviction that law as well as any other series of facts in this world may be approached in the interests of science and may be studied, yes and practiced, with the preservation of one's ideals."[6] A few months later he started the monumental labor of re-editing Kent's *Commentaries on American Law;* in the autumn of 1870 he and his brother Ned opened their own law office; that winter he was invited to join the Harvard faculty as lecturer on constitutional law. From 1869 to 1873 he edited the *American Law Review,* in 1873 he published his edition of Kent's *Commentaries,* and in 1881 gave the series of Lowell Institute lectures published later that year as *The Common Law.*

THE COMMON LAW

For all his dedication to legal studies, Holmes did not really turn from philosophy to law. *The Common Law* marks an epoch in legal literature precisely because in it Holmes turned philosophy into law. During the years between 1867, when Holmes first dedicated himself body and soul to the law, and 1881, when he published *The Common Law*, Holmes was still a Cambridge and Boston man. He still associated with William James, Charles Peirce, and Chauncey Wright, all Cambridge men. The philosophic convictions and attitudes he had acquired as a young man from his associates became for Holmes the convictions and attitudes that he brought to his legal studies and later to his interpretation of the law. "As the twig is bent"; the mind of Oliver Wendell Holmes was given its direction in its early, most pliable stage by the men who founded pragmatism. The Cambridge debating was largely finished by 1878 when Peirce published "How to Make Our Ideas Clear" and by 1881 when Holmes published *The Common Law*.

We have attempted to establish a logical consistency between what might be termed a pragmatic view of the law and the social pragmatism or instrumentalism of John Dewey. The aphorisms employed were the following: experiences are the sources of principles, their outcome is the measure of their worth; life is becoming, not being, and leading the good life is a cumulative science; development is the principle of the good life, and life has no goal except its own perpetuation. Holmes was personally exposed for a long period of impressionable years to the intellectual influences which, through the medium of published writings, did so much to mold the pattern of John Dewey's thoughts. Does there exist in the legal concepts of Holmes evidence, explicit or implicit, of the aphorisms listed above?

The life of the law is experience, is Holmes's opening aphorism. After the expansion of his thematic declaration quoted above, he continues, "The law embodies the story of a nation's development through many centuries, and it cannot be dealt with as if it contained only the axioms and corollaries of a book of mathematics. In order to know what it is, we must know what it has been, and what it tends to become. We must alternately consult history and existing theories of legislation. But the most difficult labor will be to understand the combination of the two into new products at every stage. The substance of the law at any given time pretty nearly corresponds, so far as it goes, with what is then understood to be convenient; but its form and machinery, and the degree to which it is able to work out desired results, depend very much upon its past."[7]

To appraise the contents of a book by its first page is not a procedure that recommends itself to the discreet, and yet the first page of *The Common Law* does contain its essential message. Law is more than precedent, although precedent is important in the law. Law looks to the future as well as to the past, and its basic purpose is so to formulate the present as to make of it the foundation for the building of a better future. Not only is it necessary to look to both the past for the lessons that history teaches and to the present for the problems that the present poses, but the two must somehow be fused to regulate the steadily changing, steadily developing pattern which is life. The law must provide for the present and provide for the future as well, but it must do so within the framework that the past created, and with the machinery that the past has provided. "Activity is creative in so far as it moves to its own enrichment as activity, that is bringing along with itself a release of further activities. . . . While from the standpoint of what precedes it is a fulfillment, it is a liberative expansion with respect to what comes after." The thought is surely consistent with the thought of Holmes, but the words are those of Dewey.

Just as pragmatism strove to free the future from the dead hand of the past by stressing the good spirit of experimentation as the one that would exorcise the evil spirit of determinism, so Holmes would free the law from excessive reliance upon precedent, after precedent had ceased to be pertinent. "The official theory is that each new decision follows syllogistically from existing precedents. But just as the clavicle in the cat only tells of the existence of some earlier creature to which a collar-bone was useful, precedents survive in the law long after the use they once served is at an end and the reason for them is forgotten."[8] At a time when the prevailing concept of law was the touchstone

concept, the concept that the minor premise which is the facts
of the case can be triumphantly led to a conclusion by applying
to it touchstone fashion the major premise which is the established legal principle applicable to the facts and available in a
permanently established body of settled legal doctrines, Holmes
asked the basic questions that were in such need of asking. As
his ideological follower Justice Frankfurter phrases them: "What
are the sources of law and what are its sanctions? What is appropriate lawmaking by courts and what should be left to legislation? What are the ingredients, conscious or unconscious, of ad-
judication? What are the wise demands of precedent and when
should the judicial process feel unbound by its past?"[9]

If one paragraph can be singled from *The Common Law*
which reveals better than the others Holmes's concept of the
relationship between the law and society and its institutions, and
his conviction that law exists to codify existing concepts and
make straight the path for ones that are better, it is this: ". . . in
substance the growth of the law is legislative. And this in a
deeper sense that that what the courts declare to have always
been the law is in fact new. It is legislative in its grounds. The
very considerations which judges most rarely mention, and always with an apology, are the secret root from which the law
draws all the juices of life. I mean, of course, considerations of
what is expedient for the community concerned. Every important principle which is developed by litigation is in fact and at
bottom the result of more or less definitely understood views of
public policy; most generally, to be sure, under our practice and
traditions, the unconscious result of instinctive preferences and
inarticulate convictions, but none the less traceable to views of
public policy in the last analysis. And as the law is administered
by able and experienced men, who know too much to sacrifice
good sense to a syllogism, it will be found that, when ancient
rules maintain themselves in the way that has been and will be
shown in this book, new reasons more fitted to the time have
been found for them, and that they gradually receive a new
content, and at last a new form, from the grounds to which they
had been transplanted."[10] The law grows, that is to say, by experience, and the very principles of its growth themselves grow
by experience. So does all human life, the pragmatists say;

pragmatism applies to truth the test of goodness in the form of experience. In the last analysis, Holmes maintained, the law "draws all the juices of life" from what is expedient for the community concerned. In other words, the law as administered by able and experienced men is directed to the greatest happiness of the greatest number, that utilitarian ideal which is the ideal of social pragmatism as well. Holmes was implying, says Catherine Drinker Bowen, that "a good judge unconsciously predicts a law according to the result it will have upon the community at large. Charles Peirce already had a word for this, not in law but in philosophy. Pragmatism, he called it."[11]

The Common Law has long since become a legal classic, and one so totally assimilated into legal thinking that one is prone to forget how uncommon was Holmes's view of the common law when he formulated it. Justice Frankfurter said of its contents, "More than sixty years ago they placed law in a perspective which legal scholarship since has merely confirmed."[12] Pragmatism has entered the current of American thought in many ways, but in none more profoundly, or with more significant effects, than in legal thought. The concept that the life of the law is experience, the concept that slowly and painfully made halting headway until its hour came and it triumphed, was born of deliberations by a group of highly intelligent, highly original, and highly articulate young men who met, sometimes in the study of Charles Peirce and sometimes of William James, back in the 1870s. It might not even be fantastic to say that the New Deal and such politico-economic continuations as the New Frontier and the Great Society may be traced to an ideological ancestral home in those two studies.

For twenty years Holmes served on the supreme judicial court of Massachusetts, and the 1300 opinions he handed down constitute, in the judgment of Justice Frankfurter, "the most comprehensive and philosophic body of American law for any period of its history."[13] There is no particular reason to believe that the true nature of his philosophy was understood in Massachusetts, or indeed by President Theodore Roosevelt who appointed him to the Supreme Court in 1902. He was distrusted in Massachusetts inner circles and trusted in White House circles because of what seemed an inclination in the direction of labor. He puzzled Massachusetts and he disappointed Roosevelt, a puzzle and a disappointment that arose naturally enough, except among the highly favored few admitted to the studies of Charles Peirce and William James. Justice Holmes was not inspired by the spirit of liberalism, in either Cambridge or Washington; he was inspired by the spirit of pragmatism.

The Supreme Court of the United States allowed to Holmes's pragmatism a latitude and scope it never could have enjoyed in the supreme judicial court of Massachusetts. When everything else is stripped away and only the stark essentials remain, the Supreme Court of the United States is a final umpire in boundary disputes. It exists to settle disputes about the boundary lines between individuals, between individuals and branches of local government including states, between states, and between states and the United States. It exists to limit and define the framework within which America lives. Its guide in the process is the Constitution of the United States, and obviously any guide to such a process can couch its directions only in generalities. As these generalities find application in specific cases, they produce precedents which in turn are used as legal stepping-stones to further decisions which produce further precedents. This is the organic concept of the law, a concept which everyone must accept as valid when applied to American constitutional law. The real argument concerns the limits to the validity of precedents. The present is founded on the past but must not be bounded by it, and neither can constrain the future. Law, in the judgment of Holmes, must look from the past, through the present, into the future. Legal principles and legal precedents have their validity and cannot be ignored, but the law of America is not like the law of the Medes and Persians, that altereth not. Alteration is its very essence; the life of the law is experience. "The law embodies the story of a nation's development through many centuries, and it cannot be dealt with as if it contained only the axioms and corollaries of a book of mathematics. In order to know what it is, we must know what it has been, and what it tends to become." These words, which we cited before, appear on the first page of *The Common Law*. What Holmes believed in 1881 when he gave the Lowell Institute lectures that in published form comprise *The Common Law*, he believed in

1902 when Theodore Roosevelt appointed him to the Supreme
Court, and he believed on January 12, 1932, when he wrote to
Herbert Hoover, "The time has come and I bow to the in-
evitable."

"THE GREAT PRAGMATIST"

Holmes was thought by many to be a great liberal, chiefly by
those who did not understand how he thought; he was often
called "the Great Dissenter," although the title has been challenged; he really was "the Great Pragmatist." The concepts of
Oliver Wendell Holmes were fixed early in his life, and never
really altered. He was much too ironic and skeptical a man really
to have the heart of a reformer; he was too inclined to the concepts of classical economics, certainly those of Adam Smith and
Malthus and not impossibly the wage-fund theory of David
Ricardo, to have other than the economic inclination of a nineteenth-century liberal; he had enough respect for social Darwinism, not to mention the respect he had for the entire pattern
of New England thinking of which he was a product, to think
that change comes automatically, or even easily, or is other than
a slow, reluctant process. But the heart of his thinking was not
skeptical, static, or deterministic. At the most these qualities
were brakes upon his dominant pattern of thought, the pragmatism which he adopted as his philosophy when a young man in
Cambridge and never abandoned in the seven decades of life
that followed. At the most these deterrent qualities reinforced
that judicial self-restraint which characterized his life on the
bench and was often confused with liberalism.

It is when the views of Justice Holmes are studied with the
axioms of pragmatism in mind that the full consistency of his
mental pattern is revealed. If the life of the law is experience
and experience is the result of experiment, then society must
have the maximum latitude for experiment consistent with the
constitutional framework under which it has elected to live. It
was because he believed in these axioms at a time when social
experimentation tended to take the form of legal restraint upon
specific forms of the practice of *laissez faire* by social Darwinians, individual and corporate, and at a time when the majority

of the Supreme Court considered certain specific measures of restraint unconstitutional that Holmes came to be considered both a great liberal and a great dissenter. The truth, as he frequently proclaimed, was that he believed in experimentation, not in the specific forms of the experiments in question nor in their intended ends. In one way or another he said repeatedly what he said in *Truax v. Corrigan:* "There is nothing that I more deprecate than the use of the Fourteenth Amendment beyond the absolute compulsion of its words to prevent the making of social experiments that an important part of the community desires, in the insulated chambers afforded by the several States, even though the experiments may seem futile or even noxious to me and to those whose judgment I most respect."[14]

Furthermore, in the judicial self-restraint of Justice Holmes there was always a measure of uncertainty which may well have been the product of a conflict between his consciously cultivated pragmatism and that ironic skepticism which was his native cast of mind, and, for all one knows, perhaps a fear of some jagged edge the submerged and in the main forgotten iceberg might rear, the New England conscience. "It is a misfortune if a judge reads his conscious or unconscious sympathy with one side or the other prematurely into the law, and forgets that what seems to him to be first principles are believed by half his fellow men to be wrong."[15] In the view of Holmes, objectivity, detachment, and self-restraint were the moral obligations of a jurist; "otherwise a constitution, instead of embodying only relatively fundamental rules of right, as generally understood by all English-speaking communities, would become the partisan of a particular set of ethical or economical opinions. . . ."[16]

As we said before, Holmes brought his pragmatism to the Supreme Court at a time when social experimentation tended to take the form of legal limitation upon specific manifestations of *laissez faire.* Starting in 1902 the two current and contrasting philosophies of the man-made order met in combat beneath judicial robes. It is conventional to refer to the contrasting viewpoints as the conservative and the liberal, but it is considerably more accurate to refer to them as the social Darwinian and the pragmatic. The social Darwinians on the bench read into the

Constitution their particular concept of the man-made order, the order that we have traced from its inception in eighteenth-century deism, through utilitarianism and its counterpart classical economics into the reinforcement that social Darwinism gave it. Terms such as "due process" and "liberty of process" were interpreted to sanctify, constitutionally speaking, the economics of Adam Smith and his school. Until pragmatism all believers in the man-made order, whatever their personal patterns of thought, elevated human reason and consequently tended to travel the a priori road. The pragmatist, no less a believer in the man-made order than they, but one who thought of life as becoming, not as being, and who elevated inductive experimentation as his opponents elevated reason, tended to travel the a posteriori road. If one is on the bench, one can hardly be a pragmatist without practicing judicial self-restraint; one may regard it as a juridical virtue if one chooses, but it is an obvious necessity if one is a pragmatist. It was merely the circumstances under which he donned the Supreme Court robes, the circumstances that prevailed in a Court which interpreted the Constitution of the United States after the doctrines of Adam Smith, that made Holmes a liberal and a dissenter, although he was the latter only to a point and the former only in the nineteenth-century sense.

The record indicates that the fundamental consistency of Holmes was to the experimental principle of pragmatism and to nothing else, just as he himself proclaimed. One of his celebrated "liberal" dissents was in the Lochner Case, in which a Supreme Court majority set aside a New York law limiting the labor of bakers to ten hours a day and sixty hours a week.[17] This was the case that drove what seemed to be the final nail into the coffin of *McCulloch v. Maryland*, the decision which had formulated the doctrine that a legislature is the judge of the wisdom of its regulatory acts. A comparison of the reasoning behind Chief Justice Marshall's opinion in *McCulloch v. Maryland* and Justice Holmes's reasoning in *Lochner v. New York* reveals clearly the difference between reasoning based on principle and reasoning guided by pragmatism. Marshall wrote the unanimous decision of the Court upholding the constitutional right of Congress to charter and control the second Bank of the

United States and denying the right of Maryland to inhibit its operation by confiscatory taxation. He argued on the twin principles of national sovereignty and broad construction. The former argument rested on the thesis that the federal government derives its powers from the people and not from the states, and the latter from the right of the legislative branch of government to select the means to carry out its powers. Holmes also wrote an eloquent opinion in *Lochner v. New York*, one that is often hailed as a great liberal document. It may be that, but it is clearly a dissent written by a pragmatist who believed in the right of a state to perform social experiments and disbelieved in an interpretation of the Constitution which found it the embodiment of any predetermined and fixed economic or social philosophy. He wrote in part, "This case is decided upon an economic theory which a large part of the country does not entertain. If it were a question whether I agreed with that theory, I should desire to study it further and long before making up my mind. But I do not conceive that to be my duty, because I strongly believe that my agreement or disagreement has nothing to do with the right of a majority to embody their opinions in law. . . . The liberty of the citizen to do as he likes so long as he does not interfere with the liberty of others to do the same, which has been the shibboleth for some well-known writers, is interfered with by school laws, by the Post Office, by every state or municipal institution which takes his money for purposes thought desirable, whether he likes it or not. The Fourteenth Amendment does not enact Mr. Herbert Spencer's Social Statics. . . . A constitution is not intended to embody a particular economic theory, whether of paternalism and the organic relation of the citizen to the State or of *laissez faire*. It is made for people of fundamentally different views. . . ."[18] The essential point is that Holmes was not advocating a health law, but the right of a state to experiment with a health law. His sympathy was with the experimenting legislature, not the overworked bakers.

Superficially this may seem to be a distinction without a difference. That there is a difference as well as a distinction may be seen in Holmes's opinion in *Meyer v. Nebraska*. The case involved the right of parents to send their children to a parochial school for religious instruction in classes conducted in German.

The school in question was conducted by the Lutheran Church, and it had run afoul of a Nebraska statute forbidding instruction in a foreign language below the high-school level. The "liberal" viewpoint would appear to be that the Nebraska act was unconstitutional as infringing on freedom of religion, and indeed the act of the Supreme Court majority in striking down the Nebraska statute has been regarded as one of the major milestones on the road to religious freedom in America. Perhaps the illustration of the illusory nature of the terms "liberal" and "conservative" has its own value: the majority opinion was written by an arch-conservative, Justice McReynolds, and joined by an arch-liberal, Justice Brandeis. But it was opposed by Justice Holmes, on his habitual grounds that it dealt with a matter on which men might reasonably differ and hence was one on which a state had a constitutional right to experiment. In addition, Holmes always held that it was part of judicial self-restraint to recognize the possible existence of local conditions with which a Supreme Court justice might be unfamiliar. "I cannot bring my mind to believe that in some circumstances, and circumstances existing it is said in Nebraska, the statute might not be regarded as a reasonable and even necessary method of reaching the desired result."[19] Holmes was not advocating the right of a state to infringe upon what the majority of his colleagues considered religious freedom, but the right of a state to experiment with limiting the right of religious freedom in the name of a different end. There are no absolutes in pragmatism: "It is desirable that all citizens of the United States should speak a common tongue, and therefore that the end aimed at by the statute is a lawful and proper one."[20]

The one eternal principle of pragmatism is that there are no eternal principles. Life is becoming, not being; growth is its objective as well as its essence; experiment and experience are its operational principles; that the law of life is experience is the pragmatic generalization, that the life of the law is experience is Holmes's particular application. One of his former secretaries, Francis Biddle, who was Attorney General of the United States from 1941 to 1945, put it as well as anyone in his Oliver Wendell Holmes Devise lectures at the University of Texas in 1950. "The substance of the law, according to Holmes, at any given time pretty nearly corresponds with what is then thought to be 'convenient.' He constantly recurred to this thought. Since law is but one expression of community life, you must look to the community to discover the existing notions of public policy, which are continually changing. He would not speak of justification, for that presupposed an absolute criterion, whereas the problem was: 'Does this decision represent what the lawmaking power must be taken to want?' He would have liked to get a more definite reason than that the decision was in consonance with our sense of justice, and find a more specific policy than that. Law is what the supreme power in the community wills; and all that could be expected from modern improvements is that legislation should easily and quickly, yet not too quickly, modify itself to the will of that *de facto* power, and that the spread of an educated sympathy should reduce the sacrifice of minorities to a minimum."[21]

That is pragmatism in the law, succinctly and clearly stated. No longer do the rights of minorities depend upon the doctrine of the rights of man and its enshrinement in the Constitution of the United States, but upon "the spread of an educated sympathy" among the majority. Such thinking is quite consistent with the thought of Oliver Wendell Homes when he said, "Our system of morality is a body of imperfect generalizations expressed in terms of emotion."[22]

JUSTICE BRANDEIS

The statement could probably stand that no justice in the history of the Supreme Court would have disagreed more profoundly and energetically with that extension of pragmatism which finds minority rights dependent on the spread of an educated sympathy among the majority than Louis Dembitz Brandeis. The fallacy of combining the philosophies of Oliver Wendell Holmes and Brandeis by the same link that so often bound their judicial decisions has, of course, long been recognized and is expounded in all responsible studies of the Supreme Court, its justices, and their legal attitudes. It is true that Holmes and Brandeis frequently reached the same judicial conclusions, but it is also true that they frequently did so by markedly different routes and always did so from different intellectual starting points. Holmes had precisely the correct pattern of mind for a pragmatist: he was ironic, skeptical, detached, a Yankee who didn't really descend very often from Olympus but stayed mainly on its remote heights, like an Olympian in the tradition of deism. It would be pleasantly simple to say that Brandeis had precisely the wrong frame of mind for a pragmatist, but it would not be true. Brandeis had in some respects an excellent frame of mind for a pragmatist, and yet one utterly incompatible with a philosophy that flourished on irony, skepticism, and detachment. Brandeis was not ironic but direct and sincere, not skeptical but dedicated to belief in the progress of the human order, not detached but body and soul involved. His direct sincerity, dedicated belief, and total involvement in the betterment of the human order almost kept him off the Supreme Court in 1916 when President Wilson's unexpected nomination precipitated a forensic hurricane exceeded in intensity during the twentieth century only by the typhoon that Roosevelt's Court-packing plan whipped up. Every charge conceivable was leveled at him, but no one called him ironic, skeptical, and detached. No one said that he would be another Oliver Wendell Holmes.

The truth is that Brandeis, like Holmes, was a believer in the man-made order; like Holmes, his philosophy was largely experiential; but entirely unlike Holmes, Brandeis believed in a set of moral values that are not of man's making and that provide a framework within which the man-made order is to be constructed. It is extremely difficult to reconstruct precisely what Brandeis did believe about that set of moral values, but it is not difficult to establish that he believed in its existence. On the other hand, it would be worse than misleading to suggest that Brandeis held to a pattern of thought other than approximately comparable to that of William James. Brandeis had a pragmatic cast of mind, but he was not a pragmatist after such models as James, Dewey, and Holmes.

Brandeis was reared outside formal religion. His mother later wrote: "I do not believe that sins can be expiated by going to divine service and observing this or that formula; I believe that only goodness and truth and conduct that is humane and self-sacrificing towards those who need us can bring God nearer to us, and that our errors can only be atoned for by acting in a more kindly spirit. Love, virtue and truth are the foundation upon which the education of the child must be based. . . . And this is my justification for bringing up my children without any definite religious belief: I wanted to give them something that neither could be argued away nor would have to be given up as untenable, namely, a pure spirit and the highest ideals as to morals and love."[23] When she added, "God has blessed my endeavors," she did so with entire right. Louis Brandeis measured to his mother's ideal about as well as any man can measure to his mother's ideal, and in his case the ideal can do double duty as the description of the man.

Brandeis, then, was essentially a humanist, but unlike the pragmatist Holmes there are traces here and there in Brandeis of a sort of religion of humanism that suggests a belief in permanent values of the sort enshrined in the religion of the churches. Perhaps they are most clearly visible in a letter he wrote to Robert W. Bruère of the Federal Council of Churches in America after he gave a talk to a small group in the Council. Having urged that no evil in business need be accepted as inevitable, no immoral practice need to be tolerated as inescapable, he warns against the search for the moral panacea, and especially the search for the legislative panacea. Betterment must be sought within the framework of existing institutions and first and foremost among men themselves: "Always and everywhere the intellectual, moral and spiritual development of those concerned will remain an essential—and the main factor—in real betterment. This development of the individual is, thus, both a necessary means and the end sought." And after stressing the thought that the great developer is responsibility and that no pattern of society demands the responsible individual quite as urgently as the democratic, he concludes: "Democracy in any sphere is a serious undertaking. It substitutes self-restraint for external restraint. It is more difficult to maintain than to achieve. It demands continuous sacrifice by the individual and more exigent obedience to the moral law than any other form of government. Success in any democratic undertaking must proceed from the individual. It is possible only where the process of perfecting the individual is pursued. His development is attained mainly in the processes of common living. Hence the industrial struggle is essentially an affair of the Church and is its imperative task."[24] The man who believes in the objective reality of evil and immorality, and their opposite, a moral law, and who stresses that reform comes first in the heart of man if it comes at all, is the man with the essentials of a religious faith. However it be categorized, Brandeis differed from Holmes in that he had a religious faith.

Out of this essential difference stem the other differences between Brandeis and Holmes. The man who believes in objective realities that are not of man's making has a stronger sense of the need for certitude than the man whose philosophy is essentially experiential. Brandeis came closer than Holmes to what Justice Robert H. Jackson called "the golden mean in his attitude toward the precedents."[25] Holmes, of course, had the inevitable respect for precedent without which responsible judicial action would be impossible, but Holmes was more impressed by the fugitive nature of precedent and the speed with which it ceases to be applicable than was Brandeis. Brandeis preserved a better balance than Holmes between the authority of precedent and the specific demands that the specific circumstances of a given case imposed. Brandeis tended to consider precedent applicable until there was positive proof that it was not, but then he did not hesitate to depart from it.

MORAL PRINCIPLES AND LAW

Brandeis employed moral principles as a touchstone in reaching his decisions in a way that would be inconsistent with the convictions of a complete pragmatist. For example, his opinion in a case that involved the tapping of telephone wires to get evidence of criminal activities was predicated upon what he deemed unalterable moral law. "Our government is the potent, the omnipresent teacher. For good or ill, it teaches the whole people by example. Crime is contagious. If the government becomes a lawbreaker, it breeds contempt for law; it invites every man to become a law unto himself; it invites anarchy. To declare that in the administration of the criminal law the end justifies

the means—to declare that the government may commit crimes
in order to secure the conviction of a private criminal—would
bring terrible retribution. . . ."[26] The result of this attitude was
an instinct in Brandeis to test the validity of a piece of legislation
by its conformity to fundamental moral principles prior to applying to it any other test.

If there was one central preoccupation in the life and thought
of Louis Brandeis, it was his distrust of centralized and autocratic power. He lived in a day and age when power was
centralized in big industry, and had grown autocratic under the
fostering influence of social Darwinism. But Brandeis was not a
trust buster for the sake of busting trusts. Behind his fear of
bigness was his fear of the autocratic disregard of moral principle
that bigness generates. Brandeis also knew that absolute power
corrupts absolutely, and he knew that this is just as true when
the absolute power is concentrated in government as when it is
concentrated in private hands. Furthermore, as a scholar he
knew that in the entirety of human experience, absolutism is far
more apt to be an attribute of government than of private enterprise, that *laissez faire* is a sporadic spirit that quickly generates
its own controlling reaction as it did in the United States.

There were, then, fundamental attitudes present in Brandeis
consistent with belief in a permanent and objective moral order.
Indeed, the parallel which has occasionally been drawn between the thinking of Thomas Jefferson and Louis Brandeis, a
fairly superficial parallel based upon an instinct for a wholesome
limitation upon political and economic power, may itself have a
more significant parallel of a different sort. Essentially Brandeis
was such a deist as Jefferson, one who believed in an objective
moral law but one who found himself in an intellectual halfway
house between belief in a divinely created order and belief in a
man-made order. Perhaps belief in a man-made order constructed
in accordance with objective moral principles best defines the
belief of Brandeis, with the basis for the objectivity of the moral
principles left undefined.

The result was an agreement between Brandeis and Holmes
that was essentially factual rather than philosophical. There was
also a sense in which Brandeis believed that the life of the law is
experience, but Brandeis did not understand by the aphorism

what Holmes understood. There is the celebrated remark that Brandeis made to his law clerk after they had hammered out several revisions of an opinion: "The opinion is now convincing, but what can we do to make it more instructive?" What could always be done to make an opinion more instructive was to clarify the experience which comprised the facts of the case and was the minor premise in the legal syllogism. The result is that infinitely careful marshaling of facts, presentation of details, consummate formulation of experience which comprised the celebrated "Brandeis brief" and made Holmes describe his associate as "the master of both microscope and telescope. Nothing of importance, however minute, escapes his microscopic examination of every problem, and, through his powerful telescopic lens, his mental vision embraces distant scenes ranging far beyond the familiar worlds of conventional thinking."[27]

The Brandeis brief, scrupulously accurate and minutely detailed, possessing the rarest of the legalistic virtues, the objective and dispassionate presentation of the factual background, made its appearance at the very start of his professional career. In 1879, when he was making his tentative and not particularly successful start on the law in St. Louis, he did a fourteen-page factual analysis in a case involving the liability of trust estates on contracts made for their benefit. The head of the firm for which he worked had the brief printed and submitted to the Missouri Court of Appeals as a comprehensive and dispassionate treatment of a subject passed over by the legal textbooks. Later it was revised and published in the *American Law Review* of July, 1881. Dispassionate comprehensiveness is not a primary characteristic of the courtroom lawyer. It was perhaps the greatest single legal glory of Louis Brandeis that he achieved as a courtroom lawyer what is the academic ideal of the legal scholar.

The Brandeis brief par excellence was filed in 1907 in a Supreme Court case involving an Oregon statute limiting to ten hours the work day of women. Brandeis presented the legal aspect of his case succinctly, in a few pages; the brief proper was a document over one hundred pages long presenting the factual evidence drawn from a multitude of sociological, economic, and physical studies to prove that it is physically, economically, and sociologically unsound for a woman to work more than ten hours a day. The battery of opposing arguments that Brandeis faced was drawn from the arsenal of social Darwinism: women had the right of free contract as truly as men and to limit their right to contract for more working hours a day than ten would be a limitation on freedom of contract. The Brandeis brief was essentially a plea that the Supreme Court follow to the logical conclusion the line of reasoning that had prevailed in *Lochner v. New York* and other cases involving public health legislation even though the logical conclusion this time was the opposite of the conclusion previously reached. In *Lochner v. New York* it had been held that the ten-hour day for bakers imperiled neither the bakers nor the bread. The supposition, then, was that if either had been imperiled the verdict would have been the opposite. Relying on what had at least a superficial resemblance to logic, Brandeis reasoned that a brief which proved that excessive working hours were injurious to the health of women should gain a decision on the same principle but with the opposite result. In the highly specialized and nonchronological sense in which the term is applied to the Supreme Court there were indeed Nine Old Men on the bench in 1907, but Brandeis prevailed and the Oregon ten-hour law was upheld.

THE TEST OF FACTS

The thinking behind the Brandeis brief is the thinking of a pragmatist in the most constructive and soundest sense the word can carry. Brandeis was quite as willing as the most conservative of justices to agree that liberty of contract should be abridged only when solid necessity was established. But necessity cannot be established by logic; necessity can be established only by experience. Hence the brief in which Brandeis marshaled with consummate care all the evidence to prove the deleterious nature of long working hours for women. Brandeis was introducing to American law a principle essentially pragmatic in nature: the legality of social legislation depends in part upon its reasonable nature, and the only test of its reasonable nature is the test of facts. Justice Brewer, speaking for the Supreme Court, said of the Brandeis brief: "The legislation and opinions referred to in the margin may not be, technically speaking, authorities, and in them is little or no discussion of the constitutional question presented to us for determination, yet they are significant of a widespread belief that woman's physical structure, and the functions she performs in consequence thereof, justify special legislation restricting or qualifying the conditions under which she should be permitted to toil."[28]

In the Oregon ten-hour-law case the facts supported what today is called the "liberal" position. There is nothing in the stubbornly objective nature of facts that makes them support what at any given time is called either liberal or conservative, and nothing about facts that makes them sacrosanct from manipulation by those called liberals or conservatives. As time went on and the fundamental soundness of the Brandeis brief came to be acknowledged, its technique was borrowed by those whose social objectives were very different from those of Louis Brandeis. Facts were employed by both sides in all sorts of issues, and facts listened to by the courts, as facts have been since the days of Lycurgus. There was nothing new in all this except something new in emphasis: after the voice of Brandeis came to be heard and respected, the reasonable quality of social legislation loomed somewhat larger than it had before, the legal precedent for it somewhat smaller, and the a posteriori induction based upon a study of the facts came to enjoy a greater respect than formerly as contrasted to the a priori deduction drawn from legal principles. As we said before, this is the essential pragmatism of Louis Brandeis, and its value is written large in twentieth-century American history.

This point needs to be established, because a distinction must be carefully drawn between that facet of Brandeis' personality which made him a pragmatist and the facet that directed him toward social reform. There can be other sources of pragmatism than the studies of Charles Peirce and William James, and one is the normal approach of a twentieth-century scholar to a problem. A scientific age is an inductive age, and the natural bent of Brandeis' scholarly nature was reinforced by the spirit of the age in which he lived. Brandeis was at once a scholar and a crusader, and the scholar in him inclined him to the Brandeis brief. The crusader in him inclined him to the typical cause in which a Brandeis brief might be employed. It might be employed in the cause of a limited working day for women, or a minimum wage scale for men, or in any cause that made the poor less poor and the disadvantaged less handicapped. Here the fundamental distinction between Holmes and Brandeis can be clearly perceived. Holmes would uphold a state law designed to better the lives of ordinary people because he believed in the right of legislatures to experiment with social legislation, although he had an innate skepticism about the effectiveness of the experiments. Brandeis would uphold such a law because he believed in the objective and in the possibility of attaining it. The pragmatism of Holmes had a certain limitation not found in the pragmatism of Brandeis. Holmes would grant to the legislature the right to experiment and to learn from the experience which is the result of experiment, but he would not pass beyond that point by permitting his own social and economic convictions to enter his judicial opinion. Thus Holmes never entirely parted company from the older pattern of judicial thinking which rested on the thesis that law was something received and judges were not influenced by their view of the wisdom of legislation. But the concept of the Brandeis brief rested on the thesis that the sociological, economic, and physical facts that motivate social legislation are pertinent to judicial decisions about the legislation, and hence the wisdom of legislation should and does influence the thinking of judges. The sound man, however, is never an extremist, and Brandeis recognized the necessity of proper judicial restraint even as he recognized that judges do write their social and economic philosophy into their decisions.

The pragmatism of Brandeis is best exemplified by the Brandeis brief and the concept on which it rests. But the Brandeis brief, however objective and dispassionate, did ordinarily reach a conclusion consistent with the Brandeis social and economic philosophy, and that philosophy did appear in the Brandeis opinions. Since Brandeis considered it his judicial function to marshal the facts, appraise them, and pass judgment on them— in short, to reach his own inductive conclusions and to express them in his legal opinions—he was a legal pragmatist in an active sense, unlike Holmes who was content to let the legislature do the experimenting and society reach the conclusions. On the other hand, there is unmistakable evidence in Brandeis of belief in an objective moral order which is not the product of man's experience and man's making. In this respect Brandeis is less a pragmatist than Holmes, and indeed suggests a belated eighteenth-century deist of the Jefferson pattern. Although the thought of the practicing jurist can be equated only approximately with the thought of the theoretical philosopher, Brandeis is closer to William James than to John Dewey, and Holmes is closer to Dewey than to his personal friend James.

The year 1925 found Holmes and Brandeis, for the reasons indicated, a minority of two on the Supreme Court bench. Their associates were Justice James McReynolds, whose liberalism as Woodrow Wilson's Attorney General underwent the strangest of sea changes into a petrified conservatism; Justice Willis Van Devanter, who found it easy to follow the groove of social Darwinism except for two enthusiasms, conservation of natural resources and the welfare of the American Indian; Justice Joseph McKenna, who was a social Darwinian with some misgivings; Justices George Sutherland and Pierce Butler, former railroad lawyers who never bit the hands that once had fed them or hands cast in the same mold; Justice E. T. Sanford, who brought to the bench the mentality of a Southern Republican; and Chief Justice William Howard Taft, a man of far too potent and flexible intelligence to be branded with a phrase, but one whose native bias was toward conservatism. This was the Court that was to be remade into the image and likeness of Louis Brandeis and Oliver Wendell Holmes.

The difficulty is that these two original and forthright thinkers did not have a single image nor a single likeness. Consequently, when the spirit of social Darwinism passed from the bench and the spirit of pragmatism took its place, there were two images and two likenesses. One was the image and likeness of Justice Holmes and his ideal of judicial restraint, and the other was the image and likeness of Justice Brandeis. The second is the really subtle image and difficult likeness. Brandeis did conceive of constitutional interpretation as an instrument of social policy, but he also had respect for judicial restraint and judicial tradition. Brandeis would agree with Matthew Arnold that life is both a being and a becoming. If the judicial restraint of Justice Holmes is consistent with the philosophy of pragmatism, a philosophy

whose birth throes Holmes observed, so is the conviction of
Justice Brandeis that it is part of the judicial function to aid in
the development of the law by the inductive conclusions derived
from carefully accumulated and minutely scrutinized facts.
As the social Darwinism of Justices McReynolds, Van Devanter,
Sutherland, and Butler passed, the pragmatism of Justices
Holmes and Brandeis was destined to succeed it. But their
pragmatism would flash two contrasting lights to America, the
red light of judicial restraint and the green light of activism, of
judicial cooperation with the spirit of social experimentation.

XVI
THE HIGH NOON
OF PRAGMATISM

THE SIGNIFICANCE of the Supreme Court where the impact of pragmatism on American life is concerned arises from a fundamental if little-considered fact of American life. There are two forces in America that remain in a usually uneasy balance. One is the force of established tradition and principle. One might call it, among other things, the voice of the Constitution. The other is the impact of the times, in a nation very conscious of modernity and instinctively receptive to novelty and experimentation. Continuity and change are more nearly in balance in America than in most countries. We are little given to contemplating the fact, but when due allowance is made for the fundamental changes that the Reform Bills introduced into English life, we have the oldest basically unchanged governmental pattern among the major nations of the world. The gyroscope in our ship of state has been the Supreme Court, what Daniel Boorstin calls "the American political conscience, a kind of secular papacy . . . the Great Remembrancer of our foundations."[1]

Consequently a study of Supreme Court attitudes is one major avenue to the study of developing American patterns of thought. As a rule the Supreme Court does not lag particularly behind the progress of American thought nor forge ahead out of sight of it, although both charges are intermittently hurled by those dissatisfied with its current rate and course of progress. The pattern of thinking evidenced at any given period in the history of the Supreme Court coincides at least in general outline with the pattern of thinking evidenced at the same time by a substantial part of the American people. The duties of the Supreme Court justices, however, impose upon them an obligation not incumbent upon the rest of us. They must express their philosophy formally in their written opinions, and the very weight of their responsibility insures that the philosophy will be formulated with the degree of thought and care within their individual capacities. Some justices have been more philosophic than others, some better scholars, some better writers, some better thinkers. When allowance is made for individual differences, the fact remains that a Supreme Court decision is a formal and thoughtful exposition of a legal conclusion, based upon the law but reflecting the philosophy of law and life of its author and those who concur in it, upon a matter of sufficient importance in the life of the nation to warrant consideration by the Supreme Court. What the Supreme Court thinks is not necessarily what America thinks, nor can the history of American thought be written in the history of the Supreme Court decisions, but the philosophic microcosm, the Supreme Court, offers one of the most fruitful and productive avenues to the study of the philosophic macrocosm, American thought.

John Marshall once said: "Judicial power, as contradistinguished from the power of the laws, has no existence. Courts are the mere instruments of the law, and can will nothing." Before one dismisses the concept as an outmoded and meaningless relic of an eighteenth-century attitude, it might be well to recall the foundation on which the concept rests. We have seen that all the Founding Fathers accepted as the axioms from which their political philosophy developed the existence of God and divine providence, a moral imperative divinely ordained and revealed to man in the form of natural law, inalienable rights that followed as corollaries to the moral imperative, and human equality in the eyes of God and therefore rightly in the eyes of man. This much was philosophy, or if one wishes, religion. Politics rested by its nature upon this philosophic or religious foundation. Hence a Constitution could be constructed, since a Constitution as the Founding Fathers conceived it was a contract entered upon by the several states and what were then considered their citizens to conduct their personal and corporate lives in a federal union according to the principles of natural law as translated into statute law. It was the responsibility of the legislative branch to do the translating and the responsibility of the administrative branch to do the administering. The responsibility of the Court was to pass judgment upon the way in which they did it, using natural law and the Constitution as its two sighting points.

TRANSLATING THE LAW

The result was far from stultifying where the other kind of translating was concerned, the translating of the popular law into legislative form. In its first seventy-one years the Supreme Court declared only two acts of Congress unconstitutional. One was the Judiciary Act of 1789 which specifically authorized the Supreme Court to issue writs of mandamus to persons holding office under the authority of the United Sates. In *Marbury v. Madison* (1803), which had as its immediate occasion a last-minute appointment by President Adams of a justice of the peace for the District of Columbia which his successor President Jefferson attempted to annul, Justice Marshall ruled that the Constitution did not authorize the Supreme Court to issue writs of mandamus and that in a direct conflict between the Constitution and an act of Congress, the Supreme Court had the right to declare the act of Congress unconstitutional. In its entire history the Supreme Court has never issued an opinion more vital to the fundamental structure of our national life than *Marbury v. Madison*. The other case can be quickly dismissed: it was the infamous Dred Scott decision. During the same period, the first great age in American history which ended with the Civil War, the Court declared state legislation unconstitutional in sixty cases.

The comparison with the later periods, when the patterns of thought present in social Darwinism and pragmatism have prevailed, is instructive. The Court held unconstitutional twelve acts of Congress between 1874 and 1898, and about fifty between 1898 and 1937. The comparable figures for state legislative acts ruled unconstitutional are 125 and about 400.[2] It may be paradoxical and it may not be significant, but the Supreme Court exercised its highest degree of judicial restraint, not in the twentieth century when the philosophy of pragmatism made itself felt in Court deliberations but in the earlier part of the nineteenth century when the concept of the Constitution as a charter of government and not an instrument of government still prevailed.

The explanation of the paradox, if it be one, and the true grounds for the significance of the fact, are not necessarily and exclusively the different concept of the relationship of the nation and the states that followed the Civil War from the one that preceded it. It is true, of course, that the concept called "dual federalism," which viewed as inviolable the reserved powers of the states, dwindled sharply after the conflict, a dwindling which in turn invited a closer Court scrutiny of state legislative action. But it is also true that the contract concept of the Constitution, with the implicit but generally accepted thesis that natural law underlies legislative action and administrative procedure as well as judicial decision, created an intellectual climate in which the Court assumed that an act and its administration were constitutional unless clearly otherwise. It was with the dwindling of acceptance of the natural law concept and its replacement with the concept of the man-made order that the Supreme Court began to translate into its legal interpretations the political and economic convictions of its members. It began, as we saw in Chapter XII, when the most dedicated social Darwinian in Court history and one of the most forthright, energetic, opinionated, and influential justices, Stephen J. Field, began to translate the concepts of Herbert Spencer and William Graham Sumner into the Constitution of the United States.

THE SUPREME COURT AND SOCIAL DARWINISM

The second great period of constitutional history coincides with the rise and fall of social Darwinism, extending from 1870 until the "Roosevelt judges" had a secure majority. It was the period when the *Social Statics* of Herbert Spencer (to reverse Justice Holmes's opinion) was read into the Constitution, and the concept of due process, which traditionally had to do only with procedure, took on a substantive hue. Substantive due process is the concept that there is an absolute limit imposed by natural law upon the rights of a legislature. Put in such terms it would seem entirely consistent with the contract concept of the Constitution which had prevailed since the eighteenth century, and indeed so consistent was the concept that it was seldom if ever voiced before the time of Justice Field. But social Darwinism had brought into the fields of politics and economics a new concept of natural law, the kind borrowed from *The Origin of Species*, linked to classical economics, and then applied by metaphor. *Laissez faire* was natural law to the social Darwinians, and *laissez faire* was welded to the Constitution on the principle of substantive due process by the property-minded justices appointed to the bench by Presidents Hayes, Arthur, Cleveland, and Harrison. By the substantive due process concept a legislative act regulating business had to be reasonable to be valid, a concept finally intercalated in the Constitution in 1898, when the Supreme Court found unconstitutional a Nebraska statute setting intrastate freight rates at what it deemed an unreasonably low and hence unconstitutional level.[3]

The concept of substantive due process and its ideological relative that was also the offspring of *laissez faire* economics, freedom of contract, dominated Supreme Court thinking through the years in which social Darwinism prevailed. Again we see illustrated the principle that Supreme Court thought and American thought in general are not isolated the one from the other. It was the "gilded age" in American life and thought. The Fittest Americans who survived were not numerous and their survival hardly compensated for those who, in an economic and sociological and often in a literal sense, did not survive the effects of what gilded age thinking considered substantive due process and freedom of contract. But the theses of social Darwinism were accepted as valid by many Americans who were by no criterion "the fittest," or by no criterion except their own desires and daydreams—one might recall the businessmen of Middletown who were social Darwinian frogs in a very modest puddle. Furthermore, one may accept a thesis as fully when one is rueful as when one is eager. Hence in the period after 1870, and especially in the period after the First World War, social Darwinism, *laissez faire,* substantive due process, and right of contract fused with the dim, distorted memory of what natural law really meant and emerged as the new natural law which was the new foundation of the Constitution of the United States, as seen by the Supreme Court.

The generalization is, of course, only a generalization. The Supreme Court did not necessarily apply its social and economic convictions as touchstones to determine the legality of every piece of legislation, nor did the social significance of a law always determine its fate. For example, in 1918, Congress set up a wage board with discretionary power to set the wages of women and children employed in the District of Columbia. The act was declared unconstitutional in a 5 to 3 decision written by Justice Sutherland. When Justice Sutherland, in *Adkins v. Children's Hospital*, attacked all minimum wage legislation as uneconomic and socially undesirable, conservative Justice Taft was as quick to reply, "It is not the function of this Court to hold congressional acts invalid simply because they are passed to carry out economic views which the court believes to be unwise or unsound," as pragmatic Justice Holmes was to echo his words: "The criterion of constitutionality is not whether we believe the law to be for the public good."[4]

It should not be overlooked that the same ideological pattern that so carefully protected property rights protected civil rights as well. *Meyer v. Nebraska* (1923), which established the right of parents to educate their children as their consciences dictated, and *Pierce v. Society of Sisters* (1925), which spelled out the right of parents to send their children to private schools, are landmark cases in the history of civil rights and religious freedom in America. Similarly the right of free speech was upheld in a series of cases. When a California statute outlawing the display of a red flag as a symbol of opposition to organized government was tested in *Stromberg v. California* (1931), Chief Justice Hughes stated, "The conception of liberty under the due process clause of the Fourteenth Amendment embraces the right of free speech." It is a fact that may perhaps be viewed as ironic: the foundation for the series of decisions in recent years that has so extended and confirmed the civil rights of Americans actually was laid by the social Darwinians on the bench under their concept of substantive due process. Again one sees illustrated the chameleon quality of the words *liberal* and *conservative*.

When full allowance is made for the implications of a pattern of thinking that spells freedom when read one way and restraint when read the other, the fact remains that the Supreme Court from 1870 to 1937 posed an obstacle to social legislation difficult to surmount and next to impossible to circumvent. Justice Sutherland had laid down in *Adkins v. Children's Hospital* four categories of permissible restraint on free trade. As stated by Kelly and Harbison they were: (1) statutes fixing rates in businesses affected with a public interest; (2) statutes relating to contracts for public works; (3) statutes prescribing the character, methods, and time of wage payments; and (4) statutes fixing hours of labor.[5] These were the manacles of the mind forged by social Darwinism, the manacles against which Justices Holmes and Brandeis struggled in 1925. But their hour was at its dawn. Holmes was too old to enter Jericho, but Brandeis was there to sound the trumpet.

The first cleavage in the ranks of juridical social Darwinism came in 1925, when President Coolidge made a typically safe and sane appointment to the Supreme Court. Harlan Fiske Stone had in his background legal service for New York corporations, academic service for Columbia University Law School, and political service for Coolidge as his Attorney General. There was no more reason for Coolidge to expect in him a turn toward liberalism than there had been for Wilson to expect in his erstwhile Attorney General James McReynolds a turn in the opposite direction. The Fates ironic, however, have a way of balancing off these matters, and there soon began to appear the joint dissents of Holmes, Brandeis, and Stone. Justice Stone, in taking his stand with Holmes and Brandeis, in a more exact sense took his precise stand with Holmes. Without implying that Justice Stone was in any formal sense a pragmatist, one can say that he accepted the logic of pragmatism as applied to the Court by Justice Holmes in his espousal of judicial self-restraint.

At the risk of the confusion attendant on taking things out of chronological order, we might now consider the 1936 case in which the Agricultural Adjustment Act was invalidated, a case that reveals as clearly in the contrasting opinions the cleavage between what we have termed legal social Darwinism and legal pragmatism as any case in Court history. It reveals it the more

clearly because the contrasting opinions were written by moder-
ates—Justice Roberts, a moderate conservative, for the majority;
and Justice Stone, a moderate liberal, for the minority. The case
hinged on the general welfare clause of the Constitution, which
allows Congress to "provide for the common defense and general
welfare of the United States." The precise meaning of that clause
had been a subject of debate between Madison and Hamilton,
Madison contending that it was merely introductory to the
powers of Congress that were then enumerated and Hamilton
maintaining that it was a blanket clause independent of the
enumerated powers. Roberts, an open-minded and moderate
man, conceded that in his opinion Hamilton was right, yet
found the Agricultural Adjustment Act unconstitutional because
its crop control provisions, even though voluntary, connoted a
control of agriculture and so, by implication, a denial of the
principle of *laissez faire*. "The power to confer or withhold unlimited benefits is the power to coerce or destroy. . . . This is
coercion by economic pressure. The asserted power of choice is
illusory."[6] Justice Roberts then proceeded to maintain that unless checked the welfare power could be used to buy acquies-
cence to control in any aspect of economic life, to the ruination
of the American system. His opinion, in which all the justices
concurred except Brandeis, Cardozo, and Stone, boils down to
the conviction that as a protection to the American system the
principle of *laissez faire*, appended to the Constitution by the
social Darwinians, overruled the specific general welfare clause
which had been incorporated by those who wrote the Constitution.

Justice Stone in his opinion, after rejecting as both illogical
and unhistoric Roberts' contention, which amounted to the conclusion that the government could give away money but not
regulate how it should be spent, directly attacked the supposition
that the government could buy the American people into a self-
imposed slavery. He then proceeded to enunciate the principle
of judicial self-restraint in what could have been the words of
Justice Holmes himself: "Such suppositions are addressed to the
mind accustomed to believe that it is the business of courts to
sit in judgment upon the wisdom of legislative action. Courts are
not the only agencies of government that must be assumed to

have the capacity to govern. Congress and the courts both unhappily may falter or be mistaken in the performance of their constitutional duty. But interpretation of our great charter of government which proceeds on any assumption that the responsibility for the preservation of our institutions is the exclusive concern of any one of the three branches of government, or that it alone can save them from destruction, is far more likely, in the long run, 'to obliterate the constituent members' of 'an indestructible union of indestructible states,' than the frank recognition that language, even of the Constitution, may mean what it says."[7]

These were the two viewpoints that were to meet in head-on collision until one or the other was fractured. But it is vitally important to observe that the collision was not limited to the Supreme Court. Behind the viewpoint of Justice Roberts was the entire pattern of thinking which we have traced through utilitarianism, classical economics, and social Darwinism; behind it was the thinking of Herbert Spencer, William Graham Sumner and their school; behind it was the thinking of Gould and Fisk, Rockefeller and Carnegie, and all the Fittest Americans; behind it would be the "epigoni" of the 1920s, the businessmen of Middletown, the Babbitts of Sinclair Lewis' satire that is now so quaint and dated, those who happily and greedily returned to normalcy with Warren Harding, ecstatically wallowed in Coolidge prosperity and thought there would always be pie in the sky for the asking, and then heard the strange and disquieting, and then ominous and terrifying tomtoms of destiny grow louder and louder as the sad, bewildered Herbert Hoover turned for consolation, not to the Bible and not to the mountains, but to tables of statistics.

LEGAL PRAGMATISM

But it would be equally mistaken to think that behind the viewpoint of Justice Stone there was merely the abstract philosophy of a group of Cambridge academicians, a philosophy brought to Washington by Justice Holmes, the legal luminary of the galaxy. Legal pragmatism did provide a philosophy, but not so much a philosophy of the law as a philosophy for the law. The

concept that life is both being and becoming, that truth is both
derived by experience and comprised of successful experience
and hence that progress is by the inductive method, that moral
principles are also in both a state of being and becoming and
hence are determined by the inductive method and confirmed
by successful experience which in turn is the foundation for
further induction, further experience, and further progress—the
process rolls and gathers like a snowball pushed downhill, or
like the sentence that attempts to represent the process—at the
very least lent itself to the frame of mind of which judicial self-
restraint is the product. Life will change, man will learn, experience will teach, objectives will be elevated, ideals will be
purified, but only when there is freedom to act, freedom to
learn, freedom to progress. Legal pragmatism is totally incompatible with the thesis that law exists and is discovered, not
made. Legal pragmatism is difficult to reconcile with the charter
concept of the Constitution. Legal pragmatism is at the very
least inhospitable to the concept of natural law and, in any but
an esoteric sense, to the concept of a divinely created order.
Legal pragmatism, on the other hand, is perfectly compatible
with the concept that law is the creation of man and not of
God, with the concept that the Constitution is an instrument and
not a charter, with the concept of the man-made order. Legal
pragmatism is the opposite of legal social Darwinism, but this
does not mean that because social Darwinism is a materialistic
philosophy, legal pragmatism is a spiritual philosophy. Both
deny the existence of natural law in the historic meaning of the
term. Legal pragmatism simply reaffirms the right of American
society to experiment, within the framework of its Constitution
viewed as an instrument to promote the better life, with what
may produce the greatest happiness of the greatest number of
Americans. Thought, like space, can also be round. Utilitarianism is one of the prime components of philosophic pragmatism,
and the fact shows up clearly in legal pragmatism. The Supreme
Court would slowly come around to a pattern of thinking with
which Jeremy Bentham, James Mill, and John Stuart Mill would
find little to disagree.

Legal pragmatism could never have provided a philosophy for
the law if there had not been in American life in general currents

of thought consistent with it. As we have already seen, the professional economists were questioning the eternal verity of social Darwinism as early as 1885; we have already quoted the declaration of the American Economic Association that the state is "an agency whose positive assistance is one of the indispensable conditions of human progress." But the same declaration proceeds to enunciate a concept of economics both scientific and pragmatic: "We believe that political economy as a science is still in an early stage of its development. While we appreciate the work of former economists, we look not so much to speculation as to the historical and statistical study of actual conditions of economic life for the satisfactory accomplishment of that development."[8] The social Darwinism that his fellow professionals questioned in the restrained, balanced, but highly prosaic prose which is the native tongue of Carlyle's "dismal science," Thorstein Veblen questioned in sardonic, vivid, finely readable prose in *The Theory of the Leisure Class* and elsewhere. "By virtue of their hedonistic preconceptions, their habituation to the ways of a pecuniary culture, and their avowed animistic faith that nature is in the right, the classical economists knew that the consummation to which, in the nature of things, all things tend, is the frictionless and beneficent economic system. This competitive ideal, therefore, affords the normal, and conformity to its requirements affords the test of absolute economic truth."[9]

REVOLT AGAINST *LAISSEZ FAIRE*

The lucubrations of the professionals, however, were too remote from the average pattern of American thinking, not to mention the average pattern of reader interest, to be of much significance. What was really important in the first stages of the revolt against *laissez faire* and everything it implied was the thought of men like Washington Gladden, Walter Rauschenbusch, and other preachers of the social gospel, and the thought of their secular but equally pietistic counterparts, men like Henry George and Edward Bellamy.[10] They all looked to the Sermon on the Mount as a guide to life, and they found in it no confirmation of the thesis that the ultimate reward is for the hedonist, the capitalist, the economically well-situated determinist,

or anyone else who had proved himself fittest in the late nineteenth-century form of the frictionless and beneficent economic
system. But neither did they believe that the Founding Fathers
who wrote what they deemed a charter, the American Constitution, intended to create a legalistic straitjacket with metal
ribs fashioned by metaphor out of Darwin and heavy cords from
Adam Smith.

There was something to the revolt against *laissez faire* that
echoed the revolt against slavery. It was a revolt inspired by the
conviction that there is a divinely created order, that the Ten
Commandments and the Sermon on the Mount comprise its
divinely revealed charter, that the American Constitution is an
attempted human counterpart, and that *laissez faire,* substantive
due process, freedom of contract, and all the other shibboleths
of classical economics that had been embraced by the Fittest
Americans and read into the Constitution by their counterparts
upon the bench were distortions of it. The same moralistic fervor
that had inspired Protestant clergymen to denounce the evil of
slavery inspired their successors to denounce the excesses of
industrialism. Henry George evolved his single tax panacea from
a solid background of Episcopal piety, and Edward Bellamy's
Brotherhood of Humanity had its roots in Massachusetts social
concern.

Those who joined the revolt were a motley group, held apart
by their dicta and dogmas but held together by a love of their
fellow men and usually by an acceptance of traditional principles
of Christian morality. There were the Populists, farmers and
laborites of the West, and William Jennings Bryan, the intensely
religious-minded Commoner who led them in the crusade of free
silver against managed gold. There were the muckrakers and
their media, *McClure's, Collier's,* and the New York *World,* men
like Lincoln Steffens and women like Ida Tarbell who could see
the celestial crown even as they raked the muck. There were the
Progressives who rose up for Roosevelt against Taft, and saw the
panacea for man's ills in direct popular government. There were
those who proclaimed the New Freedom with Woodrow Wilson
and set the pattern for identifying political administrations with
slogans. Even as the Darwinian phrases withered into clichés
and slowly seeped down to the businessmen of Middletown, the

concept that the evolutionary process pointed to the managed society gained ground among both those who believed in natural law and those who believed in the man-made order. The believers in a managed society had their hour with Woodrow Wilson, but a war terminated it abruptly. They had their Babylonian exile under Harding, Coolidge, and Hoover, and then entered the Promised Land under Franklin D. Roosevelt. The spirit of pragmatism, in both the better and the worse meaning of the word, was at high noon in Roosevelt's first two administrations. The spirit of reform, however, and the spirit of revolt against social Darwinism had been gathering momentum for a half century, and the spirit of revolt and reform that inspired the Progressive movement was essentially a Christian spirit, based on Christian principles and proclaimed by Christian clergymen and members of the several Christian churches. Without the antecedent spirit of revolt and the spirit of reform, the spirit of pragmatism would not have had a chance.

The basic doctrine of pragmatism is that truth is successful experience as determined by experiment. Coupled with this is the doctrine that truth is not something that exists but something that develops. As applied to politics, it implies that the social order is not something organized on principles of anterior existence but something that evolves its own principles as it experiments, learns from experience, builds upon experience, and then experiments anew. Obviously such a concept is utterly incompatible with the concept that the Constitution is a charter, just as a planned society of any sort identifiable in the twentieth century is incompatible with the eighteenth-century concept of a Constitution. But the Constitution of the United States exists and is the fundamental law of the land. Hence arises the somewhat uneasy reconciliation of the Constitution with the spirit of pragmatism, whereby the Constitution is not viewed as a charter but as an instrument flexible enough to permit the maximum of experimentation within a loosely conceived framework of national life. Justices of the Supreme Court who accepted the philosophy of pragmatism and so were benevolently inclined toward social experimentation might adopt one of two attitudes, judicial self-restraint where social experimentation is concerned or active cooperation with it. The polarity has been evident in

the Supreme Court for the past generation, with justices like
Frankfurter following the Holmes example of judicial self-restraint and justices like Black the Brandeis example of cooperation.

THE NEW DEAL

In 1934 the Supreme Court was unevenly divided among those
who held the philosophy of social Darwinism, Justices Sutherland, Van Devanter, Butler, and McReynolds; those who were
benevolent toward the philosophy of pragmatism, Justices
Brandeis, Stone, and Cardozo; and those who held the balance
of power, Chief Justice Charles Evans Hughes and Justice Owen
J. Roberts. Chief Justice Hughes was one of the most distinguished Americans of his generation, a man whose judgment
was compounded of balance and independence in a fashion respected by all, and Justice Roberts had enjoyed a successful
career as a corporation attorney without impairing the respect
of the Progressives. When Hughes and Roberts joined Brandeis,
Stone, and Cardozo, the New Deal philosophy prevailed, but
both had to join. As things developed, Roberts tended to oppose
New Deal measures and Hughes frequently did.

To recapitulate the New Deal measures, successful and unsuccessful, attempted and sustained, attempted and declared unconstitutional, is as happily beyond the province of this book as
it is beyond the scope of any reasonable definition of the word
recapitulate. To recapture the spirit of one of the most exciting
periods in American history, a period the more exciting because
it followed the drabbest of all periods, is unnecessary for those
old enough to remember it since it has never fully left them, and
probably impossible for even the most imaginative of those too
young for recollection. It took a long time for America really to
believe in the Depression. Things were always about to turn the
corner, things were always about to look up, there was always
the illusion of a rift in the economic clouds, the illusion of a rift
that disappeared and was followed by another illusion. The stock
market crash had been a lightning stroke. That was what catastrophe meant, a lightning stroke. But by 1933 it had slowly be-

come clear that when the corner was turned the vista was worse than before, that things were looking up but only for help from a vacant sky, that rifts in the clouds were a mockery and the economic blackness was absolute, that catastrophe was not a lightning stroke but a settled state of affairs. Herbert Hoover had created the Reconstruction Finance Corporation to rescue business, a necessary rescue to be sure, but not one that stirred the pulses of men slowly shuffling down a bread line, and reluctantly he had conceded that the federal government would have to help finance direct relief. But the manacles of *laissez faire* were on his hands and those of his associates. Classical economics had proved that recovery would be automatic when economic stability returned, just as terrestrial stability returns once a major earthquake and its subsequent tremors have passed. Social Darwinism had proved that all works for the best when things are left alone, that the course of human progress is as inexorable as it is inspiring. Above all, the Constitution of the United States as oriented to classical economics and social Darwinism by Stephen J. Field and all his ideological fellows and successors in the woolsack was, in the mind of Herbert Hoover, the Constitution that the Founding Fathers created. As the men shuffled slowly down the bread line, he plaintively asked, "If we are to stretch the Interstate Commerce Commission to regulate all those things that pass state lines, what becomes of that fundamental freedom and independence that can rise only from local self-government?" The bread line shuffled forward a few steps, but it was longer now and reached around the corner that things were to turn.

Then came March, 1933, and a strong, confident, inspiring voice assured a frightened nation that all it had to fear was fear itself. With the voice came action: the bank holiday which stabilized the nation's tottering finances and proved that the mysterious thing called confidence which appears on no balance sheet is more potent than the most tangible of resources; there came, in quite pragmatic fashion by a rider to the Agricultural Adjustment Act, the devaluation of gold and its retirement from circulation; the Agricultural Adjustment Act itself, which aimed at elevating farm income to prewar parity; the National Industrial Recovery Act, with its codes of fair competition designed to bring health back to the body economic; the Civilian Conservation Corps Act, designed to bring hope and health to a generation ready to enter life and finding the road to it blocked by the triplex iron bars depression raised; the Tennessee Valley Authority, which was to bring the twentieth century to a region time had by-passed; and the other measures, some of which have entered the living pattern of American life, others the yellowing pages of dead history. This was pragmatism in action, and pragmatism at its finest. Truth is successful experience as determined by ex-periment. Truth is something that does not exist, but develops. To say that Roosevelt and his brain trust did not think of the Constitution, as some said from the start and more said as time passed and it became slowly clear how much experiment is un-successful, is unfair to them. The New Dealers thought of the Constitution as an instrument and not a charter, but one should not forget that those of their opponents who were social Darwin-ians thought of it in precisely the same terms. But the entire course of the New Deal was an application to American life, in the course of the worst internal crisis in all American history except the Civil War, of the philosophy of pragmatism. It was an application of pragmatism in which the overwhelming major-ity of the American people believed in the hour when it was applied, and there is no reason now to think that they were wrong. Whether one believes or disbelieves in the formal philos-ophy of pragmatism, the fundamental fact remains that the philosophy of the New Dealers at its most materialistic was no more grounded on belief in the man-made order than was the philosophy of the social Darwinians, the twilight of whose gods was now complete. Furthermore, the spirit behind the New Deal was consistent with the spirit that began to be generated in the United States in the 1880s, that was sparked by the social gospel and the tenets of the Populists, that found a focus in the Progressive movement and successive champions in Theodore Roosevelt and Woodrow Wilson, a spirit not only consistent with belief in a divinely created order but explicitly grounded upon it. All this must be said for pragmatism at its best, because before the new Deal was over it would demonstrate pragmatism at its worst.

THE TESTS

The New Deal had to pass two tests, the test of experience and the test of the Supreme Court decisions. The Supreme Court, as we have seen, was by no means solidly committed to the philosophy of social Darwinism during the New Deal period. It had four members who might be considered dedicated members of the Spencer-Sumner school of thought, but it had three members very open-minded toward social experimentation and two members uncommitted to either *laissez faire* or the pragmatic viewpoint and very much inclined to reach their conclusions on the basis of what they judged the objective intent of the Constitution. In other words, the New Deal had substantial opposition on the Supreme Court but far from united opposition.

The first two significant Court decisions favored the New Deal. In one the Court upheld the constitutionality of a Minnesota moratorium on mortgage payments.[11] In the majority opinion Chief Justice Hughes took a position that showed more than a little sympathy toward legal pragmatism. In effect he said that emergency conditions warranted action that normal conditions would not, in the thesis that emergencies evoke latent powers. He further upheld the pragmatic position that the Constitution did evolve by growth and could not be read with literal, mathematical exactness. The four social Darwinians dissented on the grounds that the statute violated the obligation of a contract. In the other the Court rejected the *laissez faire* concept of substantive due process, Justice Roberts maintaining in the majority opinion that in creating a milk control board with powers to set a range of prices, New York exercised its right to adopt toward a business "whatever economic policy may reasonably be deemed to promote public welfare."[12]

There is evidence, therefore, that the two uncommitted justices could be receptive to the pattern of argumentation advanced by the pragmatists. Neither case involved a New Deal measure in the literal sense, but both embraced what may be considered the New Deal philosophy. But then the tide of favor began to ebb, and before very long there were barren mud flats where once the sun had sparkled on the full tide of New Deal waters. But, once more, care must be exercised by those with a bias toward pragmatism in denouncing the Court for subservience to the pattern of social Darwinism, and of course vice versa. First came the "hot oil" case and the Court decision that Section 9(c) of the National Industrial Recovery Act conveyed an unconstitutional grant of quasi-legislative power to the President.[13] But eight of the nine justices concurred in this decision, and the decision was followed by three substantial New Deal victories in cases involving the right of Congress to nullify the payment in gold clause contracts. Once more the evidence is at hand that there was no implacable hostility to the New Deal in the majority of the Court, nor does the reported jeremiad of Justice McReynolds in his oral utterance—"This is Nero at his worst. The Constitution is gone!"—indicate that the most dedicated Darwinian on the bench had unshaken confidence in the devotion of his colleagues to *laissez faire*.

The tide of favor began to ebb in May, 1935. First, Justices Hughes and Roberts joined the rock-ribbed four in finding the Railroad Retirement Pension Act unconstitutional on the grounds that railroad pensions are unrelated to railroad safety and hence not subject to the power of the federal government to regulate commerce.[14] This was a modest curtain raiser. On May 27, the Court held the National Recovery Act unconstitutional. To those emotionally committed to the New Deal and innocently unaware of what really was going on in American business, this was the day after Armageddon and the first day of oblivion. Those with lower emotional boiling points as well as all those with an inkling into what was going on in American business were not so sure that the decision had not been a well-disguised blessing for the New Deal, lifting it, with near miraculous ease, from the bottomless quagmire of regulations, rulings, and codes that had been made, remade, phrased and rephrased, and always cheerfully flouted. The whole NRA was a sick chicken when the "sick chicken" case[15] was decided, and America knew it, if it came as a body blow to those who made, remade, phrased and rephrased the codes. The Court was unanimous in its decision, Justices Brandeis, Cardozo, and Stone of the pragmatic wing joining with the centrist Justices Hughes and Roberts in a happy if by now infrequent reunion with the rock-ribbed four. The

NRA had failed the constitutional test in the opinion of all nine justices, but it had already failed the pragmatic test in the opinion of all but the purblind.

The rest is a melancholy recital that can be curtailed. As the months followed, the New Deal casualty list steadily mounted: the Farm Mortgage Law, the Agricultural Adjustment Act, the Bituminous Coal Act, and the Municipal Bankruptcy Act followed the NRA into oblivion. The view taken of the Supreme Court record in these cases habitually reflects the philosophy of the person expressing the view, and that statement holds nearly as well today as it did a generation ago. Those who remember the New Deal with nostalgic kindness, or look back to it in history as an age of suddenly opening vistas, tend to regard the Supreme Court majority during those months as waging "what is surely the most ambitious dragon-fight in its long and checkered history. The tension between modesty and temerity was temporarily resolved; the autocratic instinct was triumphant," in McCloskey's phrasing.[16] Accepting the hypothesis that the New Deal acts either were dragons or were taken for dragons suggests that something might be said for determining the identity of the dragon hunters. Four can be identified at once: Justices Butler, McReynolds, Sutherland, and Van Devanter. Presumably three are entirely innocent of the charge of dragon-hunting: Justices Brandeis, Cardozo, and Stone. Presumably two intermittently joined the hunt: Justices Hughes and Roberts.

A look at the record is revealing. During the sixteen months that started in January, 1935, the Court found for the New Deal twice and against it seven times. In the "hot oil" case eight of the nine justices found the pertinent provision of the National Industrial Recovery Act unconstitutional. There was close to unanimity in that bit of dragon-hunting. In the "sick chicken" case the nine justices hunted dragons. The Agricultural Adjustment Act was shot down by six of the nine justices, the Bituminous Coal Act by five. In each case Justice Roberts shot with the conservatives. Chief Justice Hughes did so in the first, but divided his judgment, as already indicated, in the second. The government won two of the three gold cases and suffered at the worst a nominal defeat in the third. The decision against the

New Deal which found the Frazier-Lemke Act void was unanimous.[17] The Railroad Retirement Pension Act and the Municipal Bankruptcy Act were both found unconstitutional in 5 to 4 decisions, Justice Roberts in each case voting with the conservative stalwarts.[18] These were the cases decided against the New Deal in the months before the Court-packing was proposed. In three of the seven the finding was unanimous or next to unanimous; in the other four Justice Roberts joined the conservative opinion in its entirety; Chief Justice Hughes voted with the liberals twice, with the conservatives once, and divided his opinion between the two in the fourth case. In the two New Deal victories Justices Hughes and Roberts voted with the liberals. During the period when the cloud of the Court-packing plan darkened Supreme Court skies and, to those cynical enough to distrust the integrity of Charles Evans Hughes and Owen J. Roberts, might be thought to influence their viewpoint, two fundamental measures not of recovery but of permanent reform were sustained by the Court with Justices Hughes and Roberts joining the liberals: the National Labor Relations Act and the Social Security Act. Those who view the careers of these two distinguished Americans with dispassionate eyes and the objectivity given by the passage of time and the working out of events are far from convinced that the voting record of Justices Hughes and Roberts shows any visible trend other than the dispassionate objectivity of judgment which was the dominant trend in the judicial life of both.

All this does not gainsay two facts: the Supreme Court had ruled unconstitutional a number of key recovery measures in which the New Dealers had placed an almost mystic confidence; and the American people, in November, 1936, had given the New Deal the most impressive endorsement received by any party and its program in the entire history of American politics. It was certainly not surprising that New Dealers saw the action of the Supreme Court as strong-willed obstructionism inspired by an outmoded philosophy and dedicated to the thwarting of the will of the majority to achieve what it believed could be worked out experimentally to produce the greatest happiness of the greatest number. As for the Republicans, if anything their attitude in the 1936 campaign merely lent comfort to the New

Deal viewpoint. *Laissez faire* had failed, and the notes of social Darwinism, once so strong and confident, had been reduced to sounding brass and tinkling cymbals. Alfred M. Landon's platform reduced itself to the assertion that the New Deal measures were unconstitutional and that the Republicans, with many a reservation and modification, favored them. This nascent metooism attracted Maine and Vermont, but not the other forty-six states. Not merely the result of the election but the attitude of the Republican Party during the campaign confirmed the fact that pragmatism had won the fight with social Darwinism, that the planned order had won over the automatic one. The political history of the generation that followed has done little more than confirm the decision of 1936.

The maturely ripened wisdom of Mr. Dooley, who knew that the Supreme Court follows the election returns, hardly appealed to New Dealers who were both exhilarated by the most colossal victory in the history of American politics and outraged by the most consistent and extended series of judicial defeats. In the winter of 1937 political pragmatism faced that most searching and austere of tests, the test of success. It was the expressed will of the American people that the pragmatic approach of the New Deal be the American philosophy of government. But the Supreme Court stood blocking that will, as it seemed to the New Dealers. It may seem today, as it does to many but not all who remember 1937, that the Court stood like Gibraltar, marking but not blocking the narrow strait that led from the Mediterranean of the past to the unbounded ocean of the future. To the New Dealers it was as if Gibraltar had suddenly swung into the middle of the strait, making the Mediterranean of the past an inland sea with no outlet to the shining ocean. There had to be an outlet.

There were various proposals made. One was that the vote of six judges be required to make an act of Congress unconstitutional. A second was to permit Congress to pass a measure by a two-thirds vote over a Supreme Court finding of unconstitutionality. A third and the most extreme was to take away from the Court the right to declare an act of Congress unconstitutional. But President Roosevelt chose a different device. Charging that the Court was handicapped by superannuation in its members,

Roosevelt proposed that for each Supreme Court Justice on the bench ten years, and six months past his seventieth birthday, another Justice be appointed. The Court could be expanded to a total of fifteen Justices. Since Congress has the explicit power to set the number of Supreme Court Justices and has altered the number on six occasions, the plan had both the Constitution and precedent on its side. Yet the Senate Judiciary Committee reported unfavorably on the bill and the strongly Democratic Senate rejected it by a vote of seventy to twenty. Why did the American people and its Congress overwhelmingly reject the plan?

The person who tries to explain this episode in American history in terms of tangible facts inevitably flounders in an ideological morass. A few months after the re-election of a President in whom millions of Americans had a faith nearly religious in intensity, in an election which ratified a political program by the greatest margin in American history, the American people and its Congress rejected the measure that the President advocated to bring into being the program the people had ratified. Explanations have been offered: the fact that liberal Justice Brandeis was over seventy and reactionary Justice Butler under seventy, that the Supreme Court docket was by no means crowded, that the Court did find constitutional a number of New Deal measures while under the cloud of the Court-packing plan, the fact that Justice Van Devanter resigned in May and Roosevelt could replace one of the rock-ribbed four, the fact that Roosevelt's floor manager Senator Robinson of Arkansas died a few days after Van Devanter resigned and his death weakened a far from united Democratic majority. All these facts had their significance, as they have their appeal to those who like their facts tangible, but they were not fundamental. The only true explanation is that the American people and their senators rejected a specific application of pragmatism.

The philosopher who does not accept pragmatism and the man in the street who rejects it would unite in their view of what is unsound in pragmatism, if their terminology would vary. In the ideal state the end justifies the means because there are only ideal ends and ideal means; propositions work both ways when their subjects and predicates are identical. In the ideal state, pragmatism is the obvious philosophy, since one would need merely to experiment among the available means, all of them ideal, to determine which would achieve the specific ideal end desired. In this sense most human acts are ideal. All screwdrivers are ideal means for driving screws, but screwdrivers have heads of varying widths. Therefore one experiments to find the screwdriver which is the ideal means of driving in the specific screw. But not even the America of New Deal aspirations was the ideal state, and not all political screwdrivers are ideal. The principle that the end justifies the means works splendidly where screwdrivers and screws are concerned, but not in politics and the national life.

This in turn brings up once more the fallacy that underlies pragmatism, in the view of one who rejects the philosophy. If pragmatism works in the ideal state but can fail to work in the nonideal state, there must be something antecedent to the test of pragmatism. What is antecedent can only be what is true, and hence truth is not determined by experiment but is antecedent to it. A thing is not right if it works; a thing works if it is right.

This is the sort of thinking that led the American people to reject the Roosevelt Court-packing plan. If Roosevelt had succeeded in packing the Court, perhaps certain of his recovery measures might have been re-examined and found constitutional. In the process, however, something vital in the American pattern of society would have been destroyed, the belief that constitutionality has an objective reality and that American life is conducted within the framework of its principles. The packed Court might declare an act constitutional, but the American people would not believe what a packed Court said. The philosopher who rejects pragmatism neither rejects the experimental method of discovering truth nor rejects the concept that in the great majority of human activities means and ends are both ideal and hence the pragmatic concept applies. Most of our acts do not have what is known traditionally as moral significance; most of the time we are fitting screwdrivers to screws, a process in which the saint can be a pragmatist. The same can be said, although some caution in the saying is advisable, about our corporate acts. Many acts of legislative bodies concern matters devoid of what tradition at least deems moral significance, and so can be settled on the pragmatic basis. In similar fashion, since the great majority of our daily acts are without moral values good or bad, the utilitarian principle is entirely valid for them, and the same can be said for many acts of legislative bodies. The question is, Where does one draw the line?

The scientist does not experiment purely for the sake of experimentation, but rather to confirm or reject a hypothesis. Before the experiment is the hypothesis. But the hypothesis, in turn, concerns a truth which is antecedent to the hypothesis. The scientific method is pragmatic, but it is not pragmatism. Science would be impossible without the fundamental hypothesis upon which all science rests, that the natural order is fixed and reliable. Similarly science is cumulative, basing today's experimentation upon yesterday's ascertained truth. Pragmatism is not cumulative in most who have maintained the philosophy, although an honorable exception must be made for the qualitative principle present in John Dewey's instrumentalism as it is in John Stuart Mill's utilitarianism. One may, then, be a scientist and believe in the inductive method of extending knowledge without being a pragmatist.

If this is true in the fields of natural science, it is true as well in those vaguer fields with more elusive boundaries which make up what may, with greater or lesser justification, be called the sciences of society. There has to be something constant in the social order on which to ground the hypothesis which in turn is the basis for the social experiment. In the course of history that something constant in the social order has been belief in natural law. Belief in natural law has been to the experimenter in the social sciences what belief in the reliable fixity of the natural order has been to the experimenter in the natural sciences. The most radical experimenters in the social order in American history were the Founding Fathers, and the person who argues that they were the most radical social experimenters in human history since the twelve apostles has a case. They believed, however, in natural law and all that it connoted. As a consequence they believed it possible to construct a charter of society, and they did so in the Constitution of the United States. Time has revealed that the greatest constitutional problem of all is the interpretation of the Constitution, and this has preoccupied a Court that has become and has been accepted as an equal third party in the political trinity of American life.

The Roosevelt Court-packing plan failed, and with it pragmatism passed its high noon as a philosophy of statesmanship in America. Pragmatism had lost its battle with the American Constitution. When the Senate overwhelmingly rejected the Court-packing plan, in response to the will of the people, it reaffirmed the American faith in the contract concept of a constitution as taught in the school of Montesquieu and rejected the instrumental concept as taught in the school of Rousseau. One hesitates to call it the last battle between the rival schools that dominated eighteenth-century political thought in the West, but it is the most recent and to this century of Americans the most vital. Once more, as so often in the history of the English-speaking world, the man-made order had failed a crucial test.

The time was not at hand leisurely to probe the philosophy that led to failure. Ahead were towering threats from man-made orders of a different sort, orders that originated outside the English-speaking world but inside the pride of man. There was the threat of fascism, which replaced the stability of natural law with the illusory stability of the dictator. There was the threat of Nazism, which linked with the illusory stability of the dictator a bloody mythology of racial superiority brewed out of social Darwinism and the survival of the madly fittest until the amoral superman of Nietzsche was reached, whose name was Hitler. There was the threat of Communism, far more subtle, far more pervasive; in every sense except the limited military sense and not necessarily excluding that, a threat far more dangerous. Marx also had studied at the school of Rousseau, learned some of the lessons of utilitarianism, conceived of the planned society which is the antithesis of the contractual society, and from his writings and their own plans and experiments his followers reached, in a way quite consistent with pragmatism, their shifting concepts of the social order. Ahead was a thirty years' war, and how much longer no man knows, with these deadly hostile patterns of the man-made order.

XVII
THE GOSPEL OF PROGRESS

THE CONTEMPORARY PERIOD started around 1937. Periods in history are not measured in terms of years nor is there any regularity to their pattern. They exist because there is within them a dominant spirit, the reflection, to be sure, of external situations and events, which distinguish them from what passed before and what comes after. In this sense 1937 is contemporary with 1966, but 1933 was not contemporary with 1929 nor was it contemporary with 1937. A period ended between 1929 and 1933, and a period ended around 1937. By 1937 it was evident to all who did not let their wishes guide their thoughts that the force of aggressive expansion in the totalitarian states would have to be met by the force of resolute containment in the democratic states. It was still possible to hope that this containment might be relatively free from bloodshed, although this possibility sadly thinned and disappeared. From 1937 until the hour of this writing the central fact in world affairs has been this conflict of wills and forces between the aggressive expansionism of the totalitarian states and the resolute containment of the democratic states. It has been successively the expansionism of Japan in Asia, Italy in Africa, Germany in Europe, Russia in Europe, and China in Asia. In three of the five encounters the forces of resolute containment have been successful, and yesterday's totalitarian aggressors have now changed sides and are aligned with the forces of containment. In the other two, the issue is still suspended. Thus 1937 to the present day is a period of history, and the period continues.

It is likely that pragmatism is the one possible philosophy in such a period, a period in which the only international law is that of force. If so, the greatest triumph of pragmatism in American history is the Marshall Plan, an experiment in the containment of aggression that won a victory far greater than any military victory can be, the victory that is won without a war. If this suggests that the most promising pattern of pragmatic experimentation in international relations may be the benevolent, the charitable, and the cooperative, the inference must stand. If it also suggests that the foundations of successful experimentation in living, be it international, national, or personal, are pre-existent to experimentation as the believers in the moral law maintain, this inference must also stand. Neither President Truman nor General Marshall ever had it in him to maintain that benevolence, charity, and cooperation were induced by contemporary experimentation, even as foundations for international life. A period of international tension, in any case, is inevitably a period of pragmatism in international affairs. Many things are tried, some succeed, a few lessons are learned.

On the other hand the high noon of national pragmatism passed in 1937, and it is now well into the afternoon and conceivably into the twilight. There are various reasons for this, mainly nonphilosophic reasons. For one thing, it is hardly good government to rock the national boat while one tries to stabilize the international ship of state. The nation is hardly in the mood for social and economic experimentation in a period in which national survival in a lawless world is the prime imperative. Our four cold war Presidents have been at punctilious pains to start no domestic hot wars on social and economic issues, and to put the peace of harmony before the sword of righteousness where such feuds still simmer. On the whole they have been successful.

For another thing, the change of periods that took place around 1937 was more than a change from an age in which problems were primarily domestic to an age in which foreign perils darkened the national skies. It was a change from an age of depression to an age of economic prosperity. The economists, especially those with a dash of partisanship in their veins to liven their disquisitions in the dismal science, can debate whether or not much more came from the economic pump than the New Deal pump primers poured in. Let it suffice for our purpose to say that when the period changed around 1937, the help wanted ads began to reappear after their eight-year lull. They became more numerous and took on something of a lyric quality by 1939, and from that day to this they have never ceased to be a significant factor on the balance sheets of the nation's newspapers. Whatever else it has meant, the period of international tension has been an age of high employment, punctuated only by minor and short recessions and not too gravely injured to date by the ice sheet of automation that is crawling down the economic land. An age of prosperity, whatever may have caused the prosperity, however tragic may be the causes underlying the prosperity, and however ominous the lurking threats in that prosperity, is not an age of economic experimentation. Pragmatism does better in depressions.

Then in the President of the United States there is the personal factor so difficult to gauge and so perilous to overlook. The President is a figure, not a figurehead. He is a personality, having today the gravest personal responsibility of any statesman on earth. He lives in awful isolation, surrounded by advisers, banked by telephones, engulfed in documents. It is his administration, his to make or mar, his to bear the stamp of his personality, the sign of his convictions, the signature of his belief, his will, and his way. Inevitably those whom he most trusts accept as valid his fundamental philosophy, however much they may disagree with him and with the others who advise him about its implementation in details.

THE PHILOSOPHY OF PRESIDENTS

Presidents Truman, Eisenhower, and Johnson have differed markedly in all the externals that make men different, and some of the internals as well, but each in his own way and each in terms of his personal religious tradition has attested his belief in a permanent moral order of divine origin. President Kennedy differed from them, not in this of course, but in the fact that he alone among the postwar Presidents had an instinctively philosophic cast of mind. It is not unfair to the others to say that he was more at home with ideas than they, that he had been exposed to intellectual currents the force of which they had never felt. But precisely because Kennedy's instinct was philosophic, it was not pragmatic. He did search for principles, but there is no evidence that he thought of principles as products of experimentation. It is neither easy nor safe to talk of the philosophic convictions of one's contemporaries, especially when they are only inferentially part of their public record, but the record of the postwar Presidents contains not a single act that has been considered pragmatic in the philosophic sense of the word and, politics being what it is, relatively few that have been branded pragmatic in the cynical sense even by political partisans. One might add that all four have lived in peace with the Supreme Court.

The result of all this is what could be predicted. Pragmatism won the war with social Darwinism, the war of 1933–1937. Its victory was heralded in the election of 1932 and ratified in the election of 1936. The Democratic party, as the party of pragmatism, became the majority party; and the once dominant party of social Darwinism, the Republican, became the loyal opposition. Since 1936, some Republicans, either through conviction or through a capacity to watch straws thrown into the wind, have shown a visible tendency to get on the other band wagon. It is regrettable that most political terms are pejorative—one recalls that the Tories are robbers and Whigs are derisively peddlers—but one must use the terms available and hope the pejorative element will be overlooked. The predictable result has followed, the welfare state. But the welfare state that has followed would not be considered such by anyone who really believed in the welfare state. What really has remained of the spirit of pragmatism that gave us the New Deal measures has been the process of consolidation among those which have stood the twin tests of time and the Supreme Court. On the whole, the New Frontier of Kennedy, which of course was never opened, and the Great Society of Johnson, which is still a vision, have concentrated on what might be termed the insurance aspects of their New Deal heritage. The Social Security system, for example, has been strengthened and the principle implicit in it extended in the form of Medicare. Such are the characteristic achievements of the epigoni of the New Deal, and never have they been vulnerable in the way that the Court-packing plan was vulnerable.

What can be observed, however, is the phenomenon already observed in earlier concepts of the man-made order. The deism of the Cambridge Platonists became diffused, attenuated, transformed into a spirit first of indifference and then of opportunism, and what started as a new atmosphere of tolerance which would allow England to resume its national life after the horror of civil war, ended as a cynical and worldly indifference to the spiritual values which were still perfunctorily mouthed. The utilitarianism of Bentham and Mill, which started with an enthusiasm for reform and a determination to achieve a finer life in a better England, became fused with classical economics, and what started as a movement of reform ended as a dogged defense of the *status quo*. This happened, one imagines, because the reform spirit also is subject to a tendency as in Gresham's law—the lower motivation drives out the higher. The history of the administration of such New Deal measures as the National Recovery Act shows how quickly experiments launched in the best spirit of the pragmatic philosophy can be diverted into opportunities for self-aggrandizement by those to whom every experiment is an experiment in self-advancement.

IS A NEW, CYNICAL PRAGMATISM IN THE MAKING?

There is a question which might be addressed to those commentators on the passing scene who interpret it confidently and daily through the communications media with that spontaneous infallibility characteristic of the editorial mind (the writer once had the gift, but lost it years ago). As the spirit of pragmatism has become muted and restrained on the national scene, has it not lingered and become stronger on the myriad of local scenes? One has in mind such matters as urban renewal, but proffers urban renewal merely as an example. That cities grow old and need to be renewed is hardly debatable, although European example makes one wonder if they need grow old so quickly and need renewing as soon as they do in this country. Funds are now available for urban renewal, and the country has an enormous construction industry ready and eager to remove the old and build the new. Boards appointed for the purpose have the power and the funds to depopulate entire sections of cities, level them to the ground, and replace them with structures certainly of a different type and quite possibly designed to serve a different purpose than the structures they replaced. But this can also mean that such sections will be populated by entirely different people once the process is completed. For one example, there is the West End of Boston. No Bostonian will deny that the West End was old and much of it outworn. Neither will anyone with a sense of Boston sentiment deny that a sentimental aura somehow clung around the old West End. It was one of the places in which new Americans got their start, Irish immigrants first, then Jewish, and others. It was leveled until not a stone rested on a stone, and then rebuilt with attractive, modern, high-rise apartment houses. The new West End is vastly more attractive than the old West End, especially to those who love new chrome more than old brick, but the rents are proportionate. In other words, there has been made accessible to the rich a geographically desirable part of the city along the Charles River which previously had been accessible only to the poor. The West End has been renewed, but not restored. All the old West Enders are gone.

There is the matter also of highways. It is a perversity of the American commuter that he will endure any horror that rush-hour traffic can conjure up provided he may do it alone in his car. We multiply traffic lane upon traffic lane and build cloverleaves of a complexity that has passed the baroque and threatens to outdo the rococo, and still the traffic jams pile up. In the process land takings wax and multiply until in some areas the power of eminent domain resembles more the autocracy of an Oriental monarch than the self-governing process of a democratic people. Every now and then some lone defender of Thermopylae holds out until the juggernaut of Progress levels him, like the Vermonter who defended against the new highway the house that had been in his family for generations and as the juggernaut crashed toward its approaches, set fire to the house and took his own life. How tragic, one murmurs, how futile to think that one can block the inexorable march of Progress. One trusts that if the person who so murmurs considers himself a liberal, he recognizes that he is murmuring like a social Darwinian.

Our point is simply this. The delegation of authority run riot which Justice Cardozo and his eight associates saw present in the National Recovery Act a generation ago and which made them unanimously declare the Act unconstitutional has shown an alarming tendency to reappear upon the local scene in this generation. Just as deism once filtered down, and then social Darwinism, so pragmatism shows signs of filtering down. Truth, says the pragmatist, is successful experiment. The experiment in the West End of Boston was unquestionably successful: poorer houses were replaced by better houses, outmoded apartments by sparkling new ones, crowded streets by open vistas, yesterday by today. And people were replaced by different people. No doubt the new stretch of highway in Vermont is a success, with the old, narrow, winding road replaced by a fine, broad, straight one that makes at least one strip of Vermont look like Illinois. Nothing was lost in the process but a home, a garner of memories, and a life. The test of pragmatism was triumphantly passed.

It seems to the writer that a generation ago pragmatism posed a very real threat to the American pattern of life, and the Guadalcanal that turned the tide of war against it was fought over the Court-packing plan. One trusts that the fear is groundless, but there seems to be some danger that a new, debased, and very cynical pragmatism is in the making on the local and state level. The threatened loss of federal funds as an alternative is now habitually used as an argument for projects most of which involve the use of eminent domain. One would like to think that there may still be found in America those who believe that projects are sound or unsound, right or wrong, in themselves and not in terms of the identity of the payer of the bills, but somehow such idealists do not seem to be elected to public office. One would like to believe that the American people cannot be bought, but the evidence is not yet conclusive. The diehards of a generation ago who maintained that no one shoots Santa Claus have not yet been proved wrong. In the last and bitter analysis it is not a philosophy that is involved but something very ancient that antedates all philosophies, the spirit of human greed. There are no visible shrines to the goddess Success, because they are built in the human heart. The ever present danger is that pragmatism the philosophy may foster pragmatism the cynical spirit. In the face of this real danger, however, there is the undoubted presence of idealism and belief in values not of man's making evidenced in the civil rights movement.

THE OLDEST ARGUMENT

The civil rights movement got its charter, so to speak, from the Supreme Court in a series of decisions that was based, ironically, upon an earlier series made by the Court at the height of its social Darwinian period. It got its life, however, from something very different and far more ancient, something that was before pragmatism, social Darwinism, utilitarianism, or deism came into being. No one argues for the civil rights of Negroes on the grounds of pragmatism, that the nation might experiment with the gradual extension to them of the normal rights of other Americans and thus by the experimental method reach the truth about their civil rights. No one who believes in the civil rights of Negroes argues for them on the grounds of social Darwinism, that the inexorable progress of evolution will gradually bring them into being and the process neither should be hurried nor can it be. No one argues for them on the grounds of utilitarianism, that the greatest happiness of the greatest number of Americans will be served by extending full civil rights to Negroes, although there is a lot to be said for the argument. The argument for the civil rights of Negroes rests simply and austerely upon the principle that human rights are inalienable because they are ordained by the law of nature, and that their expression in statute law as provided by the liberation amendments to the Constitution of the United States is a ratification of that aspect of the natural law.

Natural law, which was not part of the curriculum of the school of Rousseau; which was denied in any sense but the physical by the most philosophical of the utilitarians, John Stuart Mill; which was fused with the physical by the best mind among the social Darwinians, Thomas Henry Huxley; which was denied by the very axioms of their philosophy by such pragmatists as Oliver Wendell Holmes and his ideological sons and heirs in the Supreme Court, is back with us again. When everything else is said and done, the fundamental argument behind the civil rights movement is the argument based on natural law. Man has his duties to God and to his fellow man; society exists to provide the protective and fostering framework within which he may perform these duties; a duty cannot be performed without its corresponding right and without the requisite freedom to perform it. Hence the rights of free men in a free society are antecedent to the ordainments of that society, and the ordainments of the society are the codification of the rights. All men are created free and equal, not necessarily in the distorted vision of man but in the crystal vision of God. Therefore they must be free and equal in society.

The argument is as old as Cicero and older, but it is as new as Martin Luther King. This is not to say that one cannot be a pragmatist—or, for that matter, a social Darwinian, a utilitarian, or a deist—and also believe in the civil rights of Negroes. It is to say that the arguments actually used by the leaders in the civil rights movement have been consistently arguments based upon the concept of natural law. Nor is it without significance that the front fighters in the civil rights movement, Negro and white alike, have been in the main members of the various churches, and one might even run the risk of rhetoric and say that the blood of martyrs has been shed in the cause by the clergymen of the churches. The Church is the natural, as it is the historic, repository of the natural law, the law of God revealed to the heart of man.

The time may well be at hand when those who believe in natural law—and whether they are conscious of it or not the number of believers in natural law has been substantially increased by soul-searching on the civil rights issue—can challenge the confident statement of their philosophic adversaries that natural law philosophy belongs to the ancient history of human thought. Like every intellectual challenge there must be in it an element of refutation and an element of confirmation. The first may be considered first. All aspects of the man-made order have been initially formulated in the sacred name of Progress.

Deism at the outset represented progress out of the bloody quagmire of a civil war that could end only in the reign of reason or the fact of annihilation. It was the happy contribution of deism that it furnished a foundation for the reign of Reason, and England did pull itself out of the blood and mire. Decades passed, and the reign of Reason became the Enlightenment, the age of rationalism that succeeded the age of faith. England and France are different countries, and they do not always order things better in France. In England the spirit of rationalism and the slogan that became its anodyne, "Whatever is, is right," changed the spirit of Progress to the spirit of reaction, as a worldly indifference reigned in the Church and a cynical worldliness in the State. In the name of Progress, progress halted. There was a subsequent revival of the spirit of England, but it was the work of men who found their inspiration in the past and its heritage of natural law, like Newman and Pusey, or in the present and its evidence of natural law, like Thomas Arnold and Dean Stanley. In France things took a bloody course. Society never exists in a vacuum, and when the authority of God is removed the authority of man takes its place. When the "Thou shalt" of divine ordinance is silenced, the "I will" of the dictator is heard. Lessons of violence and bloodshed were not taught in the school of Rousseau, but the inevitable conclusion of its lessons were the Reign of Terror and the appearance of Napoleon.

Utilitarianism at the outset represented progress out of the wearied and sophisticated indifference of the cushioned sons and daughters of the Enlightenment into a calculated program of progress, into a better society. One neither understands Jeremy Bentham nor is just to him unless one starts with the understanding that he was essentially a reformer, not a philosopher.

Utilitarianism often worked better in practice than it promised to in theory. The slogan of utilitarianism, "the greatest happiness of the greatest number," is no contemptible one, and within certain philosophic limitations it is consistent with the objective of democracy. Utilitarianism, however, represented a concept of the man-made order, and it found its methodology implicit in the classical economics of Smith, Malthus, and Ricardo. Consequently there were always manacles of the spirit about utilitarianism, a doctrinaire approach to reform dictated by the economists, a sense that Progress was possible only upon a single set of tracks upon the roadbed laid down by Smith, Malthus, and Ricardo.

The result was the strangely varied pattern that utilitarian Progress took; for example, the pattern that led to progress in the finest sense of the word where education was concerned and to the black reaction of the workhouse where poor relief was concerned. The "cautious, statistical Christ" who never got beyond Eboli presided over its benefactions, and the charity that surpasseth all things was not in its heart. Dickens, a nonphilosopher of a very different school, caught the fallacy well in *Hard Times*, with its contrast between the patterned utilitarianism of Gradgrind, the calculated opportunism of Bounderby, and the happy, carefree, disorganized wisdom based on charity of the circus troupe. Utilitarianism designed the greatest happiness of the greatest number, but the greatest number of Englishmen were poor and classical economics ordained that they be more so. Hence the spirit of Progress led utilitarianism to the workhouse; progress out of it depended upon Dickens and his kind.

Social Darwinism at the outset not merely represented Progress but was an explanation of all life from the atom to the man in terms of Progress. Progress is inevitable, inexorable, slow but certain with the certainty of the planets in their orbits and their seasons in their course. Spring is not to be hurried nor Mars speeded in its cycle, and the Progress found in Darwin as a biological principle and extended by metaphor to the social and economic realms can neither be hurried nor delayed. Progress to the social Darwinians was a sort of disembodied and impersonal Hound of Heaven that pursued an entirely visible and material universe down the labyrinthine ways by which species appear, develop, and diffuse. The fittest survive and flourish, as the Fates have decreed, and one learns in the pages of Smith, Malthus, and Ricardo how and why they survive and flourish. Standard Oil and Bethlehem Steel were ordained before time was, and therefore Rockefeller and Carnegie; and the primal seed from which they ultimately grew was in the metaphoric womb of the Fates Inevitable. Down the centuries floated the faint echo: "Whatever is, is right." Standard Oil and Bethlehem Steel were, and therefore they were right. No philosophy but *laissez faire* could conceivably fit the pattern of social Darwinism, and, paradoxically perhaps, this fact saved social Darwinism from the determinism which was its logical conclusion. Social Darwinism, precisely because of this limitation of its logic, did conceive of the moral order as man-made, but its thinking was every bit as doctrinaire as that of the utilitarianism which in part it succeeded and in part supplanted. *Laissez faire* was at its core, and therefore in the name of inescapable Progress reaction became thoroughly entrenched in American economic, political, social, and judicial life until the stock market crash of 1929.

Pragmatism at the outset so envisaged Progress as the essential principle of life that it was a method rather than a philosophy. The great glory of pragmatism has been that it provided an alternative to the nascent determinism present, if submerged, in social Darwinism, an alternative not merely consistent with a scientific age but based on the inductive principle of science. We do learn new truths by experimentation, but put that way the weakness at the heart of pragmatism is revealed. It is not the truths that are new, but our knowledge of them. The pride of thought, however, that deems the truth itself to be new and hence the product of man's making is characteristic of the epigoni who fall heir to a school of philosophy, not to the original thinkers who bring it into being.

Peirce and Wright were methodologists, and they did provide a method for the development of thought on scientific principles that effectively parallels the method of the laboratory. William James was essentially a religious man, one who searched for intellectually satisfactory grounds for faith, and found in pragmatism a philosophy that reconciled faith with the scientific method. Furthermore, James led pragmatism into one of its most fruitful areas of development by his indication of the way in which belief in an event may bring it to pass, the way in which confidence may beget results.

Two millennia ago that confirmed believer in natural law, Virgil, found the epigram that expressed the pragmatism that is eternally true and right: *Possunt quia posse videntur* ("They can because they think they can"). But beyond James were the pragmatists whose faith was either humanistic or nonexistent, Dewey and Holmes. Both were men of the highest principles and ideals, and Holmes in his reserved, sardonic, and highly skeptical fashion was really as devoted to his fellow man as the forthright, energetic, dedicated Dewey. With them, however, pragmatism took its definite turn and became a philosophy of the man-made order. The hour that happened, the danger was born, the danger that pragmatism the philosophy would degenerate into pragmatism the cynical and unprincipled way of life. It is too early yet in the history of pragmatism to level at it the charge that it has so degenerated, but those who fear the danger find evidence that it exists. Even those who do not fear the danger are now aware that pragmatism is simply too shallow a philosophy to give answers to the deep concerns of mankind. All one needs to do is to suggest that instead of natural law principles as the foundation for the civil rights movement the methodology of pragmatism be used to determine the position of the Negro in American society, that cool, dispassionate, objective method of the laboratory whereby we "discover new truths," as the modest among us put it, and create them as the pragmatist maintains.

IN THE NAME OF PROGRESS

As we have already said, at the outset all patterns of the man-made order originate in the name of Progress. Of the patterns we have considered, deism and the Enlightenment originated in the thesis that priestcraft and the battle of the sects had brought England to the brink of disaster, as indeed they had, and that a new order of man's making alone could spell Progress. For a time it did, but Progress ground to a dead halt as skepticism, opportunism, and Erastianism became the prevailing spirits of the age. There was progress once more when men like Newman, Pusey, Arnold, and Stanley brought back the breath of spiritual life and the breadth of spiritual vision through their "priestcraft." Utilitarianism originated in the thesis that Progress was possible only by working toward a predetermined formula of Progress on the principles of classical economics. For a time progress did result but it again ground to a dead halt as *laissez faire* economics and its political implementation became the law of the land. There was progress once more when instinctive moralists like Dickens and moralists trained in the "priestcraft" of the Church of England united in effective protest against the excesses of the factory system and the degradation of the helpless victims of *laissez faire*. Social Darwinism held forth the promise of automatic Progress, but its alliance with classical economics and its metaphoric espousal of misapplied aphorisms from *The Origin of Species* soon ground its progress in America to a dead halt. There was progress once more when the preachers of the social gospel aroused the conscience of the country, and the Progressive movement, with religious enthusiasm as a major component, started that sequence of internal developments that climaxed in the New Deal. It is too early yet to complete the series and proclaim the end of pragmatism, but the series is already sufficiently extended to arouse a healthy skepticism about Progress as something within man's unguided capacity to conceive and achieve. The record of the man-made order simply does not demand of the nonbeliever a reverential bowing of the head in the name of Progress, nor is it requisite on the basis of the record of those other patterns of the man-made order which are outside the framework of this book but very much within the framework of modern life—fascism, Nazism, and Communism.

THE "LIBERALS" AND THE "CONSERVATIVES"

If the word "Progress" need not demand unquestioning reverence, the time is also at hand to re-examine the credentials of the word "liberal." In a sense the two words have tended to be synonyms, until the band of synonymity has been stretched to the breaking point, at which the word "liberal" changes to the word "conservative." Thus Lord Macaulay was a liberal, since he believed in *laissez faire* economics, the wage-fund theory of Ricardo, the food-population ratio of Malthus, the formula of utilitarianism, and the gospel of Progress. These were the planks, or, if one prefers, the shibboleths, of the Liberal party. Imported to the United States and blended with social Darwinism, they became the dogmas of conservatism. Thus a mid-nineteenth-century liberal and an early twentieth-century conservative were ideologically identical. In Lord Macaulay's time it was liberal to believe in the man-made order, but in Calvin Coolidge's time it was conservative. Before Calvin Coolidge's time, however, say in Theodore Roosevelt's time, it had become liberal to believe in the social gospel and the program of the Progressive party, and in the religious enthusiasm which was so basic to it. Now the liberal believed in the divinely created order. But the religious motivation faded out as the century progressed and the philosophy of pragmatism took its place, and the characteristic New Deal liberal, as a pragmatist, was once more a believer in the man-made order. He has continued to be such until recently, but with his new-found enthusiasm for the civil rights movement he once more proclaims his allegiance to the divinely created order.

The truth of the matter, of course, is that the liberal has continued to do what Matthew Arnold parodies so mischievously in the last chapter of *Culture and Anarchy:* he has continued to pursue whatever may be the current officially sanctioned good cause, striving always to be in the van with a frantic awareness that the devil conservatism takes the hindmost. In large measure he has succeeded, since he has made the word "liberalism" a synonym for what is good and "conservatism" a synonym for what is evil. In doing so he has definitely shifted his philosophy three times in the past hundred years and apparently is now doing so for a fourth time. The basic truth is that there is no such thing as an enduring philosophy of liberalism. On the whole, philosophic liberalism has tended to associate itself with the gospel of Progress and therefore to associate itself with the concept of the man-made order, but even this allegiance is uncertain. The hare Progress has a way of bounding off in unexpected directions. The great tragedy of conservatism is that those left behind in the chase, the social Darwinians for example, have so often been mistaken for conservatives. Historically, a conservative is one who believes in the organic growth of society in accordance with the principles of natural law; conservatism in the philosophic sense was taught in the school of Montesquieu, studied and applied by the Founding Fathers. We have a conservative Constitution, as those who deplore the fact so often point out. Unfortunately, however, in matters such as this if a mistake is made long enough it does become accepted as a truth. The historic and philosophic meaning of *conservatism* is obsolete, the identification of conservatism with social Darwinism is complete.

It would be convenient and helpful if we could identify liberalism with belief in the man-made order and conservatism with belief in the divinely created order, but to do so would be to voice one of those injurious half-truths that do an injustice to those who identify liberalism with all betterment of the social order, however motivated. It is better, perhaps, however impractical, to plead for the desirability of a moratorium on the use of both words, and with it a recognition of the fact that the desire to better the social order is not the monopoly of those who hold any particular philosophy. Our entire purpose has been to indicate that the gospel of Progress has been the illusion of a gospel, since the entire record of the man-made order in the Anglo-American tradition has been one of enthusiastic starts and sudden stops. An aspect of the purpose has been to leave the inference that belief in the divinely created order and the reality of natural law is by no means obsolete, and further to suggest that each time in Anglo-American history that the man-made order has reached the towering cliffs where Progress stops, believers in the divinely created order have found the way around to the fertile plain where progress once more is possible.

DIVINE OR NATURAL ORDER

There is something important to be said for the term *divinely created order* as a substitute for *natural law*. One does not start with a belief in a divinely created order; one starts with a belief in God. Herbert Agar said some years ago in the Preface to *A Declaration of Faith:* "This book is written from a Christian point of view. But it does not pretend that most Westerners are Christians; neither does it suggest that we should adopt Christianity as a mere convenience, because we need a faith. To disbelieve in God is a misfortune; but to insult Him is worse."

One can believe in natural law without believing in a personal Deity if one means by natural law what John Stuart Mill, Thomas Henry Huxley, and in general the social Darwinians meant. One cannot believe in the sort of natural law present in a divinely created order unless first one believes in a personal God and, to echo a phrase from the days of deism, in particular dispensation. If one does believe in a personal God and in particular dispensation, then one can believe in prayer and one can believe in a Church as a repository of faith, a dispenser of hope, a well of charity, and a guide to conscience. But it is characteristic of a true chain of thought that it can be traced in either direction, from premise to conclusion and from conclusion back to premise. If one believes in the Church, in prayer, in God, and in particular dispensation, one logically believes in the divinely created order and in natural law. Millions of Americans do not accept as valid this chain of thought, but more millions do.

We are living in an age when the Churches are trying to come closer together, to determine what is common in their beliefs, what they will share of the heritage given them two millennia ago. We are also living in an age when the Churches once more have taken the lead in a vital social movement; when ministers, priests, and rabbis are front fighters in a struggle for civil rights which in their explicit pronouncements are merely ratifications of natural rights and hence confirmations of their belief in natural law. Certainly belief in natural law is part of their common belief, part of their priceless heritage. Why, then, might not a positive affirmation of belief in natural law as the principle of the divinely created order be an appropriate and impressive manifestation of the ecumenical spirit? When all is said and done, pragmatism in American politics has taken its latest form in an attempt to buy Progress by monetary grants to individuals, communities, and states. Is Progress something built by the hands of man, or something built in human hearts? Those who believe in the possibility of the man-made order have a dubious historical case at best, and the record of history lends little assurance that Progress is something that can be bought. Those who believe that there has been more genuine progress achieved by the philosophic conservatives who believe in the divinely created order than by the philosophic liberals who believe in the man-made order have an impressive record in history to which they can point. But a pox, as the eighteenth century would have it, on the words "liberal" and "conservative." They have become fighting words, and like most fighting words they mean little or nothing. Today the Churches can again assert leadership in American thought, as the pattern of internal events once more has made men probe to find the Archean rock of eternal truth on which the human order rests. But destiny, as the ancient Greek epigram has it, wears only a forelock. Destiny can never be caught from behind.

NOTES

Chapter I. The Dawn of Reason

1. *Leviathan,* ed. Oakeshott (Oxford: Basil Blackwell, 1946), p. 92.
2. *Ibid.,* pp. 70–71.
3. *Ibid.,* p. 84.
4. *Ibid.,* p. 85.
5. *Ibid.*
6. *Ibid.*
7. In Samuel I. Mintz, *The Hunting of Leviathan: Seventeenth Century Reactions to the Materialism and Moral Philosophy of Thomas Hobbes* (New York: Cambridge University Press, 1962).

Chapter II. Natural Religion

1. *Old Virginia and Her Neighbours* (Boston: Houghton Mifflin, 1897), I, 168.
2. *Patriarcha and Other Political Works of Sir Robert Filmer,* ed. Peter Laslett (Oxford: Basil Blackwell, 1949), p. 57.
3. *Moral and Religious Aphorisms,* ed. Samuel Salter (London, 1753), No. 76.
4. *Two Treatises of Government,* ed. Peter Laslett (New York: Cambridge University Press, 1960), p. 289.
5. *Ibid.,* pp. 323–24.
6. *Ibid.,* pp. 305–6.
7. *Ibid.,* p. 368.
8. *Ibid.,* p. 102.
9. *Reasonableness of Christianity,* ed. I. T. Ramsey (Stanford, Calif.: Stanford University Press, 1958), pp. 44–45.
10. *Ibid.,* pp. 75–77.
11. *Essay concerning Human Understanding,* ed. A. C. Fraser, 2 vols. (Oxford, 1894; New York: Dover, 1959), I, 67.
12. *Ibid.,* I, 474.

Chapter III. "Whatever Is, Is Right"

1. *The Works of the late Right Honorable Henry St. John, Lord Viscount Bolingbroke*, ed. David Mallet, 5 vols. (London, 1754), V, 2.
2. *Ibid.*, V, 259–60.
3. *Ibid.*, V, 58.
4. *Ibid.*, V, 414.
5. *Ibid.*, V, 480.
6. *Ibid.*, V, 419.
7. "Essay the Second," *ibid.*, IV, 111.
8. *Ibid.*, V, 433.
9. *Ibid.*, V, 332.
10. *Ibid.*, V, 381.
11. "A Letter concerning Enthusiasm" in *Characteristics of Men, Manners, Opinions, Times*, ed. John M. Robertson, 2 vols. (London: Grant Richards, 1900), I, 17–18.
12. "An Essay on the Freedom of Wit and Humour," *ibid.*, I, 90.
13. "Soliloquy, or Advice to an Author," *ibid.*, I, 136.
14. "Miscellaneous Reflections," *ibid.*, II, 255.
15. "An Inquiry concerning Virtue or Merit," *ibid.*, I, 259–60.
16. "A Letter concerning Enthusiasm," *ibid.*, I, 27.

Chapter IV. Beginnings of the Economic Gospel

1. *The Fable of the Bees; or, Private Vices, Publick Benefits*. With *An Essay on Charity and Charity Schools*, and *A Search into the Origin of Society* . . . , 2 vols. (London, 1732; 6th ed.), I, 9–11.
2. *Ibid.*, I, 23–24.
3. *Ibid.*, I, 43.
4. *Ibid.*, I, 382.
5. *Ibid.*, I, 394–95.
6. *Ibid.*, I, 402.
7. *Essays on Freethinking and Plainspeaking* (New York: Putnam, 1905), Ch. vii, "Mandeville's 'Fable of the Bees,'" p. 279.
8. "An Essay on Charity Schools," in *Fable, op. cit.*, I, 306.
9. *Ibid.*, I, 328.
10. *Ibid.*, I, 328–29.
11. *Ibid.*, I, 350.
12. *Ibid.*, I, 363.

13. The first two essays were published under the title *An Inquiry into the Original of Our Ideas of Beauty and Virtue* (London, 1728; 6th ed., 1772); the other two as *Essay on the Nature and Conduct of the Passions and Affections* with *Illustrations upon the Moral Sense* (London, 1728; 4th ed., 1756).
14. *Inquiry*, 6th ed., p. x.
15. *Ibid.*, p. 174.
16. *Ibid.*, pp. 165–166.
17. *A System of Moral Philosophy*, 2 vols. (Glasgow, 1755), I, 266. This work was published by Hutcheson's son after the author's death.
18. *Ibid.*, I, 273.
19. *Treatise of Human Nature*, 2 vols., 1739; ed. L. A. Selby-Bigge (Oxford: Clarendon Press, 1888; 1960); Bk. I, Pt. III, sec. xvi, p. 179. References to the *Treatise* will be by book, part, and section to facilitate reference to other editions; page references will be to Selby-Bigge.
20. *Ibid.*, III, I, i; p. 457.
21. *Ibid.*, III, I, i; pp. 468–69.
22. *Ibid.*, III, I, i; p. 469.
23. *Ibid.*, III, II, viii; pp. 546–47.
24. *Ibid.*, III, III, iv; p. 609.
25. "An Enquiry Concerning the Principles of Morals," in *Enquiries Concerning the Human Understanding* and *Concerning the Principles of Morals*, ed. L. A. Selby-Bigge (Oxford: Clarendon Press, 1893; 1957). Sec. V, Pt. ii, par. 188, p. 231.
26. *The Natural History of Religion*, 1757; ed. intro. H. E. Root (Stanford, Calif.: Stanford University Press, 1957), p. 27.
27. *Ibid.*, p. 65.
28. *Ibid.*, p. 66.
29. *Ibid.*, p. 68.
30. *Ibid.*, p. 72.
31. *Ibid.*, p. 75.
32. "An Enquiry Concerning the Principles of Morals," in *Enquiries*, p. 231.

Chapter V. The Era of Stagnation

1. Cf. *Dictionary of National Biography*, art. "Hoadly."
2. *Ibid.*
3. Thomas Erastus (1524–1583), whose name is a Hellenized form of his natal Liebler, was a physician at Heidelberg and a theolo-

gian. His conviction that the penalty of excommunication was being politically abused was expounded in a Latin work published in 1589 and available in English translation under the title *The Nullity of Church Censures* (London, 1659).

4. *A Letter concerning Toleration*, in *The Works of John Locke in Ten Volumes*, eleventh edition (London, 1812), VI, 13.

5. Brit. Mus. Add. MS 32, 686, fol. 327. Quoted John H. Plumb, *Sir Robert Walpole: The King's Minister* (London: Cresset Press, 1960), p. 96.

6. Essay XII, "Of the Original Contract," *Essays Moral, Political, and Literary*, ed. intro. T. H. Green and T. H. Grose, 2 vols. (London: Longmans, Green, 1875), I, 444.

7. *Ibid.*, I, 446.

8. *Ibid.*, I, 446–47.

9. *Ibid.*, I, 456.

10. *Ibid.*, I, 459.

11. *Ibid.*, I, 110.

12. *Ibid.*, I, 111.

13. *Ibid.*, II, 157.

14. Ch. IV, *Political Thought in England from Locke to Bentham* (New York: Holt, 1920).

Chapter VI. The School of Montesquieu

1. *L'Esprit des Lois*, in Montesquieu, *Oeuvres complètes*, Texte présenté et annoté par Roger Caillois (Paris: Bibliothèque de la Pléiade, 1951), II, 233.

2. Hugo Grotius, *De Iure Belli et Pacis Libri Tres*, accompanied by an Abridged Translation by William Whewell, 2 vols. (Cambridge: University Press, 1863), Bk. I, Ch. I, par. x, i; vol. I, p. 10.

3. Robert Shackleton, *Montesquieu: a Critical Biography* (New York: Oxford University Press, 1961), p. 284.

4. The evidence for this is in Shackleton, *op. cit.*, p. 285.

5. *Ibid.*, p. 287.

6. *L'Esprit des Lois*, Bk. XI, Ch. III, p. 395.

7. *Ibid.*, Bk. III, Ch. VII, p. 257.

8. F. T. H. Fletcher, *Montesquieu and English Politics 1750–1800* (London: Edward Arnold, 1939), pp. 119–20.

9. *L'Esprit des Lois*, Bk. XI, Ch. VI, p. 398.

10. Shackleton, *op. cit.*, p. 11.

11. *L'Esprit des Lois*, Bk. XXV, Ch. II, pp. 735–37.

12. *Ibid.*, Bk. XXIV, Ch. XXVI, p. 734.

13. *Ibid.*, Bk. XXV, Ch. X, p. 744.

14. *Ibid.*, Bk. XXIV, Ch. VII, p. 719.

15. Pensée 1805, *Oeuvres,* ed. Masson; quoted in Shackleton, *op. cit.,* p. 351.

16. Quoted by the Rev. Robert H. Murray, *Edmund Burke: a Biography* (New York: Oxford University Press, 1931), p. 206.

17. "A Vindication of Natural Society," in *The Writings and Speeches of Edmund Burke,* 12 vols. (Boston: Little, Brown, 1901), I, 65.

18. John MacCunn, *The Political Philosophy of Burke* (New York: Longmans, Green, 1913), p. 1.

19. *Correspondence* in *The Writings and Speeches of Edmund Burke, op. cit.,* I, 332–33.

20. *The Philosophy of Edmund Burke: A Selection from His Speeches and Writings,* ed. Louis I. Bredvold and Ralph G. Ross (Ann Arbor: University of Michigan Press, 1960), Ch. 2.

21. *Ibid.*, p. 35.

22. *Reflections on the Revolution in France* in *The Writings and Speeches of Edmund Burke, op. cit.,* III, 311.

23. *Ibid.*, III, 359.

24. Annie Marion Osborn, *Rousseau and Burke: A Study of the Idea of Liberty in Eighteenth-Century Political Thought* (New York: Oxford University Press, 1940), p. vii.

Chapter VII. The School of Rousseau

1. *The Moralists,* in Shaftesbury, *Characteristics of Men, Manners, Times, op. cit.,* II, 101–2.

2. The importance of Holbach's hospitality is discussed in Kingsley Martin, *French Liberal Thought in the Eighteenth Century: a Study of Political Ideas from Bayle to Condorcet* (London: Turnstile Press, 1954), p. 108.

3. Carl L. Becker, *The Heavenly City of the Eighteenth Century Philosophers* (New Haven, Conn.: Yale University Press, 1932).

4. *Ibid.*, Ch. IV.

5. *An Essay on the First Principles of Government, and on the Nature of Political, Civil, and Religious Liberty* (London, 1771), p. 5; quoted in Becker, *op. cit.,* p. 145.

6. Sir Leslie Stephen, *History of English Thought in the Eighteenth Century* (London, 1872; New York: Harcourt, Brace & World, 1962), Ch. X, par. 65.

7. *The Social Contract and Discourses,* trans. intro. G. D. H. Cole (New York: Dutton, 1947), Bk. I, Ch. I, pp. 3–4.

8. *Ibid.,* Bk. I, Ch. VI, p. 12.

9. *Ibid.,* Bk. I, Ch. VI, p. 13.

10. *Ibid.,* Bk. I, Ch. VII, pp. 14–15.

11. John Viscount Morley, *Rousseau and His Era,* 2 vols. (London: Macmillan, 1923), II, 198–99.

12. *Social Contract,* Bk. II, Ch. III, p. 23.

13. Introduction, pp. xxxvi–xxxvii.

14. *Social Contract,* Bk. III, Ch. IV, p. 56.

15. *An Essay on the First Principles of Government, and on the Nature of Political, Civil, and Religious Liberty* (London, 1768), p. 10.

16. *Ibid.,* p. 13.

17. *An Enquiry concerning Political Justice and Its Influence on General Virtue and Happiness* (London, 1793); ed. abridged Raymond A. Preston, 2 vols. (New York: Knopf, 1926), I, 62–63.

18. *Ibid.,* I, 41–42.

19. *Ibid.,* I, 47.

20. *Ibid.,* I, 54–55.

21. Stephen, *op. cit.,* Ch. X, par. 135.

22. *The Rights of Man,* intro. George Jacob Holyoake (New York: Dutton, 1951), p. 43.

23. *Ibid.,* p. 44.

24. *Ibid.,* p. 47.

25. *Ibid.,* p. 133.

26. *Reflections on the Revolution in France* in *The Writings and Speeches of Edmund Burke,* 12 vols. (Boston: Little, Brown, 1901), III, 275.

27. *Ibid.,* III, 312.

28. Stephen, *op. cit.,* Ch. X, par. 121.

Chapter VIII. The Founding Fathers

1. *Autobiography,* in *A Benjamin Franklin Reader,* ed. Nathan G. Goodman (New York: Crowell, 1945), p. 96.

2. *Ibid.,* p. 97.

3. *Ibid.,* pp. 117–18.

4. See Alfred O. Aldridge, "Franklin's 'Shaftesburian' Dialogues Not Franklin's: A Revision of the Franklin Canon," *American Literature,* XXI (1949–50), pp. 151–59.

5. *Ibid.,* pp. 154–55.

6. Zoltan Haraszti, *John Adams and the Prophets of Progress* (Cambridge: Harvard University Press, 1952), p. 167.

7. *A Benjamin Franklin Reader, op. cit.*, p. 244.

8. This statement, and the entire treatment of Jefferson's thought, is very much indebted to Adrienne Koch, *The Philosophy of Thomas Jefferson* (New York: Columbia University Press, 1943).

9. "Opinion on the question whether the United States have a right to renounce their treaties with France, or to hold them suspended till the government of that country shall be established." From *Reports and Opinions while Secretary of State;* April 28, 1793. *The Writings of Thomas Jefferson,* ed. Albert Ellery Bergh, issued under the auspices of the Jefferson Memorial Association of the United States; 20 vols. (Washington, D.C., 1903), III, 228.

10. For the composition of *Notes on Virginia,* see Marie Kimball, *Jefferson: War and Peace 1776–1784* (New York: Coward-McCann, 1947), pp. 259–305.

11. *The Writings of James Madison,* pub. by order of Congress, 4 vols. (Philadelphia: Lippincott, 1865); Letter of October 24, 1787; I, 353.

12. *Letters and Other Writings of James Madison,* 4 vols. (New York, 1884), I, 162–63. The inner quotation is "Declaration of Rights," Art. 16.

13. *Ibid.*, p. 164.

14. *Ibid.*, pp. 168–69.

15. *The Farmer Refuted; Or, A More Impartial and Comprehensive View of the Dispute between Great Britain and the Colonies, Intended as a Further Vindication of the Congress* (New York, 1775), in *The Works of Alexander Hamilton,* ed. John C. Hamilton (New York: Charles S. Francis, 1861), II, 43–44.

16. Frank Monaghan, *John Jay* (New York and Indianapolis: Bobbs-Merrill, 1935).

17. *Ibid.*, p. 218.

18. *Ibid.*, p. 233.

19. *Ibid.*, p. 322.

20. Letter of September 14, 1813, in *The Selected Writings of John and John Quincy Adams,* ed. intro. Adrienne Koch and William Peden (New York: Knopf, 1946), p. 168.

21. Letter of December 3, 1813; *ibid.*, p. 171.

22. For a study of Adams' attitude toward English deism and the thought of the philosophes, based on marginal jottings in the books he owned, see Haraszti, *op. cit.*

23. *Selected Writings*, p. 118.

24. *Ibid.*, p. 176.

25. *Ibid.*, p. 30.

26. *Ibid.*, p. xxxi.

27. See "The Importation of French Literature in New York City, 1750–1800," *Studies in Philology*, XXVIII (Oct., 1931), pp. 235–51; and "The Importation of French Books in Philadelphia, 1750–1800," *Modern Philology*, XXXII (Nov., 1934), pp. 157–77. The matter of the importation of French literature is put into its broad cultural setting in Howard Mumford Jones, *America and French Culture 1750–1848* (Chapel Hill: University of North Carolina Press, 1927).

28. *The Writings of Benjamin Franklin*, ed. Albert H. Smyth, 10 vols. (New York: Macmillan, 1905–07), X, 50.

29. Dumas Malone, *Jefferson and the Rights of Man* (Boston: Little, Brown, 1951), p. 234.

30. To Washington, Cabinet Paper. Hamilton Papers, first series, Library of Congress. Quoted in Richard B. Morris, ed., *Hamilton and the Founding of the Nation* (New York: Dial Press, 1957), p. 406.

31. *The Works of Alexander Hamilton*, ed. Henry Cabot Lodge, 12 vols. (New York: Putnam, 1904), X, 45.

32. Hamilton Papers, first series. Quoted in Morris, *op. cit.*, p. 409.

33. *Works*, VIII, 427.

34. *The Works of John Adams*, ed. Charles Francis Adams, 10 vols. (Boston: Little, Brown, 1850–56), IX, 563–64.

Chapter IX. "The Greatest Happiness of the Greatest Number"

1. *Principles of Penal Law*, in *Works, published under the superintendence of his executor, John Bowring*, 11 vols. (Edinburgh: Tait, 1843), II, 10.

2. "Nam generalius et specialius differunt ut majus et minus." *De Homine*, in *Thomae Hobbes Malmesburiensis Opera philosophica quae Latine scripsit*, ed. Sir W. Molesworth, 5 vols. (London, 1839–45), II, 102.

3. Locke, *Essay Concerning Human Understanding*, ed. A. C. Fraser, 2 vols. (Oxford, 1894; New York: Dover, 1959), Ch. XXVIII, sec. 5.

4. "An Inquiry Concerning Moral Good and Evil," sec. 3 par. 8, in *An Inquiry into the Original of Our Ideas of Beauty and Virtue* (London, 1728; 6th ed., 1772), 1729 ed., p. 180.

5. *An Introduction to the Principles of Morals and Legislation* (Oxford: Clarendon Press, 1907), p. 41.

6. *Ibid.*, pp. 1–2.

7. *Ibid.*, pp. 21–22.

8. John Stuart Mill, *Autobiography* (London: Oxford University Press, 1924, 1958), p. 33.

9. *Ibid.*, p. 40.

10. *Analysis of the Phenomena of the Human Mind*, 2 vols. (London: Longmans, Green, 1869), II, 288–89.

11. *Ibid.*, II, 309.

12. In the note referred to, J. S. Mill includes a long passage from the *Fragment on Mackintosh*. See *ibid.*, II, 310–11.

13. *Ibid.*, II, 312.

14. They coalesce in Ch. XXI, sec. 2, subsec. 3, "The Objects called Sublime and Beautiful, and their Contraries, contemplated as Causes of our Pleasures and Pains." *Analysis, op. cit.*, II, 230–55.

15. Ricardo, *Works* (London, 1852), p. 358. Quoted in Emery Neff, *Carlyle and Mill: An Introduction to Victorian Thought* (New York: Columbia University Press, 1926), p. 101.

16. This is the roster of the school as given by Neff, *op. cit.*, pp. 112–13.

Chapter X. Utilitarianism in Practice

1. Frederick William Roe, *Victorian Prose* (New York: Ronald Press, 1947), p. 95. The quotation is from a review by Macaulay of Robert Southey's *Sir Thomas More; or, Colloquies on the Progress and Prospects of Society*, 1829.

2. *Ibid.*, p. 101.

3. *Ibid.*, p. 104.

4. D. C. Somervell, *English Thought in the Nineteenth Century* (London: Methuen, 1929, 1960), p. 92.

5. *Ibid.*, p. 111.

Chapter XI. Ethics by Natural Selection

1. *Paradise Lost*, Bk. VII, ll. 452–64.

2. Herbert Spencer, *An Autobiography* (New York: Appleton, 1904), I, 462.

3. Charles Darwin, *The Origin of Species*, facsimile of first edition, intro. Ernst Mayr (Cambridge: Harvard University Press, 1964), p. 489.

4. "The Struggle for Existence in Human Society," in Frederick William Roe, *Victorian Prose* (New York: Ronald Press, 1947), p. 508.

5. *Ibid.*, p. xxvii.

6. Leonard Huxley, *Life and Letters of Thomas Henry Huxley* (New York: Appleton, 1901), I, 74. Owen was Sir Richard Owen, Director of the Hunter Museum.

7. William Irvine, *Apes, Angels, and Victorians: The Story of Darwin, Huxley, and Evolution* (New York: McGraw-Hill, 1955), p. 196.

8. *Methods and Results* (New York: Appleton, 1897), p. 160.

9. *Hume, With Helps to the Study of Berkeley* (New York: Appleton 1897), p. 235.

10. See "The Scientific Aspects of Positivism," in *Lay Sermons, Addresses, and Reviews* (New York: Appleton, 1870), pp. 147–73.

11. "Prolegomena," in T. H. Huxley and Julian Huxley, *Touchstones for Ethics 1893–1943* (New York: Harper, 1947), p. 43.

12. *Ibid.*, p. 57.

13. *Ibid.*, p. 59.

14. *Ibid.*, p. 67.

15. "Evolution and Ethics," in T. H. Huxley and Julian Huxley, *op. cit.*, p. 81.

16. *Ibid.*, p. 92.

17. Spencer, *Autobiography, op. cit.*, I, 467.

18. Hugh Elliot, *Herbert Spencer* (New York: Holt, 1917).

19. *Ibid.*, p. 86.

20. *Ibid.*, p. 190.

Chapter XII. Survival of the Fittest Americans

1. Oration at Quincy, July 4, 1831, p. 13; quoted in Benjamin Fletcher Wright, Jr., *American Interpretations of Natural Law: A Study in the History of Political Thought* (Cambridge: Harvard University Press, 1931), p. 171.

2. P. 11, quoted in Wright, *loc. cit.*

3. *The Education of Henry Adams* (New York: Modern Library, 1931), p. 225.

4. Robert Green McCloskey, *American Conservatism in the Age of Enterprise* (Cambridge: Harvard University Press, 1951), pp. 27–28.

5. *Social Darwinism: Selected Essays of William Graham Sumner*, with an Introduction by Stow Persons (Englewood Cliffs, N.J.: Prentice-Hall, 1963), p. 2.

6. *Essays of William Graham Sumner,* ed. Albert Galloway Keller and Maurice R. Davie, 2 vols. (New Haven: Yale University Press, 1940), II, 479.

7. "The Banquet of Life," in *Essays,* I, 382–83.

8. "Is Liberty a Lost Blessing?" in *Essays,* I, 286.

9. "Rights," in *Essays,* I, 358.

10. *Ibid.,* p. 361.

11. *Ibid.,* p. 362.

12. "Who Is Free?" in *Essays,* I, 301.

13. "The Forgotten Man," in *Essays,* I, 478.

14. "The Challenge of Facts," in *Essays,* II, 107.

15. *Ibid.,* p. 105.

16. "Liberty and Responsibility," in *Essays,* I, 329.

17. *Munn v. Illinois,* 94 U.S. 113.

18. Richard Hofstadter, *Social Darwinism in American Thought* (Philadelphia: University of Pennsylvania Press, 1944; rev. ed., Boston: Beacon Press, 1955), Ch. 9, "Racism and Imperialism."

19. *Ibid.,* p. 45; quoted from William J. Ghent, *Our Benevolent Feudalism* (New York: Macmillan, 1902).

20. *Autobiography of Andrew Carnegie* (Boston, 1920), p. 327; quoted in Hofstadter, *op. cit.,* p. 45.

21. Robert S. and Helen M. Lynd, *Middletown in Transition* (New York, 1937), p. 500; quoted in Hofstadter, *op. cit.,* p. 50.

22. *The Origin of Species,* facsimile of first edition, intro. Ernst Mayr (Cambridge: Harvard University Press, 1964), p. 489.

23. Quoted in Frederick William Roe, *Victorian Prose* (New York: Ronald Press, 1947), p. 259.

24. *Ibid.,* p. 203.

25. *The Correspondence of Marx and Engels* (New York, 1935), pp. 125–26; quoted in Hofstadter, *op. cit.,* p. 115.

Chapter XIII. Truth Is Successful Experience

1. Richard T. Ely, *Ground Under Our Feet* (New York, 1938), p. 140; quoted in Richard Hofstadter, *Social Darwinism in American Thought* (Philadelphia: University of Pennsylvania Press, 1944; rev. ed., Boston: Beacon Press, 1955), p. 147. Ely was a dominant figure in the formation of the Association.

2. *The Collected Papers of Charles Sanders Peirce,* Vols. I–VI, ed. Charles Hartshorne and Paul Weiss, (Cambridge: Harvard University Press, 1931–35); Vols. VII, VIII, ed. Arthur W. Burks, 1958.

3. "How to Make Our Ideas Clear," *Collected Papers*, V, 261; quoted in William Ernest Hocking, *Types of Philosophy* (New York: Charles Scribner's Sons, 1959), p. 100.

4. Edward C. Moore, *American Pragmatism: Peirce, James, and Dewey* (New York: Columbia University Press, 1961), p. 96.

5. *Collected Papers*, V, 12; quoted in Philip P. Wiener, *Evolution and the Founders of Pragmatism* (Cambridge: Harvard University Press, 1949), p. 19.

6. *Ibid.*

7. Catherine Drinker Bowen, *Yankee from Olympus: Justice Holmes and His Family* (Boston: Little, Brown, 1945), pp. 220–21.

8. Edward H. Madden, *Chauncey Wright and the Foundations of Pragmatism* (Seattle: University of Washington Press, 1963), p. 8.

9. *Philosophical Discussions*, ed. Charles Eliot Norton (New York: Holt, 1877), p. 7.

10. *Letters of Chauncey Wright, with Some Account of His Life*, ed. James Bradley Thayer (Cambridge, Mass., 1878), pp. 97 f.; quoted in Wiener, *op. cit.*, pp. 40–41. The quotation is from a letter to Charles Eliot Norton dated Feb. 18, 1867.

11. *Letters*, p. 195; quoted in Madden, *op. cit.*, p. 54.

12. *Ibid.*, p. 173.

13. *Collected Papers*, V, par. 9.

14. Ralph Barton Perry, *The Thought and Character of William James*, briefer version (Cambridge: Harvard University Press, 1948), p. 127.

15. "Is Life Worth Living?" *The Will to Believe and Other Essays in Popular Philosophy* (New York: Longmans, Green, 1897), p. 52.

16. *Ibid.*

17. *Ibid.*, p. 56.

18. Perry, *op. cit.*, p. 120.

19. *Ibid.*, p. 121.

20. William James, *Pragmatism: A New Name for Some Old Ways of Thinking* (London: Longmans, Green, 1907), p. 12.

21. *Ibid.*, pp. 19–20.

22. *The Will to Believe*, p. 26.

23. *The Varieties of Religious Experience: A Study in Human Nature* (New York: Longmans, Green, 1902), p. 212.

24. *Ibid.*, p. 516.

25. *The Letters of William James*, ed. Henry James (Boston: Atlantic Monthly Press, 2 vols., 1920), I, 47; quoted in Moore, *op. cit.*, p. 116. Charles Renouvier was editor of *Critique philosophique*, in which he frequently published translations of James's

essays. James always testified to the salutary influence upon his thought of Renouvier's advocacy of pluralism and his theory of knowledge which was empirical without being skeptical or materialistic. See Perry, *op. cit.*, p. 153 and elsewhere.

26. Julius Seelye Bixler, *Religion in the Philosophy of William James* (Boston: Marshall Jones, 1926), p. 69.

27. *Essays in Radical Empiricism* (New York: Longmans, Green, 1912), p. 95.

28. *Ibid.*, p. 42; quoted in Moore, *op. cit.*, p. 145.

29. Moore, *op. cit.*, p. 152.

30. *Pragmatism*, p. 156.

31. Bixler, *op. cit.*, p. 54.

32. John Dewey, *Essays in Experimental Logic* (Chicago: University of Chicago Press, 1916), p. 165; quoted in Moore, *op. cit.*, p. 165.

33. *Pragmatism*, p. 46.

34. Hocking, *op. cit.*, p. 103.

35. William James, *A Pluralistic Universe* (New York: Longmans, Green, 1909), p. 311; quoted in Moore, *op. cit.*, p. 133.

Chapter XIV. Instrumentalism

1. "How to Make Our Ideas Clear," *Collected Papers*, V, 261; quoted in Ernest Hocking, *Types of Philosophy* (New York: Scribner's, 1959), p. 100.

2. Georg Wilhelm Friedrich Hegel (1770–1831) tried to reduce the duality of Kant, who considered nature opposed to spirit and the objective to the subjective, to unity on the thesis that difference is conceivable only in terms of an antecedent unity. One cannot conceive a full glass unless one can conceive an empty glass. Hegel aimed at the establishment of a final and eternal group of categories, what Professor Hocking terms "a sort of constitutional law for the entire course of world-events through time." Hocking, *op. cit.*, p. 287.

3. *The Quest for Certainty: A Study of the Relation of Knowledge and Action*, Gifford Lectures, 1929 (New York: Minton, Balch, 1929).

4. *Ibid.*, p. 3.

5. *Ibid.*, pp. 40–41.

6. *Ibid.*, pp. 106–7.

7. *Ibid.*, p. 107.

8. *Reconstruction in Philosophy*, enlarged edition (Boston: Beacon Press, 1948), pp. xiii–xiv.

9. John Dewey and James H. Tufts, *Ethics* (New York: Holt, 1908), p. 302.
10. *Reconstruction in Philosophy*, p. 169.
11. *Ethics*, p. 343.
12. *Reconstruction in Philosophy*, p. 167.
13. *Ibid.*, pp. 173-74.
14. *Ibid.*, p. 176.
15. *Ibid.*, p. 177.
16. *Human Nature and Conduct* (New York: Holt, 1922), p. 144.
17. *A Common Faith* (New Haven: Yale University Press, 1934), in *Intelligence in the Modern World: John Dewey's Philosophy*, ed. intro. Joseph Ratner (New York: Modern Library, 1939), pp. 1025-26.
18. *The Quest for Certainty*, p. 138.
19. *Types of Philosophy*, p. 103.
20. *Ibid.*, p. 107.
21. *Ibid.*, p. 110.
22. *Ibid.*, p. 111.

Chapter XV. The Life of the Law Is Experience

1. *The Common Law* (Boston: Little, Brown, 1881), p. 1.
2. *Ibid.*
3. Letter dated Mar. 27, 1866; quoted in Catherine Drinker Bowen, *Yankee from Olympus: Justice Holmes and His Family* (Boston: Little, Brown, 1945), p. 219.
4. *Ibid.*, pp. 222-23.
5. *Ibid.*, p. 243. Letter dated Dec. 15, 1867.
6. *Ibid.*, pp. 245-46. Letter dated Apr. 19, 1868.
7. *The Common Law*, p. 1.
8. *Ibid.*, p. 35.
9. Felix Frankfurter, *Mr. Justice Holmes and the Supreme Court*, 2nd ed. (Cambridge: Harvard University Press, 1961), p. 11.
10. *The Common Law*, pp. 35-36.
11. *Yankee from Olympus*, pp. 275-76.
12. *Mr. Justice Holmes and the Supreme Court*, p. 13.
13. *Ibid.*, p. 15.
14. *Truax v. Corrigan*, 257 U.S. 312, 344 (1921).
15. Oliver Wendell Holmes, *Collected Legal Papers* (New York: Harcourt, 1920), p. 295.
16. *Otis v. Parker*, 187 U.S. 608-09 (1903).
17. *Lochner v. New York*, 198 U.S. 65, 74 (1905).

18. *Ibid.*
19. *Meyer v. Nebraska,* 262 U.S. 404, 412 (1923).
20. *Ibid.*
21. Francis Biddle, *Justice Holmes, Natural Law, and the Supreme Court* (New York: Macmillan, 1961), pp. 68–69.
22. *Collected Legal Papers,* p. 306.
23. *Reminiscences of Frederika Brandeis* (privately printed, 1944), pp. 32–34; quoted in Alpheus Thomas Mason, *Brandeis: A Free Man's Life* (New York: Viking Press, 1946), p. 29.
24. Quoted in *ibid.,* p. 585.
25. Address at the Brandeis Memorial Colony Dinner, June 23, 1943; in *An Autobiography of the Supreme Court: Off-the-Bench Commentary by the Justices,* ed. Alan F. Westin (New York: Macmillan, 1963), p. 235.
26. *Olmstead v. U.S.,* 277 U.S. 438 (1928); quoted in *Brandeis: A Free Man's Life,* p. 568.
27. Quoted by Justice Jackson; see *An Autobiography of the Supreme Court,* p. 237.
28. *Muller v. Oregon,* 208 U.S. 412 (1907).

Chapter XVI. The High Noon of Pragmatism

1. Editor's Preface to Robert G. McCloskey, *The American Supreme Court* (Chicago: University of Chicago Press, 1960), p. vi. Daniel J. Boorstin is editor of the monumental Chicago History of American Civilization Series.
2. See Benjamin F. Wright, *The Growth of American Constitutional Law* (Boston, 1942); and the Library of Congress pamphlet, *Provisions of Federal Law Held Unconstitutional by the Supreme Court of the United States* (Washington, 1936). Both are cited in Alfred H. Kelly and Winfred A. Harbison, *The American Constitution, Its Origin and Development* (New York: Norton, 1948), pp. 540–41.
3. *Smyth v. Ames,* 169 U.S. 466 (1898).
4. *Adkins v. Children's Hospital,* 261 U.S. 525 (1923).
5. Kelly and Harbison, *op. cit.,* p. 698.
6. *United States v. Butler,* 297 U.S. 1 (1936).
7. Kelly and Harbison, *op. cit.,* pp. 87–88.
8. The principles adopted by the Association may be found in *Publications of the American Economic Association,* I (1886), 5–36. The passage quoted is in Richard Hofstadter, *Social Darwinism in American Thought* (Philadelphia: University of Penn-

sylvania, 1944; rev. ed. Boston: Beacon Press, 1955), p. 147.

9. "The Preconceptions of Economic Science," Part II, *Quarterly Journal of Economics,* XIII (1898), p. 425; quoted in Hofstadter, *op. cit.,* p. 155.

10. Washington Gladden (1836–1918) occupied pulpits in several cities and served as editor of the *Independent,* at first a religious journal of Congregational affiliation but an interdenominational periodical during Gladden's incumbency. Walter Rauschenbusch (1861–1918), Baptist minister and professor of church history at Rochester Theological Seminary, was a leader of the Christian Socialist movement. Henry George (1839–1897) is best remembered for his *Progress and Poverty* (1879) with its thesis that poverty is caused by the excessive financial return landowners exact in the form of rent and that its cure is a single tax confiscating this unearned revenue. Edward Bellamy (1850–1898) advanced his social and economic views in a Utopian romance, *Looking Backward* (1888), set in a socialized and unimaginably improved city of Boston in the year 2000.

11. *Home Building and Loan Association v. Blaisdell,* 290 U.S. 298 (1934).

12. *Nebbia v. New York,* 291 U.S. 502 (1934).

13. *Panama Refining Company v. Ryan,* 293 U.S. 388 (1935).

14. *Retirement Board v. Alton Railroad Co.,* 295 U.S. 330 (1935).

15. *Schechter v. United States,* 295 U.S. 495 (1935). Among the crimes against the fair-competition code of the live poultry industry with which the defendant was charged was the sale of "an unfit chicken." The sick chicken aroused the nation's risibilities, but the solemn statement of liberal Justice Cardozo in his concurring opinion concerning the delegation of legislative authority involved, "This is delegation run riot," aroused its concern.

16. *The American Supreme Court,* p. 165.

17. *Louisville Bank v. Radford,* 295 U.S. 555 (1935).

18. The Municipal Bankruptcy Act was found unconstitutional in *Ashton v. Cameron County Water District,* 298 U.S. 513 (1936).

BIBLIOGRAPHICAL NOTES

THE MOST ACCESSIBLE editions of Hobbes's *Leviathan* (Ch. I) are those with introductions by Michael Oakeshott (New York: Macmillan, 1947) and A. D. Lindsay (New York: Dutton, 1950). Oakeshott's introduction is challenging and controversial. Aubrey's delightful life of Hobbes is available in his *Brief Lives and Other Selected Writings*, ed. intro. by Anthony Powell (New York: Dufour, 1949). There are modern lives of Hobbes by G. C. Robertson (1886), Sir Leslie Stephen (English Men of Letters Series, 1904), and Alfred A. Taylor (1908). Among the more valuable studies of Hobbes's thought and its influence are Leo Strauss, *The Political Philosophy of Hobbes: Its Basis and Genesis*, tr. Elsa M. Sinclair (Oxford: Clarendon Press, 1936); Howard Warrender, *The Political Philosophy of Hobbes: His Theory of Obligation* (Oxford: Clarendon Press, 1957), which presents an interpretation of Hobbes markedly divergent from that of Oakeshott and Strauss; and Samuel I. Mintz, *The Hunting of Leviathan: Seventeenth Century Reactions to the Materialism and Moral Philosophy of Thomas Hobbes* (New York: Cambridge University Press, 1962).

The most convenient edition of Filmer (Ch. II) is *Patriarcha and Other Political Works of Sir Robert Filmer*, ed. Peter Laslett (New York: Macmillan, 1949). For a thought-provoking analysis of his concepts, see J. W. Allen, "Sir Robert Filmer," in F. J. C. Hearnshaw, ed., *The Social and Political Ideas of Some English Thinkers of the Augustan Age A.D. 1650–1750* (London: Harrap, 1923; New York: Barnes & Noble, 1950). The standard study of the deists, and a book invaluable for all aspects of eighteenth-century thought, is Sir Leslie Stephen, *History of English Thought in the Eighteenth Century* (London, 1872; New York: Harcourt, Brace & World, 1962). Excerpts from the Cambridge Platonists are available in Ernest T. Campagnac, *The Cambridge Platonists* (London, 1901). The most comprehensive study of their theology is John Tulloch, *Rational Theology and Christian Philosophy in the Seventeenth Century* (2 vols., London, 1872). More recent studies are Frederick P. Powicke, *The*

Cambridge Platonists (Cambridge: Harvard University Press, 1926); G. P. H. Pawson, *The Cambridge Platonists and Their Place in Religious Thought* (New York: Macmillan, 1930); Paul R. Anderson, *Science in Defense of Liberal Religion* (New York: Putnam, 1933); C. E. Raven, *Natural Religion and Christian Theology* (New York: Cambridge University Press, 1953); and Aharon Lichtenstein, *Henry More: The Rational Theology of a Cambridge Platonist* (Cambridge: Harvard University Press, 1962). Among the better twentieth-century studies of Locke and his thought are Richard I. Aaron, *John Locke* (New York: Oxford, 1937); David G. James, *The Life of Reason: Hobbes, Locke, Bolingbroke* (London: Longmans, Green, 1949); Charles R. Morris, *Locke, Berkeley, Hume* (New York: Oxford, 1956); and John W. Yalton, *John Locke and the Way of Ideas* (New York: Oxford, 1956).

Bolingbroke (Ch. III) must be consulted in *The Works of the Late Right Honorable Henry St. John, Lord Viscount Bolingbroke,* ed. David Mallet, (5 vols., London, 1754). The only modern reprint of Bolingbroke is *Letters on the Spirit of Patriotism and on the Idea of a Patriot King,* ed. intro. A. Hassel (Oxford: Clarendon Press, 1917), which contains a good thumbnail biography. The following are studies of his political career: Arthur Hassell, *Life of Viscount Bolingbroke* (rev. ed. Oxford: B. H. Blackwell, 1915); John M. Robertson, *Bolingbroke and Walpole* (New York: Scribner, 1919); and Sir Charles A. Petrie, *Bolingbroke* (London: Collins, 1937). The one study of his philosophic thought is Walter M. Merrill, *From Statesman to Philosopher: a Study in Bolingbroke's Deism* (New York: Philosophical Library, 1949). Shaftesbury's main work is most readily available in *Characteristics of Men, Manners, Opinions, Times,* ed. John M. Robertson (2 vols., London, 1900). The best life of Shaftesbury is Thomas Fowler, *Shaftesbury and Hutcheson* (London, 1882). Dorothy B. Schlegel, *Shaftesbury and the French Deists* (Chapel Hill: University of North Carolina Press, 1956), studies his influence on the French Enlightenment. The only comprehensive study of his substantial influence on English literature is in German: Erwin Wolff, *Shaftesbury und Seine Bedeutung für die Englische Literatur des 18 JHS* (Tübingen, 1960). The definitive edition of Pope's *Essay on Man* is in the Twickenham Edition of the Poems of Alexander Pope, ed. Maynard Mack (New Haven: Yale University Press, 1938 ff.; Vol. III, i); the Introduction, pp. xi–lxxx, is invaluable. See also the classic study by Arthur O. Lovejoy, *The Great Chain of Being* (Cambridge: Harvard University Press, 1936).

Mandeville's *Fable of the Bees* (Ch. IV) grew through the following stages: *The Grumbling Hive, or Knaves Turned Honest* (the original doggerel verses, 1705); *Remarks* (notes on the verses) and *An Inquiry into the Origin of Moral Virtue* (both 1714); *An Essay on Charity Schools* and *A Search into the Origin of Society* (both 1723); and *Fable Part II* (six dialogues, 1729). The standard modern edition is *The Fable of the Bees; or Private Vices, Public Benefits, with a Commentary Critical, Historical and Explanatory*, ed. F. B. Kaye (2 vols., New York: Oxford University Press, 1924). There is a good discussion of the *Fable* by Sir Leslie Stephen: "Mandeville's 'Fable of the Bees,'" Ch. VII, *Essays on Freethinking and Plainspeaking* (New York: Putnam, 1905). There is no modern edition of Hutcheson. A critical appraisal of his ideas may be found in Thomas Fowler, *Shaftesbury and Hutcheson* (London, 1882), and in James Bonar, *Moral Sense*, Chs. III–V (New York: Macmillan, 1930). The standard edition of Hume is still *Philosophical Works*, ed. T. H. Green and T. H. Grose (4 vols., London, 1874–75). The most useful editions are the late nineteenth-century ones prepared by L. A. Selby-Bigge and kept in print by Oxford University Press through successive printings: *Treatise of Human Nature* (1888, 1960) and *Enquiries Concerning the Human Understanding and Concerning the Principles of Morals* (1893, 1957). There are modern editions of *Dialogues Concerning Natural Religion*, ed. Norman K. Smith (New York: Oxford University Press, 1935), and *The Natural History of Religion*, ed. H. E. Root (Stanford, Calif.: Stanford University Press, 1957). See also *David Hume: Writings on Economics*, ed. Eugene Rotwein (Madison: University of Wisconsin Press, 1955). The best lives of Hume are John Y. T. Grieg, *David Hume* (London, 1931); and Ernest C. Mossner, *The Life of David Hume* (Austin: University of Texas Press, 1954). The following are major studies of his work, the first general and the other specific as indicated by their titles: Charles W. Hendel, *Studies in the Philosophy of David Hume* (Princeton, N.J.: Princeton University Press, 1925); John Laird, *Hume's Philosophy of Human Nature* (New York: Dutton, 1932); Ralph W. Church, *Hume's Theory of the Understanding* (Ithaca, N.Y.: Cornell University Press, 1935); Constance Maund, *Hume's Theory of Knowledge* (New York: Macmillan, 1937); Alfred B. Glathe, *Hume's Theory of the Passions and of Morals: a Study of Books II and III of the "Treatise"* (Berkeley: University of California Press, 1950); and Antony G. Flew, *Hume's Philosophy of Belief: a Study of His First Inquiry* (New York: Humanities Press, 1962).

There are no modern editions of the works cited by Bishops Hoadly and Warburton (Ch. V). Hoadly's work is entitled *A Preservative against the Principles and Practices of the Nonjurors both in Church and State* (London, 1716). Warburton wrote *The Alliance between Church and State; or the Necessity and Equity of an Established Religion and a Test Law Demonstrated* (London, 1736; 10th ed., 1846). Bolingbroke's political essays are available in his *Works* (see Ch. III), and Hume's are available in *Essays Moral, Political, and Literary*, ed. intro. T. H. Green and T. H. Grose (2 vols., London, 1875). Leslie Stephen discusses the subject matter of Ch. V in *History of English Thought in the Eighteenth Century*, Ch. X. Harold J. Laski, *Political Thought in England from Locke to Bentham* (New York: Holt, 1920) is also valuable; see especially Ch. III, "Church and State," and Ch. IV, "The Era of Stagnation." Information about Walpole's relations with the bishops may be found in two excellent studies by John H. Plumb, *Sir Robert Walpole: The Making of a Statesman* (Boston: Houghton Mifflin, 1956) and *Sir Robert Walpole: The King's Minister* (Boston: Houghton Mifflin, 1961).

The most accessible edition of Montesquieu (Ch. VI) is *Oeuvres complètes de Montesquieu*, ed. Roger Caillois (2 vols., Paris, 1949, 1951). All translations of *L'Esprit des Lois* were made by the author from this edition. The most useful English study of Montesquieu is Robert Shackleton, *Montesquieu: a Critical Biography* (New York: Oxford University Press, 1961). There is a good chapter on Montesquieu in Kingsley Martin, *French Liberal Thought in the Eighteenth Century: a Study of Political Ideas from Bayle to Condorcet* (London: Turnstile Press, 1954). See also Leslie Stephen, *History of English Thought in the Eighteenth Century* (London, 1872; New York: Harcourt, Brace, 1962), Ch. X, pp. 60–63, and Harold J. Laski, *Political Thought in England from Locke to Bentham* (New York: Holt, 1920), pp. 160–68. The best study of the influence of Montesquieu upon English thought is F. T. H. Fletcher, *Montesquieu and English Politics 1750–1800* (New York: Longmans, Green, 1940). All Burke citations are to *The Writings and Speeches of Edmund Burke* (12 vols., Boston: Little, Brown, 1901). The Burke literature is extremely extensive, and only a few titles can be listed. *The Philosophy of Edmund Burke: a Selection from His Speeches and Writings*, ed. intro. Louis I. Bredvold and Ralph G. Ross (Ann Arbor: University of Michigan Press, 1960) gives excerpts by subject heading. *Burke's Politics*, ed. Ross J. S. Hoffman and Paul Levack (New York: Knopf, 1949), is a similar book devoted to his political philosophy. The life of Burke by John Morley (1879) is a classic of Victorian biography. There are good modern lives by Rev. Robert H. Murray, Philip Magnus, and G. M. Young. Among the better studies of Burke's thought are John MacCunn, *The Political Philosophy of Burke* (New York: Longmans, Green, 1913); A. Cobban, *Edmund Burke and the Revolt Against the Eighteenth Century* (New York: Macmillan, 1929); Charles Parkin, *The Moral Basis of Burke's Political Thought* (New York: Cambridge University Press, 1956); Carl B. Cone, *Burke and the Nature of Politics* (Lexington: University of Kentucky Press, 1957); and Peter J. Stanlis, *Edmund Burke and the Natural Law* (Ann Arbor: University of Michigan Press, 1958). Russell Kirk, *The Conservative Mind* (Chicago: Regnery, 1953), effectively locates Burke in the conservative tradition.

A general survey of the thinking of the philosophes (Ch. VII) is available in Kingsley Martin, *French Liberal Thought in the Eighteenth Century* (London: Turnstile Press, 1954). The essential idealism of their thought and its ties with the past are stressed in Carl L. Becker, *The Heavenly City of the Eighteenth-Century Philosophers* (New Haven: Yale University Press, 1932). For the general philosophy of the period, see Ernst Cassirer, *The Philosophy of the Enlightenment* (Princeton, N.J.: Princeton University Press, 1951); and Elie Halévy, *The Growth of Philosophic Radicalism,* tr. Mary Morris (New York: Macmillan, 1928). Rousseau's *The Social Contract* is readily available in Everyman's Library (New York, 1947) with a good introduction by the translator, G. D. H. Cole. There is a diffuse critique of the book in John Viscount Morley, *Rousseau and His Era* (2 vols., New York: Macmillan, 1923), Pt. II, Ch. I. See also Bernard Bosanquet, *Philosophical Theory of the State* (New York, 1899). Priestley's *An Essay on the First Principles of Government* (London, 1768) is not available in a modern edition. There are two modern editions of Godwin's *Political Justice,* the edition of H. S. Salt (London, 1890) and the abridged edition of Raymond A. Preston (2 vols., New York: Knopf, 1926). On Godwin's thought see A. E. Rodway, *Godwin and the Age of Transition* (London, 1952); and D. H. Monro, *Godwin's Moral Philosophy* (New York: Oxford University Press, 1953). Paine's *The Rights of Man* is also readily available in Everyman's Library (New York, 1951). The standard life of Paine is by Moncure Daniel Conway (2 vols., London, 1892). Conway's *The Life of Thomas Paine* is a necessary book, but it is devoted rather to rectifying the public image of Paine than to discussing his achievement. Other books about Paine, marked to some degree by what seems to be the inevitable tendency to romanticize their subject, are Mary A. Best, *Thomas Paine, Prophet and Martyr of Democracy* (New York: Harcourt, Brace, 1927); William E. Woodward, *Tom Paine, America's Godfather 1737–1809* (New York: Dutton, 1945); and Alfred O. Aldridge, *Man of Reason: Life of Paine* (Philadelphia: Lippincott, 1959).

The collected editions of each of the Founding Fathers (Ch. VIII) are cited in the notes. The following volumes of excerpts from their writings are useful to the general reader: *A Benjamin Franklin Reader*, ed. Nathan A. Goodman (New York: Crowell, 1945); *Basic Writings of Thomas Jefferson*, ed. Philip S. Foner (New York: Wiley, 1944); *The Complete Madison*, ed. intro. Saul K. Padover (New York: Harper, 1953), which is actually a volume of selections from his writings; *Hamilton and the Founding of the Nation*, ed. Richard B. Morris (New York: Dial, 1957); and *The Selected Writings of John and John Quincy Adams*, ed. intro. Adrienne Koch and William Peden (New York: Knopf, 1946). The author is particularly indebted to the following studies: Carl Van Doren, *Benjamin Franklin* (New York, 1938); Gerald Stourzh, *Benjamin Franklin and American Foreign Policy* (Chicago: University of Chicago Press, 1954); Alfred Owen Aldridge, *Franklin and His French Contemporaries* (New York: New York University Press, 1957); Adrienne Koch, *The Philosophy of Thomas Jefferson* (New York: Columbia University Press, 1943); Dumas Malone, *Jefferson, the Virginian* (Boston: Little, Brown, 1948), and *Jefferson and the Rights of Man* (Boston: Little, Brown, 1951); Gottfried Dietze, *The Federalist* (Baltimore: Johns Hopkins University Press, 1960); Frank Monaghan, *John Jay* (New York and Indianapolis: Bobbs-Merrill, 1935); Claude G. Bowers, *Jefferson and Hamilton: The Struggle for Democracy in America* (Boston: Houghton Mifflin, 1946); Correa Moylan Walsh, *The Political Science of John Adams* (New York: Putnam, 1915); Gilbert Chinard, *Honest John Adams* (Boston: Little, Brown, 1933); and Zoltan Haraszti, *John Adams and the Prophets of Progress* (Cambridge: Harvard University Press, 1952). The above does not pretend to be even a selective listing from the immense literature that surrounds the Founding Fathers.

The standard English work on the utilitarians (Ch. IX) is Leslie Stephen, *The English Utilitarians* (3 vols., New York: Putnam, 1900). Vol. I deals with Bentham, Vol. II with James Mill, and Vol.

III with John Stuart Mill. For the influence of scientific thought on the utilitarians and their influence upon the classical economists, see Elie Halévy, *The Growth of Philosophic Radicalism* (New York: Macmillan, 1928; Kelly, 1952). Other major studies of utilitarianism are Ernest Albee, *A History of English Utilitarianism* (New York: Macmillan, 1902, 1957); and Alfred W. Benn, *The History of English Rationalism in the Nineteenth Century* (2 vols., New York: Longmans, Green, 1906). The *Works* of Jeremy Bentham were published in eleven volumes by his literary executor, Sir John Bowring (Edinburgh, 1838–43). There is a modern edition of *An Introduction to the Principles of Morals and Legislation* (New York: Oxford University Press, 1907). The best life is Stephen, *op. cit.,* Vol. I. There is a fairly short life with some criticism of his writings and ideas available: Charles M. Atkinson, *Jeremy Bentham: His Life and Work* (London: Methuen, 1905). David Baumgardt, *Bentham and the Ethics of Today* (Princeton: Princeton University Press, 1952), is a detailed but difficult analysis of Bentham's writings and ideas. The best study of his influence on legal reform is A. V. Dicey, *Lectures on the Relation between Law and Public Opinion in England during the Nineteenth Century* (2nd ed., London: Macmillan, 1930). There is a sound life of James Mill by a utilitarian of the later generation: Alexander Bain, *James Mill: A Biography* (London, 1882). The best study is Stephen, *op. cit.,* Vol. II. See also Benn, *op. cit.,* Ch. VII. One of the best studies of utilitarianism, useful for Bentham and James Mill as well as for its immediate subject, is Emery E. Neff, *Carlyle and Mill: An Introduction to Victorian Thought* (New York: Columbia University Press, 1926).

Utilitarianism in practice (Ch. X) and other aspects of nineteenth-century intellectual life are treated in a short and necessarily compressed study, D. C. Somervell, *English Thought in the Nineteenth Century* (New York: Longmans, Green, 1929, 1960). Francis Place, *Illustrations and Proofs of the Principle of Population,* has been reprinted, ed. Norman E. Himes (Boston: Houghton Mifflin, 1930). See also Graham Wallas, *The Life of Francis Place 1771–1854* (London, 1898). Larger libraries contain Joseph Lancaster, *Improvements in Education, as It Respects the Industrious Classes of the Community* (3rd ed., London, 1805). A life is available, David Salmon, *Joseph Lancaster* (London: Longmans, Green, 1904). The works of Macaulay were published in ten volumes by his sister, Lady Trevelyan (New York, 1898). For a good representative selection, see *Prose and Poetry,* selected by G. M. Young (Cambridge: Harvard University Press, 1952). The standard life of Macaulay was written by his nephew, George Otto Trevelyan, *The Life and Letters of Lord Macaulay* (2 vols., London, 1876). The best modern treatment of his thought is Richmond C. Beatty, *Lord Macaulay, Victorian Liberal* (Norman: University of Oklahoma Press, 1938).

The impact of Darwinism on England (Ch. XI) is treated in William Irvine, *Apes, Angels, and Victorians: The Story of Darwin, Huxley, and Evolution* (New York: McGraw-Hill, 1955). The works of Huxley of particular importance to our subject are *Evolution and Ethics* (New York, 1894); and a posthumous collaboration with his grandson, *Touchstone for Ethics 1893–1943* by T. H. Huxley and Julian Huxley (New York: Harper, 1943). See Houston Peterson, *Huxley, Prophet of Science* (New York: Longmans, Green, 1932); and Harold C. Bibby, *T. H. Huxley: Scientist, Humanist, and Educator* (New York: Horizon Press, 1960). For Herbert Spencer see especially *The Man versus the State,* published with *Social Statics* (New York, 1892), and in a modern edition prepared by Albert Jay Nock (Caldwell, Idaho: Caxton Printers, 1954). The full-scale life is by David Duncan, *Life and Letters of Herbert Spencer* (2 vols., New York: Appleton, 1908). For Spencer's thought see Frederick H. Collins, *An Epitome of the Synthetic Philosophy* (London, 1889); and Hugh Elliot, *Herbert Spencer* (New York: Holt, 1917).

The authoritative study of social Darwinism in all its aspects (Ch. XII) is Richard Hofstadter, *Social Darwinism in American Thought* (Philadelphia: University of Pennsylvania Press, 1944; Boston: Beacon Press, 1955). For the gradual disappearance of natural law as the explicit foundation of American political thought, see Benjamin Fletcher Wright, *American Interpretations of Natural Law: a Study in the History of Political Thought* (Cambridge: Harvard University Press, 1931). For its gradual replacement by the philosophy inherent in social Darwinism, see Robert Green McCloskey, *American Conservatism in the Age of Enterprise* (Cambridge: Harvard University Press, 1951). The work of William Graham Sumner is comprehensively available in *Essays of William Graham Sumner,* ed. Albert Galloway Keller and Maurice R. Davis (2 vols., New Haven: Yale University Press, 1940); it is selectively available in *Social Darwinism: Selected Essays of William Graham Sumner* (Englewood Cliffs, N.J.: Prentice-Hall, 1963). For Justice Stephen J. Field, see McCloskey, *op. cit.;* and for a more sympathetic appraisal, Chauncey F. Black and Samuel B. Smith, *Some Account of the Work of Stephen J. Field as a Legislator, State Judge, and Judge of the Supreme Court of the United States* (New York, 1881).

The writings of Charles Sanders Peirce (Ch. XIII) have been published by Harvard University Press: *The Collected Papers of Charles Sanders Peirce* (Vols. I–VI, ed. Charles Hartshorne and Paul Weiss, 1931–35; Vols. VII and VIII, ed. Arthur W. Burks, 1958). Considerable interest has been shown in Peirce, with the following works noteworthy: Justus Buchler, *Charles Peirce's Empiricism* (New York: Harcourt, Brace, 1939); James Feibleman, *An Introduction to Peirce's Philosophy* (New York: Harper, 1946); Thomas A. Goudge, *The Thought of C. S. Peirce* (Toronto: University of Toronto Press, 1950); Edward C. Moore, *American Pragmatism: Peirce, James, and Dewey* (New York: Columbia University Press, 1961); and Manley Thompson, *The Pragmatic Philosophy of C. S. Peirce* (Chicago: University of Chicago Press, 1953). The writer's debt to Moore is substantial, here and in the following chapter. Chauncey Wright has been collected in *Philosophical Discussions*, ed. Charles Eliot Norton (New York, 1877); and selectively in *Philosophical Writings: Representative Selections*, ed. Edward H. Madden (New York: Bobbs-Merrill, 1958). See also *Letters of Chauncey Wright*, ed. James Bradley Thayer (Cambridge, Mass., 1878). There is available a study of Wright to which the author is much indebted: Edward H. Madden, *Chauncey Wright and the Foundations of Pragmatism* (Seattle: University of Washington Press, 1963). The developing pattern of the thought of William James is to be traced through *The Will to Believe* (1896); *Varieties of Religious Experience* (1902); *Pragmatism* (1907); *A Pluralistic Universe* (1909); and *The Meaning of Truth* (1909). All were published in New York by Longmans, Green and Co. All who study James are indebted to Ralph Barton Perry, *The Thought and Character of William James* (2 vols., Boston: Little, Brown, 1935); and to *The Letters of William James*, ed. Henry James (2 vols., Boston: Little, Brown, 1926). Lloyd Morris, *William James* (New York: Scribner, 1950), is also important, as is Julius Seelye Bixler, *Religion in the Philosophy of William James* (Boston: Marshall Jones, 1926). Among the general works that deal with pragmatism might be mentioned Joseph L. Blau, *Men and Movements in American Philosophy* (New York: Prentice-Hall, 1952); John Dewey, "The Development of American Pragmatism," in *Studies in the History of Ideas*, Vol. II, ed. Department of Philosophy, Columbia University (New York: Columbia University Press, 1925); Richard Hofstadter, *Social Darwinism in American Thought* (Philadelphia: University of Pennsylvania Press, 1944; Boston: Beacon Press, 1955), Ch. VII, "The Current of Pragmatism"; Gail Kennedy, ed., *Pragmatism and American Culture* (Boston: Heath, 1950); I. Woodbridge Riley, *American Thought from Puritanism to Pragmatism and Beyond* (New

York: Holt, 1923); Herbert W. Schneider, *A History of American Philosophy* (New York: Columbia University Press, 1946); W. H. Werkmeister, *A History of Philosophical Ideas in America* (New York: Ronald Press, 1949); and Philip P. Wiener, *Evolution and the Founders of Pragmatism* (Cambridge: Harvard University Press, 1949).

The works of John Dewey (Ch. XIV) with the most substantial bearing upon the subject matter of this book are *Outlines of a Critical Theory of Ethics* (Ann Arbor, Mich., 1891); *Ethics*, with James H. Tufts (New York: Columbia University Press, 1908); *Reconstruction in Philosophy* (New York: Holt, 1920); *Human Nature and Conduct* (New York: Holt, 1922); and *The Quest for Certainty* (New York: Minton Balch, 1929). If one work may be singled from the list, it is *The Quest for Certainty*. The Modern Library has a comprehensive anthology of Dewey's philosophic writings: *Intelligence in the Modern World: John Dewey's Philosophy*, ed. Joseph Ratner (New York, 1939). The relationship of Dewey to his philosophic predecessors is studied in Philip P. Wiener, *Evolution and the Founders of Pragmatism* (Cambridge: Harvard University Press, 1949); and in Morton G. White, *The Origin of Dewey's Instrumentalism* (New York: Columbia University Press, 1943). An enthusiastic appraisal of Dewey in his heyday written by a perceptive disciple is available in Sidney Hook, *John Dewey: An Intellectual Portrait* (New York: John Day, 1939); an appraisal of Dewey's position in American thought shortly after his death is in George R. Geiger, *John Dewey in Perspective* (New York: Oxford University Press, 1958). See also Paul A. Schilpp, ed., *The Philosophy of John Dewey* (Evanston, Ill.: Northwestern University Press, 1939). The general works on pragmatism cited above are also valuable for Dewey. The following studies of Dewey have appeared in recent years: Irwin Edman, *John Dewey: His Contribution to the American Tradition* (Indianapolis: Bobbs-Merrill, 1955); Charles W. Hendel, *John Dewey and the Experimental Spirit in Philosophy* (New York: Liberal Arts, 1959); John Blewett, ed., *John Dewey: His Thought and Influence* (Bronx, N.Y.: Fordham University Press, 1960); and Douglas E. Lawson, *John Dewey and the World View* (Carbondale: Southern Illinois University Press, 1964).

Holmes's legal classic (Ch. XV) *The Common Law* (1881) is available in a modern edition by Mark De Wolfe Howe (Cambridge: Harvard University Press, 1963). A selection of his more significant opinions as a Massachusetts justice is available in H. C. Shriver,

The Judicial Opinions of Oliver Wendell Holmes (Buffalo: Dennis, 1940). The basic Holmes collections are his *Speeches* (Boston: Little, Brown, 1891, 1913); *Collected Legal Papers,* ed. Harold Laski (New York: Harcourt, Brace, 1920); *Dissenting Opinions,* ed. Alfred Lief (New York: Vanguard Press, 1929); *Representative Opinions,* ed. Alfred Lief (New York: Vanguard Press, 1931); and *The Mind and Faith of Justice Holmes,* ed. Max Lerner (Garden City, N.Y.: Garden City Pub. Co., 1948). The authorized biography is Mark De Wolfe Howe, *Justice Oliver Wendell Holmes:* Vol. I, *The Shaping Years, 1841–1870;* Vol. II, *The Proving Years, 1870–1882* (Cambridge: Harvard University Press, 1957, 1963). For the facts of Holmes's life see Catherine Drinker Bowen's highly readable and popular *Yankee from Olympus: Justice Holmes and His Family* (Boston: Little, Brown, 1943). The constitutional philosophy of Holmes may be studied through Dorsey Richardson, *The Constitutional Doctrines of Justice Holmes* (Baltimore: Johns Hopkins University Press, 1924); Felix Frankfurter's *Dictionary of American Biography* article and his 1938 Harvard lectures on Holmes, both collected in *Mr. Justice Holmes and the Supreme Court* (Cambridge: Harvard University Press, 1938, 1961); Francis Biddle, *Mr. Justice Holmes* (New York: Scribner, 1942); Samuel J. Konefsky, *The Legacy of Holmes and Brandeis* (New York: Macmillan, 1956); and perhaps most effectively of all in his own words, in *The Correspondence of Mr. Justice Holmes and Sir Frederick Pollock, 1874–1932,* ed. Mark De Wolfe Howe (2 vols., Cambridge: Harvard University Press, 1961). A very illuminating essay on the relationship between formal pragmatism and the law is available in Edwin W. Patterson, "Pragmatism as a Philosophy of Law," in *The Philosopher of the Common Man: Essays in Honor of John Dewey to Celebrate His Eightieth Birthday* (New York: Putnam, 1940). Brandeis' literary reputation as a promoter of social progress and an adversary of corporate bigness rests on his *Other People's Money and How the Bankers Use It* (New York: Stokes, 1914) and *The Curse of Bigness,* ed. Osmond K. Fraenkel (New York: Viking Press, 1934). The basic Brandeis collections, comprising extracts from his judicial opinions, speeches, and written articles that appeared mainly in legal journals, are *The Social and Economic Views of Mr. Justice Brandeis,* ed. Alfred Lief (New York: Vanguard Press, 1930); *The Brandeis Guide to the Modern World,* ed. Alfred Lief (Boston: Little, Brown, 1941); and *The Unpublished Opinions of Mr. Justice Brandeis* (Cambridge: Harvard University Press, 1957). The authorized life is Alpheus T. Mason, *Brandeis: A Free Man's Life* (New York: Viking Press, 1946). See also Konefsky, above.

Alfred H. Kelly and Winfred A. Harbison, *The American Constitution, Its Origins and Development* (New York: Norton, 1948) is an excellent and comprehensive study of its subject (Ch. XVI); see especially Ch. 26, "Reaction and *Laissez-Faire*," and Ch. 27, "The New Deal," for the conflict between social Darwinism and pragmatism in the Supreme Court. Among the good studies of the interrelationship among the Constitution, the Supreme Court, and the New Deal are Charles A. and Mary Beard, *America in Mid-Passage* (New York: Macmillan, 1939); Justice Robert H. Jackson, *The Struggle for Judicial Supremacy* (New York: Knopf, 1941); Dean Alfange, *The Supreme Court and the National Will* (Garden City, N.Y.: Doubleday, 1937); and Robert G. McCloskey, *The American Supreme Court* (Chicago: University of Chicago Press, 1960). The struggle over the Court-packing plan is graphically described in Beard, *op. cit.*, and in Joseph Alsop and Turner Catledge, *The 168 Days* (Garden City, N.Y.: Doubleday, 1938).

INDEX